To my grandson, Kal Michael Mclenaghan. One of the finest young men, I was so grateful to play such a huge part in his 30 years with us. It was Kal who asked me to write some more stories for him, which led me to complete my life work, *Who Cares Who Wins,* then a further two autobiographies. Kal and I blended together, he with his lovely autism and my learning problems. We read each other, sharing like boys do, age was not a difficult hurdle.

Kal passed away on 11th of April 2020. He was 30.

"Okay son, you've left me with all this paperwork."
"Share it, 'G.D' we can have a laugh when we meet again."
"Hope that's soon, son. I pray for the day I am lowered beside you."

Love you son
Till we meet
G.D.

Michael McLenaghan

Who Cares Who Wins

AUSTIN MACAULEY PUBLISHERS™
LONDON · CAMBRIDGE · NEW YORK · SHARJAH

Copyright © Michael McLenaghan 2022

The right of Michael McLenaghan to be identified as author of this work has been asserted by him in accordance with sections 77 and 78 of the Copyright, Designs and Patents Act 1988.

All rights reserved. No part of this publication may be reproduced, stored in a retrieval system, or transmitted in any form or by any means, electronic, mechanical, photocopying, recording, or otherwise, without the prior permission of the publishers.

Any person who commits any unauthorised act in relation to this publication may be liable to criminal prosecution and civil claims for damages.

All of the events in this memoir are true to the best of the author's memory. The views expressed in this memoir are solely those of the author.

A CIP catalogue record for this title is available from the British Library.

ISBN 9781786126474 (Paperback)
ISBN 9781786126481 (Hardback)
ISBN 9781528951814 (ePub e-book)

www.austinmacauley.com

First Published 2022
Austin Macauley Publishers Ltd®
1 Canada Square
Canary Wharf
London
E14 5AA

I would like to thank all at my publishers for 'sticking' with the handwritten manuscript I dumped on their doorstep!

Also, my 'inspirational' grandson who supported my strange ways, write more stories 'G.D.'

Not forgetting my long-suffering 'support team' Lorraine, Claire, Kirsten, Petra, Caroline, Mandy and many more true ladies, heroines, all.

Not forgetting my mother and father who struggled to bring me up through the struggle of post-World War 2's destitution. World travel riches now bang into destitution, disease, dementia and dodging the asylums.

How bloody rich am I.

Beware, reading this can cause severe health problems.

Born on 1 October 1945 to my father, William John McLenaghan, and mother, Jean (June) McLenaghan (née Laidlaw). Delivered by hand at the Western General Hospital Edinburgh.

"Jesus, I sound like a bloody lawyer." What a start!!!

My wee carcass was brought to the 'top flat, last door' at 12 Upper Grove Place, Fountainbridge, Edinburgh no 'post codes' to date.

The starting place, on the long 'Sojourn'!!!

What a fantastic place to be brought up in. My real-life mental features during the early years possibly started when I was about two years old… I have a clear view of my 'wee-life' looking up and out at my mother's face as I cried for help, pleading for her to remove me from the Iron-Bars that held me prisoner. Some 'big boys' had opened up the iron grating on a street's rainwater drain silver in the gutter outside my stairs, and I was 'stuffed' into this 20" deep by 12" sump with about 4" of stagnant water. How long I was down there I haven't a clue, but to look up to my mum's outstretched arms, pulling the grating away, she cuddled me tightly, and I recognised the smell of 'fag ends' right away. Well, smells are important.

She always took her hanky and spat on it to wipe whatever away from my face, especially when out in public, and I was dressed in my 'best gear': a double-breasted camel-coloured coat with leather buttons and brown/black velvet-like collar. I'd be spun-around, and without warning, it was no gentle-rub, more an abrasive, scraping motion, sometimes, adding her thumbnail to remove any heavy crusts which may have gathered from my runny nose. The smell of fag-ends which gathered in her pinny or coat pocket. The ends would be a saviour when she ran out of fags were not at all repulsive but were just another odour of everyday life! But what I could not stand and 'boaked' at was near sick, was her, or any contact on my face, and in particular on my 'lips' – *'lipstick'*.

"'O' Jings, 'Help ma 'boab'"… I rubbed my lips and even my tongue 'raw' near to 'bleeding' just to get that 'god-awful' taste away. It's not that she kissed me on the lips I soon learned to turn a cheek when I saw a woman's lips heading my way; 'yuk'. The damned stuff was on her 'hanky' too. Women always seemed to have a stick of lipstick at hand.

And hanky concealed in the hand or bag!

One of the other gauges to my age and height was the rail bridge which became a big attraction to most of the children in our street. We would gather around the sides which were too high even for an adult. The bridge stood in Grove Street at the Morrison St end. The steam trains ran from the Caley Station under the bridge and away to the West. The 'smoke' and 'steam' came over one side in huge, 'dense clouds'. Then we ran across the road to the other side in order to be the first to become enveloped with a fresh burst of sulphurous fume. What a 'great' smell, recognisable anywhere. Everybody fought over the viewing points all the time, which were inch holes in the solid-steel section panels; the only way to view the actual trains as they passed by. The holes were some 20" from the ground, and I seriously thought for years that they were purposely made for short people to view the trains. I had to, at first, stand on my tip-toes to see through, graduating later to bending-down as I grew. It was in later years that I found out the bridge builders used the 'holes' with hooks pushed through when constructing the bridge for 'lifting-points'. 'Ah well, nice thought!'

The most frightening periods of infancy, when I was three years and one month old, I was separated from my family and made or to my mind, forced to sleep in this very large, dimly-lit room, with row upon row of 'green-covered' low-lying beds or camp beds. I appeared to be entirely on my own, but I was told the full story much later in life: my saviour from this hell was my father, who told me that I was put into View forth Nursery because Mother was in hospital and only my big brother was able to stay with him as he was at school, which allowed Dad to stay at work out of fear that he would lose his job. Jean, my sister, aged four, and I were put into care. This broke my dad's heart on having to keep us apart.

One day when the nursery nurses had whole load of us bairns including Jean, and as they walked us all, myself and other younger ones 'piled-up' in prams, Jean was walking. Dad was driving John Menizies' paper delivery van; he told me in later years that as he drove along from Tolcross towards Viewforth, he came across this parade of infants and instantly spotted us. He could not help himself bursting into 'tears'; he drove alongside the nurses who recognised him, and asked if he could there and then take his bairns home, and was taken aback when he was told he could. He put us in the van and headed to his depot which was at the foot of our street, Uppergrove Place. When he got back to his Stores, he told his boss he was packing in his job to look after his bairns, but his boss told him to take us home and only come back when all was well.

My nightmare disappeared at that point in time. The cause of my mother's disappearance was soon answered, when one day, soon after the event, my dad left us in the care of my Auntie Vi and Uncle Bill McCartney, and old Granny, McCartney and of course 'Birky' the black-coated highland terrier dog. They lived only two stairs away at No. 8 top flat. Auntie Vi opened the living room window and clinging on tight to Jean and I under each of her arms, held us out over the window sill and on looking down at the street far below, she called out to us, "See that car," which had just pulled into the street. "Your mum and dad are in there with your new wee brother, Hamish…" By the time I got to our house, my mother was sitting in our living room, on an upright chair. I stood between her legs with my elbows resting on her knees, looking up at the back of Hamish's bald head as he suckled Mother!

A picture of my life from the birth of Hamish: Tommy b. 1941, Jean b. 1944, me b. 1945 and now Hamish 1948!

But there was Billy who was born in 1940 but, sadly, died as a 'cot' Death, six months later. Billy was buried in a Paupers Grave, just inside, on the left hand-side of the main gates of Morningside Cemetery.

Fountain Bridge, to its bairns, was just one big playground, which stretched eastwards to Princes St, and Edinburgh Castle areas, North Haymarket, Morrison Street to Caledonian Hotel and west-wards to 'West' Dundee St Polwarth, Canal Viewforth and south of Tolcross!

Until Hamish came along, my range was nearly always with Mum but now, 'wee-Jean', my big sister, had her work cut-out, eyes in the back of her head. Hamish was to be the priority – allowing me to escape her wee clutches from time to time; gradually, a whole lot of hours at a time. It was common, for girls were the eyes and ears for their mothers. When Mother was busy in the house or shopping, she was totally relying on the eldest girl to watch over her bairns at all times, and the eldest girl relied on the other girls also to be responsible for the younger bairns, and it worked well.

But for the boys, they were bundled in with the girls until they started school age, when depending on how well they adapted, normally 'drifted', or were 'edged' away from the girls and infants by mothers and grannies. There was no real age when this happened, as what boy would want to be seen as a 'sissy'. The Boys were 'men'. However, the boys did enjoy skipping, but as a group. By the time the boys were at secondary school, skipping was not on their mind.

As I now can see as I write, our 'fathers' were not in the frame. The division in this respect makes life look at the stage as if they never existed. 'Men' were noted by their absence. But not to play! Hindsight is a great thing, but at this point of writing, I am beginning to see two worlds coming into sight; about how a child's life was, before having to 'grow up', *both sexes?*

Our house was, as I said, the top flat, last door, and on entering it, immediately on the right in the hallway was situated the toilet, with a 'high-level system', which was normal fitment in days of old. But we never had a bath or shower in our house. On turning left when entering the house, and on your left, a door took you into the coal cellar, boards 'barred' you from entering this area, piled up beyond them huge chunks of random-sized coal buckets of 'dross-and-ashes'.

The door to the right of the coal cellar was the entrance to the living room/kitchenette; at the furthest point facing you was the 'Belfast' earthen, white enamel sink, with a single brass 'cold-water tap' to the left and a well-scrubbed wooden draining-board. Behind the sink was the window which looked down onto the back-garden. Still standing in the open doorway on the wall to your right was the open cooking range, coal-fired with the high level mantel piece, above it the gas-light and mantel, it was to be a few years before we had electric, which was installed by dad, and moving further around and nearly behind, was the bed-recess, room only for a three-quarter double bed. The recess had a privacy curtain draped in front concealing the bed. To the left wall stood the side-board cupboard and drawers. In the centre of the room stood a gate-legged table with four upright chairs, a couple of well-worn armchairs on each side of the fire place. Just on the other side of the side-board was the doorway into our bedroom, very small but managed another. Three-quarter bed which 'Tommy, Jean and I shared and a bit later Hamish, there was only room for a small chest of drawers by the window which looked out over the 'back-green'.

At this point, I should mention that our bedroom faced the bedroom (some 150 yards away) in Big Tams Hoose – later to be well famous as James Bond Sean Connery himself, but unfortunately, he was 14 years older than myself. Only in 1985, in an evening news paper, which recalled past photos published, both he and I shared the front cover of the paper! Tara! My only claim to fame.

At this point, I have not mentioned the front part of the house, where Granny Laidlaw lived.

The house was alive inside as it was in the back green on an average day. Three of us, Tommy, Jean, and myself, shared the bed in the room and later Hamish joined us when he outgrew his solid, wooden cot which was kept beside Mum and Dad till he stopped being fed by her at night. In the winter nights, the bed was draped in heavy, old 'army' blankets and an assortment of great coats (army and air-force overcoats), nice and snug, and warm. We'd 'coorie-up' to each other. We never had pyjamas, but Dad's old shirts were the next-best thing; you just curled up into a ball and pulled up the 'shirt tails' which sealed you in.

The bed itself was made up of a heavy, wooden-base frame, which had been 'well-strung' – huge springs covered with a finer layer of wire-mesh that was then completely covered by a 4" horse-hair mattress. The hair led to much discomfort, like tiny pins or needles pricking you all night, and led you in a pastime of searching out the hair which caused disturbed sleep. Some pillows were most annoying when found to also contain 'horse-hair'. The mattress was then covered with a bright-red rubber sheet, and then a cotton or linen sheet. The rubber sheet may have saved some of the mattress from the 'pee' damage, but gave you another problem. On a normal night, there was no urge to 'pee' and get out of bed and use the chamber pot, and even less on a cold winter's night. I could feel my back or feet getting warmer than the bed itself, peeing the bed warmed us up.

In the morning however, Mum had, as usual, prepared our early sponge bath for us in front of the 'open fire', and one by one she took us out of the bed, stripped us of our clothes and stood us in the small, galvanised tub, sponging us clean. We were glad when it was our turn to get out of the bed as the 'pee' had 'ponded' down in the middle of the 'bed' held in the rubber sheet, and was now 'very-cold' and the last one out of the bed would be shivering. The warmth of the fire and tub was very welcomed.

This ritual took place every morning and for some strange reason, Tommy got the blame most of the time for not getting up at the right time and use the 'po....' Poor him, so we kept a tight lip on the subject. When we eventually moved from here to another area, strange as it seems, the ritual and habit seemed to die away.

Tommy – Mum – Wee Jean – Michael (Self) – Hamish (Baby)

Hot water, which never came out of a tap as we only had a cold water supply to the kitchenette sink, however as the range fire-basket was on twenty-four hours a day and only put out four times a year, or more if required, in order that the 'Lum' was swept. This source of heat was well captured as there was always pots and pans, including as many kettles that could be accommodated on the two-hobs on each side of the fire basket, each vessel waiting its turn to be moved closer to the hotter heat and others taken to a cooler spot to simmer more gently, broths, porridge, vegs etc… a very busy, exciting spot. On lots of occasions, one of the bairns was employed to stir and keep watch over these cauldrons. What a waste of good playing time. You soon learned quickly to keep the pots turning on the right 'spot', just to even the heat and stir at the same time, a good back-hand clout on the Lug from mother brought your attention back should it wander!

Most of the time, Dad was chimney sweeping, so, for obvious reasons, he needed a bath. The galvanised tub hung on a hook against the wall up in the coal cellar; it was about 1 foot deep and 4 feet long and a handle at each rounded end, (not like the smaller-wash tub we used in the mornings) the bath-tub had three of us at a time standing and 2 sitting, Mother only allowed us a couple of inches deep at a time, anymore and we just splashed it all over the floor. It was well understood the reason for having 'linoleum' (lino) throughout the house, just a mop-up (easier said than done).

After we were finished bathing, we were dried off and into bed. Mother had the privy of the 'tub' whilst the water was still cleanest. Dad then had a good 'scrub', removing most of the 'day's soot'. He also had the job of emptying and cleaning the tub. We could hear it banging on the wall as he re-hung it in the coal-cellar.

On one night whilst Mum and Dad were out somewhere, Uncle George and Auntie Betty were babysitting us. We were meant to be tucked-up in bed, but we were having a bit of a carry-on, and before we knew it, the bed became a bouncy castle, standing up under the blankets and great coats pushing and shoving, Hamish's involuntary body bouncing about our feet and legs, pitch black, suddenly and without warning, there was a great Bang! Our world collapsed as we were all entangled, legs, arms, sheets and 'screams', fighting for breath. The next I knew, I felt a hand grab my ankle, and I recognised my uncle shouting. Then I lay on my back, on the cold 'Lino floor', completely in a state of shock. My aunt grabbed me and stood me by the window. I was sobbing uncontrollably. Next I knew, Jean joined me, and we hugged each other terrified! It was only when we were all accounted for and Auntie Betty trying to console us greeting bairns, did the 'disaster' come to light.

The bed had collapsed against the wall, letting the base of the mattress crash on the floor but only at the head-end; the foot of the bed remained attached, which meant we all piled on top of each other, wrapped in sheets, blankets and great coats. A total entanglement of bodies. We all had minor scratch marks and slight bruises. Uncle George was in a bit of a state as he heard the crash and seeing the mess, saved the day by putting the bed-back together. We recovered enough (which we waited on him doing this) by distracting our attention to the task to pick away the ice from the inside window pane which was normal on a very-cold night.

It was not long before the bed was fixed with the mattress, sheets and covers all re-made. Aunty Betty gave us a treat in giving us a couple of rubber water bottles, which Mum and Dad normally used, instead of our stone ones, and warned us not to burst them. "Sleep!"

The head of the back-green is an overstated expression used to call the areas of land behind the blade of grass. When it was wet, it was *mud*, and dry meant dust everywhere. In the first few years after the Second World War was over 1945. They demolished the air-raid shelters and levelled the ground; they left most of the wrought-iron washing poles; they were great for climbing up when they had no washing. Washing days were well self-monitored by the women, and whatever you do, don't use someone else's washing-line or poles, and you took your life in your hands if you were caught swinging on the 'ropes'. 'T' bars were a common sight in the front or back windows. Most, if not all, the small pieces of clothing hung out to dry in all weathers; the larger sheets, blankets went out in the back green area. It was bad enough if the dust blew-up, or if sheets trailed in the mud. But god help any person who passed through, or tried to play near the sacred washing; all hell broke out. There was always some old grannie hanging her over-developed 'bust' out on the window-sill… you did not have to hear them, or to feel their eyes burning into your back, your senses told you, or should have. Her warning 'call' was enough; not glancing behind, I'd shoot-off. Somehow, whether you did right or wrong, Mother seemed to know it was her off-spring who were at the rough end of the tongue.

It either ended with me or whoever being hauled up for a 'leathering (belt)' straightaway or having to wait for Father to get home from work and deal with me, but she would give me the back of her hand and a tongue-lashing. Most times, I would have preferred to just be thumped and get it over and done with. If I didn't get called up, that was easy. I'd just get on with what I was doing and let them slag each other. Anyway, in a few hours, they'd be talking to each other in the stairway. What a life! On some occasions, there would be somebody at every window, screaming abuse, and at times, more than one at each window (what we kids had to put up with!).

When playtime was in full swing, whether on the street or back-green, or wherever; it didn't matter if you were a boy or girl, if you needed to go, that would be a problem. The older ones just disappeared and came back. The infants would be taken by the older ones to one side and do what was needed there and then, trying to take them indoors would prove too late, and it happened. Me having a 'pee' right on the spot was OK, dribbling in the soil, making holes and patterns was great fun or seeing how high you could 'pee' up a 'pole' or wall was a challenge, and competed with other boys; a good game, but a 'jobby' was a bit different. On some occasions, you were caught in between having a good time that the urges were a nuisance, and you could not hold on any longer. There was no thought even at this young age of looking for a toilet! You eventually had to stand still and do it where you stood; the others just played around you not even bothering to comment 'why'… they've all done it.

It was just part of life. The only thing you might do with it after it was deposited in the dirt was to gently kick it to one side, then continue on. If you were unlucky and had your wellington boots on, you'd be very unfortunate. If it dropped inside it, 'awe jings'… Pulling the boot off was a very bad move as your heel would squash it. The simplest way to get it out was to lie on your back and point the boot in the air, letting it drip out. 'Easy'… For the girls, it was just a case of squatting on the spot to do both. It was even easy for some of the girls as a good number, like Jean, never wore pants! Unless they had older sister's hand me down.

By the time we were at school, we had them on during school hours, both boys and girls. All of this was not the question; the thing was, even in the streets, never mind the back greens, all the jobbies had just disappeared by the next day! Up until the boys were 12 years old, we were only allowed shorts, and girls, dresses or skirts.

Because we were classified as 'destitute', at least twice a year, Mother marched us up to the police headquarters in the High Street at Parliament Square, and up to the top flat, were we lined up in front of a 'long counter'. Behind it stood a policeman, draped in a long-length, brown dust coat. One at a time we were fitted out with a pair of new, all-leather black-boots, just like the soldiers had, and row upon row of steel-studs (seggs); oh boy it was great to be a destitute, not many of our pals (boys and girls) were issued 'free' boots, especially by a 'police-stores officer'.

Skidding down the cobbles all the way home was such a thrill, but short-lived as Mother had the boots off our feet even before we got into the house, and as quick as a flash, she pulled all the studs out with Dad's pliers. "But why..." There was no way she was allowing her precious, high-polished lino getting damaged! I couldn't understand her priorities jings!!!

Like most households in the street, Mother had a space booked at the 'Wash-House' (or Steamie), which was located at the top of Murdoch Terr, a bit of a long walk from Fountainbridge along Dundee St and up Murdoch Terrace. This washhouse, like many industries of the time which required a large amount of water, was located right beside the canal. Mother put Hamish in the pram, which was huge by any standards and had great big spoked wheels (great wheels for any 'Guider'; 'Guider' now known as a 'hand cart') Once Hamish was located in position, the scrubbing-board was laid across the area above his feet, then the clothing, sheets, everything that needed a 'big-wash' was then piled on top of the board. By this time, Hamish was out of sight; behind this load would be the well-bleached wooden paddle, this was a 2-foot long piece of wood which was used to lift the clothes from the 'boiling-tubs', transferring hot loads from one tub to another rinsing tub or through the mangles (rollers). Bars of scrubbing soap, soap powders, bleaches not like today's smelly stuff, just good bleachy disinfectant products. A lot of the smaller items like, whites, stud-collars, and cuffs for shirts were mostly well-scrubbed in the kitchen sink area long before this wash-day, Mum had to pay good cash for the washhouse and made good use of every 'ha' penny'.

We played around the street area beside the main entrance; inside, women dressed in headsquares, curlers, pinnies nylon-stockings at the ankles (no tights then), all in skirts or dresses, and some with a 'lit-fag' hanging from their mouth, managing to shout to each other over the din of hissing steam (clouds of it), and the general noise of huge washing machine equipment. It always seemed to be dark on the return walk home. Streets lit with the gas lamps.

What a long, long walk; Hamish was well asleep by now. Being destitute not only gave you a shoe allowance, but depending on your needs, 'assistance', as it was called, meant you were given an extra 2–4 hours at the 'steamie' but you had to use it on a different day from your normal day, and when the operator said so. In the winter months, this normally happened at night; cold and damp. Poor us but poor Mum.

Our other allowance was a bit of a treat for us, but a longer walk up Fountainbridge to Tolcross area and down into the grass market. Me, Tommy and Jean went to fetch our supply of dried milk, which came in huge (to us huge) tins, 3 or 4 of them loaded into a cardboard box. It also included our much favoured 'Real Orange Juice', concentrated; in 5 or 6 bottles all well-sealed, and the biggest brown glass jar of 'mault' (malt), all free to us destitute 'waines'. There was always something to spoil this: 'cod liver oil'. Fortunately, only a small bottle, and a spoon to be taken with 'orange juice'!!! 'What a damper!

Uppergrove Place, the street itself was, as I remember it, an area where the older children played. I always looked at these giants who played the grown-ups games, real football, some of the older ones actually wore long-trousers (boys only), and the older girls played skipping, with their skirt or dress bottoms tucked up under their blue or black knicker-leg elastic. It was a dangerous place to be hanging around with the activity going on; we always had our backs to the tenement walls stand and sit watching all sorts of games being played, 'kick the can', squares chalked on the pavement with numbers mark in each, both boys and girls hopping on one foot which was pushing an empty boot polish tin from square to square and back again. Other girls with a tennis ball, bouncing it between their legs, 'birling' around, clapping their hands then catching the ball as it bounced off the wall and back to them!!! *Stupid!* The whole place came alive after School was out at tea time, as the street was designated traffic-free from 4pm–10pm or some streets 6am. Not that our street had any cars or vans, nobody owned a car, and works vehicles were in their own yards, no one brought them home; 'hand-carts' used the streets locally, milk, bread and sometimes vegetables, even trades-men in our area used hand-carts or footed it from stair to stair. Being at that time a dead-end, most vehicles drove along up Grove Street.

Having said that Dad drove tanks during the war years, his job in the Argyll Sutherland Highlanders was to pick up tanks and other lorries from all over Scotland and bring them in convoy to Edinburgh and other areas. He was known to have brought one or two down the Street and park it up overnight, and away the next day with my Mother on board, supposedly getting a lift to work. Dad did spend 1933–39 in Palestine and returned to Stirling Castle Base, but failed his medical for further overseas duties and was limited to transport duties for the duration of the war.

St Cuthbert's co-operate stables, were situated at Grove Street, only 100 yards from our house, I spent the most exciting part of my life around them in my early years. The stables were said to have held up to 200 horses at any time. Although I left Fountainbridge when I was 7½ years old, they hold the lasting memories of my childhood. In particular when we were up the top end of Morrison Street, and just before Semple Street, waiting by the huge, twin-gates which were separated by only yards, one of which was opened by the ever watchful gateman, to let the horse-drawn milk lorry, returning with a full load of empty milk-crates and tired horse who had been out on the 'run' (wherever that was) —since very early morning; three or four am, till early pm. Inside this huge milk yard-bottling-wash plant, loading bays, horses backing the carts up to the bankings to unload the crates of empty milk bottles carts known as vans and lorries.

I'm sure the horses knew we were ready to pounce, our numbers were never more than 3 or 4, just enough to be a nuisance to them. They just ambled their way by the gutter at the kerbside, we would squeeze between what space there was at the kerb on the road and grab-hold of the 'trace' just behind the neck-collar, with both hands, swing our legs up onto the dangling 'trace', just inches away from the 'hoof' and 'scotch heel shoe', we made all kinds of cowboy noises; 'yeppee', 'giddy-up'. Folk walking past never even blinked or indeed never told us off, and I never knew anyone getting hurt. Some of the boy's managed to climb up the harness and rode the horse all the way to the stables, the poor beasts after a hard day, then us! They made their way down Morrison St, turned left up Grove Street, passing Upper Grove Place on the right, and onto the stables, we kept our position as they entered into the huge open, glass-roofed gathering area, just inside the stable opening.

The horses were then unhitched from the lorry, and shafts. All the harness remained on the horse and securely tucked-in, the Trace's to the 'brightening-stops'. Finally, the horses had their-feed-bags, now empty was attached to the reins at the top of the saddle-pad. Once done, the Horse automatically, on its own accord, wandered over to the second-gateway (twin), maybe 8 or 9 horses gathered patiently unattended, not one bothering the other. But only us yins were waiting a wee bit down the road, trying to keep out of sight of the gateman (he knew we were there all the time). We could hear the big-gate clang open and the heavy-steel shoes of the horses clatter on through. The horses seemed to know their own pecking order and kept in a single-file, and no matter what they walked at a slow pace, there was no one in sight all these horses on a main-road for the next ¼ mile to their stables all on their own, except us pests!

The horses stabled here were on all levels kept very close together in single rows, with a single bulb hanging from the roof every twenty feet or so, casting weak shadows, they were all kept separate by a 'partion panel' which was tall at the head end and tapered to the height and length of their body Row after rows of stalls, only the tails of horses showing out of them, long narrow corridors, what seemed like hundreds of horses. At the head-end lay a small-shelf where the 'hard-feed' bruised-oats or chaff was laid, and a leaf or two of hay, the horses were tethered there by means of a lead rope. Clipped onto a 'halter', the rope was short and ran down through a 'ring-bolt' fixed to a wall fitting, the end of this rope was attached to a 3" wooden ball, this restricted the horses' movements within this confined space, the horses never lay down to sleep in their whole working life.

Whose earlier arriving horses waiting on the attention of the men (stable and yards men) to remove their harness. Some had walked to a large watering trough and one by one had a well-deserved drink, we dismounted, the men completely ignoring our presence. We shot off and all the way to the 'twin-gates' for another go! When inside the gathering area of the stables, there was a walk-up long ramp, which was quite steep, it led up to a long balcony and at the end of it lay a normal size person open doorway, without a door, leading to a very dark area. Some of the horses when entering the stable-yard walked up this ramp, with their hoofs now 'clomping' and echoing every step-up the wooden ramp at a 'heavy-gait' only a 2 foot barrier kept them on the ramp, on some occasions there was a queue of horses on the balcony and back onto the ramp, the lead one waiting to be relieved of his harness, and once so walked through the narrow door. With the man barking out some echoing, non-descript orders to the horses, he followed the horses through with all the harnesses about him. but there was perfect peace and quiet for them.

The stables were not only used to keep the 'store-horses' (as we knew them). 'Roy Rogers', the most famous American cowboy's horses this time of the late 1940/50 had a lovely white tail and mane, called 'Trigger' (which I believe when he died was stuffed and on show somewhere in California). Trigger has the 'stallion' stall all to himself, down near the entrance and below the balcony and ramp. Oh boy, crowds queued up to see Trigger. I was one of the lucky ones, being a regular helper. I got to stand in the box and clap him. Roy Rogers came in a couple of times, but I'm afraid the shine came off him, as he came dressed like a real human-being! No hat. Totally normal. If it wasn't for Trigger, my dream was shattered and near in tatters. Hop along Cassidy and his mule came too, but although he was just as famous a cowboy as Rogers, hop came and went. I'm sure Rogers must have affected my trust in cowboys.

Now, when the Queen was in town, they could only house a squad of the 'house-hold cavalry'; oh boy, I could get into the stables only from time to time when they were in town, the soldiers seemed to fill the whole gathering area under the ramp and balcony. And in the morning, washed and brushed their steeds, too busy to notice me standing by the trough, warned by the stable hands, 'Don't move or you're out.' I didn't need a second telling. They had a long glove full-arm, right up to his shoulder, he went from horse to horse, lifted its tail and his whole hand disappeared up its bum (I was later in life to see this again in horse Guards Parade London, I was on parade with my Rg. (the Royal Scots Greys). I was old enough to ask the question; the reply was: 'to help empty their bowels before going on parade!' Well, I accepted this as is. When they finished all their grooming, half the horses were saddled-up; the soldiers just smartened up a bit and got on board. The horseman would take the reins of a second unsaddled horse and in these pairs made their way out of the stables, disappearing for a couple of hours exercising, returning, re-grooming, the horses were then re-stabled.

The next time the soldiers re-appeared they had their full regalia on, swords in their scabbards, looking a bit undressed with no hats as yet, still inside the gathering area, this time looking down from the balcony onto the cramped space below watching in total awe. One by one the soldiers mounted-up, as other assistants went around them fastening-buckles, handing the mounted soldiers their helmets and plumbs. Just looking down on them from this awkward angle and only a few feet from the 'cuddies', they began to take a uniformity of a kind. Things began to settle as some unseen 'Sergeant' barked out an order even the horses seemed to take note, then two-by-two they drew their swords and shouldered them, and the area soon became empty, left with loads of droppings, steaming away. I ran down the ramp in time to see the last of them turn left out of the stables, heading up Fountainbridge! What an amazing sight, on a later occasion I waited outside the stables so that I could follow them all the way up to the castle. Magic 'gangs' of us running all the way. I'm sure Mother knew when things were OK when I was kept busy playing with the horses (It was to be fifty years till I got involved with horses as closely and even closer than this period.)

Directly opposite the stables entrance on the corner of Brandfield Street, was my favourite groceries shop, where when I had two farthings to spend, I got a 'poke' of broken biscuits, a good mixture of what lay in the square tin-bins, which had glass covers so you can see what kind of biscuits lay inside, all of them were loose, and weighed not packed in wrappers. So by the time the box was empty, and you were there at the right time, all the breakages lay at the bottom ready for cheap-pickings, farthings worth filled a wee 'poke'. 'Poke' was an envelope (3 or 4 inches) filled to over filling, didn't matter if they were stale, and 1 stick of liquorice for the other farthing. What a treat. 4 farthings made a penny, 12 pennies made 1 shilling (5p modern money), 48 farthings in 5 pence. When Mother sent me for 'messages' (groceries) I'd always go to this one, as the other grocers only sold broken biscuits to the old-grannies, who used it in their pastries.

The coal-cellar housed more than baths, brooms and 'Dross' (fragments of coal-dust), the cat used this area as its litter tray, and only cleaned out when the pile of coal and dust were emptied out every few weeks in order to give room for the next load of 'big-coals', the cat's droppings were swept-up with the fine Dross of coal, and the stench was beyond telling. The cat's hard lumps were picked out, its pee was greatly absorbed and dried out in the old-coal, the hard lumps were then burned on the fire. The coal man called, and everything was repeated till the next time. The Dross was kept only to be used on the dampened-down overnight fire. Mother used the oven on the range often, when at least twice a week she would bake pies, bread and cakes. Our favourite time was helping mix all the cake ingredients in the bowl, licking our fingers, scraping the utensils clean with our tongues. There were no thermostats or thermometers on the oven so she learnt to use bowls of water or opening and shutting the oven door to control the heat, and of course her eyes, or ours.

One day, on a fine spring morning, we were all going out for a walk along the canal, for some reason I shut the oven door, the fire was on as usual and on our return when we entered the house, I can still remember the smell of cooked 'roast-meat', Dad told us all to wait in the lobby and took his time in the kitchenette, after some time he re-appeared in the lobby carrying a hessian cloth sack, dripping watery stuff, and he disappeared down the stairs leaving a trail of wet stuff. When he returned, I was given a hell of a telling off for closing the oven door with the cat inside. I had, or so I was told, roasted the cat *alive*. It was not long before we had another kitten, which was great fun for us, but very necessary, as I well remember Mother screaming holy murder as we suddenly had an invasion of mice, which took quite some time to get rid –of, when the kitten grew up to be a cat!

The kitten caused me a bit of trouble as it was the only memory I have of my Granny Laidlaw my mum's mother, my only recollection of her are her legs viewed from underneath the gate-legged table in our kitchenette. And on two occasions I was told off for annoying the kitten as it played under the table.

"Michael, that cat will scratch you!" She barked out as I chased it around the table legs, which was all I knew of her presence, till much later, some 4 or 5 years, in a totally different house. One thing was true, anybody who didn't have a cat got everybody else's mice! Mother hated both mice and cats. She found that cats were good for catching flies, which were plentiful at most times of the year, although at night, when the house finally got electric lighting, the flies would be attracted to the new bulb, so Mum got a roll of fly-tape which dangled from the light fitting. This was great to see how many flies were stuck-fast; by early morning, it was covered in black spots!

On some days of the week just after noon, we would gather at 'Martin the Bakers' bakery, which was at the very top of our street. There small delivery vans came back one at a time; we waited patiently on them reversing up to the loading-bay, only room for one van at a time. We were not allowed to go too close, so we waited on the pavement by the front of the van, just watching as the van-driver opened the back doors and another man approached pushing an open racked cage, and one by one, the driver took out 'bread-boards' and slid them onto the racks. We looked at the boards hoping to see more than just the returned loafs of bread and rolls which were not sold from the bakery shops. But all the drivers knew we wanted the 'old-buns' and seemed to enjoy playing a waiting game on us. Then without warning, he would let some buns fall to the floor and he'd flick them with his foot, making them roll down the ramp under the van towards us. Normally, a good number landed at our feet, causing a mad scamper of us kids squabbling to get one or more. They were normally iced-buns, hard as rocks, but by the time we had drooled over them, they soon softened up as a treat, and what a treat. If you didn't get one from the first van, then it wasn't long till the next one and you'd get the favoured cream or coconut buns. One of our other treats was chewing-gum, which was stuck to the pavement. There were two types; the preferred was the one spat out by whoever last used it. Normally it was well chewed and hard, but once we had it, it soon softened up, and if you were lucky, it may be sweet and even better if it had some flavour. You didn't have it long as one of your mates would want a chew, or if he found it, you would want a share. If you didn't get chewing gum, on a hot day the tar on the road melted, we picked away at it till we got enough in a 'ball' – this had a flavour of its own and you didn't have to share it, as there was plenty to go around. Destitution wasn't all that bad really!

We were classified as 'destitute' – very poor by anyone's standards. Dad was discharged at the end of the War in 1945 just before I was born. He had a series of casual jobs; chimney-sweeping, driving for a bakery and many others. These were not jobs he declared to the dole when he signed-on; none at that time were leading to full-time employment, but this other means kept us with food, but Mum said at the time, it kept us all together, as without it, we would have been all split up and put into homes. One of the jobs Dad had done was for 'charities', and that was: comedian. He somehow got mixed up with a concert party who did mostly charity work. He struck it lucky when he got a casual job as chauffer to the then Scotland's top comic 'Dave Willis', who headed the bill at the King's Theatre, Edinburgh. Dad ended up as his understudy and stand-in, but this only lasted a few months. Dave liked the whisky. They partied every day, although Dad kept a lot of 'Dave Willis' gags and sketches in his own act. As kids, we went to a number of his nightly gigs with the Variety Group, as on some occasions, they held some of their rehearsals in our kitchenette. The most remembered being the music played by our own uncle and his group of accordions and a wee side drum – us actually going to some of the venues where they played in Edinburgh. This meant we stayed up at night which was a treat on its own. I remember well when he and his partner (they had a double act – 'Kay and King' – Dad was King and his partner, another chimney sweep, Uncle Billy Hamilton was Kay) were at the Ross band stand in Princess Street Gardens. Facing the stage, which was well lit up as it was night time, wee Jean and I were playing amongst the stack up chairs just to the right-hand side offstage and when Dad came on, we rushed up to him shouting, "Daddy, Daddy." He stopped the act and he got down on his hands at the edge of the stage, looking down at us and would say, "Bed," pointing to us in the direction of home. If it wasn't for the audience laughing, we felt he meant it. Phew! I can still see his wee face – Charlie Chaplin moustache and bowler hat. We just returned to play with the chairs. There were stories aplenty; once they were doing a concert in Fife, on the way back on the ferry boat at the forth bridge they got out their accordions and drums and entertained the crew and passengers to a sing-along, unfortunately we were all in bed. Dad never succeeded, his ambition was to be a comedian full time but was recognised to be on a par with any usual stand-up comic of his age, to us he was the funniest man alive and recognised by anyone who met him to be very funny and remained so all his 76 years! In fact, none of the 'troupe' he was on stage with grew to any fame, but all the families enjoyed the best of reunions and weddings, there was plenty of entertainment.

Dad told me later in his life about how he started chimney sweeping as a young boy. In his early teens he got a job labouring to Mr Ireland down Dundas Street, where he took pity on him when his mother died. He learnt most from the other sweeps Mr Ireland employed. I remember when he started sweeping in Grove Street. He rented a shop right on the edge of the railway bridge; the wooden wedge-shaped structure still exists. We used to get covered in soot (much to Mother's annoyance) when he had to clear out the soot which he kept for sale to merchants who bought quality soot. Any rubbish that was buried and dumped in among the soot in the shop had to be removed as the merchants weighed the soot and any waste found in it meant that Dad was never paid or given inferior prices. He carried on an old tradition when I was around four years old, I was exposed to being taken on to the top of a tenement roof as part of a sweeps ritual. I do remember vaguely this occurring (this has been carried out on my son and grandsons, John and Peter on reaching their 4th birthdays).

We all learned the famous wartime song, sung by Dave Willis. I heard it many times sung by Dad, then I liked it to be my party piece although there were never many of us kids that could not sing most of the verses:

In ma wee gas mask, in working out ma plan
And the bairns think I'm a Boggy man

The girls they bring their boyfriends to see
The daftest looking warder in the ARP (Air Raid Patrol)

Whenever there's air raid, listen to ma cry
An aeroplane, an aeroplane a way up a ki
Ye'll no get in ma shelter cos it's far too wee
Ye'll no get in ma shelter cos it's far too wee

David Willis became a multi-millionaire, but he died in Peebles, broke, unfortunately he lost his money in bad business deals.

I think one of the best playgrounds around our area was 'The Canal', it captivated young and old. Our particular section in which we played was between the iron drawbridge at the top of Mill Lane, and the north side right along to Viewforth opposite which lay my nursery on the south side, also on the south side of the canal lay The Dragon boat shed they hired out rowing boats. We would lie on our bellies at the edge of the north bank and fish, using a small net on the end of a 3 or 4 long bamboo cane. We caught minnows, red breasts, sticklebacks, but at certain times of the year tadpoles, masses of them. We had an old usually damaged jam jar (which would have a crack or chip, good ones were worth money) with a bit of string tied at the neck on a handle, the jar filled with water and a wee bit of chickweed, we would fill it with as many fish or tadpoles, none of which Mother wanted near the house. Half of the fish were dead by the time we got home. Dad tried to convince us that we were cramming too many into one jar and there was not enough oxygen for them. As it turns out he was right, but it did not stop us cramming them in.

Mother didn't like finding all the tadpoles hopping around the kitchen floor. The remaining fish died very quickly, again we were told not to feed them stale bread. Oh dear!

The canal had dredgers going backwards and forwards almost daily, and some other mall barges, scooping up all the rubbish from both sides. On the North side we had the 'North British Tyres and Rubber', and below them the Brewery which our kitchenette looked out onto, huge clouds of steam and the noise of their steam hooters but both factories used the overflow of water for their cooling plants and other secondary usage of water they required. On the edge of the canal, water draw off pipes where huge sunken steel baskets designed to catch the weeds to stop them getting in the factories and clogging up. We would watch as a man with long wellies and a huge garden rake pulled out stringy clumps of weeds and piled then high on the bank, when the dredger came by another man jumped up, scooped up the weed pile onto the dredger, in the distance you could see all along the canal pile after pile of these weeds waiting to be collected. There was that many draw off and natural overflow points that weeding the pipes clear was very necessary. There was the occasional horse-drawn barge, they must have been the last of them, the barges were not long in use after the heavy industries died away.

It was a common enough sight to see people walk up to the edge carrying a hessian rope sack loaded with kittens and pups, throw these sacks far out into the water and just walk away. We and others could see the contents float on the surface moving violently around imagining the sheer panic as slowly the whole floating mass sank and the squealing and yelping slowly ebbed away till it all disappeared beneath the surface. Nobody seemed to really truly be bothered or upset and just went about their business. Also, older animals were thrown over bridges, some tied with weights around their necks so that they would sink under the surface ending it quickly, although this was a way of saving vets fees on ill cats and dogs. People would openly say that it was easier to have the animal walk to the canal rather than carry its body because they had no access to a vehicle. The dredgers were left to pick up the corpses.

On other occasions, the word spread that some poor person was feared last seen falling into the water. We would hang around getting in the way (or we thought we were helping) of the police, who had to 'drag' the canal trying to get the body to rise itself or 'hook it'. They would have a rowing boat tied on to a rope front and back, on both north and south shores others pulled the boat from one side to the other, 2 police on board with glass bottom buckets looked down into the water and a third policeman dragged a grappling hook behind hoping to disturb a body. If some person disappeared in through the ice in winter time when the place was alive with skaters and all sorts, on some occasions the police would have to wait until the ice had thawed in spring, by which time the body could be anywhere on the bottom and it took the movement of dredger traffic to get them to surface. I, and others fishing beside and under the iron draw bridge, caught sight of an old overcoat floating just under the surface of the water under the bridge, we were interested and more intent on seeing if there would be money in the pockets, as again the canal was a favourite dumping ground for the contents of burglaries, it seemed to take ages, bit by bit, we edged it away from its hiding place, but all it took was someone to shout: "It's a body!" That was all it took, everybody took off in different directions, screaming "ma maee – ma maee", slowly but surely, we inched our way back just to reassure of how brave we were.

I caught sight of a hand dangling loose under the body. I saw enough, I was off. I was later told it was of a man missing for some time.

A couple of ways to raise cash, and in particular a good source of money to buy food and other much needed goods for the house, was by saving up or collecting old woollen rags, jam jars, milk, beer and lemonade bottles. Mother never could collect them all and hold onto them, as the money was always so short! She would send us up to 'Assi-Wassi' in Freer Street. The rag and bone (and skin merchant) with all the old well-worked socks jerseys that no longer had wool that could be stripped and used by her, (mother's words 'moth eaten'). We never had any more than half a pillowcase full, but enough. 4D (3p) at a time, then wait outside the pub at night and there was always some old drunk willing to take the empty beer bottles in and cash them for you, always trusting folk, the 'jelly' jar and lemonade bottles had to be taken to a grocer who dealt with the bottling firm, otherwise they would not take them. You'd be lucky to take home 1/-d (5p) each time, but that was enough if you were lucky. Mother would smile, or even better you'd get a biscuit. Great fun!

Nothing in the way of wool was wasted, if a sock had a hole in the heel then scrap wool if that was all at hand would we stripped and the hole darned patched up in a crisscross manner. Jerseys, cardigans, any wool was stripped, 'balled' and re-used, only the most useless bits went to 'Assi-Wassi'. The most hated job I was given would be done at night, whilst listening to the wireless, it was when Mother felt very rich, she 'bought' a yard of yarn, a winding of wool oblong in shape. I had to sit with my hands outstretched palms facing each other and with the thumbs pointing straight upwards to the ceiling, the yarn was hooked onto each thumb, Mother took the loose end and started to wind it into a ball, gravity played havoc with my arms!

Most things at night revolved around the wireless, which was Dad's pride and joy, not having electric, it was battery operated a huge thing that Tommy and I had to take all the way to Haymarket for recharging a couple of times a week. The battery was called an accumulator.

Xmas at upper Grove Place was an exciting time, it built up to be party time around that time of year, at nursery we made decorations and cakes, the decorations were up and Santa called but I cannot ever remember getting presents. Not only was Xmas not seen around our streets, but not at all in our homes, it seems we all celebrated Xmas Day, not forgetting a great excitement of anticipation on Xmas Eve, the lead up to Xmas was by visiting the Caledonian Station, there at Xmas time they set up a huge model real as life train set, massive, it took up half the station interior entrance way, or it seemed that way to us bairns. Then Princess Street was decked out with a lovely display of Xmas lights, these were strung right across the street from the shops to the gardens, what an exciting sight. The shops added to this at night as they competed with their own displays. Again, being destitute we were invited to some pantomimes in our area. I remember well a regular panto held at the Palladium Theatre, at Fountain Bridge, it seemed a big affair. All of us kids arrived in a special, big bus bedecked in all manner of Xmas decorations, and as we entered the foyer, we were given an apple and orange and a bar of chocolate, what a treat! Great to be poor, our pals whose dads worked full time never had such a time, having said that, it seems the 'works' had their own party with Dad doing the concert party's we were invited to the 'halls' to see Santa, one in particular was NUR (National Union Railmen) near Roseburn. I remember being there at least twice, it was, as expected, full of Xmas and what an atmosphere, cakes, decoration and most of all Santa in real life! He sat next to the stage completely surrounded with sacks fully loaded with parcels, all wrapped in Xmas paper and one by one the names on them were read out and one by one the owners ran or was pushed with some tearful ones carried up to receive their present. I was pushed, and I'm told tearful, well he might have been Santa, but I didn't want to get that close to him. I screamed the place down, but I done what the other kids were doing with the parcel and shook it. I recognised instantly the sound of another jig saw puzzle. I remember that leaving it unopened was the order of the day, but great fun.

But Xmas at home was full of anticipation, as we all sat down to scribble a wee note to Santa, this note was to be put up inside the chimney in our bedroom by Dad, only when we were fast asleep, but before going to bed, we each hung a stocking from the mantelpiece of the 'range' in the kitchenette, then straight to bed. Mind we never had Xmas trees or decorations in our house then. Santa would not come if we were not sleeping and stayed that way. When we awoke in the morning, we all seemed to waken together, first up we went to our fireplace, "The letters have gone. Great, he's been!" then we rushed into the kitchen. Our socks were now bulging with goodies! Now sitting on the floor, emptying out the sock of its contents, an apple and orange! He's been, great!

Mum hands me a coloured box (not wrapped), I tore it apart and, oh boy, a wind-up clockwork tractor, and it had two front fixed wheels, the whole thing fitted into both my cupped hands and that was huge. I spent hours on end lying on my belly, flat out on the floor, with the tractor going around the same leg of the sideboard it circled. When I got dressed, I ran down the stairs and out across the road to show my best mate Tommy what Santa brought me. The street at this time was empty and dead to the world, but Tommy was up. His mum stopped him from coming up to mine as she thought we would still be in bed. Tommy showed me what he got, but his was a racing car, that was magic. We swapped for a while, and only parted when bits and pieces fell off the car, but that was all part of the joys of Xmas. No sweets, no Xmas dinner. That was how Xmas was in all the years living in Upper Grove, and boy it was the greatest Xmas's ever. We were all in the same boat, by the way. I think most toys were clockwork operated, mechanically operated, no battery electric motion then.

'Your carriage awaits'
Self with my pal Smokie

Although Xmas seemed to come and go, it to us was the most exciting event of the year. I was surprised with what I got, but my faith in Santa was again re-established, I got my stocking filled, even the orange, which was not a favourite fruit of mine, not that I remember fruit at all (as the war time rationing was near finished). And the letters up the chimney were away, well that cements it all, Santa did come! I cannot for the love of me remember much of the next week, as I was to learn it belonged to the adults, and New Year, which for me did carry an air of happiness and fun, but I most liked Xmas. All mums and dads seemed happy, I guess that was because the real festivities were to begin for them! But for us bairns, life just knocked us into another day and whatever it brought.

The 5 November and Victoria Day in May, known to us as 'bonfire day'. Every street around had one, no matter how small the streets were, like Freer Street, and Brandfield Street, half a dozen stairs in each, they all had a bonfire to be proud of. It appeared to be that war had been declared. Most of the time I spent with the other younger ones collecting all the scrap pieces of wood we could carry from the neighbouring houses and shops. Whilst the older gang members were out raiding the other bonies, we never saw much of this, except when they were away, we were visited by another raiding party, they'd come pouring down the streets, cudgels swinging, screaming their heads off. But the mothers and grannies came storming out of the stairs with any tool at hand, coal shovels, brooms, anything and set about the gang, but this time we had put great distance between us and the gang in fear of our little lives, but now recovered on seeing mothers chasing them off. We now joined the chase out off the street. Later on, our big gang returned mostly empty-handed from the raid! The reason was the same, if it was not from a confrontation with the other mob, it was them being chased by the other grannies. As it neared bonfire night extra dark time raids were carried out to try and light the enemies fire before the big night, but true to form, the mothers and fathers worked a shift so that there was always eyes on, and on some occasions we would arise to find someone had got through our defences and actually succeeded in starting up our 'bonie', but our night watch dragged away the burning parts and saved bonie. Some members braved it out by creating a space inside the base of the structure and making a hideout and some were to stay the whole night inside guarding it.

In one of the other streets a gang managed to set alight a bonie whether knowing or not that somebody was already inside unfortunately they died as a result. This was not a one-off, but it did not stop boys camping out inside.

Bonfires were the best way for families to get rid of all mattresses and furniture. It was a well-practised method of using smaller articles to start building the structure, keeping the much larger pieces of wood until the last day just in case they (the enemy) succeeded in lighting the bonie before the big night, that way if they did, you still had a supply of large stuff to light on the night. People cheered as more wardrobes and old 'peey' mattresses appeared. What a sight!

Everybody was so friendly and if you provided large stuff you were king or queen for the night. The next night old rivals were at it again! Once the fire was duly lit, the heat was tremendous in such a confined space, a bit of a panic got up as the flames shot skywards, sparks flew everywhere, folk were shouting that panes of windows were cracking and the paint blistered, luckily the road was of granite cobbles, but this was very much normal on bonie night. Within minutes the main flash had passed and things had settled down to a controlled fire and in what seemed minutes again, the fire was ebbing away, but you could hear the cheers go up as suddenly a mattress or another piece of furniture appeared, donated by some kind person who had had a change of heart and saved the night!

As the fire reduced finally to a glow, only a handful of teenagers hung around, turning over the bits and pieces, hoping to rekindle the fading embers.

By morning we were down there as quick as a flash, there was smouldering and wafts of smoke, we kicked around the ashes, within minutes we were black, sifting through the old bed springs, nuts and bolts which held them together, still too hot to pick up. All the kids would wander freely from street to street, sizing each other up. But the aggravation over the past few weeks had gone, so were the grannies! Everybody was back to normal, all fab, till the next time!

At this time in life, there were no fireworks in our streets even on May Day, there were just two great bonfire days.

As I grew a wee bit older my field of play widened and for longer hours each day. One of my favourite haunts with the gang was Edinburgh Castle both in and around. Although other than being a Castle it had no historical meaning for me at this point in my life. We never seemed to enter it like everyone else from the 'Lawn market' it was up and over for us, from Johnstone Terrace up the Steep grassed up cliff-face, scrambling over the western most turret cornering the moat, this being our favourite entrance onto the Esplanade was blocked when the Edinburgh annual military tattoo was on, our way was blocked by the framework of basic scaffolding with tiered row upon row of seating boards, the spectators hopefully unaware of our presence, our wee faces only inches away from their ankles peered between their calves to get a free glance at the pipe bands before we were spotted by real kilted soldiers who could out run us, but stopped short as we dreeped back over the wall and back down onto the roadway below. I never glanced back, fear alone kept me going, and fear seemed to be all our driving forces.

Talking about kilts has brought back a wee 'song' poem!

Kiltie cauld bum (cold bum)
Umbrella feet (umbrella feet)

Went to the pictures
And could na find a seat!

When the picture started
Skinny ma linky farted

Umbrella feet!!

Silly but very well known by kids.

On other occasions when we arrived in the area of the castle, we would follow the bigger boys to where the castle rock met the foundations of the outside walls looking down on Castle Terrace. Fearlessly or just ignorantly, six or more of us in single file confidentially strode out placing one foot in front of the other, walking along a narrow edge or pathway only inches wide and in some parts totally missing, which meant we had to stand back and take a wee run and jump over the gap, at one point some 5 feet wide looking directly down on the footpath at the base of castle rock along the side of the railway, the rear of Ross Bandstand and up to Princess Street itself, a sheer drop. If you leant against the castle wall somehow it was as if he knew – the parky (park keeper) – put in an appearance blowing his pea whistle! Looking all the part of a bus conductor dressed in black, tie and flat hat. There's no way he could ever catch us, after jumping the gap we all belted all the way up this rock as if petered out, arriving on the north side of the Esplanade. We scampered up the wall and over the esplanade down the other side onto Johnstone Terrace, eventually back where we started.

In all the years Mother knew nothing about this and we were never caught at any time by the parkie! On other visits to the castle we were always allowed entry over the drawbridge and never once stopped by the kilted guards standing to attention by their empty sentry boxes. We played in much of the open areas without question, climbing walls all over the site. My favourite toy was 'Mons-Meg' the huge old cannon that stood out in all-weather with a pile of original cannon balls nearby. Either we were small, or Mons-Meg was huge, but we never failed to climb inside the cannon itself. It was scary when somebody decided to come in behind you blocking out your exit and daylight, panic won the order of the day. Getting out was always such a relief.

One day on reaching the age of 5 years, Mother dragged me screaming and kicking all the way down the driveway to St. Peter's Primary School, Morningside and into what was to be my classroom, only for me to be confronted by my teacher Sister Teresa, her ugly round face staring at me from the huge swan winged bonnet on her head, her whole head hidden under a mean full-faced mask, other than her eyes, nose and mouth, no ears! I was terrified enough of Mother bringing me to this place and leaving me alone, not just fear, but terrified! And that was the beginning of my schooling nightmare.

Driven to distraction is the understatement from this day forward. I believe this pushed me away from what others say is the proper way or chosen way in life. This was not for me, and I defied schooling onwards. I hope to continue forwards on past this page to a conclusion, whatever! Just writing this page has brought on a surge of emotion and terrifying feelings that I have not experienced ever. I don't know if my writings will ever be completed. Something happened in this area of my life!

I'll continue onwards in the hope that something will rise to the surface, now 64 years later, and to get a reaction to what needs spelling out, although it is not nice, I know.

The next two and a half years at this Catholic school has left me with no nice thoughts or memories at all. Not long after, I was sitting at my desk, long bench type, seating up to four of us at a time, the desks were stepped up moving from the front to the back, I was sitting doodling with my charcoal on my slate, I was in a wee world of my own day dreaming, when suddenly and without warning, the flash of a foot rule made of wood cracked me right across my knuckles of my right hand. She had used the very edge of it, not finished at that and because I was screaming, and in such pain, she grabbed my right ear and dragged me into the centre of the room shouting at me to be quiet. I sobbed for ages; I was not allowed to even look at my hand. To finish off, I was made to face the corner wearing the 'dunces' hat, a conical shafted paper hat. This punishment seemed to last all day. Sister Teresa carried out such punishment to others who crossed her. Boys and girls alike peed themselves where they sat, too frightened to put their hands up for the toilet. Pee drifting from underneath them down onto the floor, ponding, and once spotted by her, became the subject of her furious shouts and punishments. Nobody dared look up to witness the poor kids, howling their heads off, and the sound of the leather belt striking the bare hand. Then you were stripped and stood by the radiator while your pants or whatever dried off! On one other occasion when walking in the rain, I was passing a huge puddle of water which stretched out into the middle of the road, I never noticed a vehicle coming until a sheet of water covered me head to toe. I arrived completely soaking through, in front of Sister Teresa, who stripped me naked in front of the whole class. I stood close to the radiator until my clothes dried out. I cried for most of this period in fear of more punishment, but none came! No one knew when the ruler was coming out. Although the Bible was read every day. The Catholicism was the subject which gave me and others the most hellish time and resulted in plenty of her ruler waving, screaming and shouting, most of this subject was in Latin… I only remember bits and pieces of the playground, and how we had to line up single file and march in complete silence to wherever we were going!

In one corner of the playground stood a small toilet block open to all weather, a concrete gutter to pee in and one toilet pan, no doors but the pan area had a very small roof and torn up sheets of paper scattered on the floor, no wash basins, the girls' toilet stood nearby and from the outside looked very similar. I have been told by my mum, that Jean was called to be with me when I was upset, I cannot remember, but can understand.

I always prayed for wet weather, when Mother gave Jean a 'penny' for me and to get the tram car from Tolcross to school, and if it was not raining or wet enough we had to walk to and from school giving Mum her ½ penny change, and you could not fool her. walking to school was a good 2½ miles from Fountain Bridge, up Mill Lane, Leamington Terrace, Bruntsfield Place, down Morningside and the same back, for the right reasons I cannot remember being late to school, but I did get into trouble for visiting the canal on the way home from mum!

Later on in life, Mother being a Protestant, had her own opinion of these nuns, that she would say they were just 'frustrated cows', which was the worst swearing I ever heard her say. Of course, I was well and truly much older by that stage, but it does really sum it up and I took her meaning not to be of a sexual nature. I learned some of the tricks of getting on board a tram car without paying, like sitting on the open back step when the conductor was busy at the front or upstairs. The other was to crawl along on your belly between people's feet under the reversible chairs. I was not very successful at either and was always captured, tearful as ever, I'd be ejected and dispatched with a smack across the lug and a verbal warning and on some occasions, it was common citizen doing his lawful duty. I learned, even at an early stage that I was not built for the stress of being a common animal!

Around 1952–53 dad was talking about living somewhere else, where houses were built on 'stilts' and see Uncle 'Dode', my mum's older brother and Uncle Jimmy FlockHart. As it turned out both had in the past disappeared and were now living in Brisbane, Australia. In early 1953 we were all paraded up to The Health Board at John Stone Terrace for our inoculation's so that we would qualify for this £10 immigration, I saw Tommy and Jean go up to the nurse to get theirs, but I could not see what was happening until it was my turn, they seemed OK and did not show any signs of distress. As soon as I saw the nurse with a long needle, holding it over a naked flame, that was it. I flipped and created merry hell. It didn't even matter when she dipped it into some liquid, I screamed murder, as others appeared and held me down. The ordeal was over, only a slight scratch on my arm, but I continued to greet all the way home.

My next recollection was seeing Jean at the Sick Children's Hospital at the Meadows, as we were underage, we had to see her from the Main Street, under 12 years not allowed inside hospital. Her bed was pushed out onto the first-floor balcony where we just shouted up to her and waved. That was the last time I remember seeing her alive.

One morning, I remember Mum and Dad woke us up and stood us in the kitchenette and clearly told us that God and the angels had taken Jean to Heaven and that they saw Jean raise her hands and arms up as the angels took her up to Heaven!

The next time I saw Jean was in the Sacred Hearts Cathedral in Lauriston. Her white coffin, on trestles, lay upfront of the altar. Someone lifted me up so I could see her. That evening I sat in the second row of pews. Jean lay there overnight. The next day she was buried at Mount Vernon in R44. For some strange reason and to this day, I was not at her funeral, no one knew where I got to, Mother said she got me dressed, but did not know what happened to me, and neither do I, a mystery. Jean was 8½ years, died 25 March 1953, born 24 September 1944.

She died of leukaemia, but 2 weeks before her death, Dad agreed to her receiving some sort of possible wonder drug, which would cure or kill her.

My next recollection around the time just after Jean died was visits from a grand old lady 'Granny Connor', I had great affection for her and she gave lots of loving. Although she wasn't my natural 'Granny', she was the best I ever knew. I remember being in her house at a place called the 'Newland's', an old red-brick building on Georgie-Road, right across the road from the 'Roxy Cinema'. Apparently, she helped bring-up my dad, after his mother died (my natural Granny) although it was only a ground floor flat in a block of six, and a small room and kitchen. It was full of folk, the piano was being played and a lot of tears being shed, kisses and cuddles. Then we were next on the train leaving Waverly Station, pitch dark, we had a 6 seater cubicle to ourselves, dad was busy keeping other travellers out, telling them who appeared at the carriage sliding door that all the seats were taken, on this long journey by steam train to London. Once he felt all was clear he made beds up on the net over-head luggage-racks, for Hamish and me. The next memory is of Tommy and me, running around the open decks (in daylight) on 'board the liner', 22,000 tons 'MOOLTAN', berthed in the docks at Southampton, April 1953. I recall looking over the side of the ship, watching huge 'crain men' with 'big-nets', loaded with boxes, lifting them on board ships alongside, and queues of people coming up the gang-way. Next thing we were on the gangway going back off the ship and on to a train! Mum and dad, very upset at the thought of leaving their wee girl behind, decided that they (rightly) didn't want to go to Australia, they kindly understood and unloaded our stuff. I was told years later by Mum and Dad, that if it had not been for the fact that the ship was being delayed from sailing for 24 hours, and had sailed that afternoon on time, then they might not have had time to reflect, and possibly we would have lived in Australia. But they never ever regretted the change of heart.

We spent a night travelling back to London, and then slept overnight in a police-station in London while Dad was refunded his £10 immigration fee from Australia house, we arrived back at Edinburgh 'homeless' and penny less. We were immediately re-homed in 'Duddingston Camp' which was formally the 'Polish Army Troop Camp' during the war, but now turned over to an emergency homeless detention centre, we were only there for a few weeks. I was not aware that my mum was expecting. The women and younger Bairns shared a 'Nissen' hut, along with other women and children up to secondary age, I thought this great fun - all those bairns and beds crammed into these huts. Dad and Tommy were only in the next hut, all men, I was allowed in their hut, but they weren't in ours. Tommy and I made up a 'guider' and chopped up old 'wooden-boxes' into kindling sticks, selling them around the area, didn't make much money but it was fun. Meals were brought to us, in huge steel containers.

We sat around small-tables, cramped together, Mother made sure we got our fill. Through the day, dad walked us all to 'Portobello Beach', I had heard of it, but this was the first time being there, one of the girls from the Camp who was with us, had a nasty accident when she ran through the sands. She stood on an 'broken glass bottle', she was rushed to hospital and came back to the camp with her foot wrapped in bandages.

The place was an adventure playground for us kids, we spent a lot of time round the radical road, up Arthurs Seat and fishing in Duddington Lock. Mum later commented that she worried herself sick at the thought we had too much reign and disappearing to 'God knows where', but only relieved each day when we returned to the crowded camp, she said that the adults got on with life as best, but had a certain kind of freedom to get the daily chores done without crowds of Bairns about their feet. Generally, keeping clean was a problem, but what made it worse was fleas and lice were everywhere, but under control of a kind, no one was free of them, women and girls helped with taking on the 'job' of searching our heads for them daily! Some boys and girls were going around with shaven heads, with 'purple-dye' stuff applied to nearly all of their heads. One job that I could do, and derive a wee but excitement from, was when pulling back the bed sheets and following the trail of blood-spots looking. for the fleas in the mattress, with a bar-of-wettish soap, pressing it into the area where you could see, or thought they were, smack that bit with the soap then examine it to see if a flea or more is stuck to it, if you tried to catch it, you'd probably be there all day as it jumped around.

This was an adventure for us kids, we had hand-out clothes as ours were missing, I had old shoes which were badly fitting, I ended up having yellowy puss heads, bad enough for me to be taken to the Deaconess hospital for red-hot poultice treatment, they had to hold me face-down on the table as I screamed and kicked when they applied them to both feet; what made it worse, the hospital was full of greeting bairns and most were having a poultice for one reason or other, so my screams were wasted.

Not long before we were moved to Fernieside House Gilmerton, which was an old country mansion-house given over to the homeless people, I'd never known anything like this place, big internal staircases, shared bathroom, but we as a family had one-room to ourselves, and a shared kitchen where the mothers could cook for themselves. As this was now summer time the school holidays were on, so we Bairns were entitled to free school dinners, there was a primary school nearby, we called it the Tin-School as it was made of sheet metal.

It was here we met a family who had very similar circumstances and we were friends from this time on. They were from somewhere in England, I never heard such posh voices before. The Baggarnies Uncle Bill, Aunty Kay, Cousins Clive, Kay, Billy and my girlfriend Gail.

Much of our time was spent outdoors, there were the orchards out the back, I'd never seen such a sight, we were, under supervision, allowed to pick the apples and pears, there were also strange looking raspberries and strawberries, strange because I'd not seen such the likes, even tasted them before, no wonder they drew my cheeks-in, sour was not the word. Nearby, there were even fields full of row upon row of tumshies (turnips), the local boys who we had chummed up with, were well armed with scout knives a we soon learned how to shaw a turnip (uproot it and remove the root and green leaves). We seemed to sit there for ages peeling back the 'tumshi' skins using the 4" scout knives that most of the local-boys carried, we ate our fill of sweet-juicy turnip, it would seem, everyday, and we carried as much back to the big-house only to be told off for stealing, but it never stopped them for putting them in the pot. We were covered from head to toe in mud and had to be bathed separately. Sharing the bath was not just for boys and girls separately, my best pal was Gail, we were the same age, and I was used to bath-time with Jean, we might have been 7½ years old but it didn't matter, she was like Jean, a right tom-boy, clarity (Slang for dirty) as any buy, ingrained and dirty knees. Her mother (Aunty Kay) and mine would take it in turn to scrub-us, Hamish would join us, as did other kids, bath-time was great, we'd swap rooms at night. This house had cubby-holes all over the place, hiding games were the best, we'd spend hours, day and night with our brains in different worlds, which I would not have dreamt of only a week ago.

I helped Dad and Tommy carry some wood upstairs to our living quarters, within a few days Dad made a wooden-cross for Jeans grave, Mount-Vernon was not that far away, so when he finished it we all walked to see her and put up the cross, I helped carry some water from the well which we put into jars at each side along with some flowers picked from the House Garden. (It was to be at least another 20 odd years before a stone was erected).

Whilst still living at Fernieside and school holidays finished Tommy and I had to return to St Peter's School. But there was a turning point. I did not have a nun as a teacher. All the time at school I was in the old building and was not aware that there were two more modern blocks next to the toilets, and in them were more classrooms. I was put in there and had a normal looking lady in a skirt called teacher. It did not feel right. I could not settle.

One day Tommy, his pal and I were helping in the church across the road with some others, Tommy's pal showed him and I the candle collection box was open, we looked inside and lying at the bottom were a big pile of old thrupenny-bits. We all took some. But someone must have seen us and reported it to the nuns. That night at Fernieside both of us were dragged from our beds by Father, standing there in the main stairway were two nuns. They reduced us to tears.it shocked us enough never to do it again. But fortunately, no more was done.

It was not long before we were again on the move, this time to Glenlockhart Home, part of the Craiglockhart Asylum. We were put in an old part of the building isolated away from the old people area, and right next to the laundry. There were two old wards, men in one, women and boys up to 11 years. All the meals were brought to the wards and served up by the women. I liked the porridge, it stuck to your ribs! Again, we were surrounded by countryside – our own wee world, just like Fernieside, exciting but not farmland, just hills, bushes and trees. We had a bonus – Gail and her family joined us within days. So we soon got down to games, the grassy slopes were very steep, so we borrowed some old steel bucket lids using them as sledges down the grass slopes. Gail and I found a baby rabbit and decided to bring it up ourselves. We were captured hiding it in the ward under the bed and Aunty Kay, her mother, took us back to the spot we found it and let it go. Spoil sport.

There were plenty of areas to play, even the tip was an attraction. Aunty Kay was always finding old bottles, pots and pans for use in her own home, when she got one.

The tip lay in an area between Firhill and the back end of the Sacred Heart Convent. A fine old Spa in times before.

St Peter's used the pool on special days. Even that was overseen by nuns, although it was inside, we seemed to stand around shivering, dressed in woollen trunks complete with woollen braises. Once out of the water, the trunks hung nearly around the ankles, saturated and floppy. The only good part was when they were finished telling everyone to enjoy themselves. We got a shivery bite in the form of a cream bun followed up with orange juice, complete with a paper straw that collapsed on itself as soon as it got wet, if you asked for another straw you would encourage a clip on the ear for getting the first so wet! It was better to let your shivering shaky hand spill the remainder over your chin.

Early September 1953, we moved to 113 Telford Road, Drylaw. This was a 2 bedroom, living room and separate kitchen house with bathroom upstairs. Our first complete home.

This meant for me that I had to change schools. I couldn't have been happier. I never considered that any other school even existed. There was a small price to pay, small but larger in every way. Hamish, I was doubled up with him, as this was his start of schooling age, I was in charge. The school was St David's, Pilton, no nuns. Again, I never did adjust, but Hamish proved to be a bit of a handful for the school and me. Within days a teacher came into my class and ordered me to take him home at once; the reason being he had been caught dragging a girl across the playground by her pigtails. Mother was not at all happy. That was my really only lasting memory of that school and furthermost vision of Hamish and I.

Our house was one of the first to be occupied. The whole area around it was one big building site, huge big mounds of earth and rubble built up by bulldozers and surrounded by vast areas of lochs of stagnant water. An ideal paradise for all us bairns, and it was well used, every piece of wood was used to make rafts which occupied us endlessly and all the part-built houses were a warren of a playground. We were being chased by workmen from one end of the site to the other, but always escaping their clutches. We must have been a torment to them, and that was only when we were off school. At night the poor lone night watchman could not get peace to settle with a drum of tea, by his hot brazier (fire) next to his sentry box. But one morning, we were asked to say a special prayer for this poor man that we really got to know, he was found dead as he sat in his box leaning forward and his head had burned through. He had been overcome from fumes with the coke fuel of the fire.

It was here that I first saw television. I met a wee boy from down the road, his parents were from India, but I was really taken up with this new thing, as it was then TV was limited to an hour or two a day, but I was still fascinated just watching a blank screen.

The Western General Hospital was nearby, I remember visiting it to see Mum, but I was too young to get in to see her, along with Hamish, we had to stand below the first-floor window and wave up to Mum. Then one day, I came into the living room and lying on the settee was a wee baby 'Horice'. Just tucked up in a shawl and that was that! and that turned out to be the reason why Mum was in hospital. Horice was born on Jean's birthday, 24 September 1953. Mum apparently was not very pleased at not having a girl. Life as it was for me carried on pretty much normal except when I had to be taken to the Western General A&E while playing on the rafts on the sites. I decided to jump ashore onto what looked like a safe plank of wood, but I failed to notice a 6-inch nail sticking up out of it. I felt the pain as it pierced right through the sole and out the top arch of my right foot. I was, or would have been pretty much OK if I hadn't turned around to see the nail with a piece of my flesh on the end of it, that was the end of me. my pals carried my body home. It wasn't finished when I got to hospital, they drove a spike into my thigh, more screams! What a nightmare! I hated needles before and 62 years on still do!

The first time I remember ever having an Xmas tree was at this house. It sat on a mobile trolley (tea stand on wheels) at the front window beside the door in the living room. It was dark outside, Dad was upstairs in the bath, scrubbing the soot off. Tommy, Mum and I were in the kitchen, the open chip pan was heating on the gas cooker, Mum was just dropping some chipped potatoes into hot melted lard when suddenly the whole pan caught fire, Mum shouted to me, "Get Dad!"

I shot straight to the living room door and shouted up the stairs, "Dad, Dad, the house is on fire!" Then ran back to the kitchen just in time to see Tommy flinging it out the back door.

At the same time, we would hear this thumping and bumping coming all the way from upstairs down to the bottom, then one heck of a crash, followed by Dad shouting, "The lights, the lights! Switch off the bloody lights!"

We rushed into the living room to see Dad lying naked with the Xmas tree and lights lit on top of him. Mother pulled the plug out of the wall. I got the blame because I shouted the house is on fire. He apparently shot out of the bath and as we had no carpets on the stairs or elsewhere his wet feet never gripped the top step lending him to miss much of the stairs and shot through the door and into the tree with full power on. Tommy saved the day, and got a slightly burnt hand. Chip pans were just a large pot full of grease.

Again in this new house, we had the countryside right outside my front door, no more than 30-ft away just over the other side of the old road, wheat fields all the way over to Craiglieth, up to Groathill and down to Crewtoll, where now the fire station is sited. On this site we would play with real gypsy bairns, who lived there in their horse-drawn bow wagons and real campfires. We were always warned by our folks to stay clear of them, why, I don't know!

We played as other bairns and were treated the same.

Tommy got himself a paper delivery job at Craiglieth paper shop. So we took a shortcut across the wheat fields tramping our way from the house. The wheat on those days stood the same height as us. It wasn't long before we fell afoul of the law! When we knew a policeman was searching for us, we crawled about the wheat trying to hide from him, and all the time he followed our every move just by watching the movement of wheat! Eventually we had to come out and it was dark and he shined his torch and somehow even knew our names. Crying did not impress him and with threats of all kinds hanging over us, we took the road way round.

But I think Jean was never far from me at night in the dark. I would creep out of my bed in my night shirt and climb up on the wide window ledge. I'd sit curled tight and just stare out over the wheat fields and over the tops of the far off Craiglieth bungalows and know somewhere in that direction was Jean, alone and afraid in the darkness. I cried for someone to bring her home.

8 Year Summary

At the point looking back over the past eight years, I find it hard to establish just what is or was wanted. Mum later said I was always clingy, silently crying, and going to nursery I found stressful and school was worse, even before Jean died! I could never understand exactly what was right, what did I have to do at school.

When you got something correct after a while they would say, "See I knew you could do it all the time!" What they didn't know was I never knew what the hell I done to get whatever it was 'right'. Nobody showed me. Now I feared getting it wrong again, and get bawled and scolded once more. It was a serious vicious circle and I could not cope! I got the thumping and belting no matter what. But slowly and now conscious of it, I attuned to accept the physical pain without question and at some points it was a welcome relief. The verbal, though not as bad as the paperwork theory just had to be taken and hope it stopped soon.

I could not understand the Latin copying words verbally, such as songs, and the singing seemed easier, reading it and trying to hold on to it was impossible.

I was finished more over the subject of homework revision, all impossible, I must have at some point at the early stages missed the point and slowly drifted apart of the reasoning for this subject. The harder I tried the worse it got, and less was achieved. Punishment increased. My sums, tables I could call out without any problems, but again writing it down was more than difficult, and I never caught on what. This was to get worse when it came to calculations from the board, simple adding or subtraction. I could see the answer if I closed my eyes and write it down in the sum but failed when they would tell me to put it in the carry or subtracts. Somehow, I can now. Out came the belt.

In very recent years I was told I was dyslexic.

Mother was not happy in this area or environment and Dad's health was suffering as well, all these stresses were building up. Then we got the news, very early 1954, we were moving once more to a top flat 63/5 Stevenson Drive. Three bedrooms, living room, kitchenette, bathroom. Six houses on the stairs, the home to 19 children in all. I was now 8 years old and boy, this was different again. Looking out of our bedroom window straight onto huge trees that lined both sides of the drive (Stevenson), all the way up from Balgreen nearly up to Stenhouse Cross, and viewed as a driver would see it looking down the tree lined tunnel, they arched together at the top and when fully leaved was eerily darkened. Thankfully at this time of year only the buds showed their head, so I got a full view through them into Saughton Park on our side, just inside the spiked railing which circled the park where 4 rugby pitches. I'd never heard of rugby, let alone see it. Beyond them lay all the muddy football pitches. So many to count, but well over 16, a huge vast area.

Right at the furthest most part of the park you could see another line of trees and just in front a structure which was later identified as the bandstand, and on my extreme right, a much closer line of trees had the viewpoint into the enclosure, where special football and running track events were held.

The bedroom and living room shared this view that was to the front. The bathroom and another back bedroom looked out over the back green, they were truly greens, sectioned off fencing, some of which was lying flat, this gave us access from one garden to another, they were mainly drying greens where the grass was kept short for mothers to get access in all weathers.

All the tenements around those greens faced backwards, so their kitchens and bathrooms faced into them. In the centre where all the greens met were mounds of grass-covered earth works which were the remains (some complete) of air-raid shelters. This is where the bairns hung out, away from the washing.

The kitchenette was located between the living room and bathroom, being on the gable end wall it was small and had a window which looks down onto 'The Plantation', some 30-ft X 20-ft completely penned in and grassed (lawn), this section of land with half a dozen or so small trees whose branches stretched nearly up to the windowsill. In spring time they all had cherry blossoms, a display much loved by us all. Dad nicknamed the kitchenette our '4 apartment kitchen'. It was the focal point at most times of the day and night. The cooking was done on an old upright Edinburgh cast iron gas stove, with an eye-level grill. Posh. A stove enamelled twin tubs with a centre board, on which Mum fixed her splendid hand wringing mangle 2 rollers with a winding handle, the washing hauled up and out of the larger wash tub, fed in between the rollers, squeezing out most of the water, filling up the smaller one, repeated back and forwards using cleaner water each time. It was not long until we could actually afford a 'Dean' washer, which had a gas burner to heat the water, and an electrically operated agitator which swished the water and washing together backwards and forwards, and it had an electric roller. Wowee! Mum's pride and joy. This was the first of firsts where we were to be ahead of anyone else in the stair.

Crammed into the kitchenette was a gate legged table where we would eat all our meals in shifts, such was the size! The living room had an open fire place, a small range with a couple of kettle swing hinged stands, which allowed us to have another hot water source. The main living room window looked out to the front, but a second smaller window had the same view as the kitchen. The folk below us were the Hardings, Ma and Pa and three grown up bairns in their teens, Hilda, George, Tommy and below them the Deas, Ma and Pa, Ian three-year-old, his two sisters, Lorna and Shena.

Opposite the Deas was Ma and Pa Neely, sons George 6 years old, Douglas months, and my girlfriend, Elspeth 8 years; above them was McIntyre and her Downs Syndrome son Donald (nice pair) and finally next to us Ma and Pa Leitch, 2 daughters, 1 boy.

With moving to Stevie Drive, all of a sudden, I found I had real aunties, uncles and cousins living nearby and my 'Granny Connor' lived only 10 minutes walking distance away. Everything seems to be working better, at least from my eyes. Dad had started to do chimney sweeping for himself and he had an old mate helping him, Oli Taylor, typical of all the sweeps I got to meet, they were always 'black' engrained with soot. Poor Oli, he was handicapped in two ways, he had a very bad stutter (impediment) and only 3 fingers on each hand. It never stopped him from playing the drums on a full-size kit, but better still, he was a 'roper' and climbed all the roofs and lums, and with no difficulties even worked with the sweeping ropes which were like grease when wet, and that would be most of the time. He was well respected in the trade.

They walked everywhere, carrying the ladders, brushes, ropes and sheets (tookies). Dad couldn't afford a van at this time.

Mum was a book-keeper in earlier days. She handled all the paperwork and went from door to door delivering business cards and taking in the orders. I even went down to help. 'The Wee Shop' at Balgreen where Mum had an agreement with the owner, which the owner took thrupence 1½–2p for each customer they booked on to have their chimney swept. There was great anticipation when I brought the order book home, just to see how much Dad was going to earn that week!

On a number of occasions, I had to get up and go out with Dad at midnight, after he bought a small van it was loaded with soot from the sweeping just done the day before and it had to be dumped at the tip before he could start another days sweeping. Between the hours of 12am–1am, the tip 'Hailsland Tip' was open to all trades, they would not go there until the sweeps were finished. His sweeps were sometimes was late, I took their place, this was just great by me. Dad and I travelled in pitch dark all the way from Stevie to Longstone, when we got there the watchman swung open that wooden wire meshed gate and waved us in. it was spooky. The van slipped and slewed down the winding track way littered with rubbish on my side and just a big black hole on the other. Eventually when we got down there it was great to see, in the headlights, other sweeps shaking their sheets emptying them in huge cloudbursts of soot. Dad opened the back, all the time exchanging words with the other sweeps. He pulled out the sheets loaded with soot emptying them where they fell, great stuff we were wallowing in. I was sneezing, my nose was running with the miffing acids. I folded the sheets in a certain manner and then stacked them in the van, there was no stopping. Back in the van and back up the track, this part of the quarry was up to 150-ft deep. The watchman held the gate open and gave us a wave. It was back home, Oli always turned up, I always enjoyed when he was late. Mother always gave me a bath, followed by a big bowl of porridge. That was great.

Mum even took on a job as a cleaner at Haymarket in a lawyer's office and how I know this, I was roped into helping her. She started just after midnight. We had to walk all the way there and back through Murrayfield, Roseburn and up Grosvenor Crescent to the old Victorian style buildings, it covered three floors. My duties were the same, all the open coal fires (which heated all the rooms) probably 8 or 9 in total, had to be red-out (cleaned out) and set (ready for relighting). Each fireplace had its skillet (coal bucket) any coal in it was tipped out onto spread out newspaper, making sure the fire was completely out. I'd lift out any pieces of part burnt cinders and put them to one side, then with a poker rake out the other cinders shoved them up into the skillet then brush and cleaned up ashes. Mother would then follow me into each office room after I had got rid of the dusty job, she then started to dust down. I'd take the skillet down outside, empty it keeping clear of the dust (stour) which blew everywhere, refill the skillet with good sized pieces of coal (large and small sizes), also kindling sticks pieces of wood (chopped up to 4 or 5 inches long), take the lot upstairs. Then taking newspaper sheets, twisting them into knots placing them into the fire basket, then a layer of criss-cross kindling sticks, a scattering of small pieces of coal, well placed then that was a fire 'set' for the first person in and only have to put a match to it. One fire done 7 or 8 to go. If Mum was happy, so was I. Having said that, this could be done by any person who had an open fire in their house, a daily task for most folk. Mother worked fast, she could dust and polish in a flash. Then it was home, and a quick tub, then bed!

This place, Stevenson Drive, had loads of areas which were just a haven for us bairns where we could direct our unspent energies instead of the games in the park, like footie, rugby none of which interested me in the least. Hearts of Midlothian would appear training, just outside our window in the park. I only have one clear memory of them when a bunch of us kids crossed the pitch that they were training on and one of the older bairns shouted to Willie Bauld, the then No 1 named football player in Scotland, "Gone yer sel Willie." Willie shouted back: "Get the f**k away!" We all took off. not waiting for a second telling.

I think this was the first time I recall such a swear word ever used even in this area. That as my everlasting and only memory of the great man. It just cemented my lack of interest in football, I was more interested in the 'Burn' (water of Leith) which held many different adventures like Tarzan swings, swimming, rafting. I bought my first raft from big boy Clive Bain; he was about 10 years old and lived right next to the Burn at Fords Road. He lived in a house above the stables (2 Clydesdale Horses), his dad was the local butcher and very rich!

Back to the raft, Clive wanted 2/6d (12½p) a lot of money. Never short when I needed it. The next Sunday, I went around to the back of Tynecastle Gorgie football ground by the school. The football match was the day before. I climbed up the 10-ft wall and as expected, piled so high that I didn't have to reach down far to lift up the top handful of empty beer bottles a well-known spot for the local boys who were skint. I needed to take 1 d worth of screw top or 1/2 d for wee bottles that meant 30 screw tops or a mixture (beggars cannot be choosers, as the saying goes). After a few trips up and down the wall, I found a place in nearby long grass where I could hide them till the next day as the pubs who took back and refunded empties were not open on a Sunday in those days. Next day I caught some old men who were going into the Tynecastle Arms Pub and pleaded my poverty, (bairns and women were not allowed in bars). Trustworthy as usual they came out and gave me the money all 12/6 (12½p). Straight back to Clive, deal done. I was surrounded by would-be pals (crew) and filed onboard the platform, raft 4 oil drums tied together with planks of wood and I was the captain and owner. We pushed off with long poles and out into the middle of the Burn a bit of shoving and pushing going on, within seconds my world turned upside down and I surfaced just in time to see the bottom of the oil drums sink below the surface, all of us screaming and shouting. If it weren't for the overhanging branches of trees to grab hold of, me and the others would have gone under. I didn't get any sympathy from any of them, just a good slagging. Mother wasn't very pleased and I got a wee thumping for telling lies! She didn't believe my story that big boys pushed me in!

One morning I was awakened by mum shaking me awake, "Michael, Michael! Hurry up and get dressed." She half called and shouted to me. I thought it was Dad needing a hand with something. "Come on hurry up, he's waiting on the street for you."

I was pushed out the door and taking the stairs two at a time, I ran out the stair passage. Glanced around looking for Dad in the street, and all that was there in the darkness was the milkman beside the horse and cart. He just said, "Michael." I recognised him, I'd seen him before, he then pointed to a milk basket (12 pinter) with a full load of empties, it lay on the ground beside his feet. "Can you put that up there?" he said, pointing to the back of the cart.

I walked up to it (without question) lifted it up and pushed it on, then stepped back. Glancing over my shoulder looking for Dad.

"Right, Michael, 4 o'clock am, tomorrow at the Roxy, we won't wait!" With that he walked up to the horse's head, clicked his teeth, then just moved away.

I ran back up the stairs. Mum was waiting for me in the kitchenette. Then she told me that one of the milk boys had left school and another boy failed to turn up to take his place, so she put my name forward. I don't think I could take it in, I'd just been told I had a job! That was the highest point in my eight years... to last 60+ years.

With this move to Stevie comes another school! I don't think it even registered with me to have any emotional feelings about whatever school it was, neither up or down, like or dislike. By now my attitude was submissive to come what may. That was to stay with me onwards!

St Cuthbert's R C School, Hutchison, Chesser! The only lasting memory St David's other than Hamish's issue was that I never got the belt or remember any down side. I succumbed to whatever they gave me, and they never responded to my negativities.

Here at St Cuthbert's they decided that they would have to hold me back one year because I had failed their assessments, whatever they were. I do not remember some sort of exam paper when I got into the first week, but if that was their way of assessing me, then they too missed the boat, as I never even attempted to complete it. I was not, I think, finding a way out of the system, staying inside it in the knowledge that corporal punishment was their only defence.

This place even had its own smells very different from Fountainbridge, which was rubber from the tyre works or well-kept odours from the breweries and others that all blended together. I never even thought there were more varieties either, not for a moment! But now, still a lingering sniff of horses, but lost somewhat in the stench of Cox's Glue Works on Gorgie Road, it really took ages to understand how animal hooves stank putrid when boiled, also the Tannery in Ford's Road – I can't even describe it. My favourite variety of mixed smells was when in Slateford, the whole place aired of farmyard, not that I was ever in one at that age. The slaughter house smelt of pigs, sheep, cattle and other farmyard poultry. Every Tuesday was market day, herds and flocks gathered in every available pen and road space, either waiting for re-sale or slaughter.

On a hot summers day with the breeze coming from the south, Mother complained of the stink of the market and going around the house slamming the windows shut!

I was well and truly amazed one morning in spring when I got up on one of my first days of the milk run to find the farmyard came right up to our house. I thought I was hearing strangely familiar sounds outside, I got out of bed and up to the window, I couldn't believe my eyes.

There, across the road behind the tall iron railings; sheep, millions! Well definitely hundreds, all over the park as far as I could see and even more being driven by the shepherds walking down the road waving the hooked-crook in the air shoving the sheep and calling instructions to the dogs who were running up and down, in and out. Organised chaos!

Oh boy, I was down there in a flash. Just in time to see the last load being shepherded into the park with the gates clanging shut behind them and a pack of sheepdog running madly up and down the outside fence. I had to take the long way around the park to work.

Now a milk boy, this was my first paying job, not that I was to profit from it for a number of years, Mother oversaw that. I cannot remember exactly what my first weekly wages were for a 4am to 7am shift, 7 days a week including all holidays (working them) and for the next 7 years until my 15th birthday. I remember when I was given an increase possibly after the first year, they went up to 2/6 d weekly (12½p). The other two boys working from the cart were a couple of years older than me, and had been working this run well before me, they just ignored me for what seemed months, and were well in tune with handling every part of the routine. Although I was quite small for my age, I managed fine, and soon learned how to reach up to the tail end of the cart and pull towards me a fully loaded '12 pinter' basket and gently lower it in to the ground at my feet.

The crates piled up to four high, five or six wide and six the whole length of the cart, each crate held twenty-four bottles full of milk and if kept upright (as they should) an inch or two of cream would gather at the top. And it was important that the customer got it delivered with the cream on top, it was a treat for the man to get the cream, the infant or for baking. With no refrigeration it had to be used quickly. The milk boy would get the blame if the milk and cream were to be disturbed and unsettled. It was therefore my job to see that when I got my baskets of milk that they were all OK.

My milkman would stand at the back end of the cart and take the bottles one at a time and load them into the hand carrying baskets, some of which held six up to twelve pints but ½ pints of milk were asked for by my regular customers, they were carried in our hands separately. The bigger more experienced boys could use the 12-pinter baskets.

The 12-pinter baskets were mainly used for the higher populated tenements on my run at Westfield Road, Gorgie, 16 flats in one stair as a 6 pinter we used with main doors and smaller tenements. I was well balanced with the 6 pinter in each hand but my milkman would place a 12 pinter in the well of a tenement for me (impossible for me to carry when full, but OK when bringing back a full basket of empties). In the big tenements my milkman would leave me 2 full baskets in the middle of the well entry and I would load up my smaller 6 pint basket from it and go around each door where the owner would leave out an empty (very clean bottle, if greasy, no milk). Each empty bottle meant one full would be left.

With my company, The Store or St Cuthbert's Co-Operative Society, the policy was to collect the money on the doorstep, if it was cash, the norm was to wrap it in a small piece of paper and jam it on the neck of the bottle. The correct amount had to be left, the milkman was not for stopping to handout change at any time. To get over this the customer would calculate how many pints they needed each week, they then needed to buy tokens from the Store when they got their rations. The tokens came in different colours but were of a size to drop inside each bottle. The people were very trusting. I cannot remember anyone stealing money or tokens on our round.

Most of the tenement stairs with long passages, nooks and crannies were very spooky. I needed eyes in the back of my head and lived on my nerves when in them. On one occasion when I entered the long entry into one tenement, I could see 2 baskets placed in the centre of the well right below the gas light which flickered overhead, as I leant forward my hand stretched out to pick up a pint, slowly a hand emerged from the darkness attached to a long bare arm, it nearly touched the back of my hand. With a scream, I turned on the spot, and heard footsteps running behind me as I shot out of the stair and straight into the middle of the roadway where I collapsed with fear and relief, rolling around the cobbles I looked up to see one of the older milk boys standing in the stair doorway rolling down his sleeve, roaring with laughter and I could hear my milkman shouting abuse at us to behave and get on with our deliveries. If it wasn't cats, rats and mice darting around at that time, it was the other boys. Anybody's nightmare. The bigger lads tore me to pieces (mentally), I must admit I grew to enjoy their attentions in this area, it all ended as a big laugh. I am sure my milkman had a quiet snigger!

The run always started at 4am sharp, Mother had me up in plenty of time and a steaming hot plate of porridge was on the table and well salted as usual. No tea, toast or biscuits in those days and not even a piece (sandwich). In the summer, my footwear was someone else's (hand-me-downs) black rubbers always great to have them on your feet. The rest of the year it was always wellies which never fitted, and if they didn't have holes in the soles, they soon would have, and a cut-out insole of cardboard slid in place. This was replaced daily as the damp had the best of it.

My clothes were always some old grey long-sleeved school shirt, well-worn at the cuffs and collar! Holed on the elbows or patched up. A pair of school grey shorts, well repaired or worn, with all the pockets sewn up (Mother always sewed up all our pockets, most mother's done this from new!) again as I was not at secondary (and in second year at that), we were not allowed to wear long trousers till over 12 years old. If and when I had a jacket, it would be an old school one. I never had any bother getting up and out leaving Tommy still sleeping in the bed settee we shared. He was excused these duties because of all the operations he was to have on his ears – cold, dust and even rough playing could cause him serious problems. To me, he had the worst job by looking after the family when Mum and Dad were out, he turned out to be a great cook and home keeper, he could manage any situation around the house, and of course, he was 4 years older than me. So all his hand-me-downs came to me.

I just had to grow into them. It helped that I had a few male cousins of my age and size. Once I was up, fed and dressed for work, I'd head out of my stair, cross the road and enter the park (Saughton) which was always locked up at night. My entry by way of the bent railings., just enough to squeeze through, and head off across in the pitch dark to the furthest away corner of Balgreen, exit by the old paddling pool where another hole in the railings happened to be, out of there over the red bridge crossing the water of Leith onto Gorgie Road and away along to the Roxy Picture house, 10 minutes on a fair day well in time to be ahead of the milkman. Even the journey to work never really gave me a problem in the dark cold days of winter. The railings stood 5 foot 6 inches, and sometimes when it snowed, it drifted to the full height, making it impossible to get into the park. I then had to go down Stevie Drive to Balgreen School and down the road, circling round the park.

I never thought in my wildest dreams I'd be a milk boy and actually working with the familiar horse and carts, also the clinking and clatter of the milk bottle and getting paid to be part of it with the feeling I was helping Mum by earning a wage. The milk round covered the same route each day, from the Roxy along Gorgie Road flats, left down Westfield Road (tenements on one side), round and along Stevenson Road and Avenue, to the paddling pool at the park, this is where we hopped on board and had a ride up to Stevie Drive and all of Whitson, zigzagging in and out of the streets till finally finishing up the top of Whitson Road and the junction of Stenhouse Woods at 6.30–7am.

We normally met up with another milk cart at this point, where this was the point, they too finished using the boys in time for schooling. Also, a motorised lorry met both carts with a refill of milk crates taking away the empties. The milkmen continued on their own to finish the remainder of the run, and no tenements involved, mostly main doors.

The horse was, on special occasions, taken out of the shafts, his van driving harness tied up in a fashion so it would not get in a tangle, he (the horse) was let free to graze the grass in one of the enclosed plantations, what a treat for him, being a change from the dangling nose-bag full of dried food, chaff or bruised oats, causing him to snort and blow and a many more, only getting relief in a pale of water.

One of our favourite pastimes on the run was on bucket day, when the households put out their pails full of mostly ashes, as most waste would go on the fire, but some things in better-off houses went out in the bucket. I had my favourite customer who used to tie up bundles of old newspapers, but she must have had bairns because included in the bundle were some comics. I could not afford to buy '*Dandy* or *Beano*'s', it didn't matter how much ash and tattie peeling they were covered in, I bagged them. This was the highlight of my week. Tommy enjoyed them before they were handed down to my pals.

On one day our horse threw a shoe. The milkman went to the phone box at Balgreen, he made contact to the office on Fountainbridge who sent out the farrier, who arrived half an hour later in his splendid horse lorry. We all sat on the open cart frozen to death with only a nearby streetlamp illuminating the area. The farrier set to work, removing the remains of nails from our horse's front hoof, he disappeared into the back of the lorry where he had a coke-heated, small furnace here he heated the shoe, and re-shaped it on his anvil, clanging away till it was re shaped, coming out and burning it onto the horse's hoof. Smoke curled around nearly making him invisible and the horse just stood there without even moving, balanced on three legs.

It was all over in ten minutes, and back to work, glad to get my blood moving back into my purple kneecaps. That was the only time we used the mobile farrier, and if a horse took lame, then a replacement was brought out using the lorry. As like one morning our horse was spooked and when our milkman tried to steady it, it took off! Lucky it didn't get more than a few yards down Wheatfield Road, when one of the bigger milk boys managed to catch up quickly, he grabbed its halter and just hung on for grim death, shouting at it to "Stand, stand!" and to our surprise, it quickly came to a halt, but not before empty bottles crashed all over the place. Luckily no full bottles were damaged, just as some full crates teetered on the edge. A few yards more and it would have been a disaster. With borrowed brooms we set about cleaning up the mess!

All the horses were trained to obey the same words of command, as the milkmen spent most of the time standing at the back of the cart loading the baskets and being 15 feet away from the horse's head and blind to the horse because not only its blinkers but the structure of the cart. When we were finished at one stair ready to move onto the next, he would call quietly to the horse 'walk on'. The horse obediently just walked on, and the regular horses automatically stopped at the next stair; they knew the rounds very well and if you wanted to stop it then a simple 'halt' was all that was needed, the horses were very smart!

In the first years, Xmas Day was not a holiday, and for me it was just another morning. The only noticeable difference was, it was really the only time I remember getting tips or a sweetie in the form of a fairy cake or actual single chocolate sweet complete with wrapper. From special customer who took the trouble to listen for you coming and getting out of bed, only a very small handful did this, actual money. Tips were usually a ½ penny wrapped up separately in the bottle, but most were given to the milkman, even your customer bypassed you to give him the tip. He never shared anything with any of the boys (old bugger!). Even the horse got fresh bread or a carrot for Christmas!

One of the most spectacular presents I ever witnessed was a Shetland pony. On the corner of Whitson Road in the fenced off plantation in the darkness of Christmas morning stood a black Shetland pony, it was a Christmas present for Gypsy Car Dealer's daughter Charlotte. The family were known as gypsies, not that it mattered to me, I thought that this was possibly the best Xmas present someone could get. (I was to get a job with her dad washing cars at his second car showroom at Ford's Road Scout Hall. This is where the pony was left, Champion was his name. For a couple of hours' cleaning, I got 9d (3.75p). My job after the milk round, also my second ever job and the first where I was allowed to keep the money). Charlie, Charlotte's father, who gave me the job cleaning his cars later bought a cottage in Gorgie Road near Cox's Glue Works and named it after his only child 'Charlotte'. She was killed in an accident at Hillend, her horse and her were struck by a bus and both killed, she was in her late 20s. Charlie was a broken man, he had a stroke and spent the rest of his days in an electric wheelchair, wandering along from the cottage, his fine long white hair and beard. When I first met him, he had a shiny full head of jet-black hair. Poor man!

A bit of a wee money earner for the milkman was the horses' dung. We carried a small metal bucket and shovel on the back of the cart. When the horse dropped some dung, whoever saw it was tasked to shovel it up and get to it before any other person. The dung was well sought after by most folk for their garden vegetables and rhubarb. (Dad used to say he preferred custard on his). Woe betide any of us who missed it. Our milkman was well rewarded at the end of the year for his supply of fresh dung! I was to meet another milk boy who was only 3 weeks younger than me, he was James Cavanagh. Jimmy lived at 9 Whitson Crescent. We knew each other from school, but when I met him at the end of my run at Stenhouse Avenue West, he was attached to another cart, when we crossed runs at that point and on recognising each other, we became 'blood brothers' and firm family friends for the rest of our lives. Although we normally finished at roughly the same time every day, and at the same location, some days like holidays. We stayed with the cart right up to late morning just to help our milkman get finished early and also get a wee bit extra pocket money, which was great. We finished at Fords Road end, some of us would stay on the cart just or the fun of it all the way back to the milk bottle depot at Gardner's Crescent, Fountainbridge. Getting to the depot was at the time a wee bit exciting to say the least for us, but not the horses. A walking trot was the normal pace all the way. But it changed once the milkman caught sight of another cart well within catching distance. Two or three of us sitting on the foot plate of the shafts, bobbing up and down to the rhythm of the horse, keeping clear of it farting in our faces. We would be ordered up and onto the cart behind the milkman, so we could steady the rattling milk crates in fear they would fall to the ground. The horses thundered with their clattering hooves as the two galloped full tilt along Gorgie the Wardlaws streets passing on the right, heads turning with looks of disgust on the locals faces. Even at midday there was not any traffic compared to today, not even a bus in sight. Fortunately, it wasn't our luck nor the horses to have the speed to overtake the other cart, we, or should I say the horse only had enough energy left to tackle the very steep brae of Henderson Terrace, and what a climb. The driver judging the junction correctly, had the horse set a good pace in order to get up. They only had one go at it, I never heard of any failing. I think it was more how fit the horses were rather than the ignorance of the milkman in charge.

On one occasion when we got to the top of the brae and onto Angel Park Terrace, where it was very common to meet a couple of carts on the road ahead as this was a major road junction from Slateford and other outlying areas, we found ourselves in a traffic jam, the likes I have never seen up to that date, only a trickle of traffic coming towards us. As we crowded around the road bends that took us onto the straight road of Dundee Street, we were faced with sight I've not even seen since. A policeman was directing all the traffic around a stationary horse milk cart, not unlike ours, this one's shafts were pointing in the air and a heap of crates and smashed empty bottles had already been swept and piled alongside. On our left stood a small row of tenements (2 stairs) with a small area to the basement flats and open stairway, this was fenced off by a 4-foot iron spiked railing with an 8-foot drop into the basement flats (as they were known).

What happened was at Yeaman Place, a street going straight off Dundee Street and opposite the areas, a horse coming down Yeaman lost control on the downhill slope and could not turn right. So with the railings in front and being pushed by the cart tried to jump the spikes and was impaled by its belly. It was decided the horse would be shot and as we passed by it was covered by a tarpaulin. All I could see were a couple of its legs, it was a very bad day.

The tale soon spread that the driver actually drove the horse down the hill at speed. I have heard of horses having to be shot for all sorts of reasons whilst on the rounds and now this. True saying 'seeing is believing'.

Once we got to the dairy depot, a yardsman took over the reins. There were about 6 or 7 loading banks where we had to wait our turn until a place was available and when one was, the yards man began backing the horse, still in the shafts, up to the banking and no sooner had the tail of the cart made contact with the bank, the brakes were put on. The banks men with long hooked poles set about pulling the empty crates onto the bank. Whilst this was going on, the yards man unfastened the horses' traces and britchings from the shafts, secured all the loose ends of harness on the horse, and gave the horse the command 'walk on'. The horse knows exactly where to go and wandered over to the huge exit iron arched gates where there were other horses gathered. Waiting till enough of them were there, the gates opened, they moved off to the waiting bank of nuisance bairns ready to rush them and swarm over them like a rash.

At the time I followed my milkman and entered a smallish dark room where there was a gathering of other milkmen, a lot of shouting and bartering (vocals), as they huddled around these clattering pieces of machinery which counted all his tokens. He just poured all the tokens in one go into the top and alike magic they were counted. Whilst this was going on others were counting their coinage on shelves which were on most of the walls, they all had the same type of diary type books constantly flicking pages back and forth, adjusting figures with pencils and those that were done with all this, they joined a long queue where they waited in turn to have their books and money checked-in, and then they were finished their shift. Only to return at 2am and start another shift with a full load of milk and a much-refreshed horse.

When I started schooling at St Cuthbert's, I never felt happy or at ease with it. They were building the new school across the roadway, so my classroom was in the old stone-built building similar to St Peter's. but no sign of nuns, although it was right next to St Cuthbert's Church, and strangely I had a man for my teacher, he turned out to be a bit of a hard task master and in my eyes a bully. He'd shout and bawl at everybody, his face always seemed red with rage which for me (and not alone) made me fear every day. His greasy long black collar-length hair always seemed to fall over his face and he continuously swept it back with his hand and his strap which he used for punishment seemingly every other minute. Both girls and boys suffered and feared him. I cried often and had to try hard not to as this only got him into a rage, and lead to more slaps on the ears, only to be relieved when I thankfully got the belt. Which, when not lying on his desk, hung draped over his shoulder. I saw the belt as a relief. I could not understand the lessons, in particular the sums. I just did not know or saw what they were about, and couldn't make sense or reason of them. So again, it was easier to take the punishment than make an effort, or so it seemed logical to me. I'm sure this was now the beginnings of my defensive strategy, purely nature's way of dealing with this problem. I can now say that on reflection, sums seemed to give me the biggest problem, and I'm sure all other subjects just fell into my defences. Easier not to succeed with them just accept the punishment! And my whole time in primary followed my theory from start to finish. Although I was no longer using slates, but pencils and notebooks.

Once the new school building was opened, I escaped the teacher for a Mr Early, he was a very nice man. I cannot remember ever once getting the belt from him or even him getting angry, in fact he always seemed to have us laughing. I still kept up my defences as it seemed to be accepted of me and my reports always had me at the bottom of the class. This was my position and by now, I was very happy with it.

Even at that age (8 years) and developed attitude, having full and clear knowledge that I had my milkman, I never heard one word, either way from the schools that working was a problem; it was to me never even mentioned. I wasn't the only 8-year-old doing the same job. When I met Jimmy Cavanagh, who not only lived around the corner at Whitson Crescent and on an adjacent milk round, he attended the same school. He too had only just moved to Whitson from Watson Crescent, which is just off Yeaman Place (where the horse was shot after trying to jump the railings). Our play areas where the same and our mothers used the same steamies. We had a lot in common. By the time Jimmy was 22 years, he was to lose all his family. When I was first invited to his house at Whitson, his mother was already bed ridden, his father was a seasonal painter (outside painting was not done in winter) he also suffered with a bad chest, coughing all the time. His sister Margaret was about 20 years older. She was at home looking after her mother and father, after just returning home from her first trip on an ocean liner where she worked on board in the ship laundry. She had travelled all the way to New Zealand and Australia. She held us in a magic spell telling us the fantastic stories. Margaret was, as most young women, a great housekeeper, she could set and kindle a fire in just a minute.

Not long after I met Jimmy, only months, he disappeared from both the milk run and school. Days later I met him in Whitson, he told me that he had found his dad dead one morning and was buried at Mount Vernon. He said his dad had choked on his own phlegm (spit). I was horrified. Jimmy said it didn't bother him as he used to hit him a lot. Margaret had decided to become a nurse and was studying. She gave up her world travels to look after her mum and Jimmy. Jimmy got up one morning to find Margaret dead in bed. She apparently died of an accidental overdose of sleeping tablets. She was going to sit her final nursing exams next morning. Margaret was also buried at Mount Vernon.

Up until this point, we had a pretty exciting life. We spent most of our playtime at the park or up Corstorphine Hills, we had similar imagination and we used them well, if it wasn't his mind working 10 to the dozen, it was mine. One of our favourite areas was up a tree on the edge of Corstorphine Wood above Balgreen Road. We'd have our supplies of food and water which were a few pieces of white bread buttered and well sprinkled with sugar or covered in used chip tasting lard, washed down with a mouthful of real tap water drank from an old lemonade bottle. We'd spend many an hour up that tree talking about what adventures we'd get up to. One of which we actually carried out - 'Live on an Island'. We made an attempt with a borrowed tent, bussed it down to Cramond Island with our pieces and water. We spent hours on the island, but in the evening, we pitched our tent back on the mainland, we were only meant to be away a few hours, but it was well dark when we decided to head home. We walked up through the deserted village streets and it started to rain very heavily, so we sought what shelter we could under a small bush next to the bus shelter. After a wee while, about three or four police vans were coming from the direction of the city, they drove past us at speed and disappeared down into the village towards the shore then out of sight. We did not think much of it, and our bus came along.

We arrived much later in Stevie Drive, and oh boy, there were more police vans at the foot of our stairs. We were in luck; my dad knew the inspector in charge of search and rescue. We were grounded for a couple of weeks and under some threats of one kind or another not to even talk at work or school. It must have been a powerful enough threat because we kept our distance from each other for the said period, it didn't take us long to get involved with some other schemes, but less adventurous! Well, not altogether.

After this episode, poor Jimmy was to have a serious life changing accident. One day at school in the new playground another boy picked up a railing spike and threw it up in the air like throwing the hammer style. Jimmy unfortunately walked into its path and it pierced his head entering his brain some 2 inches. He never got well enough to return to school, indeed it took some 5 or more years for him to get back to the milk rounds.

I had by this time added another job to my weekend tasks. After I was finished my milk round on Saturday mornings, I volunteered myself for another 9d (3½ p) to be an extra hand on another milk cart with the other mob from Dumfriesshire Dairies milk. This was a much easier route and I was helping out in the last 2 hours of the shift, with no tenements, around the back streets of Roseburn near what is now the rugby stadium, then only a dual mound of earth enclosing a running track with crossbars for rugby in the centre next to the ice rink. I was to sell toffee apples on this mound when the Highland Games were (as we know them) held there a bit more earnings to give to Mother. Even at this age, I did not have a great interest in money, but being offered a job was exciting on its own. This cart was huge, all boxed-in proper seats behind and above the horse and a huge canopy which came up from behind you, up and over your head giving you cover from the weather, with a roof over the milk bottles on the flat bed behind, the only other difference was I was handling money all the time as the customer paid there and then, and not milk tokens, there was continuous running back and forth to the milkman who never wandered from the area of the cart. I was only allowed, like the rest of them, to deal with one customer at a time, so that the money transactions were dealt with singularly, no mistakes. The milkman's head was in his books and his other hand delving into the many deep pockets of his heavy leather money bag draped around his head, feeling and counting the coinage for change of the correct size. Quickly I ran back with the change and back again for more milk and the next customer, and so it was for up to a couple of hours. He finished at Balgreen Corstorphine Road end, and then back to Mother who was waiting for me with a huge shopping list. Some called this a love-job (unpaid). Three or four big shopping bags and I raced all the way up to Stenhouse Cross, a complete circle of all the shops needed.

I'd handover a bag and shopping list to whoever was behind the counter. I was not the only bairn waiting in the queues to get their households stuff. I'd run from shop to shop (bakers, fruit and vegetables or whatever and leave a list and bag at each, then I'd run all the way up to Stenhouse Primary School and join the boringly long queues to pay mum's house rent, clutching the book and precious money which was sealed in an envelope. Oh boy I was always glad to ditch the money safely into the hands of the housing officers who just sat there glum faced with his rubber stamp at the ready and thumping it hard into his inkpad and then on to the rent book. Once this was done, I'd be off like a bullet, back to the shops, pick up the bulging bags, heavily laden my arms pulling on my sockets, stopping every few steps to rest and adjust my handholds, just dying to get home and finished, the rest of the day was mine.

I had my own defences when it came to Mum and Dad, and that was just to submit to whatever pleased them, the 'yes' word seemed the best way in keeping them happy and off my back! Strange as it may seem, doing all the chores asked of me, and with me not kicking up a fuss made me actually feel good, they were not all stressed or phased out (most of the time) that pleased me no end. Mind when Mother at other times produced a pen and paper, I could see what was coming, and tried to make a sneaky exit, down the stairs quietly closing the door behind. But she was always one step ahead, when I showed myself creeping out of the stair, a voice from above shouted: "Michael! Get back up here, now!" And no matter what or how I felt, I surrendered to face the music.

On one occasion, when I got to the top of the stair, she was ready for me, thrusting an empty bag in my hand and shopping list enclose. She pushed into the palm of the other a well folded up note 10/- (50p) a wee fortune and with a warning that this was her last. "Don't lose it!"

"Yes Ma." And I left, 4 steps at a time down to the bottom, running all the way to Balgreen shops. When Mr Robertson, the greengrocer, finished filling my bag, he asked for the money. I suddenly realised that I couldn't find it. I searched my pockets and found no holes for it to slip through. He sent me on my way and worst still he kept the bag till I had paid. I searched every inch of ground all the way home. I cried my head off. Finally, I must have plucked up the courage to knock on the door, Mother answered and in an instance, she flew into a fiery rage with arm and hand in full swing at my head. I thrust my arm up and in doing so opened my clutched fist to protect me from the blow, out fluttered the 10/- note, still tightly folded, strangely that seemed to enrage her even more, but I was quick and put a flight of stairs between us! With more words of encouragement, I was re-warned and sent on my way with a fresh skip and jump. I completed the initial task.

As the dark winter nights came in, word got to me of a wee job at an indoor bowling alley. My first ever hearing and sight of such a thing. This was in a ramshackle hut at the side of the burn, near Murrayfield Ice Rink. My job was to put up the skittles on the two first lanes with another boy, who showed me the ropes.

Jumping up and down of the barriers at the bottom end, rolling the near impossible balls back to their owners and as fast as you like, putting up the pins (skittles) before another ball was thrown in your direction. This job didn't last all that long, as I never let on to Mother my whereabouts, coming in wet on a dry night didn't help me hide it, as playing at the Burn after the alley was my downfall. My pay was mostly by way of tips 6d (2½ p) or 8d (3½p) a time (or night) one or 2 nights a week.

Summer time other than weeks off school, always seemed to be endless days of sunshine… or it would seem that way as my sun always shone and no better time as when Betrammills or Mr Chipperfield Circus's came to town. It would all start with word of a few lorries arriving at the car park of Murrayfield, an advance party of men who put up smaller tents. I was down there like a bullet. They always seemed to welcome us and set up some small tasks like fetching and carrying endless pails of water from the Burn to fill up even bigger buckets which was scattered around the empty site. I never found it boring and could do it till the cows came home, and did. Our numbers soon dwindled to just small handful and it was us who turned up day in and day out! With fresh lads turning up by the hour, just to be turned away. We had established ourselves.

Each day the site grew, a good scattering of all sizes of tents, some filled to the roof with hay and straw. Pathways linking each one to a main walkway through the dirt and mud, whole families filled the huge shiny mobile caravans. Trapeze artists and clowns practiced their acts in some of these tents and we were VIP spectators. We were never challenged as to why we were there but accepted as one of them, others were chased away.

On the 'big day' when the whole site was ready, so was I, arriving early with other boys and most of the circus crew, we gathered at the railway bridge of Chesser Avenue at the entrance to the slaughter house or cattle market, awaiting the arrival of a very special train. In the distance you could see the stream of smoke and steam, the sound of its ear-piercing whistle. Crowds gathered on the eastern side of the bridge, as that was where all the action took place, even us experts were not allowed down on the ground by the loading ramps and holding pens area. This is where the real men mingled, having a last gasp on their fags and pipes before the serious part of their work was to start.

As the train grew closer, we were getting more than a wee bit excited, there came into view the clear outline of the tops of the elephants and giraffes sticking out of the wagons that held them. The crowd cheered them all the way into the stock yard, the animals were more used to all this noise, more than we were to them. Some elephants blasted out a good trumpet in reply. The train had to stop on the east side of the bridge as the bridge was too low to get the larger animals under, so the unloading was done this side. It was at this point and just after the elephants were unloaded, us wee circus boys were given a small shovel and pail. Our leading role was to follow the herd of elephants as they walked in a line head-to-tail, some ten or more adults and some childlike down to wee baby ones, the big ones walking single file linking themselves trunk to tail, the babies keeping close to mums. Just like the horse dung we had to quickly scoop up their dropping, some of the lumps we had to lift with our bare hands, they were too heavy for the wee shovels.

One of the circus workers would appear now and again with a replacement empty bucket, relieving me of the heavy load. It was great fun and made me feel important and wanted! By the time we got back down to Murray Field, it seemed like hundreds of men had taken up the whole area, the Big Top had arrived and was laid out in section (flat) with the whole roof in the centre. On the ground were lots of ropes and pulleys had already been erected giving a skeleton shape of the tent, and a central pole taking pride of place. The men all heaved and pulled on one rope, they leant back as if in a tug of war, digging their heels in, all of them working as one. Slowly, but surely the giant canvas was hauled up foot by foot. They worked into and through the night! They must have, cause by the time I got down (as soon as I got out of the house before Mother captured me) the whole site was up and running. The whole sounds and smells of the place was fantastic. I could (and considered) see why so many young people, children and all ran off to join the circus. It was only minutes before I had a job to do, sweeping, shovelling, pushing or lifting no problem. Who said, 'hard work's not easy'.

One day I was called to the open door of one of the long caravans. The man standing there asked if I could polish his boots. Yes. He went inside and came back out with the biggest pair of boots I had ever seen. Coloured, bright yellow and red. The toe caps flapped about; they were even twice the size of his feet. I made a meal out of washing and waxing them. He didn't look like it, but they were his boots, as he was the clown. I really thought I had made the big time when I told my mates what I had just done. I thought the best job up until then but was walking and scrubbing the elephants in the Burn, that was up until now 'the top job'. After this I was allowed into the 'ring' between acts and stunts, in front of the live audiences and clean up after animals or whatever needed doing. It was to be in my twenties before I actually sat ring side, and had to pay to get in!

Back at school I detested anything to do with religion or churches. I never saw anything of the nuns, but it still had a very negative thing for me, the fear of dying and what went with it scared me nearly to death!

Fridays were the same at previous schools with a parade to morning service. This one was at St Cuthbert's church. To me, these services were unexplained boredom. Looking towards the altar, the women and girls with heads covered sat on the right and on the left the men, and the boys all put to the front, dare fidget and the priest brought the whole service to an earthly silence and addressed the culprit, reducing whoever to a state of quivering jelly and a red kip face) to boot!

When I had to go to confession, that was just a gimmick although I took every inch of it seriously. Once inside the confessional box, I rattled my brain to come up with the closest lie to the truth as I could just to get out of that damned room, 3 Hail Mary's later and I was recharged for another week of clean lies.

I can never ever remember Mum and Dad attending church or chapel. I assume they did for Jean's burial service. I cannot remember although they made sure I did. When Dad prospered on Xmas Day, we had to first attend Mass before we were allowed to open our present. I remember quite clearly being in a shop next door to the church on Xmas morning with Hamish in tow and he was captured pinching sweets off the counter. He started young at only 5 years old, fortunately it didn't go any further, thank God, I reckon it would have been me who got it in the ear. When Mum could afford it, we got 2d for the collection plate instead of the usual 1d (½d in each collection normally 2) so I would get the 2d changed into 4 half pennies pocket 1d and that left me 2 x ½d for the collections. I never thought of this as stealing but god knows. But I never let on to Hamish feared he would bash me.

I could never understand that when we had a visit to our classroom by the local priest (dirty beast as Dad called them, but not until later years) and as part of his talk he would always ask of us to put our hands up those who had thought of becoming priests when grown up. I'm sure that as young as they were, the majority who did put their hands up were the bullies, loud mouths, or scruffy buggars, again just looking and watching the priests; maybe they fitted the needs of the priesthood. I was later told that poor Jimmy's mother was given a very rough time for it after his dad died. His father said he wanted to be cremated when he died, his mother wanted the priest to handle the funeral but, as it was then, they totally refused and if she went ahead with a cremation, she would be kicked out of the faith. She relented and had him buried. Say no more!

No wonder I nearly always choked to death when the bread was put onto my tongue at Holy Communion. He (the priest) even at that stage of the Mass, would try to give me a clout for miss behaving, I was not.

I think it is fair of me to say, now 61 years later, that I had mentally established an openly clear route away from the reality of schooling as it was seen and applied and very much accepted, although I agreed with this but established my own coping strategy which they saw in their view, I was just lazy and disruptive, without ever trying to take me or my views on board. Was I dyslexic? I still haven't a clue, I don't really know the meaning of it! A pleasant distraction at the old building of St Cuthbert's was now and again whilst out in the playground, we would climb up to the stone wall which acted as a barrier to a side street with tall stone tenements. Peering over the wall sat an old man, trampish, a common sight then, but he sat there weaving cane baskets. Piles of cane tied in bundles around him, pulling out one at a time, twisting and bending them into this framework. By the end of the day just before we went home, we had a last look, just in time to see him wandering off with a couple of finished baskets and tying up what remained of his canes. Not a word did he say, just a friendly toothless smile and goodbye wave. A magic moment.

The bandstand near Fords Road end of the park. During the summer months and on a Tuesday night at around 7pm, we would gather around the area of the bandstand which housed a complete brass band, and on the lawn sat the older folk, tapping away at the loud music, the 'parky' was always around to make sure we behaved ourselves. But we knew better, and kept the peace in case we'd be sent home and dare miss the pipe band. Oh boy, we could march up and down with them and make as much noise as possible, what a great night that was.

On a warm sunny day, the word spread that the 'parky' was going to fill up the paddling pool which was at the other end from the bandstand down at Balgreen. Crowds of us bairns gathered there, some in swimming costumes, if you had one, the majority were hand knitted by mothers and normally done from spare wool, tied firmly at the waist, it soon drooped around my knees when wet! We would have a grand time but could never rely on it being open the next day for sure someone would smash a glass bottle in it and the 'parky' would have to drain it, and clear it out and he would keep it shut down until every slither of glass was washed out. It was safer paddling in the Burn. At least we had the swings to keep us occupied.

In November near the bandstand but just inside the park, the council erected a huge scaffolding for the annual 5th November fireworks display, it was local to this side of town, and hundreds turned out no matter the weather. We were lucky with a grandstand view from the windows. My favourite spot was inside the enclosure, this was where the organisers would hope all the fallout from the big rockets would land, where no members of the public were to be. We watched as the rocket exploded high above up and lit up the whole area, but we were hidden by the high surrounding banking and bushes, that's when we could see the rest of the boys and girls 15 to 20 of us running all over the place trying to guess where the rocket would land. The place would return to pitch black and near silence. Keeping an eye on where the rocket finished, I followed a tiny red glow which was all that was left of it. It got closer and closer, finally fading out completely, if its last sighting was near you, curling up and being as small a target tensing in expectation of it hitting you a smack, thump, was all you heard, homing in on that sound and if you were lucky to be first, you had the prize and sometime you had to fight for it. The rocket was a monster, and hot to handle. The stick alone was about 5 feet long and the firework itself heavy and took up 1 foot of the stick and heavier than a pint of milk (full). It's a wonder no one was every hit by one, it would have killed, no wonder the 'parky' aimed them here.

I had an unexpected break from work. One Saturday just after my 10th birthday, in October 1955, I found 2 empty jelly (jam) jars so I treated myself to a visit at the Tivoli Cinema along Gorgie just before Dalry. I handed them over the counter in the ticket office, they were as good as real money. The whole place was full and the only seat vacant was at the front, after only a wee while, I got up to go for a pee, when I came back someone was in my seat. I told (Hitler) as the old usher was known, he couldn't find me another seat. I protested too much, next thing I found myself out on my ear and in the wet drizzly street. I just got on a No 1 back-door single-decker bus home. It must have been playing on my mind, when I got to my home stop, on the park side of the road, I walked around the back of the bus and in the darkness never saw a van coming from the opposite direction. The driver I was told never saw me; the van hit me. I only remember being laid out on our settee by a lady who happened to be a nurse. I just lay there in a daze (shock), the nurse made me drink some hot, sweet tea. This was apparently to help treat shock. Ambulance men came and took me to the sick kids at the Meadows. I was treated for broken ankle (Potts fracture), it meant I had a full-length plaster cast and a three week stay on the same ward that jean died. What I remember of that stay was the constant fear when the nurses, hour by hour, marched up and down holding a huge needle, looking to give it to someone. All that time in there, and I could have enjoyed it! And I never got one! And when I got home, Hamish just used my sticking out leg as something to jump over. Most of the times he fell over it, my screams made Mother furious. But it did hurt!

She told me often enough that they had someone to do my job until I was OK. When eventually the plaster was removed, I had one skinny leg and another just skin and bone, it was the turn of the year when I was back at work. But Dad had a surprise for us all! My accident had struck gold. He had made an insurance claim. He got £34 awarded. The lawyer apparently took £17 and he got the rest. So he bought our very first television set, 12-inch (diagonally corner to corner), real black and white pictures. TV up until that day, had only been seeing my mate's grannies around the corner and that was only when he was visiting her, which was not often, but now we had our own, and what a way to achieve that! Viewing was only a few hours a day and one channel BBC! 12pm–1pm the high spot of the hour was the *Larry Marshal Gang Show,* with special guests of the day, very much a Scottish show. Then it was off till the next viewing 5pm–6pm, children's hour, good viewing. Then the adults viewing 7pm–10pm, they would stay up viewing even the 'dot' as it was called, this was because the TV was full of large heated valves, when switched off, the picture was slow in disappearing and as it cooled it diminished down to a whitish dot in the middle of the screen. It was known for TVs to catch fire while cooling down. Some fearing that this would happen, would not go bed until the whole screen was clear, even when the TV was disconnected at the wall from the mains electric. After a few weeks of having it, we had heard the news of a 2nd channel, STV. I saw it on my mate's grannies new TV, we couldn't get it on ours as it needed some work and aerial. Dad went to work and with a long length of cable attached to the TV and the other end to the toast rack off the cooker, he hung it out the window, then with a long 12 inch knitting needle of Mother's he poked a hole at the bottom of the TV itself, pushed in the needle all the way and like a screwdriver turned it and like magic a new black and white picture came to life and it was *Robin Hood* himself great, I didn't have to go to my mate's grannies. Dad had fine-tuned our TV.

One of our other areas which occupied us for a wee while was Carrick Knowe Golf Course which was a bit of a risk to get to it, down Whitson Way cross Whitson Road and sneak behind the tenements and back greens up and over the spike iron railing, climb a slight embankment that's if it was not on fire. The driver of the steam trains shovelled out red-hot cinders from the boiler fire and regularly caused the grass verges to catch fire, if the way was clear we had to hop skip and jump over two tracks and a high wall barred our way to the golf course. If a steam train was coming before we managed to climb it, he would blast his steam horn so much that it deafened us for ages. We cowed down tightly hugging the base of the wall and the heavy thundering engine rolled past only some six feet from my head, it was terrifying and never ending as the clanging rattling wagons following behind frightened us all the more. As soon as they passed, we scrambled over dropping down onto the long grass verging the golf course. At least with the steam trains had a good chance as you could see it clearly and hear it. But now we had the new electric train (to be known as Diesel) which was silent, and we had to keep clear of some electric wires somewhere (no one really told us what to look for). Wires and cables, we were not impressed with them, no action, lifeless things.

Once on the course, we had to be on our best behaviour and were, to cross from one area to another, you dare not even walk (or get caught) on the fairways and you feared to go near the tees, many a boy caught by even a golfer was subject to being turned over to the police as we were trespassing. You were sort of ignored if you behaved and stuck to the rough better still if you successfully helped find a lost ball, but don't ever touch it. I obeyed all the rules, fear.

If I went down to Balgreen I could have and often did use the proper crossing at Balgreen Halt (station) much safer, but I normally took the Whitson shortcut if we were going to the zoo by the back door. The Halt was a well-used commuter station and a favourite way to go to Portobello Beach with the whole family.

To get to the zoo we'd crisscross our way over the golf course, till we came out at the Corstorphine rail station 'Pinkie Hill' areas Corstorphine Road, up and over the huge wall, up behind Scotius Academy School, to the top of Corstorphine Hill and the back of the zoo, after climbing the 10 foot high fence, which had a few strands of barbed wire, on one occasion we climbed where there was an old stone wall much higher, but an easy climb. When I got to the top, I saw this statue of an eagle, I'd never really noticed before, I reached up to it and was about to touch its claw, when it turned its head and just blinked its eyes at me. The boys and I screamed, I was down and out of there, fortunately into the zoo side and ran all the way, yelling my head off pushing past the visitors and not stopping till I found this old man keeper. I blurted out my story. He seemed just amazed to see the whole gang behind me, however, he was pleased with my story because it just happened that the eagle escaped when he entered its cage a few days before and thought it had left the whole area. I felt chuffed.

The bird was captured a couple of weeks later, its progress and movements were followed in the evening newspaper we never got a mention. Like lots of the local bairns, we spent hours at a time running about inside the zoo always thinking they were evading the keepers because none of us had paid, but they knew and treated us as part of a day's work.

30 years later while working for myself I received a call out to sweep out a chimney in an old building next to the elephant house. I knew the building well, a grand old mansion, but we were to ask for its occupier Mr and Mrs McGibbon.

I thought this was a wind up, it took a lot of courage to go up to the front of the queue at the main gate and ask to see Mr McGibbon. And yes, he was real and the new curator.

Jimmy had been off the scene for months and was moved from a general hospital somewhere in Edinburgh to a psychiatric hospital miles west of the city. One day, Dad turned up with a funny sort of bicycle, a moped where you peddled it and when it reached a speed (10-mph) a wee motor engine kicked in and it zoomed away without peddling. I climbed on board, he took me for a spin, I put my arms around his waist clinging on for dear life. Without worrying where we were heading, out of the city and never stopped until I found us zooming up a winding steep brae. In these huge grounds with old buildings spaced out amongst open grassed parks, a few people sitting around in the sunshine. Eventually we arrived at a long low-lying bungalow structure. When we stopped, he told me this was Bangour Hospital Psychiatric, and Jimmy was in this building used for children.

Jimmy was excited to see us, he told me he had only seen his mother once when they sent her out in a special ambulance, but she found it too much.

He had a huge scar on his left temple, but to me he was the same old Jimmy, like me hyper! While he and I ran around in the woods, Dad was having a cuppa. When he was finished, he took Jimmy for a 'backy' on the bike, they drove down the hill out of sight. Jimmy over excitedly waving his arms about moving about on the back. No helmets in those days. They both disappeared out of sight, and when Dad did arrive back there was no Jimmy. Dad was a bit more than amazed! Just then Jimmy came running up the hill, I was glad to see he was smiling. He told me that Dad slowed to take a bend, Jimmy thought he was going to fall off, so he put both feet down on the road and the bike just slid away from beneath his bum leaving him standing in the road and Dad not knowing this opened the throttle and took off at speed up the hill! We left him in a very happy mood, but it would be a good while before we met again.

When Jimmy and I became blood brothers, it was at his insistence and done in the old Indian style. I was terrified of needles, never mind a knife, it took him some time to realise it was not going to happen this way however it was by chance that I somehow cut or pricked my thump and as quick as a flash, he stuck a thorn into his thumb and before I knew it we had put the bleeding thumbs together, if he wasn't quick in acting and thinking, I don't think we would have been blood brothers.

The thing that always amazes me about him was his knowledge in outer space. He could tell you all the planets, their sizes, distances from each other. One of his favourite toys was a gyroscope, and he could tell me how it worked. I just could not understand any of it. But after his accident, he could still remember most of his subject but did not add to it or even apply it to any extent. He was home sometimes to stay with his mother, but I was not aware of any support. I used to go up to the house, his mother was still alert but bedridden. She allowed him to get a budgie, blue and white, he called it Billy. He was very fond of it and had it very tame and talking. His mother could not keep it when he returned to hospital, so my mum and dad volunteered to watch Billy till Jimmy came home again. It worked out fine and we had it often and it flew around the living room. Mum did complain of the mess it made beneath its high perch and onto the floor, but Dad was washing all the windows one day and failed to notice Billy was flying about, till he flew past him and out the open window. We made up a story to Jimmy that Billy was now staying with my auntie just to keep her company.

It was many years before I accidentally let the truth slip. I was amazed to find how emotional he got, and I got a telling off for telling lies. As it turned out, Jimmy took full care of his mother, without any help, he cleaned, cooked and helped with her personal care. She instructed him from her bed. I witnessed this when I visited. My mother offered to help as did some of the neighbours, but Jimmy had developed a frame of mind that people were just interfering, but cope he did. Again, he drifted into his own wee world and we separated. I later found out that he was taken into the brotherhood near Falkland Place in Fife.

One Sunday, with two other pals I cycled all the way there. I met Jimmy who was not happy there being taught and fed by these priests, he showed us down in the cellars where he and others who were being put on punishment duties by polishing rows of black leather shoes housed in the dark arches, alongside this was the long wooden dining tables set ready for his tea. The place was spooky. We left and cycled all the way to Kinghorn, it was getting dark so we were planning to sleep in an old barn if we found one. We called into a chip shop and only got a few yards eating our chips when a wee van pulled up beside us. The driver told us to pile in, bikes and all, it was just a tangle. He told us the chippy owner told him of our problem as the last ferry boat from North Queensferry would be gone. He managed to catch it just in time and drove us all home. All I know it was after midnight and not much was said, as somebody had phoned the police to say we were all OK. I don't think that we really got upset about it as it was an adventurous thought sleeping in a barn.

Dad was doing great stuff at the chimney sweeping, he bought out two well-known local sweeps, Stanley and Jones for £90 as they had to pay back taxes, along with it came a van and a telephone number "Cra 4835": in full "Craiglockhart 4835" and a good number of regular customers. There was another local sweep Dougie McLean who covered most of Stenhouse, he was a well-known sight, working on his own, pushing his bicycle with his rods tied to the crossbar, a sooty black figure.

We were the first persons not only our stair but the whole front block to have a telephone. Mother had a wee money box alongside the phone and she charged the going rate to persons who came to the door to use it and she timed them. It worked, the only other phone nearby was the telephone box at the street corner, but there was always a queue of about 2 or 3 waiting. She did turn away a good number who tried to take a liberty.

At one point she had a small padlock fitted to the dialling mechanism, it must have been for Tommy, as we never had anyone else to phone. We even began to have holidays, one was camping. Mum, Dad, Hamish, me and Tommy (Horice was too wee, and was left with family). Laden down with pots and pans, blankets, sheets, clothes and food also primus petrol stove, we caught the buses (SMT

Scottish Motor Transport) all the way to just north of Galashiels, the bus unloaded us all on the roadside near the Gala Waters, we climbed over fences and with the local farmers permission we set up the tents right by the fast flowing river. We got flooded out after a heavy rainfall which burst the banks of the river, we were very lucky that Dad had pitched on slightly higher ground but the river swelled so much it circled us and we were left on a new island. Luckily some fishermen came by and carried us all to the far banking where we reset our camp. This was great fun for us bairns. Once we got the new one up and going, Dad kept us busy collecting wood for the campfire. He dug a shallow hole that was to be our toilet, he surrounded it with larger tall tree branches to keep us hidden and private. At night when he lit the campfire, we put some potatoes beside the hot cinders and when they were ready, I pretended to like mine, Yuk! A lot of picking out ash. In the morning, Mum marched us to see the farmer and get milk and eggs. On one morning, Dad and Tommy were in the smaller tent which was used to store the food, dry clothing and bedding, it was raining a wee bit, so they decided to do the cooking inside this tent using the petrol primus stove which has to be pumped so that the fuel lights properly, but something went wrong. As we watched out of the open flaps of our tents, suddenly and without warning, we saw the two of them scramble out of the tent, they were followed by flames. The whole thing was ablaze in seconds, but with some quick thinking the pair pulled away the top of it and put it out, this left all the contents piled high on the groundsheets. After that no matter the weather, all the cooking was done on an open fire. Luckily none of them were hurt, all the stuff was covered with spare groundsheets. Our tents in those days did not have groundsheets only canvas tops waxed to make them waterproof.

A few days later, Dad and Tommy got a bus all the way home to fetch more gear, which included some long lengths of chimney sweeping ropes and an old car inner tube, this really made the holiday. Dad had it blown up, tied the rope to it and floated it down the river with the three of us all in it. Mum made all of our meals on the open fire since the tent fire, including mushroom soup using the fresh ones we picked ourselves one morning. The farmer let us pick some fresh vegetables from the surrounding fields.

On another camping trip, Dad had his wee van, he emptied it of the sweeping gear, the 5 of us set off on a Highland camping trip and so it was we went over the Forth to Fife on the ferry and all the way to a place called Glenfarg. He continued to drive, eventually pulling onto a small track. There was no farm or stream never mind a river, but inside this forest there was plenty of wood for the campfire. For our water supply there was a cottage not too far away. Tommy and I fetched water in pails from the owner. It was much like camping at Gala.

One day Tommy and I reported back to Mum and Dad that we had spotted a few fields away in the distance a bus, just like our Edinburgh ones. Dad came clean, it was a Corporation bus, we were in a place called Riccarton and the bus was at Sighthill, Edinburgh. It didn't matter to us; we still had a great time. Tommy and Dad drove home to get more blankets, and we were all given a treat. When one day, he took us all to the (flicks) pictures near the zoo at the Astoria Cinema.

When it came to weapons, I have 'guttys' (slings), knives, air guns, bows and arrows, and for a very short time real bayonets. I used to stay home some nights on occasions but only if I had somebody to cover the milk run and anything else. My pal David Farmer lived up James Court in the Lawnmarket, immediately above Glenns the bagpipe maker and at the back in the court itself was the blacksmith and farrier. When the noise of clanging and hammer beating down on the anvil from the blacksmiths coupled with the tuning of bagpipes, which seemed to go on day and night accepted by all as every day part of living. A tenement up the road was either being demolished or renovated. But true to us bairns, we had great fun inside it. When no one was inside it we took over. In the attic place we found loads of guns, .303s, rifles, 18" First World War bayonets and a handful of pistols, but luck was on the good citizens' side, no ammo was found. There was us up and down the street (High Street) fencing with all the bayonets and struggling with the guns. We decided to stash this lot for the night. No one seemed to care, such were the days. We hid them under a workman's hut for the night. The next day they were all gone, another gang pinched them.

My favourite knife was the sheaf, most boys of all ages had strapped to the hip on a belt a double bladed knife. Some of the boys joined the Cubs or Scouts so that they could carry the more expensive bone handled more like Jim Bowie knives. The knives were single edged, four-inch blades with tin, wood or bone handles. We used them for any reason, peeling apples we'd got out of an orchard, or just whittling wood (carving). We had a game we played using them 'knifey' where two of you stood 3 ft apart facing each other, legs together. One would throw the knife to the left or right of the other and continue doing this only if the blade stuck in the soil first. Each time he would move a leg out to touch the blade, eventually with his legs spread wide, he had to jump cleanly in the air spinning completely and full with his back turned. All this in one move and both feet never touching down till the whole move was complete. He would be the winner. The number of throws taken set the pace of the game. So close was this that your opponent was nearly doing the splits. I've heard bairns getting a knife in the foot and had a few close calls.

The 'gutty' or catapult (catty) if you could afford one was made of steel, rubber and a piece of leather to hold the stone or what was to be fired. Mine was usually a 'y' shaped branch of wood and elastic bands. I was a 'hot shot' for a few days when I took a pot shot at a water rat climbing up a twig of wood sticking out of the Burn near the bandstand. Smack! The rat shot straight up in the air, and plopped back into the water and swam away. I scored a hit, but my mates after cheering declared I had only hit the twig, but I was chuffed. Other gutties were made using our thumb and first finger, linking them with an elastic band used to hold our socks up and a folded piece of paper. Your pal was then fair game or vice-versa as a target. Boy it stung!

Air guns were very common, our family had one or more in the house for target shooting or vermin. I remember when a mouse ran about the bedroom, Mother was making the bed and started shouting and screaming about a wee mouse. I grabbed the air rifle and shot it. I thought I was hero.

One Sunday we were having a picnic by the edge of the Burn, Mum, Dad, Hamish, Tommy and me. I played beneath a bridge that crossed the Burn, jumping from stone to stone. Tommy unknown to me was up on the bridge firing his air rifle. I put my foot out to touch something floating down at the same moment Tommy fired the rifle at it. The pellet (slug) hit the nail on my big toe and penetrated it through to the bone. I screamed and hollered! Dad took me into the A&E at the Lauriston Royal Infirmary. The worst part was when they injected my toe to freeze it, then the feeling of whatever tools they were using to dig out the remains of the lead pellet, scraping on the bone! And finally, another jab for the prevention of infection. Of course, I got the blame for it all and Dad warned me not to tell my school mates or teachers what really happened in case the police got involved.

Pistols were just as common, some using coloured feather darts we used on custom made paper ring targets, good fun, and others used 'wasted' (inferior lead pellets) pellets, we were allowed to carry a rifle and or pistol the police never bothered us, but nobody seemed to abuse them or get caught doing damage except tommy on me.

I had a school mate who got into trouble for using streetlamps as targets, he deserved it. Only a telling off. I never knew of any boy or man who didn't, at one time or another have a gun of some sort.

Rats were the most common target, they swarmed anywhere there was the slightest signs of a tip in some parts of the back greens where all sorts of garden compost piled up, the Burn saw many rats running up and down the banks at all times of the day, then there were the quarries, Hailes, Ravelston Quarry and some other small ones, you had to stalk them, for some reason when you went near them without a gun they just moved away giving you space, as soon as they saw a gun the seemed to sense it and scatter. It took hours of waiting before they would come out of theirs holes again. The police never ever bothered myself or anyone I knew with a gun or knife, although we never were allowed to touch cut-throat shaving razors or Italian flick-knives. Dad still used a cut-throat razor for shaving and a leather strop (strap) to sharpen it. It was just not done to be carrying one. I never liked the look of them and to scrape it on your face, yuk! Both the razor and the flick-knife were carried by the older boys as weapons for gang fights. The flick knives had a spring button on the handle, on pressing this the blade hidden in it 'flicked' out and locked out ready to use. The much older teens and young men carried them and were quick to use them in fights. We never ever attempted to even get one.

The weapon used most of all was the bows and arrows. We never bought them, it was all rough and ready, a bow made from, a sapling type branch from a tree, hacked off using the sheaf knife. A length of string tied to either end of the stick and you had a bow. A good bit of bamboo cane was normally found lying around any back-garden area, supporting the peapods, not for long. If you soaked it in some water for a few minutes then it could be straightened and made a fine arrow and even better, a stiff rusty old nail stuck down on the end and tied off with a bit of string, keeping it in place. This was the next thing to the real McCoy. The nail and string on that end of the arrow made it fly better to its target. Again, it was all fun and nobody got hurt or offended as long as it was not miss-used. Everything in this area was accepted, it taught us how to respect people and property, also a huge respect.

In the really cold weather when there was a big freeze, some of the lassies in our stair would carry pots, pans and kettles of hot or warm water out into the park and just pour it over the grass. It was great, sheets of ice formed. Those of them who had ice skates enjoyed showing off their skills out there in the open, now and then we boys had fun sliding in and around them, this sort of thing kept on going for hours, every now and then and another pot of water was added.

Winter or summer, when on school holidays, I had free school dinners, this was to make sure we had at least one meal each day. I went down the road to Balgreen School where we had to line up, boys in one and girls in another, also separated from those who paid. It was the colour of the ticket that mattered, this was my favourite part of the day. School dinners to me were great, mince and tatties, broth soup, semolina pudding, I couldn't stand the black flies they put on it, yucky stuff. Raisins my pet hate. I'd spend ages getting them all out in a line around the rim and if I got to help the dinner ladies collect the dirty dishes, I was in for a second helping mince and tatties of course.

We didn't have much luck with kittens, we were getting overrun with mice as everybody else in the stairs had cats, we got their mice. They were getting into the larder, a concrete fridge size box high off the floor with a door on it, somehow the mice got in and were even swimming in the big bowl of water which the cheese and butter were kept submerged in to keep them fresher. This was the normal practice to keep this produce not only cool, but being under water kept the air from turning it, the milk was also kept this way, but it was already in bottles. Mum had a new Deans gas boiler with an electric mangle (roller) she was busy washing away when she got somehow distracted, and left the mangle turning to go and do something else, when she returned screaming her head off. The wee kitten Dad had brought in to catch the mice the day before, was trapped dead between the rollers. As I was the only one in the house with her, I was given the task of removing it (mess as well) and bagging it. We never had another cat again, just loads of mouse traps to set. It was a novel way of catching them, all you heard was a gentle 'click' or a loud snap. A loud snap meant it was caught normally alive by the foot or tail, so you had to be careful not to get bitten. A click meant a full body part and could be messy trying to release it down the toilet. With that done, resetting it was left to Dad, you could have very sore fingers. Only a small piece of well smelly cheese or meat was needed as many as 3 or 4 could be caught over one night.

Horice was only about 6 months old and sitting on the floor when we heard the squeaking of a mouse, on turning around, he had one by the tail suspended in the air, another scream from Mother, I grabbed it and flushed it down the toilet pan. Horice looked a wee bit confused.

Dad was doing so well at the chimney sweeping, he bought a wall safe which looked almost like a wall electric socket, he fitted it to a blocked-up fireplace in Tommy and my room. Fortunately for him no one was in when an inspector called one day to do an annual check on the plumbing and electrics in the house, they left a card saying they were calling again. I don't know what he did with the safe, but we were left with a drafty letter box opening in the wall.

Getting a short back and sides was always a must for us on a regular basis to keep Mother happy. Dad bought a pair of haircutting shears to save the expense. He made a bit of a mess trying out what was called the 'bowl cut', he got hold of a baking mixing bowl, put it over our heads and cut off what was sticking out of the bottom. Mother went mad and decided to keep sending us to the barber at Balgreen until I went with my mate, the barber refused to cut his hair because it was moving with lice. I unfortunately sat too close to him and brought a couple home. She bleached my head with purple dye and got going with the fine-toothed nit comb, after that it was back to Dad's bowl cut.

When my leg was healed enough to return to work, I had to take up with another milkman on the new 3-wheeler electric van and the competition Dumfriesshire Dairy. Their depot was at Harrison Park, that was the battery plant, van and cart storage. The horses were stabled along Watson Crescent beside the park, behind tenements facing the canal they kept up to 90 horses. Jimmy was born and lived here before moving to Whitson. But this van run I was on ran alongside the one I was on before and I met it at the Roxy picture house also at 4am. There were good points to working with the 'Dummy' as it was known by all, we didn't have to keep our eyes on the dung or deal with collecting money or tokens, all we done was deliver the milk and collect the clean empties. The van had a doorless cabin where we could escape the weather and it was upmarket to be seen in one. My milkman had a good 'handle' (name) Jock-Smith-Cameron-Smith! He was a gentle giant of a man, but anybody was gigantic to me. After we finished our day's work, he continued on till he completed the run, which finished up near Fords Road, then he had to back track over it to knock on doors and collect any money. There were 2 other older boys with me at this time, and within weeks they left and two new boys started, one of them lived in the next stair to me, Alan Currie. I had seen him around but this was the first time we talked. With a lot in common also the same age we became great pals, with Jimmy still missing at that point in time. Alan and I went everywhere together. The other lad Joe Taylor, we were all the same age, but Joe and I never had a lot in common, but it never stopped the three of us having fun as a gang.

On a Saturday morning sometimes after finishing my chores for Mum I used to go to the Roxy picture house matinee, which was great, it started at 10am till 11.30am. If I was on time the three of us would get there together and only one of us would pay, the other two sometimes with other pals would go around the outside, down the side to where the exit door was. Whoever was inside took a seat after giving his ticket to the usherette, he'd sit in the stalls near the toilets and wait for a minute or two, then get up and walk into the doorway of the toilets then up a couple of steps to face the double exit fire door, lift the handle bar, the daylight blinded you, a swarm of bodies had normally gathered in amongst them Alan and Joe then we all took up seats. We got away with this for ages, then one day when it was my turn to wait outside, unknown to any of us the exit door had been wired up to a switch, that when the door was opened, a flashing red light was on inside the main cinema above the toilet doors. We never knew and when the door opened 8 or 9 of us stood ready to file in. we were all taken aback by the amount of bodies coming out, yelling and bawling, pushed out by two ushers shoving from behind, even boys who were having a pee were all chucked out, the door slamming closed behind us. Alan along with the others ran around to the ticket office protesting that they had really paid. That was the end of a good thing!

The Saturday matinee pictures were great, it entertained us bairns, not only with cartoons and films, but live shows yo-yos hoola-hoops, quick on the draw, cowboy demonstrations, tap dances. The full-length *Tarzan* or cowboy films were shown 10 to 15 minutes each week. The cheering, clapping, shouting, roaring noises filled the whole theatre. In the summer time the park would hold a variety of children's shows.

Mother took Hamish away from the Catholic School and put him into Balgreen Prodie Protestant School. Then she turned her attention to me. It turned out that Dad was the Catholic and Mum, the Prodie I too was told I was coming away from the Catholic schooling! I felt great because my new pals, Alan and Joe, were also leaving primary and were already talking about going to Tynecastle Secondary on Gorgie, but I was in for a shock. Mother had decided not to put me to Tynecastle, but to her old secondary school that I never even heard of, Darroch Senior Secondary at Viewforth. I kicked up a stink, but I was defeated.

Jimmy, still up in Fife, was never to return to normal schooling and only put in an appearance on the holidays.

Tommy left school for good and started his apprenticeship as a baker and confectioner with Liddles the Bakers at Gorgie Road, Chesser.

This was to lead me to another job, it was only casual, covering for roll delivery boys who were off for one reason or another. As normal, bakers started at 1am to make and bake everything for the day. No fancy cakes, cookers or machinery, most of it was hand done.

When I was called in to do my duties as a roll delivery boy, I would do this after my milk round 7am–8am. On occasions some roll boys had early duties cleaning and clearing out the rubbish from day before, even setting mice and rat traps around the back yard which fell away sharply to the Burn. Crossing the park once the gates were shut at night, until they were opened the next morning, it was against Scottish law to enter even though there were bent railings you could get through.

At 1am Tommy and I went in through one of these bent railings opposite our stairs, when no one was in sight, in the pitch black, we ran over to the cover of the enclosure hedge and high fence, keeping close in the shadow of it, feeling our way along and over a small metal railing fence, squeezed through it with the high twin gate up front of it, which was not safe to climb over the other side into the Fords Road Bridge as to our left sat the head park keeper's house, so instead we scaled the 6-ft barbed wire topped stone wall, Tommy was first up, I took hold of his outstretched hand and he pulled me up, on the other side of this part of the wall was the gable end house garden, the last house in Fords Road we had to be very quiet, we had done it a good few times, as we balanced on the wall avoiding and gingerly wobbling over the coils of wire, I lost my footing and fell back towards the park, my foot slipped and I fell head first down off the wall. My foot and leg shot through the coil of the wire which tightened around my bare thigh and closed around my bare skin. I was left totally dangling upside down, screaming my head off.

Tommy was down like a shot; the words were not of sympathy. "Shut up, shut up!" he shouted back at me. shouting, "The parky!"

I must have obeyed, he struggled to untie me, lifting my body up eventually struggling to be released. Up on the wall again, we managed to escape over the bridge and away from any trouble. Just over the bridge we scaled a smaller wall down the other side with the river shining in the moonlight and hugging the gable wall on our left, we edged our way along a muddy footpath on the high bank, passing the stinking dying tanks of the tannery! Then trying not to upset the scrap dealers' snarling Alsatians gnashing and choking on their chain leads, snapping at our faces. Then we arrived at the back area of our bakery shop. I never got paid for this job breaking up cardboard boxes, scraping out huge mixing bowl, mopping floors and most exciting, lighting a rubbish bonfire, all of it on own by the Burnside, washed down with ladles of milk and so many cakes and buns as I could eat. All left over from the day before. Twice a week the bakers made up huge flat pastry trays, 3 foot by 2 foot in size of base, then a nice thick complete covering of fresh custard! Tommy's job was to put on a thin layer of crispy crusty pastry and cover it all with white creamy icing, then cut away the outer edges, the wastage of the vanilla cake (slice). Tommy always made sure I got a nice wide piece, the rest was for the bakers to share. I'd walk down Gorgie Road to start my milk round all messy and sticky stopping at the Stanky Burn beside the Roxy to wash away the mess from my face.

I'd either do the Chesser run or the Saughton Prison one, depending who was on leave. On the Chesser run I had the use of the big black delivery bike with the basket on the front, I would never keep my balance on it. When I peddled around the corner, I could never understand why when I turned the handlebars whichever way, the basket never seemed to turn with the front wheel. I always ended up falling off skinning my knees and hands, picking up and re-bagging the rolls. I ended up always walking the thing!

The prison run was easier, as it was only a handful of rolls, so a smaller wicker basket was needed! The prison got 2 well fired rolls every morning. I had to ring the big bell at the old small picket door which was the walk-in part of the huge wooden arched doors only opened for big motors and prison buses taking prisoners to and from the courts. At that time of the morning as coaches come out with loads of prisoners, I'd get loads of waves from them, once inside the big door and at the other end of this short, high arched tunnel were a couple of iron gates with an uninterrupted view into the jails internal cobbled square, where the big gallery blocks which housed the prisoners were. Bodies walking around at a fast pace, prison officers with silvery chains dangling from their pockets, but I was only delivering 2 well-fired rolls to the wee gate house just inside the first gate, up a couple of steps and welcomed smile from the officer behind the counter, I just managed to see over. All the doors upon the wall behind him opened I could see row upon row of different size keys. Handing him his rolls, I'd get on with my run.

One day I arrived at the main gate to look back down the main driveway up to the prison from Stenhouse Road, I could see and hear a large crowd of people gathered at the bottom, everything seemed normal as I got in and handed in the rolls. When I got back to the shop, I was told that there was a hanging. I was told later that it was the last hanging in this prison. Decades later I was to be a prison officer here.

1957 saw me in Darroch School, grand old red sand stone building, a boys and girls separate playground. The only new things I wore that day were a school tie and badge sewn on to a well-used jacket. I was still clad in shorts and would be like all the boys in the first year. In the second year we were allowed to wear long ones for the first time ever in our schooling. My class was to be 1TD (technical drawing), I was the second from the bottom class in the whole school. mixed sex classes but we were kept separate in the classroom itself. The school was hidden from view behind Gilmour Place, Tolcross and Viewforth, this was taking me very close to my place of birth, I knew of other schools in the area, but how this managed to escape me, I'm damned! Maybe it was just hiding from me.

Mr Kennedy was my headmaster; he was a well-built man. Anybody bigger than me was huge, but he was. Grey white hair and moustache to go with it, he only showed himself now and then, or if you were sent to him, woe betide!

My register teacher was again bigger than me, but smaller than Mr Kennedy. He had a fearsome look about him. His cloak not like the head's, long and flowing, his was all torn and threadbare which seemed to cover his whole bodily frame, misshapen, greasy hair, continuously sweeping it back from over his eyes and forehead. He spoke with a foreign brogue almost spitting all his words, frightening, and he lived up to this. He never smiled and always appeared to like his own aggressive manner (a chip on the shoulder), and lived up to his name (nickname) 'Doc Soc'. We thought and only knew him to be German but looking back as his facial expressions I would now see him as Polish, not that it really matters, he was a bully and swine from day one.

My schooling and education was doomed from the start, just being in a class full (30 plus) of kids, who did better than me at all levels, some seemed to try their best, but none ever were to escape the verbal abuse and use of 'Doc Socs' belt. My big ears were my weak spot for me (and others). They were known as the 'handles' for the FA Cup not that I knew what the Cup was for. He would just walk up to you grab at your lug with his thumb and first finger, twist it, this forced you to stand, he would hold on even though you were on your toes to gain height and ease the pain. He ignored your screams of pain and continued this pose whilst he lectured the class, then equally with great pain he would twist suddenly in the other direction, forcing you back down into the seat. This was for me the worst part of the torture inflicted, although he was wicked with the use of his belt. I could take more than of it!

The girls, they could at times get the same type of punishment, but they had a good defence, that was crying and screaming. When he made a move towards them, verbally or whatever, he seemed to get satisfaction in their reaction and was happy with that! This I think just re-cemented my views or observations of what schooling was all about and religion had nothing to do with it. I could not find or feel a baseline or understanding as to what this was all about and when was this nightmare going to end?

The only thing outside school was working, which I continued to do and was happy with. I could not see a future beyond Chimney sweeping and rolls or milk which were doing fine without school. I had to leave my work every day to attend school. Got thumped, sums, write and whatever. But it did not tie in with my work. I was not aware of any other jobs other than what I was doing. Maybe if they had taken the time out to relate how school could get you other jobs, then told us or showed us what a plumber, electrician and others done, and asked us if we thought that we may like to be one. No, they didn't. Maybe I thought that the job I had and had been doing over the past 3 years or more were the only ones and nothing else out there existed. The way they were going about my schooling, trials was not a good example of life to come, or even a target to aim for, if I had a role model of any kind at this point in time, then I was working alongside them. If I could achieve the tasks they gave me without any problem then that was easy. Yes, there was lots of shouting, but if that was used to get a job done then it didn't happen for long, they were sacked very quietly and never with fuss. They just got told not to come back or you never saw them again. Just don't argue, do what was asked or told and you kept our boss happy. Orders were given sometimes in a loud voice, but if the tone was right, then that was OK, for the teacher to bawl and shout was not a problem, it just did not wash with me and some others. It soon lost any value or effect but for the girls a man shouting in an aggressive manner was a wee bit more than enough. 'Doc Soc' was about to find out how non-effective the belt was on me.

Fortunately, I could spread myself about in the system and I was able to use the other teachers time awarded to me to my advantage. I don't think this was a conscious thought on my behalf, but it was nonetheless my saviour and theirs.

My only favourite subject, if you could call it that, was music, the singing part. I actually achieved this with the help of my teacher, Fanny Fuller. This poor woman was the subject of as much abuse as me. She had one leg shorter than the other and the shorter one was lengthened by a huge boot with a massive sole, she would clunk up and down. She wore a skirt (or blanket) dark woollen (brownish) and unfortunately for her, she stank of pee, which was not unusual then for older women to have that odour about them. But she didn't stand any nonsense from anyone or let her be held back. She could give out the belt as much as the others, this was for others, I got on well with her. It was under her tuition that I was able to sing now and again at morning assembly in front of what seemed the entire school. Up on the stage, no microphone, just me her and her piano, she told me to sing to the clock way up high on the wall at the back of the hall. I did enjoy it, and one song in particular, My Love is Like A Red Rose, the reason my career went away was easy, my voice broke. I wondered what the heck was going on, and my death was nearby!

I did handle the practical work better, like metalwork and woodwork, although it never excited or inspired me in the slightest and quite frankly achieving anything was as far away as ever. The only thing which was noticeable, I never got told off or the belt in these classes, the same as the others who most of the time, never got the belt. At least this was a plus factor on my scale!

One of the places I had most fun when at Darroch, when we had spare time, was the canal, where else, if someone could afford it. The rowing boats near the drawbridge, you were only allowed to stay within the bridges the other being the View forth Bridge where my former nursery was. Once or twice some idiots tried to row under this bridge, on one occasion hanging about on the roadway above it were a gang from Burghmuir High School, our enemies! But our lot were out smarted when attempting to row underneath, the gang above chucked huge stones down on top of them slightly hitting one, but drove holes in the bottom, sending them all in the water. More were seriously hurt but had to make up an excuse for abandoning school, go home to dry off, no wonder we weren't allowed to hire a boat.

One winter the whole canal froze over as it normally did, 3 of us skipped returning to school after dinner, we had great fun, but we failed to check the ice sounding as we walked from Viewforth Bridge on towards the Yeaman Bridge. We should have been chucking thick pieces of ice ahead to hear the echoing pinging which would have told us where the ice was good enough to walk on, if you got a dull clunk, you never waked on that bit. We just kept on playing and running about till all of a sudden Rellio, my big Scotch-Italian mate let out a yell, in slow motion, he disappeared through the ice and just as quickly his head surfaced only to go down again, then he rose up, trying to pull himself up to the edge, for it only to break away under his weight. I lay down as near to him as I could get, terrified that I will go in, the other lad took hold of my feet. Rellio got hold of my jacket sleeve, after what seemed an age, he inched himself onto thicker ice. When we all got onto the towpath, Rellio, dripping, frozen and crying, more worried what his mother would say. We hatched a story and used it on his mum. Some bullies from Burghmuir School threw him into the canal and we rescued him. We had to repeat that to the teacher the next day. We were heroes! Sweating buckets in case we were found out.

Behind a close mouth on Lochrin Place was another milk dairy plant, Murchies, they had a bottling plant and creamery based there. As far as I know they only sold direct to shops who distributed over the counter milk and cream. Behind them Tollross Tram Car Depot, housing a drive through covered area and tram turning point all in one. It was a very busy, noisy and dangerous area. Coming back up towards Lochrin Place from Tolcross itself and just at the crossroads stands the King's Theatre, where only the 'top of the bill' acts from all over Scotland were allowed to play. Dad actually was understudy (stand-in) for Dave Willis there. Coming back along Lochrin Place again towards my school stands an old army barracks hall. This is where we did all our gym, parallel bars, vaulting horse and met a regiment Sergeant Major (retired), Mr Jeffery's. He was a great laugh, but very tough and strict, his sense of humour was very warped if not sick. My pal David Farmer was the same height as me, but to be kind he was bloody fat! There's no nice way of putting it. David could not run, jump, even walking gave him difficulty. I was always sympathetic towards him and he sort of shadowed me (understatement). I think somehow the RSM noted this.

One day in the gym he got a bit fed up of trying to encourage David up a rope, with me trying to lift one leg of his off the ground which was too much for me. The RSM ordered me to give David a high shoulder down the whole length of the hall, I made a very serious attempt. Stuck my head in between his legs and somehow managed to get both his feet off the ground. Poor David just tilted over and hit the concrete floor and never even bounced! A scream came from him instantly. He frightened me speechless. The RSM just barked out orders, which I obeyed. I got dressed. Poor David's whole right shoulder was black and blue. I had to get him dressed as well, then home to his mother. Up at his home in the Lawnmarket, he cried all the way. It turned out he had dislocated his shoulder! He came back to school in a few days, arm in a sling.

Once a week we would be bussed all the way to Meggetland for field sports football and rugby. We all had to have proper footwear, whether it fitted or not didn't matter. So I had Tommy's well-worn and over-sized football boots. I couldn't even run in them, I was, and I knew it, useless at football and worse still, I had never even known the first thing about rugby, other than the goalposts were different and that was my limit for both games. As this was the whole of our field sports and we were forced to play. It was fear of being hurt that was my biggest problem, and when I picked up the rugby ball with screams "run" ringing in my lugs, I caught sight of this charging mob closing in on me. I got shot of the ball and ran. The RSM was fuming. I got ordered back to the dressing room where I joined odds and sods who also failed to achieve, both sexes. Those of us who had a good reason to fail, what was asked of us was sit to one side. The rest, well we got the belt, no matter who was watching or crying. I didn't mind him dishing it out, it was more of a tickle. He actually seemed not to like giving out this punishment. I liked it…

Mum talked me into taking on a paper round after school. I wished I hadn't. Humping a satchel of Scotsman and Evening News. Broad-sheet papers up and down, in and out of five-storey tenements along Polworth, although she convinced me it was on my way home. Home seemed far away! You had to write their name on each one, fold it, put it in the bag in the correct order, don't put the wrong paper through the letterbox! You got it in the lug from the shopkeeper, then the customer lay in wait for you just to remind you! Oh boy. My hands were black with the ink, again Mum knew what I was earning, there were no tips! What a bind! Fortunately, I took the job on very near the end of my schooling days.

I was in the last year of my schooling when for some unknown reason, I found myself in the most impossible and challenging part of life to date. The bully of the whole school threatened me with a fate worse than death and I didn't doubt him for one moment.

He told me he was going to put me in my coffin! Threats and dog's abuse in front of everybody in the playground. But he wanted me after school by the canal. I was crapping it solid, my arse was going in and out like a fiddler's elbow! I was there first, on the side by the rubber mill. I didn't wait long for him to appear over the iron drawbridge. What I can only call a lynch mob, 30 or 40 compared to my 2 or 3 bodies in support of me. I just wanted to throw in the towel right there and then! Up until now I had dodged this guy Hendry Wood 'Woody'. I'd witnessed him on a few occasions fight his way up through the ranks of other bullies, and now it was my turn to face him, just to survive and get it over with. I just didn't know what to do, this was my first fight ever. I could only picture how they done it in the movies. I took up a boxing stance as he got to within a couple of feet, as he closed in on me, I noticed him trying to raise his feet at me. His hands remained near to his side, reluctantly and half-heartedly I thrust a fist in the direction of his face with no danger of ever hitting him. He actually backed off. Backing off so much that before I knew it, we had covered about 30 yards and come over the canal bridge and into a side street. Not a blow was struck and he was very verbal about how he was going to kill me. With a tightly moving group and their bikes, I tripped over one and he took this chance to lay the boot into my head, one such blow hit me on the face. I suddenly became aware of an adult voice shouting: "Let him up! Let him up!"

I then saw the man pulling Hendry back from me and telling him not to kick when I was down! I got up in a flash taking up my stance and seeing red blood coming from my face dripping on my sleeves. I put blow after blow in the direction of his face. He curled up screaming from me to stop, but I never made contact with his face, only his hands that stopped me getting through. I then backed away and let him straighten up, he did this and the next move he done was running into the crowd shouting as he disappeared into the throng of bystanders. "I'll get you tomorrow!" Then he was gone, leaving most if not more of his followers surrounding me and cheering.

I felt quite good, but not for long! Next day in school I was given a hero's welcome. He saw the attention I was getting, I really hated this, it just was not right. Up until this point I was the school 'Bam' and was quite happy in that level, knowing exactly where I stood in life. This was very strange, not ever hating him other than his bullying ways, and he never really bothered me up until this point, in fact we got on, no problem. So I went over to the other side of the playground where he and some of his gang stood. He actually took a defence step back as I went up to him. I've never had an effect on anyone like that before, I felt uncomfortable so I put out my hand, offering it as a peace gesture, gingerly and with a measured look of amazement on his face he took it slackly and I told him I was not a bully, he can have it back and we'll forget all about it. Walking away leaving him to work it out for himself. Nobody else said a word and I felt great. I was no longer the bully, having said that, I had more people talk to me and without a doubt less bullying.

Close on the heels of this. Doc-Soc turned his attention to me, when at one of his maths lessons he chose to put the answer to a sum up on the board, then asked his class to give him the whole sum without writing anything down. He looked around at all the expressionless faces, all was quiet. I thought I knew so gingerly, I put up my hand. He brought laughter to the whole class, pointing to me with his finger, "Ah McLenaghan, what is the answer?" this even shocked me to even dare try this. So I verbally said what I thought it was. He was seen to be dumfounded and said it was correct. "Now come out here, boy, and show the class how it works out on the board."

I said I couldn't, he came at me blue with rage, and dragged me to the board by the ear! It was like any other time, I couldn't work it out on my paper, but for some reason I had it all worked out in my head. Why on earth I put my hand up, God only knows! He got so angry, then seemed to lose the plot, out came the belt and he started with it. After a few 'whacks' I turned and walked out the door, quick on my heels he ordered me down to the head's office where Mr Kennedy was waiting for me. He took out his belt, I counted 16 lashings, I called him a 'bastard' and walked out of the office and school. No one followed, I walked all the way to Slateford Cattle Market, watching the sales, waiting till it was time to go home. If Mother got to know of what happened, then I would have got the sharp end of her tongue and more!

She never knew for years. When I went back to school the next day, I never heard a peep, not a word! It was not long after this happened that Doc-Soc failed to appear, then a replacement teacher arrived, it was great. This was truly the first time ever in this registration class that I could relax, not that I learnt anything other than Doc-Soc had shingles; it was said to be painful, and he would probably not return. Fantastic, wonderful!

It was after Tommy joined the Territorial Army when I was not long at Darroch before our bedroom took on a change, his bits of uniform hung on every available hook and place in the wardrobe. he became a drummer shortly after joining the TA Royal Artillery 432 LAA Regiment. The smells of polish and Brasso stank our room. He really took a pride in the smart way to look on parade.

I couldn't wait till I was 16 years old; on being in uniform not withstand dad was in the Boys Service and served in Palestine for 7 years with the 1st Battalion of the Argyll and Sutherland Highlanders with 2 years before that in the Cameronian Rifles. He had the tattoos on his arms, and he was a very snazzy dresser. Also all my mates' dads served in one or another. It wasn't long till it came in my direction, but I was to find more to schooling and another direction running in parallel, and that came in the form of the Royal Scots Grey's Army Cadet Force, based at Chesser, just up the road over the park. The commitment was, seemed easy to me, to turn up every Wednesday evening and Sunday 11am–4pm. I was issued with all of my kit at once, coarse hairy battledress with a couple of shirts to match the dress, ankle gaiters with brass buckles, 2 ties, white lanyard, one bluey black beret and one grey. 2 eagle collar dogs (badges) and one Regimental Cap badge, along with that ammunition pouches and back pack with cross straps finally the last of the webbing, waist belt, all with the brass fittings and buckles.

Tommy came in handy with spare Blanco khaki and white for our lanyards, Brasso and boot polish with yellow dusters. This was the best clothing I ever owned or called mine!

Dad and Mum were from the start laying ground rules, they would show me once how to keep my kit clean, but under no circumstances were they taking any responsibility. Dad showed how to scrub and Blanco the brasses. Mum showed me how to iron and wash the rest. Tommy showed me how to get good box sleeves in my tunic using only brown paper and iron, instead of a wet tea towel and hot iron. Between them and the cadets, I soon learned how to get good marks when on parade. Razer creases in all of my tunics and shining toecaps, heels and underside of my boots, all spit and polished with good instructions from Dad. There was always good competition, even looking at the turn out of my NCO's. I wanted to be like them and I was, but they always pushed for more. I was in my element, although I never achieved a rank, just being well on top of this was enough, even the drilling, marching on parade felt great. I wanted nothing more! Apart from square bashing dress parades. I enjoyed the weapon training, good practical hands on stuff, on parade marching with .303 rifles at the shoulder, to stripping cleaning the Bren gun and Stens till they nearly wore through. We never ever got to fire any weapons in this country. Our parent regiment was in Germany and we were told that a visit to be with them was being arranged and for those of us who could afford the trip – £4.00. Then Mum and Dad decided to put my name on the list to go, but like so many others, they could not afford a down payment and struck a deal to pay 2/6d (Half Crown or 12½p) each week for the next few months.

Two of my mates also joined the cadets after me, Alan Currie and Joe Taylor, it was only Alan who wanted to go to Germany. Joe didn't last long with the regiment. I thought I had problems. Joe just didn't know his left from his right, always threw the whole parade out of step! The RSM always addressed him as a Sack-of-Tatties, that did fit the bill, but he just could not be bothered. His mother was back-a-fronted. When one morning poor old Joe threw the towel in. The thing that bothered me, he was meant to be brilliant and top of his class. We were totally opposites. Poor Joe Soap.

About 30 of us all ranks, led by Captain Taylor, boarded the overnight train July 1959 from Edinburgh to London, most of our belongings stowed away in the guard's van, our photos taken by the Evening News on the platform. We had breakfast on the train, excitement all around as we arrived in London.

Out kitbags were loaded onto the waiting 1 tonner army lorry which took us to the Calvary Barracks of the Blues and Royals, Queen's Regiment, where we spent the whole day with them. On parade taking a salute at horse guards parade we were turned out shining bright in front of a member of the royal family.

After helping stable and groom the horses later, we helped the troops polish up their breastplates and long leather black boots. Then an early night in our allotted bunk space. After a big breakfast we were loaded onto another 1 tonner and on our way to Harwich where we boarded a troop ship along with hundreds of regular soldiers making their way up the gangway onto the huge ship. Most of them carrying a .303 rifle and steel helmets. The place echoed of tacky steel studs from our feet as we slipped and slithered on the steel decks, going down below where we were allocated a bunk bed three high and row upon row. Everything was orderly and we were treated as equals. The next morning, we had to queue up waiting in turn, everybody stripped to the waist with our towel and washing kit in hand, trying desperately to keep our footing as the whole ship rose and crashed down in the heavy rolling seas.

Many of the soldiers were violently sick, we were all standing in vomit, only a few of us were OK. Later when we were up on deck hanging over the side rail getting a thrill out of the rolling waves and fresh air until a soldier went upwind of us and threw up, the wind blew it all over us. Yuk!

For us young lads this was our first trip away so far from home and every minute was a true adventure. In a couple of hours, we were collecting our kit from down below, down the ramp and putting our first foot in the Hook of Holland! Another train journey all the way through Holland; fantastic new sights. Hundreds of bicycles at all the level crossings. Had my first cup (tiny cup) of very thick black coffee, nice! The countryside was as flat as I had heard. I never noticed it, but we must have at some point crossed over into Germany.

We arrived in Hamburg. We were again loaded into another 1 tonner truck, driven all the way to just outside the camp gates in Detmold. We were ordered off and told to leave all our gear on board. We quickly formed into 3 ranks, right-turn, and marched in through the security gates. This was the first parading since London, and before we knew it, we were in the central parade ground inside the barracks. RSM Moss marched and drilled us for what seemed ages, a bit of a gathering of Royal Scots Greys tank men watched our well-oiled drilling.

We felt great and done ourselves proud. We were I noticed the only ones in uniform wearing our famous grey berets, the reason was soon clear. Most if not all were busy working on and around the huge workshops on all kinds of armoured vehicles, an assortment I'd only seen in war movies. They wore black berets with shining eagle cap badges. Others walking and running between those sheds, they wore the grey beret at other times.

We got to meet up with these men in the mess hall where plain old good grub was served up in such amounts that I had only dreamed of. The men took us all on board acting like fathers to us. At night we would move to get all our kit scrubbed and ironed ready for the next day, then if all was well, play football or swim in the stagnant outdoor swimming pool waters. It didn't bother us much only the hidden dangers beneath, rubbish and ropes submerged just waiting to entangle our feet and legs, but that did not put us off – great fun we had.

Slowly but surely, we were getting some sort of messages that somewhere there could be a war about to happen. Also, a wall being built in or around Berlin; this so-called war had a name: The Cold War, but this was only some talk amongst the regular soldiers in the camp and elsewhere. We never at any point took anything on board.

There were some busy days of sightseeing, on one to visit a Sinalco soft drinks factory, again always in uniform, and whenever marching right up to the front door always drawing an audience of some kind. On one occasion while marching in public on cobbles, we were given the order to 'halt', and we all did manage this, even with hobnail boots on, except for our Alan, he was in the centre and halfway up the ranks behind me, when a heap of bodies fell past me, just missing me. He had skidded and like bowling pins, took out the lads upfront of him. They all quickly recovered, but even in front of the spectators Alan got a roasting from Sergeant Goldie, our boy. We had a laugh later at his expense.

At night we as usual had a bit of spare time back at the barracks after getting organised and preparing our equipment the next day. Sometimes depending on the time, we were allowed to join the troops in their NAAFI bar area, not much went on. I think we got in their way. We sat there drowning in Coca-colas or orange. I think the ice was more novel than anything else we had never seen much in the way of ice, except in big screen movies in stars there drinks. But there was a juke box sat in the corner, and we were a bit anti-social with it that indirectly on one night we were the cause of a punch up. The top hit no 1 song then was 'Running Bear' and it was our favourite. When we had the time and money, that record was repeated over and over again, much to the annoyance of some, they had had enough of us and literally pulled the plug on us, so no one could play any music. The trick worked, and we left. But a fight broke out between the remaining troops over the state of the juke box, we were banned! I'm not surprised that the hit was our theme song everywhere we went, in particular when we were in a lorry.

We spent one day visiting the Black Forest, the only thing they could find of interest to show us was a giant of a statue with holes and dents in it when it was used as target practice during WWII.

It was planned for us to go on an exercise with the regiment. The whole camp was full of armoured vehicles all the way around the square, and foot soldiers galore, I'd only seen the likes in a war movie! I could only get on board a Ferret Scout Car. The lorries and Saracon troop carriers were full and I was not complaining. I was to travel outside the body of the scout car lying on top of the camouflage nets inside the basket attached to the sides. Just before we boarded, we were all (cadets) taken to the stores and issued with tank suits, it made me feel like a real soldier. The suits had zips up and down all the way round it also, when zipped properly, formed a sleeping bag. Then we took up our places, and off we went, it was just great lying there just feet from the commander sitting in the turret speeding in file waving to the passers-by. We ended the first part of the journey on the steep banks of a wide fast flowing river, where there was already lots of vehicles, huge things unlike I'd ever seen just queuing up. We were ordered off and over to one side above the brownish river and behind us at the top of the bank a Dense wooded ridge. We sat and lay there in the hot sunshine watching men in boat like craft laying out heavy steel locking cables from one bank to the others already on the other, they were the royal engineers. The noise was deafening smacking of sledge hammers against steel containers and bars, they were putting out floating pontoons to carry all of us and tanks, across the other side as part of the exercise. Suddenly a sergeant came from one of the lorries shouting and waving his arms at us, we didn't wait, got up and moved in the direction he was pointing to. The noise around made it impossible to hear any instructions, without any indications or whatever we all turned to look up behind us as one, and again as one we ran down stream. I could hardly believe my eyes, tanks, not stopping to count them at that point, but when we felt safe and stopped, 4 of them in a line on the ridge behind us, only 20–30 feet from where were just sitting, their tracks crushing the bushes and small trees and we never noticed a thing. But what a sight, great! It wasn't long till we were loaded back onto our vehicles and driven over the completed floating pontoon bridge. We travelled down back roads out over hills and ended up in a very heavily forested area.

We had been issued Dixies, forks and spoons, in an opening in the forest we gathered in a queue behind other soldiers, this was the field kitchen. Our Dixies were piled high in lovely smelling stew, mashed tatties and peas. We first sat on our bums in a wee group and scoffed the lot. Starvation is good kitchen. No sooner had we finished and washed up that we were given a very quick tour of the forest areas, and warned very strongly, not to stray into these areas after dark, which was fast coming. We were quickly shown where at one corner was the infantry (the Argyll and Sutherland Highlanders) and another regular German Infantry, then our own troops quarters and that sometime later they were having a mock battle. We were then shown to some tents where we were to stay all night and not to show our heads, if we did then we risked being killed. I did not sleep a wink, wrapped up in my tank suit the sounds of men, guns and engines was truly real, it was all around us and at times I thought we were going to be overrun and killed. I'd wish I had stayed at home. At some point the battle slowly drifted away, at one point they must have encircled our camp.

In the morning we were back in our allotted transports, some of us were given a map which had coloured lines all over it, I was told to follow the red lines and before I knew it I was sitting in the commander's seat with headphones and microphone which I was told linked to my driver. I was more in fear than the night before. Unfortunately, I was not told the driver knew exactly where to go, so as far as I was concerned when we took off going over a cropped field through fences and onto what seemed to be very private gardens, he was following my map instructions. I was more than worried. As it turned out the British forces had all rights and paid farmers compensation for damages caused. I didn't feel any more relaxed at this!

A day out with the 98th Panzer Division was one of the best. After a breakfast of the new crispy flaky stuff with milk, hot or cold (cornflakes never heard of them), and sugar, slices of toast, well buttered, layered with heaps of crunchy melted sugar! The whole day was spent around their base near Saltou tank ranges, getting rides on their Panzers, halftracks, live firing machineguns on the ranges, Lugar pistols, all the stuff we had seen in the movies. Absolutely fantastic. The difference being we never got to use weapons with live ammo with our own troops. The day ended with a march past; we were all tidied up and marched past the Panzer regimental flag pole giving it a smart salute. They in turn paraded past us and gave us a salute, they were well turned out, but we were gobsmacked when they burst into a very stirring marching song, striding our smart erect bodies, resplendent in their blackish uniforms and caps. What a day they treated us all like equal soldiers and friends.

On another day we visited the Mona Dam, the location of one of the Dambusters daring bomb raids during WWII. Only a good repair is to be seen. We were bundled into the lorry again ending up at a place named Belson Concentration Camp. I had never heard of it as like others in our group, however, we were soon brought up to date. The whole place appeared at first to be a small forest area with birch trees and bushes around long man-made flat-topped mounds of earth, freshly done with the only obvious difference, a solitary small post mounting a piece of what looked like plywood sign with the figures 16,000, and that was all. Other than a couple of men mixing cement into buckets building what seemed to be the base for a monument as they told us to be a pinnacle in remembrance of those in the mass graves. The other thing I noticed was the absence of any wildlife, birds or noise of any, and that was all we could see or hear of Belson Concentration Camp where thousands upon thousands were murdered only 14 years before. It was not until we left the immediate area did I realised just how spooky it was, only what seemed hundreds of yards away in a war grave cemetery, and the place seemed more noticeably alive than Belson.

We had a good reason to be in this graveyard and that our CO (commanding officer) promised families back in Scotland that he would try and find the headstones of the troopers' graves sites who died during the fight for Belson, take photographs of their final resting place. The hillside was a sea of white graves, it took us what seemed like hours of searching row upon row until we were satisfied none were missed. The final roll call was 28 Scots Greys and NCO's, we all felt chuffed that our duty was truly done in honour of them all!

The day wasn't over, we piled back into the truck, after a while it pulled over into what seemed a small village. We were told to do any shopping but not to wander too far. Shopping was not really something we could do, not only had we not brought money, but there seemed only to be one tiny corner shop. So we followed some of the other cadets up a track between two houses, at the top the view opened up to find ourselves on a towpath and in front a canal. Some boys had already gone off to the left, so we (3 of us) followed others already a good few yards ahead to the right. Somebody pointed out that the what at first glance we thought were electric pylons, were in fact East German Machinegun towers. Immediately on the other bank were what appeared as if a whole forest of trees had been cut down leaving bits of stumps behind. The immediate tower sat back about 200 yards behind the far bank of the canal, I could see other towers staggered at gaps of a few hundred-yard intervals lining the way in each direction following the canal. For all of us this never caused us any concerns, that was until from behind us from where we had just come there was the high-pitched sound of what I though was police whistles blasting away, followed quickly by alarming shouts and the sight of all our cadets running back to the pathway where we had just emerged.

I didn't hang about and ask what was happening, the boys behind me shouted as they pushed past me and others. Tracers, tracers!" One of them looked skywards glancing towards my left. Again, he shouted "Tracers!" I looked up to where he pointed and saw coming from my right a couple of streaks; white like shooting stars and sounds like a fire cracker, whatever was happening had an effect on us all. Down at the truck a couple of regular soldiers were helping us climb over the tailgate being actually piled on top of each other scrambling to get on the bench seats. It was all very frantic! Within seconds, with everyone still in a daze the canvas covered truck where normally the end canvas was rolled up, being the only window we normally looked out of, was now completely wound down with only bits of daylight coming from the edges and corners. The truck pulled away. In the near blackout conditions, we looked at each other fearing something. We sat in complete silence only broken by the two regular soldiers who flung us on board speaking to each other. They then told us out loud that someone had buggered up things in a big way. The driver or whoever had taken us right up to the border of East Germany. British soldiers in uniform were not allowed to go within 3 miles of this border. I still at that moment could not take on board what had just happened let alone the consequences. I reckon the driver and regular soldiers were keen to put 3 miles between the border guards and us all.

The day never ended then. We went to our beds nearing the end of the whole tour, fast asleep when suddenly some of us woke up to find our dormitory lit up like daylight. Then as quickly back into pitch dark except flashes of light in the sky, lighting the whole horizon like someone flicking a light switch off, on, off, on, it reduced some of the boys to tears, we were frightened. Was this the war, the Cold War? we feared that we were not getting home, even when it was explained to us that it was an electric storm, no way, this was totally war. Within days we had retraced our footsteps, right back to the troop train at Harwich and home.

In the next couple of months, I had to leave my milk job and other jobs behind for good. I was told by the schools that the sooner Michael and schooling parted company, the better for both of us! Mother, always one step ahead, had my name put forward for an interview and exam as an apprentice grocer. This was a job well sought after. Being a real grocer with full size apron, expertly cutting up cheese using a long wire weighing and packing sugar, flour, peas, into different coloured bags was a job I only dreamed off. Yes a grocerer. I sat an exam along with others, for some strange reason, I was told that I had done the best out of all who were with me, and they therefore wanted me to attend their store at Leven Street opposite the King's Theatre at Tolcross. It was not what I had thought it was like, I got a white apron and full sleeved jacket to match, that is the only part of it which was familiar, no full-length wooden counter or sacks of flour, peas and such. I was told that I had done so well in the exam that they wanted me in their prize store. Self-service, one of the first with a wines and spirits counter out the front, I was not impressed, this was the first time I had seen such a store in my short life. Women behind the cash checkouts as they were known.

My job was to stack the central isles or gondolas as they were known, marking every tin or jar with the price using a pencil. Any eggs found to be cracked or broken were collected and up to 5 at a time placed into an empty jam jar with a piece of greaseproof paper on top held in place with an elastic band, they were sold off mainly to women who used them in baking, nothing was wasted.

One job I truly hated was cleaning the massive glass frontage doors and windows. Escaping on the big local delivery bike was a favourite alternative, having learned how to handle it at the bakery. On one outing I cycled all the way up to Herriot Watts School up by Tolcross when I tried to cross the driveway up to the main school, a huge black limousine (car) cut right across my path bringing me to such a sudden halt I nearly hit the side of it. The driver never even looked at me and pulled away but the passenger sitting behind him smiled, leaned forward and waved. I had just met Philip, the Duke of Edinburgh. I was flabbergasted and left standing all on my own and no one to share this moment with.

From time to time I would have some of my old school pals come by during their breaks, it didn't make me feel any better being in this job.

One day I was out delivering up the road at Brunts field Links, there was an army recruitment tent for the Scots Guards or any other regiment. I was very taken back by it but had a look. I was told to sign some papers and did, then told to attend a medical the very next day also to bring my birth certificate with me.

The next day I dared ask Mum, "Could I see my certificate?" She must had twigged and made a swipe at me as I ran down the stairs.

When I got home, Dad was waiting for me and I got a roasting from him telling me the Military Police were at the door looking for me and why had I failed to turn up for a medical? That was the end of military for me.

But there was one old woman who took a shine (liked me) to me, no one else male or female went near her. Why? Because she stank of pee, it was strong, she created an atmosphere that you could smell she was in the store before you saw her, and she always had a ragged appearance, but she was always pleasant. She always looked for jars of broken eggs and when there were none on the shelves, I would go to the back shop open a big cardboard box and check to see if any were broken and if there weren't any I'd give it a heavy kick, first checking no one was around. She would always give a big smile when I appeared with a jar full. No one else got this treatment.

I was looking forward to having my working days (like others) reduced to 5½ each week down from the 6, with only Sunday off, but as most shops still worked a full Saturday, we closed on the Wednesday afternoon. I couldn't get up to much, a bit lonely, my pals were all at school. Even my money was well down, with all my jobs before this one my earnings were 23 shillings; to Mum and 2.25 shillings in tips for me. Now down to 17 shillings a week. Give Mum her due she gave me 1 shilling and 6 pennies pocket money nearly a drop of one third of pay weekly. Mum now could afford a Provident Cheque, but only an £8.00 one, this was repaid back at a minimum of 2/6d (12½p) weekly, the cheque was usable at certain shops and stores, buying anything up to its full value. We all took it in turns when one Provie Cheque was finally paid off, it meant I could get new well-fitting shoes or underwear. On one such cheque I got the lot to spend on a new three-piece suit made to measure from Jackson the Tailors at the top of Leith Walk on Leith Street. To get one made by them was equal to the top tailors Burtons (at that time, old saying 'gone for a Burton'), when Mum asked what colour of grey or black was the cloth I stood back and quivering with fear told her it was tartan jings. Did she not lose the rag! But when she actually saw it (as normal with any clothing she always had to approve of the sizes and types) on me at the fitting by the tailor, I was taken aback, not one word did she utter, the drain pipe narrow legs, the small turn-ups at the bottom, and even the wee belts on both the back of the jacket and waistcoat. It was a nice dark-Campbell tartan, he took it back for 1 week to make final alterations. My pals decided to upgrade their suits to tartan!

As I had arrived at my fifteenth birthday (15th) it meant me being of age to go to the Palais De Dance at Fountainbridge, but only the matinee, only those over 16 years were allowed in here through the week. Some of my pals who were still at school but 15 years old had been here before me, so I just followed them in through the main doors. Crowds of girls all dolled up, I'd seen and met the odd one or two, but this was different, even the pong of perfumes (pongs). After getting tickets at the foyer a short number of steps led us into the main ballroom itself. Windowless high ceiling, and a huge mirror clustered ball hung from it, throwing flickering light images bouncing off the walls on whole ceiling. Up on the right side, groups of bodies had gathered and some seated on the balcony, which extended to the stage was on the back most wall facing me, it took the form of half-moon sticking out on to the dance floor, the other half hidden behind.

Today the local rock band thundered out their tunes, and at half time, Nat Alan and his jazz-band took over with continuous music at half time the bandstand revolved, one band disappearing as the other appeared. Great stuff! Real coke-cola with ice was served in the balcony bar, but no alcohol was ever on sale at any time! My work only allowed me Saturdays, holiday periods, time off to enjoy this.

Dad's business was doing great, I moaned and groaned about my job, Mother was not having any of it. She knew I wanted to be a chimney sweep. Dad was taking on sweeps galore (John Flynn, Ollie Taylor, Captain Hughes, Pat Lunn, Albert McShane, Geo Kemp, Davy Black, just to name a few), he was known as Mr Lums-Dun, he applied for major chimney sweeping, army, navy and air force contracts, doing anything from domestic house and Nissan hut chimneys in their hundreds, four times a year, including Edinburgh, Stirling and Fort George Castles Lums. Thankfully he was that busy as happened before and now men failed to turn up for work. This was a welcomed break from groceries! Mum managed to give my boss a good excuse for being absent again, but I was now working with the cream of chimney sweeps.

Whilst working up in Edinburgh Castle I was sent with one of the old bottomers to sweep the chimney in the old cookhouse, this was single storey detached building sitting on the castle ramparts. Being small meant I only had to carry the wee jinkie ladder, 6-ft extending to 11-ft. the bottomer went inside to sheet up the fireplace, I climbed up to the roof stepped gable, climbing up through the pea-soup thick mist, the top of the chimney was way more than 18 to 20 feet from the bottom, but I had to grope my way up the stepped stones till I arrived. Completely working blind, the bottomer shouted, "the lum, hee, he, he," I gave him a "hee" he in reply then dropped the ball and brush to the base, then up again. I just happened to glance around over my shoulder, I nearly fell backwards, the mist had suddenly lifted, I found my heels were hanging over the edge of the chimney with virtually a sheer drop of over 150-ft right below me, I froze for an instance, or it may have been longer, because the bottomer came out shouting up to me: "What the hell are you doing? Where's your three knocks?" (meaning I finished) banging the chimney pot 3 times signalled the bottomer I was finished. I must have looked a sight; he came up to free my fingers from the chimney pot

When doing Glencourse Army Barracks chimneys on Dad's first day here, he had 900 lums to sweep all in one day which was pretty much normal. Seven of eight flue pipes inside the Nissan huts with multiples fireplaces in the married quarters. My job along with bottoming was scouting ahead preparing the way for others, getting and making sure the occupiers were in and ready. Our sweeps were in and out within minutes. One roper constantly hopping from one roof to another and as many as 6 or more bottomers, all go!

Then Dad sent me ahead to prepare the way for the last 400 lums (or vents as we sweeps called them). Apparently, they were located in an area closer to Penicuik about 1 mile from here. For the love of me I couldn't find them, there were a number of soldiers around. But none could tell me where the named barracks were. Dad eventually turned up ready to continue. I was glad to find he too was flummoxed. Oh boy, Dad was not happy!

Nobody in this military base could say where these barracks were but just to confirm the area of land marked on their map was the same as his instructions. However, a few days later Dad got a phone call from a major telling him to report immediately to the GHQ (General Headquarters). He was a worried man. What's he done wrong?

However, the major signed (to his astonishment) Dad's job sheet saying he was satisfied all 900 lums (vents) were all swept, but adding a verbal warning swearing Dad to secrecy not to say a word about the 400! As after the 1st World War plans to erect barracks on the site went ahead up to the point of construction, however the 2nd World War shelved the physical erection of them, but somehow the paperwork went into the system including some of the ongoing maintenance work, such as chimney sweeping which had been on paper, signed for ever since, so much so too many heads would roll to stop it at any stage! Dad had this contract for a few years and lived in fear that he would be caught. It was my task every Xmas to take a bottle of whiskey to the commanding officer's clerks house from Dad!

The 'Pali' although not my favourite venue was a must to be seen at, at least have a common knowledge of, after all the to be famous (James Bond) Big Tam or Sean Connery, once a local at this place., had by my time got weaned from the place. The most notorious mob were the Yanks, the resident lot were based at Camp Richie out by Currie, who regularly (in uniform) smashed up the whole place. I witnessed one such happening on the first visit when I turned 16 years.

Luckily for me I was already sitting up on the balcony sucking on a straw finishing my coke, when suddenly the dancing crowd right below me erupted into a fighting frenzy. Air force Yanks in uniform seemed to rush into the whole crowd, bodies pushed, shoved and some desperately trying to scatter. The reason soon became apparent. Behind me a number of Yanks were chucking full, empty and part-full bottles of coke out over the edge, down onto those below. One of them grabbed the bottle I was happily sucking on and it too disappeared into the crowd.

I glanced over to see lads and lasses and Yanks lying, running, just covered in blood. I focussed on getting down the staircase, just in time to miss the returning bottles coming up towards the balcony and mostly by the uniformed Yanks. Broken glass, chairs, tables, the screaming guys and girls who were still standing now fighting and pulling each other to get outside. Some who had already got out, plonked themselves immediately on the steps, this blocked the paths of the ones behind causing a pile up. I somehow got myself clear and away from the main mass, but only to see a group of Yanks already in the roadway gathered round a stationary black taxi and all in one move on one side turned it right over and onto its roof. It was then set on fire.

Again, another panic took over. I joined most of them and ran in fear of my life. I had heard of these and other episodes when the Yanks took over. The city took control and banned Yanks in uniform from the pubs and clubs.

It was worse when the US fleet anchored in the Forth.

As the 4-piece band rock band played their heart out during their turn on stage at the 'Pali' one Saturday morning, I sat looking down at them from my usual spot. The lead singer was giving the old Elvis songs a good thumping, twanging away his electric guitar, I was fairly impressed, and envious. Crowds of guys and dolly birds surrounded the stage jigging and gyrating to his actions. The singer took hold of the microphone with his free hand and instantly dropped to his knees laying completely backwards, his head about touching the floor behind him. What an act! He held that pose for what seemed an age, the crowd looking up at his waving their hands in the air. What a guy! Magic stuff!

I then noticed another lad push his way to the front of the crowd. I thought he was a wee bit over excited. All in one move he lunged at the feet of the singer, grabbing hold and pulling loose the cables. The singer's body just flopped to the floor. He was being electrocuted! How that guy managed to work out what was actually happening I still don't know. The singer made a complete recovery!

At another session Tommy being a military drummer took up the challenge with the group to enter a drumming competition and he won it! That was uplifting for him, only that week the whole family had gathered up on the Castle Esplanade to see him in all his splendour on his first appearance with his regiment dressed in regimental blues (blues – dress uniform).

We took up a position next to the moat wall as the band played, coming over the drawbridge from the castle, led by the brass work bugles blaring out. Couldn't see him yet but did hear the drum's bringing up the rear. A loud bang echoed out! Then a small side drum rolled between the feet of the leading bandsman, rolling on its own away down the Esplanade. When he appeared, drum-less, keeping in the true tradition his sticks going through the full motions. Mum was horrified and the rest of us speechless with laughter. Poor Tommy!

Mother never gave up on me. She didn't want me to be a chimney sweep. I would have been more than contented to have achieved that. One day she sat me down at the table, in her hand was a letter. She put a blank sheet of paper in front of me and gave me no chance to question it but: "Copy it now!"

I hadn't a clue what it really was for but another letter of application. I'd been through this boring subject before, for me the future was the present. But this job was just for an apprenticeship as a gas fitter with Scottish Gas. This really flummoxed me. I hadn't a clue as to what kind of person this title was applied to, not a damned clue and dare I ask. Again, I just done what was asked. Life was on us!

Shamus arrived just like Horice, just a wee package lying on the settee (31st May 1960) I hadn't a clue, we were expecting any new arrival. Life was too busy to notice these events. More to the point, I received an unexpected surprise from Dad!

A jet-black Ford Escort. Red leather seats and running boards. But I couldn't even drive, let alone hold a licence. He took me out for a few instructions and that was that. He had rented a lock up in the mews in Belford Road, Haymarket, where he kept most of his tools and just managed to squeeze this car in. it didn't take long for it to wear off, too young to appreciate so much. He sold it on to my uncle for £30. Having said that, if I'd been able to keep it nearer the house it may have been a different story. He'd never obviously considered insurance, a good lot of my pals were getting motorbikes and scooters and writing them off with no mention of insurance, it did not seem to be an issue!

I unfortunately received a reply to my letter of application to Scottish Gas asking me to come to an interview and entrance exam. I was not impressed with this. Mother was over the moon that I got a reply! The reason she forced me into writing for this job was in their advert they stated that normally they would be looking to have only those who had passed the school Leaving Certificate. But on this one occasion, they would open it up to those who failed or never got any exam results, and in their opinion felt there were possibly some lads were just as good and deserved this chance!

It didn't impress me. However, on the allotted day I went. I was told that they were only accepting the top 10. I was not at all troubled with this. About 30 of us went into a huge room with single desks spaced out. The whole thing took about 2 hours. I did notice that most of the questions wanted only an answer. Anyway, that's all the answers they got from me. I never felt pressured and for the first time in my life not only did I not turn the papers upside down or face down, I actually think I at least answered them and one of the first out of the door.

I got home and told Mum about the algebra and geometry, she confidentially replied, "Oh for Christ's sake! That's all I wanted to hear!" And with other words of wisdom told me I'd better keep a clean sheet with the store job and forget the gas and I instantly did!

They were preparing to take Hamish, Horice and Shamas on holiday to Kinghorn in Fife. Tommy and I being at work were left to look after ourselves and behave. It was only a few days later when the postie dropped a letter through the door, it was from the Scottish Gas Board, saying I had passed and offering me an apprenticeship with indentures and a date to start. I immediately got a train over the Forth Bridge to Kinghorn. I don't know how I managed to find them, but I did.

I've never known Mum and Dad to be speechless! I was in a bit in shock myself for days I wondered what had I done right, when everything seemed to be wrong. I wished that I could see these papers, questioning myself over and over, maybe they felt sorry for me, this never ever happened. I mean these were subjects way beyond me, I found it difficult to feel confident and failed to see this as an achievement and soon fell back into my own pattern of life that I could handle. My level and standards that I could keep pace with. Unknown to myself or others, I had set my own unchartered standards.

As it happened on my 16th birthday 1961, I attended my first training session at Scottish Gas Training Centre, Lower Calton Road, just down Tolbooth Wynd, the High Street, Edinburgh, along with 29 other lads (10 from Edinburgh), from as far away as Falkirk and Glasgow. They were to travel once a week on an early train to spend the day here, returning home all in their own time, but got fares. Only about 9 or 10 of us were new starts. We shared our day mixing with 2nd and 3rd year students (big getts bullies) bullies. My instructors were old Jimmy Simpson, a solid old tradesman who showed you all that wasn't in the manual, a good hands-on man. Then Stuart Farquson, David Crawford, both by the book, qualified gas fitters themselves, everything as per the book! But well-disciplined men.

One of our first issues was a hard-covered book the 'Holy Bible' of gas! The gasfitters manual. They frightened me near to death when I was, told, that if we completed the next 5 years as apprentices then we were going to have to know this book from cover to cover. I just went off this job! It didn't help me any, to find out I was not alone!

He started right away with a history of gas and its manufacture but went on to drag on to his table what he termed a gas meter. One what was even then in the history books. It was called a 'wet meter' boring stuff. It was a huge round object which he said was filled with water which operated the mechanism. Why on earth drag this object in and tell us how it worked? When all the time it was redundant, why?

Out of all of us, I was the only person (including the instructors) whose future was to be built on it, internationally so! Pay attention Mike!

The mornings were spent in the classrooms, where I was to struggle, but after lunch I felt things coming together and for the first time what was on the chalkboard earlier was now coming into my vision, although it was only my mates who most of the time would bully me verbally. I never had to be disciplined by the instructors. I was to see over the 5 years that many were, a couple were sacked, and a few lost their indentures (their essential papers that were with the London City Guild) to say they were of good character. They were regulars to be put before the big bosses.

I was not ever given any punishments or warnings by bosses or instructors at any time! But being allocated an area I was to work in, as we all were to work within the locality where we lived, mine was District 5 (one was in the old and new town). 5 was west of Haymarket, north to West Pilton including Murrayfield, Queensferry, Corstorphine, Winchburgh, Newbridge, and RAF Turnhouse (now Edinburgh International airport); a huge area with a wide range of type of housing from tenement bungalows was District 1 was mostly tenements.

I'd get the bus from the house to my mobile workshop which stood at the bottom end of Morrison Street, Haymarket. This vehicle looked like and was the size of a single-decker bus, the front had two side bench seats with a central doorway leading through into a huge storage area, housing larger tools, spare parts for most jobs.

My supervisor Jock (John) McLennon, no matter the weather always wore a soft old-fashioned hat and long work trench coat. He was soft spoken and a very fair man and fatherly figure to us apprentices. But the tradesmen all seemed to be in their 40s, and military men who fought in the 2nd World War. Most were bib and braces overalls and old worn tweed jackets, all of them wore ties and bonnets. There were between 8–10 of them with about 6 apprentices of all ages and experience. All of the tradesmen had served as plumbers before the war and now took on the role of gasfitters. Two of the older apprentices, George Robertson (Dode) and his mate Gordon Minty, had just come back from completing 2 years away doing the National Service with the army. Their apprenticeship was put on hold for that period, like most young men after the war now they were in the final year, but still classed as apprentices.

We all met here at 7.30am. some got their job sheets, tools and material, if lucky allocated an apprentice for the day. Within minutes all who were left were us who were going on bigger installation jobs, which meant too much materials to carry or going a good distance which was going to take too much walking time. So, we'd get dropped off but if there was no room, then it was padding the hoof, walking no matter the distance, nobody owned a car or van, the only other way was by bus, but it rarely went in our direction. It was bad enough having to carry their tool rolls, a square sheet of leather 3 feet by 3 feet, with all the tools, and junk neatly folded in it and carried over your shoulder like a huge sausage, just balance there nice and comfortably balanced, although it weighed anything upwards of 20 lbs. After a while you forgot it was up there and could walk for miles and did! These men were well used to doing it, and never seemed to complain! I never then found reason to, I was well broken by the milk run!

One of the first things you had to remember on your journey was did you have his tea and supplies on you before your set out to the first job. Never mind if you hadn't, the simple task of making his tea (coffee wasn't invented), no matter what the heating supply was whether a cooker in a house or an open fire or your blow lamp you had to follow the same ritual.

The teapot was an old syrup tin, trades name 'a drum-up' (large) with the top inner rim cut off with a loop of wire from lip to lip at the top, more than ¾ or full, bring to boil, carefully put in a level teaspoon of dry tea (he had 3 teaspoons full to do him all day) you had to remember enough was kept by for his afternoon break, the same applied to the sugar and milk, which he had in a very small whiskey bottle, nothing was wasted. Before putting in the milk or sugar, you had to put in a matchstick, all the scum on the top gathered around it, tipping this out trying not to waste any tea, you then had to swing the drum 360° rapidly over your head on an extended arm and stopping when it was down at knee level, this made all the tealeaves settle to the bottom. What a great brew! Once you had finished, dare not scrub out the drum that was where the flavour came from!

Now that everybody was working a 5½ day (44 hour) week, half day off was now a Saturday afternoon, just like my pals who were working.

Alan had just started as an apprentice electrician in the papermills in Currie. Our wages were similar, but way short of what we got on the milk run, 19/6d less National Insurance stamp which left me with around 17/9d (88p). Mother seemed to understand and only took 10/- (50p) which was the most pocket money I'd ever had to date!

So, Alan and I along with Joe (Joe Soap) decided on a holiday to Butlins camp near Ayr west of Scotland, £8.00 for the week each, Spain and any other of these holidays were only dreams. Scotland's trades holiday rotated around Edinburgh Trades fortnight being the first 2 weeks in July, followed by Glasgow the other 2 weeks. The English holidays were normally the whole of August. Edinburgh mostly travelled to the west coast, Gourock, Alexandrea and up the Clyde, or stay at home camping, Kinghorn or Portobello.

When Glasgow has what they called the Glasgow Fair (last 2 weeks in July) they flocked down to Portobello thousands of then. You could tell they were around by their accents.

Butlins holiday camp grew up in the 1950s, but at that time we could only dream about it! We booked up for the Edinburgh Trades; the first week as we needed a rest in the second week. The other reason being, we would have spent all our holiday money before the second week started!

I had a whole £5.00 to spend. We all did. Our mothers told us well beforehand that no one was to have more than the other. We paced ourselves penny for penny, day by day, and they were right. It spun out well.

On the day we'd get to the travel shop at White Park in Gorgie Street next to the Hearts ground. Where at 8am sharp we boarded the waiting double-decker bus. Mums, dads, bairns and us full of excitement piling up the stairs hoping to get to the front seats. We travelled all the way to Carnwrath where we stopped at the toilet and a wee café for the driver to get his tea break. As usual we had a poke of chips minding not to break into our £5 note. This was money saved separately for this stop. All aboard, this was the best part of the journey, everybody pointing out the recognisable landmarks as we neared the final stages. We'd waited a year for this view, as the Headland (the heads of Ayr) came into view, losing sight of it as the bus dipped into a wee glen or behind some trees, each time when it again came into view, it grew closer and larger, till the run down the brae and what a spectacular sight, the whole camp spread our below us. Cheers went up from the whole bus: "Butlins!"

Other than my tartan suit, we all had a pair of light blue jeans, they were all the trend brought on by the great group, The Swinging Blue Jeans. The whole camp was full of lookalikes and winkle pickers, with a huge boff hairstyle like a huge coil of sprung hair dangling down the front of my forehead to the near tip of my nose! We had such freedom. All us teenagers were crowded into the furthest most chalets. Just to give the others peace and quiet.

Inside they had a bunkbed and single with sink and mirror above. At the foot of the single stood a box like affair with screen curtain, our wardrobe! All we had was a wee case each (and we were lucky), as long as we had our comb and hair cream, Brylcream (white grease), but we had a small metal waste basket (it had a hole in the bottom). We soon learned to use the sink. Poor girls, a couple of them a few doors up were captured in the early hours when their sink came away from the wall, they got away with it somehow. That was an offence which along with getting caught with a girl or she with a he! You were shown the gate out and your name and chalet number announced over the tannoy system! It did happen, that is if you were unlucky. If you were daft enough and stay long enough to fall asleep and not hear the shouts: "Maids, maids!" and get caught by one of them, oh boy! They just tipped all your belongings out along with whoever else's stuff into the grass verges and they just enjoyed it. They got paid for each skull captured. But the worst part was you'd have to have a good reason for being home that early!

It wasn't only us lads that were under strict instructions, both from our mothers and fathers, if you take a woman out it is your duty to make sure that she got right home safely and never cross the threshold unless invited, by her parents only. We never had to think about that, or was it an issue, it was just part of life to most of us, but I was made very easy to comply with, no matter what strange urges come over you or her. She too, was under the same directions, and everyone I and the boys met, resisted all temptations. But it didn't stop the stories flooding on.

On one night we met up with some girls. I had had my fill of 3 pints of beer (no lager on tap then). We all went our separate ways, but mine wanted to walk down by the seashore with the lights in the camp behind us and the sea breaking in front. But being pitch black, I could only hear it.

We sat on a wooden bench now and then another couple would wander by in silence kissing and hugging, Yuk! I was getting cold with the sea breeze. What happened next was nothing to do with me, she started kissing and her hands started to wander. I hadn't a clue what to do, or in which order. Then she took my hand up towards her chest, she must have lifted her bra up first, oh they were warm, for the first time ever I held and squeezed a soft warm breast, but I couldn't get excited. Between the beer and cold, all I could think of was my bed and sleep. She tried everything, in and out of my underpants and for some strange reason to me anyway, she repeatedly took my hand off her breast and down into her knickers, holding it there, squirming her bum over the seat. I preferred to be up top! Eventually thank god, it was all over, and we split up (I'd just had an encounter with a torn mattress). My bed was a welcome sight.

The next morning after roll call we were walking to breakfast, when a group of girls caught the lads eyes, they stopped and were chatting away for a few seconds. When we left them, they turned to me and all started pointing and laughing at me.
"Jings Mike," Joe laughed at me. He continued, "She's an old crow."
"What, who is?"
"Your bird, she must be 40 or 50!"
Alan chipped in, "That's the girls old auntie you had last night!"
As the week went on a horrible picture grew. As we met this group nearly every day, yes it was the poor old sow, this horrible event went home with me. I've been abused, she's taken my innocence, oh Mother! But as far as I know and told, I was the only one of us to get even 'sticky finger' and no way was I going to brag about it.

Back to the reality of the holidays. After a big fry-up breakfast, there was plenty of things to do, competitions and prizes to be won. One of which the three of us entered was the Palace Theatre, where the Red Coats held a singing competition where the prizes for over 15s were cigarettes, a pack of 5, 10 or the ultimate 20 fags and not just plain old fags but filtered!

I never won 20, but did get a 10, that was worth a wee fortune. After cutting off the filter, throwing it away, using my penknife, I'd cut up the remainder into 3 parts, and at cut price sell them to Alan and Joe. Fags were the main prizes and if you were under 15, it didn't matter as long as you have an adult to give them to, no ID required, and you didn't have to produce an adult.

They had a large indoor heated pool with huge areas of plastic jungle, along with Tarzan swings, lots of swimming games and competitions, no guessing some of the prizes! Same prizes to be won at the fair ground. Right through to the very last hour of the week, the place was alive and full of excitement. From the Pig and Whistle Bar loaded with quiz games, to the Beach Comer Bar with live variety shows, you had to be early to get the best seats, but the booze was dear. But the older ones sneaked their own supplies in but sat in fear of being caught. They even enlisted us to go into Ayr town on the tour bus, they paid our fares to smuggle back in a couple of half bottles. We only had to ask some trusting elder on the bus to get them from the local shop (the camp was about 2 or 3 miles from Ayr itself), and honestly they weren't for us mister!

Some were so skint or mean, they could not even afford to buy the first drink in order to get a glass that they kept the same glass all week. Nevertheless, we scored a free pint for our efforts! Only if Mother knew!

The rock ballroom was the favourite place to go at night. Better still if you were on the first sitting for meals, you shot back to the chalet and into your gear, plenty cream on your hair then board the chairlift up to the ballroom which was well placed on top of the hill out of the road of the main camp. It was a very likeable noisy place to be. Plenty of lively rockers and bands. I spotted the old one now and again and the boys kept nudging me in the ribs!

Jimmy was at home with his mum. He has missed all his schooling, but has started full time with the St Cuthbert's Milk learning to be a full-time milkman. His father said years before that he would be proud to see his son with his own milk horse and cart. I never saw much of Jim at this stage only on the passing.

Part of my apprenticeship agreement was to learn other areas of the administration, first was at the Scottish Chairman's Headquarters at 26 Drumshuegh Place, near the West End. We had to be smartly dressed, learning filing, posting, all garbage, a waste of time! 3 months of life gone by. Then another few weeks in the main distribution warehouse where all the appliances came through. This was located behind the Training Centre at Calton. Lifting and loading all types of appliances, general labourer.

One of the best areas to work in was the gas meter return and repair shop, to others it was just a hovel. It was a very small room, dark and dingy, full to the roof of battered old meters. This area was also gas lit and had no windows, only one doorway which had no door, a work bench about 8 feet long with a couple of wooden stools. On one sat 'Hoppy', an old man, and hung dangling on the bench were two wooden walking sticks, which belonged to him. He was badly injured during the 2nd World War and could only get about using them but he was perched on his stool most of the day including his breaks. No matter his disability and complete lack of teeth, he seemed to smile and laugh all day, never a word in anger passed his lips.

One of my jobs was to empty meters of the pennies and count them, take a meter reading and label the details on the meter. That meant putting the key in the padlock which would puncture the paper seal showing it had been opened. But Hoppy showed me a way to open the meters without a key and breaking the seal. Well I'll be damned, all you done was taped the side of the lock and the bloody thing fell open, dip your sticky wee hand in, grab some pennies and re-snap it shut. Nobody was any wiser! No wonder he smiles all day!

However that I found that was not the only method of his income from this wee room, other than meters coming in to be emptied of known cash, our other way was the meters that came in empty, not even a padlock but the problem was the coin operated mechanism was not working, not all on closer inspection were faulty but just jammed up with unseen pennies as many as 3 or 4. We could collect up to 10–14 pennies each day, a small fortune! He would keep me happy with a good supply of mince pies and sweets, washed down bottles of lemonade!

I established a side-line, that was melting down all the off cuts of lead which were coupled to the meter supplies into ingots the size of small ladles. Although it was a sacking offence stealing metals, I never really at that point thought anybody else wanted this lead, but I became a bit of a hoarder! So much so as I just threw them into the coal cellar in the house where I kept my smelly gas clothes along with Dad's soot clothing. These ingots were beginning to pile up. Unknown to me, Dad was beginning to have worries.

When one day, I get up to find them all gone – the lot. I was told by my mum that he (Dad) and one of the sweeps took over an hour to remove all the ingots down into the van. He was so scared that at 1am they motored up to the canal just outside the town, and emptied them over a bridge into the water. He brought to my attention later that the ingots I had used was stamped SGB (Scottish Gas Board). That was as good a reason for dumping them!

Hoppy did however teach me the skills of using the soldering bolt, how to file it, clean, heat it, applying the right amount of flux then tinsman solder, without dripping it all over the place. Filing and preparing the tin case of the faulty meter then running in keeping the bolt and heat on the move, with the final lifting off without leaving a huge lump of unsightly solder behind, but more importantly, not have to go over the surface twice! Finally applying a coat of battleship grey paint, our national colour for gas meters, tried and tested on our fleet. I was in my element getting these instructions from master craftsmen.

Gas by law has to have a recognised smell, so that it can be identified for what it is by everyone! All gases had their own peculiar odour, but towns gas and now natural gas are doctored with this new distinct smell well known as 'gas'. This smell is deliberately put in at the start of distribution, only small amounts are used as like any perfume. But in the 1960s, a gas worker from Granton Gas Works stole a very small bottle of the stuff and went on to empty it down the Mound and Princess Street disrupting the whole area for days. The roads were dug up, shops evacuated. At least the stink proved its effect!

The coin operated gas meter or technically known as the 'pre-payment' was a great way of paying for your gas as you go, it was also used as a piggy bank by most. The meter man called every two months to empty the meter, he would read the meter, and measure the amount of gas used, then a quick calculation told him how much to keep, the remainder went back to the customer, who would be standing over him watching his every move. She knew how much had been put into the meter since last time (he didn't till counting) and she had a good idea how much gas was used. All hell was to pay if she thought he was diddling (fiddling the books). He was in for a tip if the figures were in her favour, if she had a good rebate, we were in for a treat that night.

House breakings were very common, and the meters were a great target. In most they were the only reason. Mother kept what went into the meter a bit of a secret and only let known when she heard the meter man was on his rounds. Sigh's all round!

Most folk who still used coal fired ranges were slow to change. The first thing they wanted gas for was a large boiling ring, which sat nearby the open fire, a large ring because it could take the largest and smallest of cooking pots. Others chose a more standard hotplate cast iron top which fitted snuggly beside any open range. Another useful gas invention was the Poker which could plug in alongside the rings using the twin bayonette valve connector all high-fi for this period. The Poker was a time and mess saver, just put it in the fire basket, cover it with coal, Bob's your uncle, Fanny's your auntie, everybody wanted one!

In the average home with fireplaces in each room and central heating not even on anybody's map, to have a gas fire in the living room was a thing of the future, but not really that far away. The expensive part was affording the supply pipe from the meter to wherever it was needed. In the early days of my apprenticeship the cheapest way to run a lead pipe was around the walls and a work of art neatly following the skirting, corners or raggled into plaster deep enough, the surface of the pipe cleaned and polished to a standard befitting the elegant fire. Folks took pride in their metal work, not just the brasses leading the grates or polishing the copper, most set a standard and you followed.

Newer types of heaters (space heaters) for the hallways, bedrooms, using only a fraction of the gas of any fires. With only a small jet or multiples of them giving off convection heat circulating up and around the room and with no ventilation needed, in those days they were a must in any home. Again, the expense came where pipes were needed. But we were kept busy.

With electric supplies becoming the thing, the gas lights were fast depleting. We were not at this stage involved with central heating, as this was still in the land of the gentry and a very specialised calling.

Gassings, whether by accident or deliberate, were quite common. Before I had become an apprentice using gas for suicide was well-known to the point that one of my pal's mum took her life in this manner. Like others before her, she just put a pillow inside the oven, turned it on, and let the unlit gas carbon monoxide ease her problems. Firstly, she made sure that there was enough money in the meter. Others who survived ran out of gas!

Others worried themselves sick with fear of an explosion. The coin meter saved the threat of explosions by a fair margin. The meter ran out before there was enough gas in the room to cause one. Explosions did at times happen, yet again the smell forewarned of such.

Before entering the gas industry, I'd only found refrigeration in butchers and fish shops and they were electrical. At first, I found it strange to find gas fridges, coupled with the fact that heat from burning gas produced ice!

Worst still my mates thought I had gone bonkers; it wasn't long before there were more of them in the domestic household than electric. (The gas fridge died away with the change of gas to natural gas). Folk had done away with their larders to make way for this gas fridge, they were even encouraged to do away with their pre-payment meters and accept a quarterly billing. The reason for this was simple. They would not have the problem of the fridge defrosting once the meter ran out of money. Now natural gas came. The flame on the fridge was very unstable and could snuff out at the slightest draught and only noticed when the fridge started to defrost, or a build-up of gas occurred so it became dangerous.

There was no way that mum was going back into the area of using a larder, the move to electric fridges was very swift. The gas industry realised that a flame sensor or flame failure device would be too costly, and it would not deal with the defrosting issue. Electric won. Within a couple of years, gas fridges disappeared.

In my first year of apprenticeship, I was working in an old man's house in Corstorphine. My tradesman gave me all the tools I needed to carry out welding on a lead pipe joint in a very tight space under the floor space. But first he turned the gas off at the meter in the kitchen. Once I crawled on my belly, one hand leading with the candle (no torches for us at that time) lighting the area and the other dragging my tools behind. I cut through the ½ inch diameter lead (composition lead) pipe, using my penknife I heard a slight 'puff', which was the pressure releasing, great. As I worked away, paring the pipework (cleaning it), my head began to hurt. I felt sickly very unwell. I became 'faintish', without another thought, scrambling out of that space, just managing to drag myself out of the hatchway on to the floor, I collapsed in a heap on the floor, gasping for breath. All my tradesman kept saying was get the hell back down and finish the job. The old man hanging around in the background repeatedly asking, "Do you two want a cup of tea?" The tradesman answered him, "No, not until we get the gas back on."

He replied, "Oh, I've got it on."

I went over to the meter, he was right, he had turned it back on! I was half-gassed. The gas when working (on) is at such a low pressure (towns gas/coal 2.5 water gauge) not much more than me breathing, you can hardly hear it in an open area. Fortunately, not enough for the naked flame to do damage! I recovered in minutes. Nobody I knew had any major gassings or explosions, although we all had our share of minor mishaps.

Working with naked flames in very confined areas was an occupational hazard, your instincts were your safety zones!

One area I disliked most was the vacant building sites in wintertime. When it was too cold or wet for the brickies to work their cement, as a result the sites closed down from October to March, huge lay-off of tradesmen in all skills.

Jimmy's dad was an outdoor house painter, he was one of those men who had no work all winter. We were lucky in that gas work to a degree could carry on in any weather. With the only man officially on site watching your every move was the watchman, normally 'crabbity'. Always appearing to be an abandoned site. We found what shelter we could get, normally in the most completed (hopefully roofed) house or structure and hope it didn't have a completed floor, let alone windows. Howling gales and snow driving through, on the bare soil which was to be the underside of the floor using the gathered wood, a wee fire (creature comforts) was kindled and a drum was always on the boil. Knowing where you were going, a visit to a bakers on the way, buying a couple of pies or even a stale loaf of bread to toast was a great warming asset to these cold sites. No matter where you went, or window you looked out of, he was there, the old tramp like bugger of a watchman shadowing your every move. The place was a ghost town of foundations whole or part built, heaps of sand, stacks of loose bricks, riddles, shovels, lying around forty-five-gallon drums of water, and only us two with the ever-present Scrooge lurking about.

This is one time I never complained of working the blow torches, the only problem we had would be to run out of methylated spirits used to run them. At least one thing at having the site to ourselves, was that when in the summer time and all the tradesmen on site, everybody had to down tools at the same time to have their break. Everybody no matter who, ten minutes mid-morning and afternoon, and 30 minutes at lunchtime.

An old retired tradesman known as a Nipper as he nipped over here and there to collect all the shopping lists of the tradesmen and others and to go to the shops, bakers mainly, others brought their pieces with them. The Nipper collected all of this and drums for their tea, he had to have this all set out in the right place within the communal hut, where everybody had been given their own space to sit. He had to have everything in place when the 10am whistle blew. Down tools everybody, and a mad rush to the hut and in an amazing silence for the period hardly a word was spoken. Reading their Daily Record doing the crossword, this was repeated each time. The Nipper called up if someone was noted to work on, normally a new man, they would sit in complete silence until that person arrived at the hut, his face full of embarrassment. No word of warning was needed!

The Nipper was paid not by the hour, but by a portion of the whole sites bonus. It was important to keep them working, the bonus was based on an hourly production, known as the 'grip'.

One of my tradesmen, Charlie Wilson, was in the navy during the war and always brought a smile to my face. He had the looks of Popeye the cartoon sailor, and always in a happy mood. Charlie lived just up the road from me at Saughton Mains, he was very shrew with money and like the rest a stickler for good dress and time keeping. He was also the trainer for Hearts junior team. With tools on his shoulder he never walked down the road like us all, he always had an old fag packet at foot, dribbling it all the way, off and on the kerb on his own oblivious to traffic and all.

Like other tradesmen we sometimes ended up at their house for lunchtime and you were then treated like one of the family.

Charlie's was no different. On one of our dinner times in his kitchenette, I was introduced to his triplet daughters, all resplendent in matching uniforms and probably about 13 years old then. I had heard of them. They or one of them was trying to cadge a ½d (eighth of a new Penny) as two of them had 1½d and the other ½d, it was amazing, he stood his ground over this and refused point blank and never gave in.

The next time I'd see these girls a few months later was on TV singing, they were known as Carlin Sisters! I knew of the Carlins, but never the connection with Charlie. In a couple of years, he was to be the first of my tradesmen to own a car, a Morris Traveller, the only day he brought it to work was on a Friday because we had to travel all the way back to Calton Roads, as that is where we were given our wages. Under normal circumstances the big mobile would pick us all up from various locations on District 5, cram us all in, but we would have to get the bus home. When Charlie used his car, I would travel free! But any other passengers would have to pay his going rate, which was measured exactly to the furlong and a good guess as to the petrol used. He was much sought after on that run! When I finally met Charlie, he was in his 70s, he didn't know me, he was suffering from dementia!

I learned to play the chords on the guitar, it was my passport to joining 2 other apprentices, Roddy O'Neil and Ian Bannerman. Although none of us were really any good it didn't stop us thinking different. With an amazing amount of self-confidence, we managed to talk an estate agent into leasing out a very small sub-sub-basement area in York Place to use as a rock club. Roddy had a mate who was supposed to be great at drums, once we got all the gear down and set up there was only room for six others. Our groupies (Bints birds).

My ordeal at Butlins was still in my head. When one night I got attached to a lass who worked locally, and the boys knew her well, after thumping out some

Beatles numbers (or destroying them), the bird and I walked all the way down to Leith where she lived as this was me doing my duty. All the way down to the foot of the walk and beyond. The shore wasn't far off with the sounds of familiar waves ringing bells, but this was different. We ended up in the back dark passage of her dimly lit stairs, at least I was prepared for a wee bit of kissing.

This was getting interesting, her hands wandered, my excitement increased. She never even attempted to stop my hands moving over her. (Roddy was right!). Then without a word of warning she hitched up her skirt, and I stepped back as she needed room to step forward, with the flick of her hand she stepped clean out of her white knickers, rammed them into her paper carrier bag she had with her, not a word was said and we took off from where we paused.

It wasn't long before my fingers relocated the nylons on her thigh, then her suspender button. I was once told that above this point the guy should feel the moist torn mattress. I felt the warmth, then as she parted her legs, and my fingers probed for the cavity, nothing! Suddenly again she shoved me back (I really thought I'd buggered something). Unbelievably, I thought I was seeing things, another pair of white knickers came off and into the bag! Jesus, I knew it was cold!

Then we were into it! I found the mattress! I let her lead. It only took minutes before I began to realise I wasn't enjoying this now very painful experience. Oh no! when without warning a voice (female) shouted down the stairs, "Are you down there?"

"I'll not be long, ma!" she shouted back.

Her mum saved my bacon, or I should say willy, Oh Jesus! It felt as though it had been run up and down with sandpaper! This was my first experience with sex. I was now totally in favour of the priesthood.

It took me a couple of weeks to feel confident that all was OK, but no way did I have plans to seek medical help or female company!

Jings, what do those guys go on about! I gave up the guitar instantly.

1st October 1962 – my 17th birthday. Nearing tea time leaving a gas job up in Ravelston on my own, daydreaming not a care in the world, on arriving at the Pelican Road crossing at the junction of corstophine Road and Saughton Hall Road, as I waited at the black and white striped crossing a large lorry drew up to a halt, the driver leaned forward and waved me across. I walked out with it on my right, one step beyond bang! I woke up sitting on the floor of the shop I had just been in!

The next thing I heard Mother say loudly, "Michael what's the mark on your face?"

In between mouthfuls of mince and tatties, I said, "A car struck me on the head." Oh Jesus, all hell broke loose.

My next recollection was lying in between the sheets on a bed in the Royal Infirmary with a nurse at the foot saying, "Happy birthday."

I spent a few days there. Once I got home to find that a 3-wheeler Robin Reliant (Del-Boy) car, was behind the lorry, instead of stopping overtook it at speed, and the corner of the roof stuck me on the right temple. I was carried into the shop when I regained my feet, the driver offered to take me home, and dropped me at the foot of the stairs, the rest is history!

Apparently, I suffered amnesia, loss of memory… also when Mother phoned the police to report it, they told her they and an ambulance were looking for me. To this date I still have no recollection. (2 knock downs, 2 dates). No awards don't know if anything happened to the driver.

It was not long after this happening that my long-awaited military ambitions began to come to fruition. Ma at last gave in, I was accepted after a medical to join the 15th C Company (Scottish) Parachute Regiment, TA – No 23999316, 15th, Easter Road. Edinburgh. There were three companies in Scotland. One in Glasgow, the other Aberdeen. The only reason being for picking them was purely because they were the smartest turned out on most parade grounds this side of the border. The other regiments just seemed not to be eye-catching when on parade, a bit raggedy around the edges.

I would have fancied the Marines but as far as I knew there were no Territorial in UK.

I was issued two separate uniforms, the normal battle dress as with the cadets. The other being my working one which was used 90% of the time, but I had to be like the rest turned out immaculately on all occasions no matter what state it ended up each week. The second uniform was made up of a camouflage smock, net scarf camouflaged olive-green trousers with ammo pockets. Boots with longer ankle support, and putties (wraparound bandage like gaiters) to support the ankle when jumping. When they gave me my so-called dress boots, not forgetting my steel helmet (Tinlid), the only thing good about them was the steel studs (seggs) a right scrappy Second World War rejects. I never realised that Mother had kept my old ones from the cadets, she had them stuck away on a shelf wrapped in old rags at the back of the coal cellar. Well done Mum, I was chuffed to pieces when I unwrapped them! Studs and all shone bright after only a few minutes refurbishing them. I could not have had a better start!

After the first few weeks with the main parade being on a Sunday morning. Regimental Sergeant Major, Davie Adams, a short stocky erect man made to measure brought the whole parade standing in ranks of 3. He took up his place in front and centre facing us all, then he called out my name (I was in the rear rank), he ordered me front and centre, to march all the way around the company and take up a place beside him facing the troops. He then gave me a reddest kip I've ever had, lecturing them, all the time pointing to my turn out. But the guys were great. Even the older troopers gave me a pat on the back. Some of these men were retired paratroopers with 20 years' service already. I did make good friends with other new recruits like myself, wee Ronnie Campbell, a great character.

I was in my element, down at our barracks in Easter Road. They had an underground rifle range .22 at least this time there were real bullets. We practised our shooting skills and most of our square bashing here on the Wednesday nights. Saturdays and Sundays were spent weapon training. Very familiar grounding. The major difference was all the weapons had intact firing mechanisms, everything from Bren guns, Stein guns and new to me, self-loading rifles (SLRs),

3.5 rocket launchers or bazookas (anti-tank), stripping oil from Energa, grenades and hand grenades. Removing their base plugs, putting in the primer detonators ready for use. (hand grenades know as Mills Bomb or Pineapples).

The real thing for me was when we used them for real up at the practice ranges on the Pentland Hills at Dreghorn on the outskirts of Edinburgh. Loading the magazines and firing them at targets 25 yards for the Steins and 300 yards for the Brens. All those years of handling them and now they came to life.

After a couple of months on the Bren gun I was told I had gained marksman status! But I wasn't smart with the hand grenades. Just a sergeant and I standing behind a 2-foot-high brick wall as I was 3rd or 4th now to go through, the others taking shelter in the adjoining brick shelter. The flat bedded coal ash, throwing pit lay in front. As I just pulled the pin he said, "Stop," and pointing into the centre of the area, he said, "see that grenade out there? Well, see if you can get close to it."

Until this point I had only my nerves to deal with. It was amazing, a grenade took on a whole new meaning once you removed the pin, thrown it and spent only a second upright to see the thin smoke saying you had 2 seconds to get down to cover. But this one showed my cowardice. Oh shit, only a tiny part of somebody else's grenade showed just above the cinders. It all happened in a flash of dust. I threw it before I could see where it landed, in the same instance he grabbed and pulled me down by my webbing and tucked up by the wall, in time to feel the full smack and thud of the second grenade exploding on the other side of the wall. We were both showered in ash bits and dust. Our helmets and tunics were completely covered in dust.

As calm as you like, we got up and dusted each other down, all he said was, "Next."

I disappeared into the hut, the next passed me by. When it was over, he said I threw it bang on target, my grenade took most of the blast deflecting the shrapnel and bits away, but it sent my bomb back in our direction, fortunately not high enough to get over the wall. Phew! The soft ashy pit took the main blast. 2 in 1 shot.

Now being recognised as Bren gun marksman I was No 1 completely responsible for every part of the weapon and its use from, carrying it, cleaning, ammunition etc. I had a No 2, we shared most of the duties but his main part was carrying all the spare parts and ammo, a good pair of second eyes, he could spy the surrounding area for trouble, he'd be changing red-hot barrels, replacing empty magazines, as I held position on an existing target. The barrel had to be cooled as quickly as possible, a good pee done the trick that was the only water around. As I was only 9½ stone and 5 foot 8 inches going on a route march, anything between 20–22 miles over rough tracks and hills, never gave me much of a problem with being No 1 on the Bren. I had to carry it. I must have been seen to be toiling sometimes as without saying a word, a corporal appeared from the line of the marching troops, exchange my Bren (weighing 28 lbs) for his SLR rifle (9 lbs), I felt as though I was walking on air. The same act of camaraderie was shown to my No 2, great stuff!

These marches were usually done on a Sunday and it was common for us to take our own weapon home and clean it thoroughly and bring it back with us for inspection on Wednesday. No problem of turnings of heads by the public or law.

For nearly every weapon training we went to the live rangers at Barrybudden, east of Dundee. The place was a mass of sand dunes. Here I got my skills using the Energa grenade, Mortar and Bazookas, just to find out facts that I had been taught and told, that these weapons were a killer to us as much as the enemy. Once you had firmly thumped the butt off a .303 rifled with a blank bullet up the breach with the muzzle pointing skyward in the direction of a tank or whatever, sliding the working end of the grenade over it, keeping your face and head as clear away as possible, your left hand steadying the stock, using your right hand trigger finger with a flick of it on the trigger instantly clearing the finger and away before the violent kick on firing broke it, as it was well known to break your finger. The mortar was more purpose built for the job, and had a short rope lanyard attached to the trigger assembly near the base. But the blast and any fins that may have come away from the bomb itself as it exited the tube, could at worst kill a member of the team. It was essential that everybody duck down away from the exit, instantly the bomb shot out of the chamber. But the bazookas (3.5 rocket launcher) perched on my shoulder and about 5-foot long, kneeling on one knee and about 40 foot from the already well ruined tank acting as my target. Anybody standing within 30 foot of the rear would be seriously injured or killed. Again, a number two loaded the rocket into the rear, and attached 2 wires which were activated by the trigger, he then gave me a tap on the helmet for the OK.

Aiming at just under the turret, Swoosh, it was off with a very positive kick on the shoulder. The rocket took off in what was slow motion. I could follow its full arch to the tank, it fell short of the whole body, bounced once, and rose slowly into the air, over the top, slamming into the sand dune behind without going off. Thankfully the CO (commanding officer) decided he was leaving all unexploded stuff for the bomb disposal. Thank Christ!

The SAS (Special Air Service), I'd heard of them, but my encounters with them were always nearly the same, their favourite exercise was 'escape and evasion'. On one such evening we set up lines on the eastern slopes of the Pentland Hills, Edinburgh, I'd spent all afternoon digging a silt trench on the right-hand, the last and extreme flanking position with the whole company dug in on my left, the furthest most being another Bren man. In between rifle and Stein gun men had also dug in. We were well warned that the two SAS men were on a final leg of a course and if they got captured, they would have to go all over the past 6 months! But it was our duty to capture them regardless. Keeping in mind the stories gone before them of their enemies (us) they did not lie down without a good fight, broken limbs or not!

In daylight and after the field kitchen closed and the CO emptied a full bottle of dark run into the communal tea urn, we scooped up a full mug, sugary, milky and horribly tasting substitute for tea. Being under 18 even in the paras were not allowed alcohol, but this was supposed to be different and if this was what rum was all about, Jesus you can keep it.

As it grew darker, even my No 2 sharing this trench near disappeared in the blackness and the voices and noises all faded away, only the silence being broken of the solitary sergeant moving up and down the line of trenches, giving instructions on the possible whereabouts of the SAS guys and don't stare as the silhouette of trees or bushes or for sure they will bloody move! And he was right, they did appear to.

With no way of keeping time, the tension grew, our eyes hurt, what little light came from the moon which was well hidden behind the thick black clouds, his last warning to me was that he had sent out a 6-man patrol and they were due back.

The bushes kept playing havoc with me and No 2. Then from my left a voice commanded, "Halt, Halt! Who goes there?"

I swung my Bren round to where I thought the voice was calling to then a reply came, "Patrol coming in!"

The challenger asked the patrol leader to come forward and identify himself I peered into the dark, I could just make out a figure rising out of the nearby gorse bush and with rifle in hand move towards our lines.

Then as the figure came right up to our lines, I heard a brief exchange of word, followed by the patrol!

My focus was back on the area to my front and right. Without much warning other than a shout of what seemed warning shouts from my left, came the clatter of rifles, Steins and Brens, all opening up, I didn't wait for an order, the bushes in front seemed to move, so I opened up using 2 magazines (56 rounds) before silence fell. The air stank of cordite.

The sergeants were busy running up and down the lines, shouting orders of all kinds. But it turned out the SAS guys had shadowed the patrol and at the right time took up position inside the numbers and when challenged to come in one at a time, easily got into and through our lines. It was only because they placed themselves within the first 6 men, did they succeed. Six men went out eight came back, two too many.

We only did our job as trained, that if one more than the number came back from patrol, Open up. They got through the exercise was over!

Every 3rd weekend we journeyed by train through to Yorkhill Territorial Barracks, met up with not only the Glasgow Company but some of the Aberdeen Company who made this trip. Arriving there on Friday nights, we'd prepare our bed for the night, taking any available space on the floor. No mattresses or pillows, only a couple of heavy army issue blankets. After laying out our kit, our priority was to head for the arcade in the city centre. We were left to our own devices. On the odd occasion we were escorted by one of the Glasgow Company just to make sure we behaved ourselves. This was my only opportunity to get underage drinks, 2 pints and I was anybody's.

In the morning we were on parade, a full complement, 3 companies. We'd spend the whole morning split into sections, going through anything from gym, map reading, rifle and other weapon drill. After eating whatever was prepared by the cook, we'd pile into 1-tonners lorries and in convoy head to various locations around the Glasgow countryside (among our numbers and not yet famous, Glasgow musician and comedian Billy Connolly). We'd carry out the same exercises as we'd do in Edinburgh and Dundee, but this time with a full complement of 3 companies. Then without warning one Saturday morning we were lined up and told that this and the next day was to be our pre-para course! Fail any one part and we failed the lot and no resitting.

We did not even know of such a course, never mind having the slightest idea of what was to come. Within a few minutes the inside of Yorkhill and Drill Hall was transformed into an assortment of ropes, climbing mats and narrow walkways suspended between balconies and scaffolding.

I was thrown right into it, by climbing hand over hand up a rope with screams of encouragement that installed fear. Once I got to what I thought was the top, and ready to make my way down the 25 foot again he screamed "No, no!"

My mind in stark panic, I eventually understood that I had to grab hold of the iron bolt which secured the rope at the top most part. My hands and arms ached. When I finally got within my feet touching the concrete floor, he yelled into my ear, "Don't dare! Get the f*** back up!"

It seemed impossible to instruct my muscles to obey the hellish order, but somehow, I did. The agony of getting to the top a second time was more than unbearable. My mind seemed to blank out as about just below halfway down my hands and arms could no longer grip the rope, with half grip I slid right onto the concrete, crumpled into a heap. I could feel hands pull at my smock bundling me out of the way to make way for some other sod.

Not a word was said, I lay there. Within what seemed barely a couple of minutes, I was thrust along with others into doing press-ups and with not a word of 'pass or fail'. It was up the flights of stairs to a balcony with a 3-foot barrier between me and a 35-foot drop on to the concrete below. This was the scariest thing I was about to do in my 17 years to date. With a tower scaffolding at about 15 to 20 feet away, linked to the balcony by a 1-foot type of planking linking the balcony to the tower. I was first to meet this challenge, only a small stool to the ledge and straight on to the planking. Once I got on to it and only the voice of the instructor on the ground shouting up instructions to me, "Stand to attention. Look straight to your front and do not look down!"

Jesus, was I shitting myself? Knees getting wobbly, the next command was madness. "Quick march!" So I did, desperately wanting to look down to see where my feet were, as I did so again, he screamed, "Look straight ahead." I just got to the middle when up came another lecture, "Halt!" I obeyed, wobbly and swaying from side to side. Next came, "About turn!" As clearly as I could, wobbling, I did it! No longer had I completed that move, facing to where I had just come from, then another order was shouted. "Walk backwards and in step!" I hadn't even done this on the ground, and at a very shaky place I just shook from step to step feeling my way backwards and thankful when my hands touched the scaffolding! I just wondered where this was going to end. Then ordered to attention and march off all the way until I reached the relative safety of the balcony. Then it was their turn.

The whole day was intensely full of more ropes and bench work ending in carrying a man in full kit up and down the parade ground till my knees folded beneath me. Still no word of failing, and I didn't even think of it.

Up early next morning, we crammed on board the waiting lorries, not a clue as to what was coming next, nobody knew and we didn't ask. We arrived at a location north west of Glasgow at a spot down a track way none of which was familiar to me or anyone else. Pretty rough and very hilly country.

This time I was given an RSL (rifle) as like the rest. Once we had kitted up, webbing, ammo pouches, backpack, full water bottle and tin lid strapped to my waistband. We took off along a track in two single files and at an easy jogging pace, we had no clue that this was a measured course over very rough terrain 3 miles long, which included climbing up and over very steep hills which were topped with a craggy cliff faces, some 80 to 100 feet high. Although there were plenty of hand and footholds, the weight of my kit made my joints feel as if they were about to tear out of each socket.

The downward slope should have been easy, but my legs were like jelly. More of us by now well strung out (every now and again a none soldier, instructor, came into view and just pointed and yelled in the direction to take) who knew where this nightmare was going to finish! A wide river came into view following the track down to it, and before I knew it with rifle held high above my head just following some others in front of me the water up to my chest. On the approaching bank, only a few yards away and just beyond a high stone rubble wall were a few men already climbing over. Canvassed topped trucks could be seen.

Once I scrambled over it a waiting soldier grabbed hold of my rifle yelling at me that I'd finished, telling me to join the others now grouped behind one of the lorries.

I felt great; I'd done it!

We all lay about in the grass having a fag and chatting or untying our boots, wringing out our socks. Then without much warning we were ordered to our feet. Removed of our webbing and packs, smocks and helmets, just standing there looking like drowned rats. Marched over to the open car park, we were divided into groups of six. Lying a few feet away were a number of telegraph poles with pieces of rope attached at even intervals. We were ordered six to a pole, take hold of a rope (toggle) which each had a small wooden peg on the end. Then we were told that we were to re-run over the same entire course 3 miles and at no time should any man fail to keep hold of the toggle or rest the pole on the ground. Should they do so, he or the whole team will be dismissed from the regiment. Nobody said a word.

After about only 10 minutes rest we were back on the start of the track again. Surprisingly the pole seemed quite light, but not for long, even getting up that crag was impossible, not a word was uttered between us. My concern (as later to be as the others) we couldn't keep it from hitting the crag face, thinking failure. We struggled on till we were at the top only to be faced with a screaming ab-dab of a sergeant. Even when crossing the river, we tried stupidly to keep it high out of the water. I kept losing my footing, spending most of the time under the surface choking and gulping water in huge amounts with my hand still with a grip on the toggle trying to keep the other up and under the log, totally oblivious to the others. We staggered coughing and splattering up the other banking with the wall only feet away.

Shouts from the instructors, "If that log touches any part of that wall, then you've all failed!" and it didn't! now screaming at each other we all got over, or should say fell.

With hardly a word said, we grabbed our already soaking kit and got dressed. We split up into our own companies, boarded our respective lorries, when we found all our gear we left at Yorkhill stacked up in the back!

When back in Edinburgh, they generously dropped us each on our doorstep. The only thing strange was a couple of the guys were missing. Between us we worked out they had failed, but then again, we were kept in limbo, or was it all of us?

When I got to my house, the sergeant who sat beside the driver leaned out of the window, shouting, "Mind 6.30pm Wednesday's parade," with a broad smile and thumbs-up.

I only assumed I'd passed. What happened to the others, God only knows!

After this course, Sergeant Major Adams asked me when my summer holidays were, I told him first 2 weeks in July 1964. OK he said, have your kit bag packed by then, you're off to Parachute Training School at RAF Abingdon, Oxford.

Two of us who had the trades holiday travelled by train first to Birmingham New Street Station then crossed over to Snow Street Station a short distance away. Both of us in working uniform (smock etc.) and kitbag with webbing. Feeling a bit hungry, we went into the station café, we only had 2 Scottish £5 notes, but unknown to us Scottish money was taboo! The lady at the till charged us both 2/, 6d taken off for handling charges. When we asked for our full change, she refused. No matter how much we complained (17-year-old soldiers away from home), she refused.

Once we were out on the platform, we saw a policeman, he marched us back inside, and told her to refund us our full change and she did when he threatened her with arrest. Apparently, we were told later, never take Scottish notes south of the border, reason being the English receivers could not give it out as change, and could only take it to the local bank, so a 6d in the pound was charged (unlawfully). But many English got away with it! The English pound however was accepted in Scotland, part of the problem was that Scotland had many different banks and notes at that time. British Linen Banks, Bank of Scotland, Royal Bank Scotland, Clydesdale Bank, Commercial Bank, Bank of England.

Jack and I continued on our way, arriving via Oxford station in RAF Abingdon at about midday. We found the place a hive of activity, air display day. Crowds of public all over the base. We found the throng after leaving our kit beside our single bed. We appeared to be the first of the troops to arrive and were not officially under any orders till Monday.

We mingled with the crowds on the warm sunny day. All excited to see all that was happening, I'd never been to an air show only ever seeing so many aircraft familiar on the big screen war movies coming to life. We pushed our way to the front ropes of one crowd, looking out over the grass and seeing what was a tarred wee roadway just yards from us, and a couple of hundred yards beyond a huge open doorway of a hangar, loads of people crowding into it, so we just slipped under the rope and walked along the tarred road which seemed to wind its way to it.

The crowds we had just left now on our left. We smartly strode out at pace, to our surprise we thought 'they' were waving to us, so we waved back. Two smart paratroopers in uniform, what else? Then simultaneously something caught my eye above my brow, I looked up just in time to see a pointed thing emerge into view, it made us stop still looking upwards, turn our heads and behind, we both took off. It turned out to be a Vulcan Bomber plane taxiing behind us, it was huge, the biggest bomber in the world we were told. We just happened to be on a taxi runway and it wasn't stopping for anyone! We spent the rest of the day losing ourselves behind the ropes.

However, Monday 5am, I was up and my bedding made up into a bed block (sheets and blankets all interfolded into a nice square block) placed neatly at the foot of the bed along with all our kit ready for inspection. When the corporal or whoever was finished venting his anger, throwing articles about and this sometimes included beds and bedding, because something was not up to his standard! Then at the double we were on the parade ground in ranks. The first order every morning was for anyone who wanted to report 'sick', only a couple of guys fell out to see the MO (medical officer) at 8am, but they were given duties in the barracks to keep them occupied: scrubbing for us one hour of square bashing drill, followed by a couple of miles running in and out of the empty runways. Then breakfast.

The Territorial soldiers were housed within the inner areas of the base and the regular full-time ones dotted around the outer quarters. One good reason was that we only had 2 weeks to complete the whole course. They had 3 months and classified as residents.

We only met them on the aircraft when jumping or after a day's work was done. We ate with the RAF in complete comfort whereas they had their own mess halls and own cooks and food.

It followed that our level and timing of training was miles apart. As they marched us TAs to the nearest hangars, I could see away at the other end of the airfield a couple of small helicopters hovering high above the ground with ropes dangling from then, with some soldiers sliding down to the ground. It seemed a very active area. I was totally taken aback at the size of the inside of these hangars. Rubber matting covered most of the concrete, wooden chutes which terminated 6 or 7 feet from the ground, parachute harnesses hung from the ceiling beams. We got into groups of 8. Learning to land properly was the first stage: feet, knees and legs together, arms up, elbows tucked in, and with a slight bend of the knees, twist and roll to one side, front and then back. After hours of this it was onto the chutes and harnesses to put in some speed and motion for reality.

Slowly the morning fall out on sick parade was to increase to more than 50%.

After a few days we moved on and upwards mock up fuselage of the aircraft, where and how to approach the door, in a line of men (stick) when getting out of the door, a hand left sticking out, getting caught in the slipstream (70 miles an hour rush of air) even a loose helmet or equipment strapping could cause serious injuries. Everything is checked and double checked. Fitting into the parachute harness is quite simple, except when you fasten it all into the central buckle, and then tighten the whole thing up, you find 2 large rectangular buckles end up in between your legs, they help to hold the seat strap in place. On the practice rig in the hangar when your swinging around from it, your body weight is carried by these straps. All is fine until the instructor screams at you to keep your legs firmly together. Oh shit! Your crown jewels get instantly crushed, the pain has to be experienced!

The bastard knows, but refuses to let you make an adjustment and prolongs the agony until you are out of your seat strap, before you get lowered to the deck. In reality you'll break your legs if you land for real whilst in the strap. Later when back in the barracks there's a rush where we check our 'jewels' and compare the bruises.

Within a few days we moved into another hangar where we graduated up much higher off the ground, some 40 to 50 feet, up at roof height, where another mock-up of aircraft exit door. This was the 'fan' jumping assembly. After putting on a harness, I climbed a vertical wall ladder which terminated inside the enclosed space, waiting for me was one of the dispatchers (chucker out). He gave me a reserve chute which I clipped into the D rings on the front of the harness. Once at the doorway, he clipped on a fastener to the back of my harness, this clip was attached to a wee cable which in turn was attached to a huge fan which was to simulate the speed (22 miles per hour), that was the average rate of fall during a jump from a plane.

I didn't doubt that, but just standing in this open doorway looking directly down at the sea of faces of those waiting their turn to climb the ladder, I couldn't believe how mad I was to be up there. I nearly froze.

"Don't look down!" a voice barked in my ear. "Go!" he screamed in my ear.

I shot forward without another thought. Before I even knew it, I was on the mat in a heap. such a mess. I was ordered up again instantly. This time still shitting myself thoroughly, but with my eyes open.

"Up again!"

Fuck it, even after 4 or 5 times I still ended up a crumpled heap. The last time, scared shit-less, I did it my way, once I knew he hooked me up, I threw myself out the door, not waiting for his command. I landed perfectly; nothing was said!

There was nowhere for us to go at night on the base. As we were well warned the paras were banned from most pubs. The only way around that was to wear civvies, but we have none. However, 6 of us after teatime found a wee local bar who took sympathy on us, so we decided to buy a round each of some stuff from a barrel which was on the counter, Scrumpy. I'd heard of the stuff. But he warned us that it was up to him when he thought we'd had enough, fair do's.

So I bought the first, my god it was worse than vile. Jesus, how can anybody drink this vinegar? But after a few sips, I had another sip, then another. I remember getting halfway through it, then waking up at 5am sick as a dog!

Apparently the six of us didn't even drink 2 pints, we were that stewed, me in particular. They managed to talk the guard out of putting me on a charge of being drunk in Her Majesty's uniform, were it not the fact that I was more sick than drunk!

I couldn't remember a thing either than I was on my second pint, then lights out!

One morning 5am, we all paraded as normal, the exception being everybody was out on parade including regulars, paras, marines, the only ones excused were the small complement of SAS. We were then all marched in ranks of 3, out on to a taxi runway running parallel to the main runway. After nearly marching the full length, we were brought to a halt, a right turn now facing the runway. An order for us all, some 200 men to look closely at what covered the tarmac. I saw something strange (from this distance anyway), then we were told it was bread stolen from the kitchen during the night. They were Halting all take off and landings and whoever is responsible was ordered to take one pace forward.

For what seemed a wee while, there was complete silence and no movement. Then at last, I couldn't see, but was aware of a happening to my right. It turned out to be a good number of marines took a step forward. They were marched away. All of us were marched back to the parade ground minus all the marines who were left to clear up the mess.

The reason was the poor menu they were having.

Another half day was spent getting used to handling all our equipment, main chute – 30 lbs, reserve chute – 15 lbs, and weapon container – 70 lbs, this was fitted against your leg once the chutes were both already on you. The container sat just on top of your foot and up to the waist, where it was clipped on with a strap and release pin at your ankle connected to another at the waist, also a coil of rope 15-foot long attached to a D ring on your harness, the other end of the container. This being jettisoned (released) when you're in free air space and before you hit the ground. Pull the pin, it falls away and dangles 15 feet below, swinging away, but make sure nobody's below before jettisoning the bloody thing and don't fall on it when it lands before you.

Now and again when moving around the base, we noticed a plane fly in circuits, straightening out and a solitary parachute exit where we dare ask what was going on, the answer was: officers do their jumps on their own, completing the whole course in days.

By the Friday of the first week we boarded a lorry along with our main chute and reserve. After about 20 miles we arrived at our DZ (dropping zone) to do our first jump up in the Barrage Balloon, a huge silvery skinned balloon like the ones used for anti-aircraft defences during the war. Suspended under it by steel ropes a square box like thing covered in canvas top, with only an open doorway (without the door), it swayed very gently in the light breeze. We were told earlier jumping Was only done in winds up to 15 miles per hour (not a clue how that was meant to help me).

The chutes were already given serial numbers when stores issued them to us which we then signed for. I suppose if it failed or whatever we could exchange it.

As the container only took five of us and a dispatcher at a time, the remainder took up a sitting position upwind to await their turn. The DZ was a huge parkland area empty of life except some old RAF looking concrete sheds to our rear. At the farthest point downwind there appears some moving cars and such like on a boundary road. Beside the balloon stood a heavy RAF winching lorry with a heavy-duty cable coming from a cylinder tethering to the balloon. The front five walked in line, with the last man disappearing inside followed by the others and finally the dispatcher. Above the noise of the winch loud voices could be heard, but not distinctly enough to understand. Suddenly with a loud clunk the winch wheel slowly turned.

I watched in awe as the balloon rose up and away, taking up a slight bit of slack which carried the container to slightly slide over the grass surface and upwards. The door turned out of sight. At about every 200 feet the winchman clipped onto the wire a small yellow flag, 3 in all to indicate usually that the balloon was now at 800 feet. The wheel stopped with a jolt as he switched it off.

One of the remaining RAF dispatchers walked away from us whilst all this was happening and took up a position some hundred yards further again downwind, he clutched a megaphone. I could hear faint voices coming from the balloon, the "go!" instantly followed by a body, feet first, falling at one hell of a speed, trailing behind him his static line and parachute unfolding from his back. Just as his feet neared the first 200-foot flag and with the whip cracking smack, his chute opened. He drifted from us and the dispatcher spoke to him through the phone, guiding him all the way to landing.

We saw that this was repeated with the three others. When the balloon came down, out stepped the fifth man, we thought he must have had problems with his equipment, wrong!

Feeling just a bit nervous, it was my sticks turn. We were called forward and given a final once over. I was to be No 2, so No 5 led the way into the dark box. When I entered, No 5 was already hooked up standing in the back right-hand corner. No 4 was in the left-hand corner, both facing the door. No 3 stood in front of No 5, then the dispatcher hooked my static line up. I stood with my back to No 4. No 1 in front of me close to the door. The dispatcher stood next to him, his huge frame blocking the doorway with his back to us having a last word with ground staff outside. I noticed a gap of about three feet between me and No 3 and 5, we had a rail between us. On the floor of this space it seemed to have some sort of covering.

In a very loud voice the dispatcher shouted, "Up 800 feet, five men jumping."

With face full of shock, I looked around at the others for some kind of reaction, nothing! Left with my own reaction that it included me. I was one of the 5 men jumping with no time to react. The box lurched, and I could see the head of the guy standing outside disappear under the doorway. The whole box tilted from the back down to the door making us all grasp the upright supports fearing we were going to fall out the door (the reason for this was to help us exit).

The whole cage vibrated to a halt. "No 1, stand at the door."

I could only look at the back of his helmet as he struggled just to turn into the door. Once he steadied himself, with a slap on his back to help him, "Go!" He seemed to just fall out, not jump, as I expected to see him do it. Then a horrible stifled scream came up to you, followed instantly with the crack of a whip. The dispatcher all this time casually leaning out of the door watching the proceedings and looking happy with his work, he waved (I take it) to the crew on the ground.

Then turned slightly to me. "No 2 stand at the door."

My mind was in a locked-up turmoil, gingerly shuffling forward, terrified I'd fall out.

"Look up, straight to your front," he bawled out.

The first thing I noticed was the roadway was no longer at the very end of the DZ, but right below and made me wonder if I was going to have to drift over it, but no. Out of the corner of my eye I saw No 1 chute collapsing on the ground.

"Go!" and I did. Oh Christ! I was totally paralysed as like a bullet and my head flung involuntarily backwards. All I saw was sky (I was told later I screamed loudest), followed by a gentle tug, and the familiar crack of a whip. Bit by bit the whole world took on its familiar shape, after doing all my checks (chute open and looks OK, look left, look right, nobody there, and nobody below, wriggle out of seat strap, done). I could see I'm on my side of the roadway, this is great. Then I heard a voice.

"No 2, No 2, pay attention!" It was the dispatcher with the megaphone. "Legs together, knees bent, and hands firmly up high gripping and steering, pulling on the front lift webs, elbows tucked in."

Slipping into a perfect sideways landing. Great!" Oh shit, the ground sped up to meet me. Wallop! The grass just slammed into me. After gathering up my chute, I joined the others who had completed their jump on board the lorry. The excitement now running through my veins was so much that I couldn't even speak for the remainder of the day. I wasn't the only one as the journey was done in near complete silence.

When we got back to the barracks, I found the empty bed spaces were growing in numbers, those who were injured or refused to take part, or those who just refused to jump any more, were we envious of them having the courage to say no to the RSM.

On the Monday morning we arrived back at West-on-the-Green for the second and last balloon jump. I foolishly never wore my trouser braces relying on my belt instead. If on Friday they told me then to do my 2nd balloon jump, no problem, I was very high. now given two days to go over the first jump, I was now more than petrified! It must have played in my mind.

However, this time I was No 4, oh God, then at the last moment we were told it was to be the hole in the floor jump. My mind was fully in tune to the bloody door exit! I forgot the routine for the floor. Too late, we were all on board. On the way up this dispatcher was a bit of a joker, he was singing the old song,

'Please Help me I'm Falling'. As best I could I kept a close eye on the first man out after the cover was removed revealing the oval shaped hole. With arms folded over his reserve chute on the command 'Go' he put one foot out over the hole and shot straight down with the familiar yell within a second or two his chute opened and he drifted out of our view.

No 2 was called forward, this guy was like how I felt, legs and hands all over the place. The dispatcher tried to reassure him he'd be OK, then when all was right, "Go." He hesitated, then sort of jumped, down he went, then came to a halt, he managed to put both hands out to the sides and held on, shouting. The dispatcher grabbed hold of the static line on the back of No 2's chute, said, "OK son, I'm going to pull you back up." He had to repeat it a few times, saying, "You'll have to let go first, I've got you." Even I believed him. No 2 seemed to obey and relaxing his grip, shot straight down and drifted away. I was so spaced out, I just followed No 1 and stepped out.

After landing and rolling up my used chute again I felt high, very high. I did notice however that some members of the public had been watching the proceedings from the safety near our trucks. I felt like a prize fighter walking towards them with my chute on my shoulder and helmet on my head.

I squeezed my way past a crowd and up to my lorry. As I was bending down to put the chute on the grass, I suddenly noticed to my horror that my trousers had slipped down from the waist to above my knees and only held in place by the tail of my smock, which served its purpose. The tail before putting on the chute is unclipped from the waistband at the back of the smock, it's pulled through between the legs and that end is clipped on at the front, so as when you're swinging about and reach up to alter the lift webs it stops what has happened from happening! Hence the back-up braces. I somehow managed to escape being put on a charge for not wearing my issue braces!

Come Monday morning parade, it was amazing only a few of us stood to attention, those reporting simply fell out and limped away. But they were running about and playing football all weekend, they never got away with much. When I got back after breakfast the barrack rooms inside were spotless.

Later in the morning with main and reserve chutes on, we were marched to a waiting aircraft, propellers turning. This was, as for many of us, the first time on a plane, and having to jump from it. I had only seen the likes of this in the war movies. The aircraft, a Hastings, sat on a low tailwheel, with the nose looking high. In second place we approached the doorway and small metal ladder, the noise from the 2 propellers on each wing was deafening and the draught created tremendous. Excitingly. As I was 2nd on board and we were loading on the left-hand side (port) we had to climb the ladder turn left, walk up the steep floor up to the entrance of the pilot's cabin, duck under the static line cable, which went all the way down the centre of the fuselage to the floor on the tail area. We had to walk (or staggered under the weight of the chutes) down the starboard (right) side to the doorway, then pull down a paddle spring loaded seat. It was awkward trying to sit straight, because of the tilt inside the fuselage.

But once it rolled down the main runway, the tail lifted, then slowly it rose up. My first flight, what a thrill! I was taken aback at the view I got looking out over the open doorway opposite. I couldn't believe it was happening to me. The men opposite, our knees only a couple of feet apart, a lot of sad and worried looking guys. This was our first jump from the aircraft which meant a stick was of two men on each side going out at a time. The aircraft would then turn around dispatching another 4 until it was empty.

I was No 2 on my stick, a couple of dispatchers squeezing up and down the rows of troops kept my mind busy, just sitting there with the weight of my main chute resting on the bare framework. The only thing at that moment in time that caught my attention was the sight of the plane tail wing was much lower than the base of the door, I didn't get time to think.

"Action stations!"

Both of us rose to our feet with all the good training now being put to the test. I clipped my static line onto the strap attached to the steel cable, as again in training, I checked the guy up front's main chute and harness so he was clipped on properly, and on command I about turned. He then checked my gear (double check), again face the back. I could just see the red light above the door was still on, then the next command, "Stand at the door!" Barely heard above the racket of the engine.

I shuffled up close, to his chute nice and tightly, he completely filled the open doorway. My right hand gripping my static line above my shoulder and left one across my reserve chute. I could hear and feel the pilot had suddenly changed the speed to slower. I nearly lost my footing, as if someone had slammed on the brake in the car, followed by a loud shrieking noise. I never saw the green light, but, "Go, go, go," and I was out!

The wind and buffeting also a black flash (found out later that was me going under the tail wing) I just seemed to curl up tightly hug my reserve chute, then complete silence. Getting bumped about on a cushion of cotton wool and looking up at a blue sky. Suddenly the now familiar crack of whip. The horizon and green field swung into sight. I looked up to see my chute beginning to open fully, it seemed great. Then completed the rest of my checks and out of my seat strap using my lift webs. I managed to steer clear of the other three, looking for a fixed point on the ground and not a moving object. I could see which direction I was going in which was backwards, in stretching up, grabbing hold of both front lift webs, pulling them down hard, I was able to land perfectly with a slight forward drift and a wee bit hard. The other three guys were well spaced out, after wrapping up my chute and making my way to the transport, I stopped with the other to watch the aircraft fly back on with the next 4, but only three jumped. The plane came round again, some of the guys around were shouting up, "Jump, jump!" nothing happened. It flew around again and four jumped. We had a good guess as to who has refused.

We returned to the airbase to be re-issued with chutes and marched towards another Hastings. We never got any warning what was next. Just followed the crowd.

Jump aircraft Beverly

This time I was No 5 in my stick No 4 and No 6 (the one in front and behind me), I'd never seen these 2 guys. I couldn't' have missed them at 6' 3" each they were twin brothers and both SAS. I was only 5' 8" and 9½ stone. I was totally dwarfed between then, but I just accepted it.

We were jumping in stick of 6 (12 in total). When the command, "Action stations," were given, I started my double check on the one facing the tail, I had a wee bit difficulty reaching their shoulder straps, but luckily one of the dispatchers squeezed by both sticks and completed it for me. But when the order, "Stand at the door," was given, I attempted the shuffle step as taught, leading foot forward, sliding the back on up to the heel of the front, in order no one falls. Everybody in step. Then "Go" that's all I heard, sandwiched between these.

The guy up front with a huge stride created a gap that I tried to close with my short step, next thing I knew the one behind started to violently push me forward. He was very impatient.

As I tried to turn to him as we moved, all I knew next was daylight. I fell out the door, the slipstream caught my arms and legs which had not had time to assume a tight position, spinning me into a twist. I was lucky to kick myself out of it just before I hit the ground, unhurt but in a daze. I never saw hind or hair of these two at all anywhere.

We were told that there was a maximum limit of 6' 3" for anyone parachuting. These guys were certainly on the limit.

Jump No 5 was again from the Hastings. After marching up to the awaiting aircraft with all engines turning, we were shuffled into single file. I found myself to be first in line. I didn't know if I felt frightened maybe nervous, as I sat on the starboard side with the door opening. I had to put my left foot out to the side, normally there was a body at that side, now nothing. I slipped my left hand by my side groping for some support. When I made contact with the doorframe Christ it was way near the middle of my back. I looked around at the dispatchers for reassurance, that I was sitting correctly, what with my leg out for support, they busied themselves, eventually coming up to me. He grabbed the safety net (I forgot about it) and secured it on my right as normal. Nobody seemed to take notice of my worried look. The only reassuring thing I noticed was No 1 opposite, only a couple of feet from me, his right leg and foot seemed to take up the same angle of support as mine, also nearly a third of the right-hand side of his body was over the door opening, as was mine.

It didn't make me feel any better. I didn't feel very secure as the plane suddenly lurched forward, taxied on to the main runway and just roared down. Within seconds the tail gradually lifted up off the ground. I felt better now my legs and feet were naturally come together. Glancing out the door opposite the ground and horizon slowly fell away and the skyline grew. I just managed a brave glance round to my left and down, my worries and fears turned to a rush of thrilling adrenalin. There was no horizon, everything below was in miniature, cars, lorries, people and roadways. It was like watching the films and not real.

Jump aircraft Hastings

The red light was very much on. I must have lost track of time. Suddenly, "Action stations." Now face to face with my opposite, we never exchanged glances. Hooked up, double checks done. "Stand at the door." Turning left and half a step, with my left hand over my front and on my reserve, my right-hand palm, extended arm just outside the door frame. Left toes jutting out of the door and my right holding steady. But my head was slightly outside. I could no longer see the red light without learning back. The aircraft was flying straight and level.

Now a thought struck me that I was in the unfortunate position of being more outside the aircraft than in. On the left these huge propellers noisily cutting through the air, such a fantastic sight and thrill. What gave me a wee bit of concern was on my right. The tail plane seemed only some six feet away and level with my feet. It'll cut me into two! Thankfully my thoughts were as I felt a hand grab my shoulder clothing, and in the same instance, the noise of the engines changed noisily the wing dipped and the ground took on different angle. Woodlands suddenly appeared, and getting bigger by the second, before I really knew it the craft flew straight and very low. This was really exciting stuff. My mind fully concentrating on parachuting, he had taken us for some unexplained reason to skimming some 50 feet above the trees then I recognised part of the landscape as Weston-on-the-Green DZ (found out later there was something obstructing the DZ). Seconds later the plane banked away and upwards soon began a run in. I took a slight step backwards to have a reassuring glance at the red light which thankfully was still showing. I caught the eye of my dispatcher who gave me a wink (ma pal). He released his grip on me.

He was now flying straight and level. The engines pitch changed at the same time. I felt the plane slow up followed by the stall warning alarm whine. A slap on my back followed. I jumped.

The black flash of the tail plane went over me as the slipstream hit my feet putting me on my back with both arms across my reserve. Looking skywards being buffeted about in the slipstream, crack, my chute opened. The ground swung into view, reaching up taking hold of my lift webs, . Suddenly I was being completely smothered in parachute silk!

I tried to grasp it, but quickly I was faced with rigging lines. It was just a mass of material around me. I tried to fend it off. I looked down, to see my feet standing on top of a helmet and face looking up at me screaming and yelling. Looking up all I could see was the inside of his half of his parachute and part of my chute. Both of us had what appeared to be half a chute each. I fought and wriggled to get myself on the outside of his rigging lines. All I could see was the ground revolve at speed.

My mind froze as my arms and hand worked in a panic, then I was bodily free, but my reserve was still entangled as the last thing I saw was the ground hurtling at me. I never had time to position or brace myself.

No pain, nothing. Just lying there still. Bodies with parachutes falling around. Just a few feet away lay the other paratrooper. It was the guy in the next bed to me, Spud. He lay there like me in silence and dazed. Then within an instance. We seemed to be lying there for ages, when all around us the other guys were up and about rolling their chutes up, totally ignoring us.

Out of nowhere appeared our RSM (Reg Sergeant Major) screaming dogs abuse as us. I must have lost the plot and told him to f*** off, to my amazement, he did.

Within a couple of hours I was back at the base and harnessing up another chute, marched out again, but not to a Hastings but to a Beverly, which to my mind's eye resembled a tadpole sitting there on the runway, square on its wheels, huge square body, long high tail with twin end booms, and this time we had our weapon containers. Again, I was in the first 10 to climb aboard. The bottom of the doorway was some 5 feet off the ground, it was huge inside. We were told about them, but this was the first time near one.

With the weight of both my chutes and having to drag the container to the centre inside the body of the plane was difficult to say the least. The dispatcher shouting to us over the noisy engines and pointing to a very slim and flimsy ladder on the inside of the plane fitted hard up against the wall of the doorway I had just entered. I followed the man in front of me who was up and disappearing through a hatchway above. My God, shit!

We were crammed 12 of us into a cigar tube like space, our knees touching, just enough space to stand up in and right at my feet the aperture jump hole. I sat there looking down only 12–15 feet to the runway hurtling beneath. There were a lot of worried faces.

Only minutes into the flight one of the dispatchers appeared up out of the hatch squeezing by the guys holding a rectangular frame like panel, placing it over the aperture hole, then disappeared down the hatch without a word being said and not even a glance, leaving us in near darkness.

There was secondary lighting coming from framework above the floor hatching. Sparks and engine works spanning from the engine bridging housing, flashing and noise like a fireworks display. Then a head appeared up the hatchway, it was the dispatcher. Nobody could hear what he said, only his hand signs were being followed: four would clamber down not long after the engines died back, then with a deafening roar we swayed to it pulling away again. Knowing it had just dispatched them. He reappeared more went. I, without even being aware of thinking, undid my harness and chutes, that was it, enough! I had no thoughts, a complete blank other than I wasn't putting the chutes back on. Then a dispatcher took my chutes down below.

I then agreed to go down as I was the only one left. With no chute on, the RSM who was on board made me stand at the open doorway, with both hands gripping the sides tightly, standing in the open doorway all the way at 1000 feet, banking and turning. I just stared over the view below. After what seemed an eternity the ground loomed up, finally and still standing there, it landed, hurtling down the runway, slowing and turning in to a taxiway alongside some hangars and at speed. Without warning, the RSM pulled one of my arms away from the door, without a word, threw out my chutes and weapon container which landed on the grass verge. Screaming in my ear, "Jump!" without faltering I obeyed. Five feet to the ground and at about 15 mph, landed in a heap, no injury. My first thought was why? Then I looked back at my stuff lying scattered about, adjacent to the chutes store. I'm now thinking he done me a favour. My mind was in a turmoil. After re-checking my gear, I found myself walking across the parade ground. He was for some reason taking me to see the RAF commanding officer.

Suddenly the bugle began to sound the retreat and the flag was being lowered. Everybody as usual came to a halt where they stood saluting, all facing the flag. But I didn't, I kept on walking, nobody stopped me. Normally you would be on a charge for this. I was not in my right mind, call it shock, I don't know. Under no circumstances would I even consider doing anything like this.

I sat in front of this old kind gent, the CO, he quietly told me how even Gurkha's had such accidents and refused to go on, next I was taken to see the camp psychiatrist for a few minutes. When I came out, I found a jeep sitting there waiting for me, on board was all my gear, the lot. I was now on my way home!

Now there was another empty bed.

I was 2 jumps short of my wings. But now I had acquired a completely new change of character – controlled aggression! What's happened to me, my respect of authority has gone, I've never answered back, certainly not to those I held in high respect. But it still wasn't like that, my reactions are spontaneous and not thought through. But what a relief, free, why… life changing!

Not long before I joined the paras, I met a cracker of a lass, instant love! Bert, one of the older apprentices on my gasfitters crew bus, was married and then living at Wardlaw Place, Gorgie. I never liked his wife much, she was '*voicie*' and loud! They had a young daughter. Then out of the blue he moved to Whitson Way our living room and kitchen windows were only feet apart. It was shortly after this move, I met Senga, his wife and sister Dolly. She lived with her mother and father in a top flat in Dalry Washington Place Lane.

After going around for a few weeks, it was time to meet the family. Her mum and dad invited me to their 25th wedding anniversary at the house. They had outside catering, which was an upmarket thing to do at that time. The event was delayed waiting for the pair of us. The flat was a room and kitchen with outside toilet on the main stair landing shared by 4 other flats. The living room was packed with laid out tables and people. We sat together with our back to the wall after climbing over everybody and facing the doorway we had just entered. Everybody was in the party mood.

My worst nightmare was about to happen. The door opened and instantly I recognised this guy as he squeezed into the room. The man most feared in Stenhouse, Whitson area. Before I could even speak, he looked at Dolly and asked if I was with her. She said I was and from that moment we were pals. I normally took to my heels when I saw him coming. It was her brother, Boris. Oh boy! Nice girl, hen!

She told me later he was out on a day release from Wellington Boys Borstal or Penicuik.

Her dad, old Boris, was a very nice person. I like him, he confided in me that he was in the Royal Artillery called up at the beginning of World War Two, and at Tobruk and then captured by the Germans at El Alemain, Egypt and spent 4 years as a prisoner of war in Sicily, north of Rome and finally Germany. He escaped once and was on the hills in Italy, recaptured by a couple of Germans on a motorbike and sidecar machinegun carrier. This was verified by one of his boyhood and army pals. I never doubted him in any way. He never spoke to his family about it, they did show anger that he spoke to me and not them!

Young Boris stamped his own card that weekend. He broke into his mother's gas meter and buggered off. Police got him; he was returned to Wellington Farm. His mother never brought any charges against him.

It was only a couple of weeks later when Boris (younger) put in an appearance. Dolly and I were in the house on our own, when at 10pm Nisbits, the pub near the foot of the stairs closed, we could hear all the voices singing and laughing echoing up the stairs. Dolly went into the wee lobby to meet the crowd all hell seemed to break loose in that small space.

Just a mad swarm of bodies, with arms, shouting and swearing. They all disappeared into what was the tiny bedroom. I heard Dolly screaming. I rushed through and squeezed past three men just standing there watching her mum lashing into Dolly who was lying on her bed on her back with arm raised trying to fend off blows from a wooden stick her mother was attacking her with. I moved forward and grabbed hold of the stick, only to find myself under attack from young Boris and her uncle George. Old Boris grabbed them both while shouting to me, "Run, run, Michael!"

I did but managed to grab hold of Dolly by the wrist, and we both shot out of the main door and down the stairs. I only noticed then she still had her pinny (pinafore) and slippers on. We walked all the way to Whitson where she stayed with her sister. Bert told me later, welcome to the family

After my time with the paras, Dolly and I agreed that we should up our income as she herself was still a trainee typist/clerkess and me an apprentice. We applied for a job at night and weekends (Saturdays) as an usher (me) and her usherette at the Edinburgh Palladium Theatre at Tolcross.

I was issued with a two-piece purple velvet suit, flat hat with peak, and bowtie, as doorman. Dolly had similar colour skirt and jacket also headband. She was dishy in it, all the part of an ice cream usherette. Both of us had standard issue torches. We worked Monday to Friday 6pm–11pm and Saturday 4pm–11pm all for 19/- (95p) each week, and free complimentary tickets for a Monday's evening dress rehearsal show. Saturday had two sittings. It was normally a variety show with the resident performer being then the legendary comedian Lex McLean, one of Scotland's top.

The top venue was always at the Kings. He was meant to be too loud to appear here and this was as he would rise in his career. That's what they (the establishment) said. He went on in later years to have his own successful TV comedy show.

We lasted a few months in this job until one night, Dolly never showed up. I suspected something was wrong, got permission to go home to her place in Dalry. When I got into the street, she and her mum were standing in the shadows of the stair. Dolly had a towel wrapped around her hair, her mum told me they were waiting for someone and told me old Boris was upstairs and to wait with him. I thought she had just washed her hair.

I went up to see him sitting there in the chair, his shirt and hands covered in blood. Then he told me, her younger brother Dick had hit her on the head with the brass candlestick which was lying on the floor. By the time I got downstairs the ambulance had gone. The next time I saw her, she was lying in a hospital bed, she was kept for a few days, the back of her head well stitched up.

After that she decided to stay at Whitson, the travelling and cost of extra bus fares made us give the job up.

We saw each other nearly every day, done a lot of babysitting. After a year together, we got engaged and I had to ask her dad if I could take her hand in marriage. I was never so nervous, standing there in front of him not knowing what his reaction was. "Aye, fine," he never even looked up from his paper! But at least I'd asked, unlike the others.

We didn't have an engagement party, but, this time with her mums' permission we did have a week's holiday at Butlins. but boy, did she not (her mum) send me off with a flea in my ear to bloody behave myself. I think she should have been talking to her daughter, she had taught me well to enjoy the female breed and put to rest my first experience. And all in practice, not a book of guidance in sight.

Her mum's warning seemed to strike home, we had chalets right next door to each other and not once did she allow me into hers, and she never came into mine. Not that I didn't try! We'd have had a better time at home. We did hold hands.

Before getting engaged, I made it clear that when my time was served I'd be off to Australia. It was inbred in me. Dolly knew before we got seriously involved. We treated ourselves to another engagement expense, that was for her first flight and my first civilian flight, a return flight to Glasgow Renfrew Airport from Edinburgh Turnhouse Airport, the old original one. It was BAE British European Airways. The plane, a four engine propeller Vanguard aircraft, much more noisier than the Hastings even with the doors closed. I lit a fag up as it trundled down the runway, I'd never finished it when I was asked to put it out as we were now landing in Glasgow. It was the furthest she had been from home other than Butlins. The return flight was four hours later and duration the same, minutes, all at the cost of 18/- for both of us.

However, I was to get a bit of a damper in my life long plans to Australia. I failed my intermediate exams for the London City and Guilds. I had sat them only 2 months or so before. Failing badly the theory parts, but I came top in the practical. Unfortunately, I had to pass both sections, but worse was I had to re-sit it the next year, both theory and practical and that was the rules, also I was the only one in Scotland to re-sit. And I did and passed.

I only know that I had to wait until I was 21 years of age, then I was free to choose to get married as this was the accepted age. I was very self-confident that the job I was doing or even the qualification I had didn't give me a problem, so was not pressured to succeed in gas fitting. I'd never failed in working or keeping a job, but to me this job was not going to hinder my future no matter!

Jimmy had himself well and truly a job which I was envious of. He proved himself to be a great worker with only his poor bedridden mother to support. He no longer worked for the milk, he just seemed to get the best paid jobs. Having worked for the British Tyre and Rubber Co, Mill Lane, Fountainbridge on the assembly line doing the final requirement to tyres and later Garden Hoses, then for Burton the Bakers biscuits at Sighthill.

My 3rd year apprentice pay was £8 per week. Jimmy's £20, he had the best of clothes tailor made, also a growing collection of Beatles records to go with them he had a Triumph Herald convertible, cherry red car and like me no driving licence.

One weekend, not long after the Forth Bridge was newly opened, he'd invited me for a spin over to the Dunfermline in Fife. We'd never been across the bridge. Everything was OK on the way out, and no traffic in those days. This didn't stop him losing his way on approach to the bridge on the way back, he somehow managed to get himself into the wrong lane, facing the oncoming traffic. Jimmy thought the oncoming car was in the wrong lane, even though the guy stopped. Jimmy continued head on into him with no seatbelts then. How he never got injured let alone killed, God knows! The guy's car did not look too proud. Jimmy's bonnet was folded back squashed into two. The police came, helped to secure down his bonnet.

Jimmy's spike accident at school left him with an aggressive argumentative attitude that most folks could not handle. even the motorist and policeman struggled, getting him and the car out of the way was their priority, without charge. After the exchange of details, ignoring the steam from the engine, he got to Whitson. I was in his house when the car insurance agent called.

The poor man tried to explain that he should have had a qualified driver with him when driving, let alone 'L' plates. Jimmy true to form, told him he didn't (and genuinely) know that a person with a provisional needed to do that. The insurance paid out. What a guy!

A small group of us were one day rounded up by some older apprentices. They grabbed hold of one, who struggled a fair bit, but we watched on as 5 or 6 of them bodily lifted him into the work bench, spread-eagled him, tying him hand and foot to the four corners. One hell of a lot of shouting. One of them undoing his trouser belt. Jesus, he was screaming and wriggling. They were piling on top of him shouting to him to behave. I was mind boggled! I like the others had my eye on the door.

"Don't even think about it!" came a warning from two of them.

Without warning, his trousers and pants at his ankles, one of the guys appeared with an open pot of red lead, which we use for sealing joints and washers and a big old paint brush (well used). And in one move dipped it into the pot, the brush dripping the red paste was thrust straight at and over his private parts, followed by a second dose. He was struggling, squealing, effing and blinding.

Even after untying him, he was swinging his hands and fists in all directions trying to make violent contact with the big ones. After watching this, it was my turn, but I was like a lamb to the slaughter and never struggled. I knew that we were at some stage to face our initiation, but I'd never have guessed this was it! I let them help themselves and didn't put up a struggle. I don't think Mother had this in mind when she warned as to always 'wear clean underwear'.

When the guys were finished, Christ, what a lot of scrubbing took place with our willies and knackers hanging in the Belfast sink, not even the privacy of toilets. We scrubbed ourselves raw. Worst was my white underpants were stained blood red. There was no way I was taking them home to Mum. I binned them and forked out for new ones.

Dolly had the pleasure of helping me clean what I couldn't see!

I, like all the tradesmen of the time, worked happily with lead, as it was commonly used at a material for plumbing, gas fitting and roofing. As lead piping was the most used by us, the standard gas piping was normally coils (rolls) of ½ inch diameter thin wall, sometime ¾ inch. The heavy thick-walled lead pipe was used for water and the joints then were lead to lead or lead to brass. Copper was gradually introduced more than halfway through my apprenticeship. I liked working with lead, roll of 20 feet or more, carried over my shoulder, sticks of tins man solder, hand held brass, mouth operated blow lamp used for these soft joints (lead to lead) and in some situations portable gas fired furnace (oven) was used to heat my solid copper soldering bolt. Once handling lead, it took only minutes for your hands to turn black with a silvery sheen. By habit we copied our tradesmen when a break time came, to use a bit of paper (any kind) and not your bare black hand to handle your pie or piece, but no one said why. Likewise, when we used to saw through asbestos piping. We were instructed to have a bottle of water at hand to dampen down the dust we created when cutting the pipe or sheet asbestos. But no one said it was dangerous, just dusty. No masks then.

The only harmful thing for me and others was when we had to work with molten solder, whilst heating or making a joint, the only way around that which was not at all fool proof was to follow by example. In the training centre behind the instructor's backs one of the older apprentices, took a full ladle of molten lead and poured it over a young lad's hand. Three of us in fear of our health due to a similar attack took to hiding in caves up Calton Hill,

An instructor came up threatening us with the sack if we didn't return. All of us young ones threatened to 'down tools' if the big bad boys were not brought under control.

The gas board did provide us apprentices with a year's graduating amount of tools, but we supplied out own clothing. There was no order of dress, mine, an old jacket and a pair of well-worn and patched up jeans or corduroys, whatever was available. It was very hard for Mother to find a replacement. Trousers were well-worn hand-me-downs from all family members. Lastly if there was any wear left in them then the that's what we got. As for washing them, even this was a problem. Mine were too greasy (worse than sweeping cloths) they had to be washed on their own and away from the washing machine in fear it got contaminated and any new wash was stained. So it only got a pot boil.

It was great when she got her hands on a pair of jeans, and she cut off the back pockets for knee patches for mine, and this went for elbow patches for jackets or skirts, matching or not.

Dad and I had to strip off as soon as we got in. We had to share a space on a shelf in the coal cellar for our work clothes, even at that we had to have a wee bit of space between them as mine were smelly of gas and oil. The smell was so bad that sometimes when a stranger called to the house, they'd bring to Mum's attention they could smell gas, but Dad's clothes were sometimes soaking wet.

I was once asked by a bus conductor to get off because some old 'wifies' on his bus were nagging him about a gas leak!

I was not an exception in dress, but the rule. There wasn't a trade at that time or tradesman who didn't expect to be clean, in fact, it was the opposite. You never came out to work to stay clean, but it was always a priority that the site was constantly kept clean. No tradesman can progress a job that is untidy or dirty no matter. This was the apprentice's job learning how to use a brush and shovel, also keeping the pipework clean, lead, brass and copper was all well shining at the completion. There were no priority on personal hygiene.

With all this metal work, thieving was rife. But if I got caught then my job was on the line which did happen to a couple of apprentices. It wasn't worth it. However, it didn't stop those outside the gas company.

We got a call that some old dear in Gorgie complained her gas lights had stopped working. When we got into the attic space, we found that somebody had been there before us. They had flattened the lead (block tin) pipe from the meter below using a knife, silently cutting away all the pipes in the attic.

In my fourth year, I re-sat my Intermediate London City and Guilds for the second time on my own and passed both theory and practical. This was my first ever certificate. But next year I had to sit the final exam as I was always kept informed that it took both to fully qualify and without it, I would not get my Indentures.

I learnt many skills from my tradesmen, who themselves were taught plumbing and gas fitting only by practice so was with most trades there were no off-site classrooms and they were not confident or trained to instruct. They were known when qualified as time served after completing 5 years. After completing five years you could get proof that you had indeed spent that time in the industry, preferably with the same employer. When (and only if you had behaved) you would be very reluctantly given your letter of competence. Not forgetting the tradesman you served 5 years with, he was using his name up front, to say that you not only served five or more years, but you reached whatever standard to work and in which area. Normally he would nominate one are, domestic, commercial or industrial, it was your misfortune if you spent all of your years learning in an industrial site, nobody would want to employ you in the housing (domestic sites), they would not want to retrain you. Whereas a marine plumber could use your skills.

Like my trade, after your time was served as apprentice. for Christ's sake, don't' fall out with him before you get that bit of paper. Some of the crafty buggers deliberately kept it from you, they didn't want to lose you. It didn't matter if you were the best, you'd have been cheap labour. In any event they would have had another one 2nd junior apprentice a couple of years behind you. Whatever happened you were only on the first rung of the ladder in your calling. And it wasn't only the Freemasons who had their trade secrets. Every trade had them, joiners, brickies, roofers and slaters never mind plumbers and joiners or gas fitters, from town to town they had a different saying, signs, and name for each tool or piece of material, fitting or joint. The way it was used, sharpened or cleaned.

One strange one the chimney sweeps used, even although I was brought up with them, they never let on, not even my father told me straight out, he never thought his own bairns needed to know. However, it was a 'dancer'. I heard them speak of one often. A dancer used in the terms of sweeping was an empty house. An empty house meant that there was nobody living in it, so it had no furniture or floor covering (lino or carpets) so a bottomer did not have to put a sheet up over the fireplace, which meant the roper could sweep it and make as much mess as he wanted. Although we were his sons, his men would not like it if he shared the secrets with us until we proved ourselves.

I could have my head in my hands from a tradesmen whilst I was on a site with my own tradesman and caught being idle, they would be suspicious and tell my boss to "get that bugger moving". They hated anyone watching, so you learnt to keep the peace. I never knew and certainly my own tradesmen did not know how to keep a batch (mix large or small) of plaster from going hard. We only mixed up enough at a time to fill very small holes. Jesus Christ, no sooner had you mixed it up it bloody went solid before it got to the hole. What a nightmare!

But Dolly's dad, old Boris, he was a plasterer's labourer, labouring to James Bond, 007's wee brother, Neil Connery on the building sites all around the city.

I was amazed how these plasterers could make up a bath tub full of the stuff and leave it lying, go for their ½ hour dinner break then start to shovel it into buckets. It never set (blown off hard). My tradesmen and others thought it was some special plaster mix!

The old bugger (Boris) refused to give up the secret for decades. Bit by bit, he fed me clues, which centred around a 45-gallon drum of water they used, always taking their supply of mixing water from it. Whenever I got the chance to see plasterers on sites, my eyes were on that drum. I noticed only they used it, I'll be buggered when he told me (by which time it was on the DIY shelves) it was a bar of Fairy scrubbing soap which was kept in the drum, they would always wash their hands in it. The soap was a plasticiser and it bloody works! It was a well-kept secret indeed, but now it's sold in bottles and very pricy. The plasterers have the last laugh. Buy a bar of soap!

When I sat the Intermediate London City and Guilds exam the theory took place James Gillaspie School at BruntsField. I was the only one sitting the gas fitting. I haven't a clue what the others were doing, about 20 of us. This time I decided to do the paper my way and not even as the present adjudicator said, "Start at question one!"

One of my tradesmen told me to pick the easiest ones first and don't get stuck, move on to the next, and bugger the workings. I couldn't care if I got caught. I didn't and for once I actually enjoyed it, not knowing if I had the right answers. Eventually the paper was finished, and every question had to have an answer, better still, I was in amongst the first to leave although that did concern me. I thought that had to mean you've failed, but tough! I was just glad to get out.

It was only a day or two later when I was confronted with an adjudicator and instructor up in the training centre to sit the practical part. I was quite at ease. I did feel this was a complete waste of time as I was convinced the theory was gone, although I never said this to anyone. In fact, in a way they made me feel a bit special. We were all pals. I had to check the tools and materials were correct as listed on my practical job sheet I also had to check the work bay, three whitewashed walls representing a kitchen set up, cooker, fridge, boiling ring, poker point and an over sink water heater. I had to note any marks on the walls or holes, (screw holes) points would be deducted from me if I left any. So I checked there are none first. Once that was done the place fell silent.

Out came a stopwatch and clipboard, there were no distractions, it was great! No gas or water leaks, all the pipes and screw heads shining bright and not a mark on the walls. Without a word the adjudicator looked over my shoulder as I set the gas pressure, he finally asked me if I wanted to make any adjustments before I signed it off, the bugger! I thought and looked hard and long, was he telling me something was wrong? Now, for a moment he truly had me stumped. It was then I caught the eye of the instructor (who all the time seemed to busy himself in other things and ignore me), he sort of glanced past my head and behind me, with a slight nod of the head, I turned to look behind me thinking he was in contact with someone to my rear, but all I saw was the exit. I never realised at that moment he was telling me to scram – beat it! I did, and I passed both. It meant our class was still complete. I had had a year to wait for the finals next year 1966. I couldn't give a stuff come what may, I was off to Australia!

Dad's business was doing very well, so much so he had brought a few cars over the period 1963–65, Rover 90, Austin Cambridge, all what were known as family cars. This was great for me, he always had them spotless inside and out, at the weekends when I was free the job landed on me to wash, dry and wax them at 5/- for a couple of hours suited me fine.

This and any other spare cash went in the bank. We were planning to get married. As it was then, the women got to choose how and when, and their mother was to organise it all and also pay for it but her mother completely refused any financial help from anyone.

My dad said he would help pay, he felt responsible. But he was turned down. It's my daughter's wedding and I'm paying, but that was the normal way of things in those days. They didn't want a Catholic church wedding (I never thought of one too). But Dolly went to Sunday School CE so we were to join the church in Stenhouse. I wasn't really a hypocrite, but I enjoyed a laugh. Of course we were joined in every church lessons.

Senga, they didn't have to ring the bells when the church was in session, just open the door and let her vocals out.

We even had to attend Bible studies at night and she was there too.

We booked a hall up near the old ERI at Martins the Bakers. Her mother had to fork out £5.00 deposit. In the meantime, Dad was teaching me how to drive in his new second-hand car, two-ton green Humber Super Snipe. It was previously owned by Sir William Younger (McEwens) the brewery tycoon and chauffer driven, fully automatic, with wood panelling, as much a Rolls Royce as any. It took me three attempts to pass the driving test and each time it was my old friend the theory that let me down.

Dad hired a caravan and towed it using his car. When he came back, he unhitched it in the roadway outside our window so that we could tidy it up before he took it back. Both him and I went inside to see what was to be done. Both of us went to the back window of the caravan, then he wandered over to the front and I followed him.

"Oh shit, Michael, Michael!" he's shouting.

All I knew, I was falling straight over him. Within a split second we ended up lying arms and legs all in the air, struggling to fight free of our entangled predicament only to find we were looking up at the back window, and all the loose fittings and ornaments all about us. We clung onto each other dazed and wondering what the buggery is going on? Both of us now virtually standing and touching the floor in front, we edged out way back up the floor and slowly the caravan began to tilt level, it was then he suddenly shouted, "Feet, Feet!" Oh yes, Dad, smart arse, left the undercarriage up (feet). What a beamer in front of all the neighbours.

Back to the wedding. Things were just not working out; this was our first try at a wedding and it was hijacked and getting a bit beyond our I control. So I told her I wanted a Registrar's Office wedding. She said she was planning that as well, noses went out of place, but life at last returned to a wee bit like normal.

Things were slowly moving towards our goal – Australia – although things with this respect were blowing hot and cold. It was a subject we had to talk about when on our own. We secretly visited the Australian house in Alva Street, I chose her mum's home address for a mailing contact.

My mother for some reason took it all out that we were planning to go away. I don't know why! They too had a chance.

After a medical, all was well, we had been accepted, but first they advised that I wait and try and get my finals. We were getting married first, the date, 8th October 1966 one week after my 21st birthday.

Australia was magical, mystified, its name conjured up everything in my imagination, it was the key thing, word, on my mind in my life until now, nothing will shift it. My whole being was turned and revolved around it. The more people that questioned why I wanted to leave Scotland and disappear around the other end of the world only made me dig my heels in, they were the fuel that fed my fire. I was bloody going! It made me stronger also built me a solid foundation.

Failing the paras allowed me more room mentally to focus on the year ahead.

I just realised how much I had tied myself up with the paras. Part of my signing up was to do a jungle exercise in Malaysia or the Yemen Desert, both war zones. I chose Malaysia, as it turned out, 16 TA paras were killed between both countries. Not aware of the full implications of this, I was looking forward to the exercise. Now things had changed, and I was moving on.

Australia, City and Guilds or not, bloody try stopping me!

Thank goodness, I never thought I would get through to this point, never mind having two sets of London City and Guilds, it was bad enough having to sit all the exams at the training centre. There were night classes we had to attend in the first couple of years but it wasn't that bad coming home from work, having my tea then heading for Tynecastle School in Gorgie, being there 7pm–9pm up to twice weekly, but as things got more advanced the venue was changed to Leith Academy School at the foot of Easter Road, where they had more science rooms, not only was it along journey both ways leaving home at 6pm and not getting back till after 10pm, what a drag! But it was always freezing cold. I should have been well contented, the next posting was to Portobello (end of the earth) and Ramsay Technical College, they seemed to have every bloody boring piece of equipment that I never really wanted to see. Everyone who I had met who also attended this place, not one had a good memory of it, other than the day they were released. It took 4 buses to get to and from this dump, all gone.

Dolly's mum and dad moved away from Washington Street Lane (it was being demolished) to west Granton Gardens, right opposite the Gas Works entrance gates. A brand-new build (maisonette), 3 bedrooms, bathroom, kitchen and living room. A far cry from Dalry and change of venue. It was a long way for me to travel although now she had room of her own, our love held fast!

With Australia well on our agenda, I first had to sit the London city and Guilds gas fitting finals, May 1966. There were about 20 of us lined up in the classroom at the Gas Board Training Centre, Carlton Road. Theory in the morning, practical after lunch break. All seemed to go well, but I couldn't give a toss. My plans were already in motion.

Late July came a word that one person had failed, and the fingers pointed at me. Who the buggery cares? Then mid-August, the postie delivered the results: I had passed!

We were well on the way to our wedding day – 8 October 1966. My mate Alan at the last minute decided that he couldn't be my best man, his wife was due the baby any day soon. So instead of asking any of my other mates, who were not as long standing, Jimmy said he would do the honours. We had a bit of a problem, although he had good money, the last thing he treated himself to was a suit.

With only a week or so to go, he and I shot off to Jacksons the Tailors, picked a wee suit off the peg, with a few minor adjustments he was brand new and chuffed, so was I.

Her best maid was her friend Carol.

We were having the reception in her mum's house at Granton. The original order for the large wedding cake for the white wedding was never altered, so we ordered a huge tin box from Scobie and McIntosh at Fountainbridge so that we could take the cake or what was left of it (expecting it to be most of it) to be shipped to Australia, opened on the occasion of having a baby! Only the immediate family were to be at our reception as it was in the house at Granton.

A keg of beer was the mainstay of the alcohol and a few bottles of spirit. My dad supplied 2 x 24 cans of beer and gave them to old Boris to be held in reserve in case they ran out.

The big day came around. We all met up at the Registrar's Office in Haymarket. Jimmy and I on a bus from Whitson, Dolly and Carol from Granton.

Everything went so well that I never remembered a thing in and out. Some photographs on the front doorstep, tooting horns from passing vehicles. Dad was out in the road with his new movie camera. After all was done there the four of us got a taxi to the Carlton Hotel at the bridges for morning tea and sandwiches, really to pass the time, as all hell was breaking loose at Granton.

We were told not to arrive till 1pm and bang on time, we did. As we had already said to folks, just give us money instead of presents because in less than four weeks, 8th November 1966, we were flying to Australia and had no room for baggage.

We had to leave the main party for 3pm to catch the train to Blackpool via Preston for our honeymoon at Butlins hotel on the seafront.

Bang on time, we left them to enjoy themselves. We were later to hear of a near battle at some point, they ran out of beer, or so it was said. Old Boris, the old bugger stashed away the 2 cases of canned beer for himself under the bed. He never mentioned it to anyone, he was captured a couple of days later supping on a can stretched out on the bed. Mother-in-law gave him a corker of a black eye.

But we were on our way at last, the journey from Edinburgh to Preston except we were in the eye of most on board our carriage, still a bit of confetti in my hair and wearing my buttonhole. Dolly with her lucky chimney sweep in hand. When we boarded the link train to Blackpool at Preston, what a shock. Christ, the train was nearly full of other newlyweds going to Blackpool. What a sight! The place was heaving. Most, if not all were English. Two of the couples were going to our hotel. Friends.

We got to the hotel at about 8pm, dark and bloody windy, wet. What a memorable hotel, not a bit like Butlins, crap! Bed and breakfast and a bar where we celebrated with her a tomato juice and me a pint of milk!

The next morning after breakfast, we were treated to a wet and windy boring Blackpool. I don't know what all our friends shouted about? Somebody told us we had come at the wrong time of year. That says it all!

We did meet an old couple at the hotel. They must have took a shine to us, or just felt very obliged to take us under their wing so to speak. They were there for other real reasons, it was the Tory (Conservative Party) conference which was held there annually. We got a mother and father lecture from them as to how to trust each other, in particular with money. They gave us their rosettes (lapel) for to wear when out and about, which we did. Not that we were really aware why, it just looked good and it worked. When we were in a long queue to get into to blackpool tower, the usher at the front came right up to us (I thought we had done something wrong) took us aside and escorted us right down the line, past the pay desk and into the lift. Before we knew it, we were on the way up.

We did manage to get to an evening show and see our family favourite TV funny man, Ken Dodd, it was great! We found him a great act to follow.

After four days we packed our bags and said goodbye to Blackpool.

Of course, we weren't expected, but as planned returned home to Granton on a working day in the afternoon with no one in, dressed in my wedding 3-piece suit, I climbed up the drainpipe and entered through an open window much to my mother-in-law's consternation. Well, gives her something to greet about. Mum in law had news for us as soon as she got over the excitement in finding us back so soon, she told us that her dick raped his girlfriend after our reception. Was I not glad that Australia was on the cards, the quicker the better.

There was a bit of real excitement on the Sunday before we took off. It happened in the building site compound in the area of land immediately behind the flat, inside the high perimeter fence where all the tradesmen's huts where their material and tools were stored. Old Boris stood in the kitchen beside the window overlooking the large area, he called on us to take a look. Jesus! One of the huts was ablaze. He said some youths had just set it up. Within minutes the fire engines started to arrive. Next thing there was banging on the front door, it was the police, telling us the whole of the building was being evacuated. There were gas bottles stored in the huts ready to explode. Right enough, the whole building shook. We didn't wait to be told twice. There must have been at least 100 of us stood 50 yards away beside the gatehouse of the gas works. Looking back at our block of houses, by this time 5-foot-tall propane gas bottles were going up in every direction from the compound behind. Firemen were now running over the flat roofs with hoses attending to the bottles, spitting flames that landed on them. Quite frightening!

Somebody asked, "Where's old Boris?"

Nowhere to be seen, until the all clear was given. There he was, still in the kitchen by the window struggling with the 13-amp plug. He just glanced up at us, gave a disapproving shake of his head, then returned to the damned plug as he muttered. It did later occur to us that he was involved in the heavy bombardment of the creeping barrage in the North Africa campaign. This was just Mickey Mouse to him, and we were running for cover!

8th November 1966, saw us on board the overnight train from Waverly, Edinburgh to London. Our £10 each immigration to Australia was on. We were luckier than most folk before us, in that getting the choice to fly all the way to Sydney was pretty new for even childless couples and single folk, as the others still had to take the six-week boat trip.

The horror stories of that journey were believable, especially when husbands were put into completely different areas of the ship for the whole journey, only with the agreement of the other occupants could a couple have time together for an hour a week if they were lucky. Thankfully we avoided that trauma.

We never got to see anything of London, we just managed to find our way via the underground to the airport and board the Qantas 707 jet plane. We'd heard about their new jets. I think I was the more nervous of the two of us when the plane thundered down the runway.

When we got on the plane, we introduced ourselves to others who were also emigrating. Some older couples dotted around but sitting next to us and behind us, were three others all aged 19 years of age and none of them knew each other till now. One was a lassie going to meet some long-lost cousin. She was beginning to regret leaving her only family behind, a sister (younger) hoping to go ahead and set up home. Then, two boys, orphans, one was being met by some church minister who helped look after such people and get some sort of work. The other boy had no idea where he was even going to sleep that night and didn't have any contacts anywhere in Australia. Just before landing we all had to fill in all sorts of immigration papers. We had to help the last boy and the girl fill in the form and read out the questions to them. The girl could barely write her name. it was, even then, heart breaking. We were later to learn that the Big Brother movement was known as an abusive organisation.

We stopped in five different countries for refuelling: Athens, Persia (Iran), then Bangkok, as at every stop we were given a complimentary ticket for a cake or orange drink. The terminals were then much the same, small, single storey buildings only the lingering policeman on duty and quite empty, except here in Bangkok. We were halfway through our drinks when suddenly we were all ushered out onto the runway and down to the far end where our aircraft was waiting. Around us there were soldiers running all around, and on a nearby runway another military style plane with troops clambering up into it as it moved, the whole place was surrounded by jungle. The air was humid. We'd never been so hot. As we started to climb the steps up to the jet, I glanced around to see red flares shooting up out of the jungle, and in the sky above, fighter jets diving down into jungle. We were last on board, the door closed behind us and as quickly as we were seated the plane took off. Things were back to normal.

However, after getting to Sydney, the papers were full of the Guerrilla army having captured Bangkok International airport and I was there, missed all the action.

Our third stop was New Delhi, and fifth Singapore which was less eventful. But the pilot thought we were over loaded so before he let us all on, we had our weight taken one at a time on a set of bathroom scales. We never got the results, but were soon on our final leg.

Sydney. I was taken aback looking down on the outer suburbs at how green it was, lawns, gardens, not a bit like the scrublands shown in immigration pictures and film nights, not one bit.

We were to be met by a couple, Margaret and Donny, who Dolly knew in Edinburgh and had just emigrated to Sydney some six months before. They wrote to us earlier that they would find us somewhere to stay.

We landed at 9am a warm sunny spring day and they were there to greet us. They actually had their own car (a huge step up the ladder) driving us up from the airport heading north into the city, not a bloody clue, but I was gobsmacked at all the palm trees lining the roads. Skyscraper buildings, and the smells of vegetation that hung in the air. It wasn't until we turned a corner and above up a short motorway that I couldn't believe my eyes!

It was real! The Sydney Harbour Bridge, and I never believed it real up until that point, and now we were going across it. We were kids with a new toy. This was at that point the highest point of our lives and I never even knew that there were trains crossing, truly amazing!

Once off the bridge they immediately turned off and onto a side street only some couple of hundred yards from the bridge itself, and this Whaling Road, was where they had rented us a small flat. A bedsit, shared shower, penny in the slot gas meters. We had the top floor flat of what was known as a 'colonial house' and what a view! Straight out over the Sydney Harbour, the bridge to our right, at the other side circular quay ocean liner immigrant terminal and the city itself, with the half-completed Opera House. The ferryboats scuttling to and from the surrounding terminals. It was now we found out that we were living in an area known as Milson's Point, on the northern shore or North Sydney.

Once we had put our cases into the flat, they took us on a wee drive around the area. It was even better than we expected, all these folks walking about in short sleeve shirts, shorts, bare foot in their sandals. Wooden weather board colonial houses, painted greys, greens and white. We ended up going for a walk in the adjoining local shopping centre of Crow's Nest, this was very novel looking 2 storey buildings, normal shops below and single flat above with an awning covering the whole length of the walkway looking like a scene out of a cowboy movie, upright posts holding up the front of the awning where you tie up your horse.

As we waited at the lights on the pedestrian crossing, we were at the front of the queue facing those on the other side, we were well warned not to cross before the lights tell us, or we'll get lifted (jay walking). I looked at a guy on the other side, he caught my eye, he was waving at me. Jesus, somebody knows me (I was thinking), I did wave back, but he just continued. So did I. When we walked towards him, he continued to wave, right past me. I commented to Donny, he told me how stupid I was and I'd get used to it. The guy was only swatting flies away! Oh shit!

At about 1pm they told us we were looking tired. We agreed with this as I cannot remember us getting sleep on the planes 36-hour journey as it seemed to stop every few hours, and we were on a high most of the time.

They left us alone in the flat. I never thought for a moment that we would sleep at that time of day, but sleep we did.

It was midnight before we woke up. With a nice cup of tea, we sat in the darkness by the window. Jings, what a sight! It was like a picture postcard view we'd seen of New York with all the tall skyscrapers, light in all the windows, but here twice the size as it reflected on the harbour waters with the flickering lights moving over the surface. The ferry boats, we sat there watching as daylight came in then a strange sight as the morning drew in. The movement of people on the pavement below us increased, some walking down the roadway and reappearing with a shopping bag. Some reading or just carrying newspapers, but the strange thing was they seemed to be dressed in pyjamas or some women in night dresses. We got dressed properly and followed them to find the shop. I felt quite embarrassed at first, not very sure where to cast my tender wee eyes. What a sight, the folks back home would never believe this everyday sight. We never saw or heard of this in the adverts Welcome to Oz.

We got the Sunday papers and milk. Huge paper seemed like 100 pages and more, a section for every aspect of life. But the headlines reaffirming the rebels had indeed taken the airport at Bangkok was so unreal that we had just escaped in time. There was some news of a murder, reading like something out of a gangster movie. Some man was shot in the back as he walked up the step to his house by a gunman passing in a car, he then got out of the car, walked up to the wounded guy and shot him in the head then drove off. It was a few days later when we were told that it only happened at the foot of our road and indeed, it was a Sydney Mafia execution. Oh shit! Where have we come to?

We had a few days of sightseeing, one place in particular in the city centre became our favourite venue, Paddie's Market, it sold all produce from the country garden, chicks, chicken, snakes, lizards, the lot and every nationality.

Planning ahead, I managed to find a small shed in North Sydney to let to store our meagre belongings which were following behind us by ship.

After being at the Paddie's Market, I spied something that I thought I could make a few dollars from, a box with 24 live wee yellow chicks, not a clue how to bring them up, but at least I had the hut to keep them in. Doing my best to fatten them up, I grated some breadcrumbs and left them to settle in. I called in the next afternoon to feed them only to find them all dead. I think it was to do with the heat and some smart git mentioned water could have helped. A waste of $2.00.

By the end of our first week, Dolly had full employment as a secretary with a pharmaceutical one-man business. It was only her and her boss. Her job varied from general office and filing to manually handling individual tablets (painkillers, sleeping etc.) and lotions/creams, packing them, posting, ordering etc., attached to a small lab and storage. Pills then were loose, not in silver sealed packets, just bottles. She got free samples to give to friends or whatever.

It was only a couple of days later when I got lucky. Only 500 yards from our flat was the headquarters of the North Shore Gas Company. After a short interview, I was offered the job as an appliance service engineer, a five-day week at $39.00 (£25.00). the fitters rate back in Scotland was £12–10/ a week, this was double, and it appears the cost of living was to be just the same. Also, I was to be given a wee van, there were none available just now.

We'd landed in heaven!

In the meantime, I was issued with a small brown suitcase which contained my tools also a trench/dust coat to protect my clothing and map of the area in the north shore, not too far away, jump on a bus then off.

Given four job sheets at a time with the only instruction on it being it was a faulty gas cooker, oven, fire or fridge, and new to me, bath heater for the hot water and shower, with a small storage hot water heater at the kitchen sinks. All I was armed with were washers, diaphragms and grease to slacken controls, that was it. I really had an issue and self-doubt with my new job, and that was I'd never done this type of work before, the skill for this we done and only covered in a few hours in the training centre, but the guys in the UK who done this work were known as maintenance men, who studied for 3 months to do it. We were gas fitters whenever an appliance breaks down well you passed it down to these guys.

Christ, I was now having to learn their job and learn I did!

We started at 7am, Monday to Friday, only 50 yards or so there was the Aussie pub, dark and light brown tiled, inside and out with a huge central oval shaped bar. One huge public toilet and it was bloody full. Loads of them swigging the skooners (third of a pint) of new and old beer, they were very social.

I recognised and was recognised by some of the faces when I got off the bus at the stop beside the open doors, they waved me in. it was embarrassing to always say no, only once did I join them, it was great. But we had to go to work, they were in tune to this. I was just getting started.

I had to get off at the bus stop before in future. But I learned a lesson, I honestly thought these guys including bosses were coming to work half cattled from a party or something from the night before and never gave a thought they were straight from the bloody pub!

As I was without transport, I was called in to double-up with these guys from time to time and without a doubt a drink was top priority. One older guy Stan, in the first few weeks seemed to ask for my assistance nearly on a daily basis. Stan was a likeable character, but booze, jings. I'd thought I had seen something, they told me he was a prisoner of war of the Japanese and had a tough time. He was about 5' 3" tall, stalky. He was every bit a true-blue Aussie, rugged with a rough raspy voice to go with it, but very likeable.

When we went into a house for which we had key access because no one was home He would immediately abandon me to sort out the gas appliance while he raked through every drawer and cupboard in the house until he got his hands on their grog or spirits, then he sat about with the bottles, being careful only to take a few swigs from each, then replace them back to wherever they came from. His eyes were like looking at pee holes in the snow. But the bugger was never up nor down although he got captured one day when he was on a job and the customer came back unannounced. All she saw of him was his feet and legs sticking out from under the bed where the booze was. His excuse was he was trying to trace a gas leak and smelt underneath the bed. He got away with it after the boss had a word with him. Within the next couple of weeks, I think most of the guys had the use of my experience. I began to take note that this side of the Harbour Bridge was occupied by white Europeans and more obvious no coloured or blacks, notwithstanding. The fact of the times is that in the whole of Australia they only let blacks in when they were seamen on board visiting ships and only allowed ashore for essentials hours at a time. The aboriginal was not allowed into the towns or cities south of the bridge and the city housed huge communities of all others, Greeks, Turks, Italians, Chinese etc. There were in my time only a scattered handful north.

One guy Olaf Larson, who worked in the company used my labours regularly. He was a cheery lanky (half breed and born Aussie/Norwegian) he was the most regular, more because he was a lazy bugger for a man of 25 years. The first thing we done on the morning was to drive all the way from the company depot to his aunties (Magg) house in another area, Mosman. His cousins were getting ready for school, so we joined them for breakfast, tea and toast. I was surprised that this house like most then were pretty rundown weather boarding and dark inside, poorly furnished, not like the immigration films and photos. However, folk seemed friendly.

On a couple of mornings, his mum, father and his girlfriend, Margaret (18) were already finishing their breakfast as they all stayed here overnight and were ready to go home (as they and Olaf actually lived south, Punchbowl), some 70 miles away and were only here on a visit. They were very friendly, his dad originally came from Norway (escaping by boat 1940) wee Maggie, was only 18 and been going out with Olaf (25 years old) since she was 12 years old. Strange as it may seem to a lad like me from the backwoods of Scotland, this was not common.

Our evenings were getting more and more occupied visiting Donny and Margaret, extending to some of their immigrant friends, Toni and Avril, Beryl and Martin, English couples from Suffolk who had been here only 7 or 8 months, they were our advance party. Through them we were introduced to the beaches.

The first was Long Reef, what a sight, huge breakers, where to one side were the surfboarders, the swimmers the other all having great fun. White Sands and the Aussie beach patrols sitting high up on the tower and a land locked lagoon, teeming with shallows with small fish trapped there with the receding tides. It was on this reef and surf where I learnt to swim and dive (scuba) the warmth of the water made it easy, surrounded by confident snorkelers it wasn't long before I was snorkelling down some 30-foot holding my breath for up to just under 4 minutes. We were regulars, even spending our first Xmas Day on this beach. A far cry from failing my swimming school exams in Dalry swimming pool with only 5 feet of disinfected water, the instructors could not convince me I wasn't drowning!

On the reef itself, when the coral was high and dry, I spent hours messing about in the pools, catching or trying to get a grip of the trapped fish. One thing I was totally gobsmacked with was the octopus, which were about 2 feet long, they were known as the 'blue and pink ringed', to say I hated the sight of them was an understatement. The local guys were playing with them as if they were pet monkeys letting them crawl all over their legs and arms, but by Christ, it was only a month later that a young soldier on rest and recreation was killed by a pink ringer on this reef. It turns out this was the very first recorded death by that octopus, they discovered that they had a hair poke in their beak (shit I never knew they had a beak) from this they injected a poison into the nervous system stopping the heart. This guy had it on his arm and just collapsed (I'm going back to Dalry Baths). You don't have to venture into the water to find death.

Only a hundred yards away we heard a bit of a commotion on the beach itself, when a crowd attacked one of the beach patrol who shot someone's dog dead for being on the beach, again it was part of the law. Any dogs found on beaches or in the water will be shot. The reason being that their body sweats and stinks attracted sharks, seemed a reasonable thing to do! But the dog owners were out to get this guy. The police chased them away.

The patrols did have one good job. They were allowed to measure the outside hip of any female's bikini pants, there was a legal size on the narrow side and asked to leave if it was too skimpy. Bloody laws!

But my Dolly was well covered by hers and a cracker. She was worse than me in the water, she couldn't swim at all, but she showed no fear when one day one of our friends arrived with a surfboard. It was huge, some 6 feet in length, and took two of us to lift it onto the water, none of us could go on the bloody thing except lie on it even at that, not for long, and struggled to get back on board. Dolly was messing around with it when we realised she was gone. We ran up and down searching in the huge surf, when someone spotted her away out offshore some 200 yards sitting on the board in amongst a gathering of other surfers waiting to catch a wave. We swam out, she was as happy as a 'pig in shite'. I was so knackered I had to hold onto the board for support. As we escorted her back in, she nearly had a hairy canary when she realised how far out she was out. That was the end of surfing. She returned happily to sunbathing which bored me out of my skull, lying there covered in oil with layers of sand getting into your creases. And how the hell our female species suffered or enjoyed getting sandpaper rubbing in theirs was beyond me.

For a short while I tried to learn the art of spear fishing. But not for long when I found I was being followed by sharks of all varieties. I was following the practice of keeping my speared catch in a Hessian sack, tucked out of the way at my side on my weight belt around my waist. When I was told the tales of some guys and sharks following the traces of blood seeping out and without warning striking. In most cases only a thump in your side would be felt as it took your catch. In some cases, a chunk or all of the diver would go too. Keeping an eye on each other was seen to be the best defence. I had another one, bugger off and leave the fish!

I got a wee shock of a letter from the Aussie Armed Forces to go to the nearest post office and register for call up to serve in Vietnam! I nearly dropped my ashes in my underpants. I thought wrongly that it was only America's war, wrong! All immigrants on setting foot ashore here were eligible for call up. I went to the PO just to be told, my birthday was on the wrong side of the 1st October 1945, I was too old!

It made me wonder about the other two lads on our plane, they were younger than me,

In the coming months I was to meet another two lads, one born in Scotland and the other here in Sydney but of Scot parents. Both of them died in Vietnam. Sad.

Just before Xmas 1966, we got ourselves a wee flat at 116 Mowbray Road, Willoughby, which was a few suburbs north but still on the north shore of Sydney. It was a living room, bedroom, kitchen and shared toilet and shower. All the back half of a brick and weatherboard bungalow, the Italian owners had the rest. Nina, Carmen, baby Mario, like us immigrants. I near forgot old Grannie, always dressed in black, only the bairn could speak English and Italian very well, so we spoke most through him!

We had our own laundry area out the back, a brick built shed, which housed a huge 20-gallon copper bowl-like pan with lid set in a framework of bricks and a gas ring below. On this we boiled our load of water, alongside this were two big scrubbing and wringing tubs with cold water supplies between the tubs a larger than life hand-wound mangle with wooden rollers. A bit of a novelty.

To start with I was in the house one night, Dolly came running in shouting for me. I thought the house was ablaze. Following her into the darkness and the laundry, where I would see the gas burner was lit. I sensed we were alright, with great caution I let her lead the way and take the lid off the steaming copper, she pointed in. Oh shit! There swimming around was a lizard. I done the right thing, called Nina and the bairn (Mario). In a flash, she scooped it out with only a rubber glove for protection.

Then only a week later in this laundry Dolly bloody found my worst nightmare, only it was in one of the big empty tubs, it was like a re-run, only a spider! At the time totally unknown to us it was a Funnel Webb (or Black Widow) and it was bloody big! Standing as far from the edge of the tub as possible and on tiptoe, I gradually peered over the lip down to where the long hairy legs first came into view, bit by bit, closer till the whole thing appeared. Jesus Christ! What a size! There was no way I was going to call on spider-Mario or his mother. I braved it out, grabbing hold of a mop in the corner, plunging it blindly over onto the depth of this tub, thumping it over the inner base, corner to corner, removing the mop head above me. We moved closer for a peep – nothing, it was gone. We looked at each other, I caught her eyes squinting towards the mop head, and me now turning to the mop in my hand. Shit! There it was face to face, not for long. In one move the mop was off to one corner, her and I out the door into the night. Some 30 minutes later we braved it up, searching the inside of the laundry, it was gone. Where? I never told her, but I was awake all night waiting for it to creep up the covers!

My workmates told me the next day that the area I was living in at the time was one of the only areas where the Black Widow was to be found in all of Australia. What with the bloody octopus what was next!

We spent our first Xmas here. For the big day we bought a (hire purchase) stereo unit much like my dad's, it cost us $45.00 ($8 down, $8 per month), it was hard work trying to prove our credit worth as immigrants got a bad name. Come the 2-year point for release of their passports and those wanting to go back to GB, for whatever the reason, who could not afford the fare, took on loads of HP and then sold all the gear to get the cash!

Although our immigration we knew was conditional, that we surrendered our passports for the two years, or buy it back for the cost of the Australian Governments cost, fares etc. some folk saw better to wait the two years and use the HP as their ticket! I got my stereo and paid it off. Although it was very tempting.

As Xmas neared, it was not the same feeling. It was getting hotter. The radio blasted out to us British warnings of over eating on our heavy foods on Xmas Day in this heat, they tried to educate us into salads, yuk! On the big day itself, we tried to make it like home, but there was just no atmosphere, no trees, just a wee breeze from auld Reekie, a wee draught. We made up for it in plenty of well wrapped-up presents.

The Italian family were away for the week. Dolly made our dinner, broth, tatties and a wee roast. The place was that hot that she was dressed in her bikini. We didn't have a TV then so made good sitting out in the back garden with our radio on an extension lead. Later Donny and Maggie came up and we headed to Long Reef. Had a great day but not Christmassy!

I was given another Xmas present. After passing my Australian Driving Test, theory only as I had my GB one. I was given my own company works van, a Morris 1000 pick-up (utility) for private use as well. Adding to this it meant having a two-way radio, I had all my work issued over it, the jobs were all around my doorstep. But I was in for a wee bit embarrassment minutes after getting my first van and driving it out of the works depot at North Sydney. Motoring along the Pacific Highway on the right-hand lane of the 4 lanes, positioned to turn right at the junction ahead, only me on the road with a black and yellow single decker bus to my rear in the inside lane. As I slowed, he whizzed past my left-hand side. Without warning the Aussie bastard, pulled out hard in front of me. I slammed the brakes on. Crunch! Shit, his rear bumper clipped mine. He drove on leaving me in complete shock, my nice new chrome metal bumper was bent in half, worst still it stuck well up in the air. It was of good thick metal; I couldn't pull it down to a less obvious embarrassing position. Driving it back to the works garage was truly weird. I had a red kip trying to explain it away. They didn't bother their buckie, just gave me another van and sent me on my way.

This wee van gave us a bit more flexibility. We went to our first ever drive-in movie. It was strange to be sitting there alongside your allotted post which held a box with extension cable, you opened your window, unhooked the box and re-hooked it to your wound down window, wind it up, sit back and watch the movie screen up front high on a white board. You had your own volume control on the box. When the movie was finished, I done the expected. Drove forward with the box still inside which broke loose the cable, but with the chaos of the other cars I managed to sneak back the box to its holder. We never went back in the van in fear of getting spotted.

Our first New Year's Day was a strange affair. Nobody seemed to bother about it.

A new man arrived at the gas company, Mick, an Irishman with his family who arrived just after us (by boat) and had to live in one of the immigration camps that we, as a single couple, managed to avoid. They invited us to their camp on New Year's Day, which was based 70 miles south-west in an area of Liverpool. We travelled by train and bus, it was a stinking hot dry day. As we travelled further away from the coastal sea breezes, great big blowflies seemed to gather around your whole face, in particular mouth and nose and no amount of hand waving moved them away. We were used to it but not so much on this grand scale (one thing we did learn about these blowflies was they loved boiled eggs, if you had an egg at a BBQ beware, when it travelled from plate to mouth it could suddenly change from white to black before you could bite it!).

Mick met us at the gate of the camp with his two young children, what a shock! The place was indeed like he warned me it would be. It resembled a Second World War prison camp, completely encircled by a high wire fence with nothing but dry bush surrounding the outside. The ground was hard packed rock and bush dirt, rising up and away with row upon row of Nissan huts, all around were wooden board walkways, very similar to our Polish Army camp in Edinburgh.

People wandering around, kids at play in the heat. He showed us the toilets and shower blocks, no sewers or drainage for the loos. Just corrugated iron seat upright, one hinged with a place for your feet (concrete slab) and a small metal drain with some chemicals poured in to prevent disease. He had to provide us his own toilet paper and a loose-fitting board to sit on.

This was the Aussie 'dunny'. Then there was the communal dining hall, just another huge Nissan hut with row upon row of cluttered tables, kids climbing all over the place dropping or spitting on the duck board floor covering.

The four of them and what belongings they came with were crammed into a small corner section of their hut, and no movement of air in any of the places. His wife just wanted to return home! A couple of months later she got her wish. He didn't even hand in a notice or left word. I don't blame them, what a culture shock. Homesickness was not only an illness but a killer. There was much talk of suicides 'what the hell!'

We both had our moments, even though we were better off than before and after seeing their situation we had better insight into just how lucky we were.

I was restricted to only using my wee van within the North Shore, I saw a car in the newspaper for sale at $80.00, I phoned this guy and bought it over the phone. This wee rust-bucket arrived on our doorstep. All excited he departed with my money. The first thing I done with it was a good clear out of the inside. Then a coat of paint I got from Carmen, my landlord and that was the inside done. When it was dry, we settled in to take it for a spin. Fortunately or unfortunately, I turned the car across the busy road doing a three-point turn, done the first part, only to find for some reason I could not find reverse gear! Half-blocking the road, a police car pulled up, one of them got out. He just swore, then it got stuck in a forward gear. He got it into neutral. We stood watching as both officers pushed the car into a neighbour's driveway thinking it was ours. They wouldn't pay attention to us pointing to our house. When leaving they threatened to book me 'if that effing car goes near the road'. One of them came back with the phone number of a car wrecker. We didn't argue. An hour later it was towed away which cost us another $16.00.

We had made a good number of friends, with Dolly's 20th birthday coming up and being away from home it had to be a special affair. With the help of Nina our landlady I planned a surprise party for her. Luckily it was on a Saturday, arranging as many of our friends as possible which was about 20 in all. I left Donny and Margaret with a list of goodies, including beer etc., as I planned to take her off into the city as a treat, a bit of shopping and a visit to the wrestling match live, our favourite viewing programme. We were always watching it on someone else's TV at that point.

I planned to keep her out till at least 5pm, a long bloody day! Phoning back to Nina whenever I had a chance. We took the morning train from along the road at Chatswood over the bridge and into the city. I never got bored, yes I did, but had to keep up appearances. I spotted a smashing bright orange 2-piece suit, and she was a cracker in it. I just managed to get her to keep it on, although she wanted to keep it clean for a special occasion. Keeping cool, I told her today is my special birthday present and all that shite. All she wanted to do now was go home.

I don't know how I managed it, but I did, we walked down town into the Sydney Kings Cross area, thankfully the wresting was on early pm. I agreed with her that it was better seeing it on TV, that bloody started her off again. After pretending three times about going to the toilet (phoning), I got the all clear for our 2-hour journey home. By this time, it was pitch black.

We entered from the back of the darkened house, in through the kitchen. I followed her as she started to open the living room door. The place was dead! I thought I'd made a mistake, shit! All hell broke loose! Yelling, screaming, I couldn't believe my ears when the live bagpipes blasted out. It turned out a great night.

Olaf Larson and his wee girlfriend turned up later with two others from the gas company, typically Aussie's, they brought their own grog.

The sad part was the young piper, an Aussie by birth, but his parents are both Scottish, he lived in the hills area west of Sydney. We were at his farewell party flung by his family later, he had been called up and was heading for Vietnam. Poor lad was 'killed in action' three weeks later.

Dolly became unwell, had to stay off work, I called in the doctor (Dr Bligh) who said she was suffering from a chest infection which was making her a bit depressed. On the way out, he turned and said we should really be planning a family.

A few days later, we got large newspaper in the post from her mother. It was our first sight of the Edinburgh news and it was special. Splashed across the front page was a story of her brother young Boris who was up in the High Courts for rape. It was a shocker at this time when we were getting settled and her not well. We couldn't understand why she wanted to send us this. It was the first and last we got from her, everything came through old Boris and his was full of good news. I think his loneliness from the prison camps showed through.

Olaf was asking for my assistance more often now that I had my own van and area. Most of the guys that I helped were not calling for me. The bosses did call me in for a wee word. There had been a complaint, they told me. When I was on foot with my wee case and using the bus, my average daily job complete total was 16 which to me was OK. I didn't find any problems, they did. Their average each day with a van was 8. I had a bit of a panic going on. What the hell were they saying? They must have seen my face. Once then saw me out the front door and with a friendly smile, hinted that I should keep my snorkelling gear and picnic ice box in the van well up. 8 jobs was more than enough It was getting to be the same routine with Olaf. When I got to the job where I was meant to help him, the bosses called a 'double-hander', it was no more than one of his set ups. He was just wanting me to see that he had come across a Sheila (female) he had the hots for and he would be getting all excited if she was in her nightie or worse! But if it was not this, his other weapon of pleasure was a double compact mirror he kept, using it attached to the tongue of his shoe he tried to manoeuvre the female so he could look up seeing what she wore or not! He even boasted of spiking their drinks and getting his way with them!

Everybody in the trades knows or speaks of someone who 'knows' he was just a joke that wouldn't go away, can't do a thing about it. Shared this with Dolly.

Her boss was Noel Kalusi, he spoke like an Aussie, he was a nice guy. He lived in the hills area out Katoomba Way west of Sydney. He moved into a new wooden type bungalow completely surrounded with real bush. I volunteered to take on the job to clear it as his wife said he was too lazy or busy. So I gave them a rough idea of what it would cost going on what he said, half a day's work. Dead keen to impress, I got stuck in, it was dense and 'jaggy', I clobbered it and cut my way through it in 2 days, they kept me going with jugs of iced orange juice. I was not long finished when he told me the truth. He was scared to do it because of the number of snakes he's seen crowding about. I hadn't seen any. He reassured me that would be because of the noise I was making scares them off. Had I known I wouldn't have even considered it! Mind you $40.00 was a wee fortune.

I got the shock of my life when on a job up some 30 feet on a ladder a gas wall flue pipe suddenly and without warning burst. I got a whack on my cheek and biting pain. I nearly fell off. Instinctively I grabbed my face, shit! I had a handful of some prehistoric creepy crawly massive beetle now clinging to my hand. I slammed it against the ladder, the bugger even survived this and flew off! I shinned down the ladder three rungs at a time, I fell over backwards on the scrub-like garden below. Oh shit! Staring at me only feet away from my head was a snake. Shitless with fear, crawling away, I recognised it was a Blue-Tongue Lizard as it scurried into another bush. This thing was nearly the length of my arm, then it disappeared as quickly. It was only a few days before we had visited Taronga Park Zoo and saw one in a cage. Big buggers!

When I picked up the courage to tell my workmates about this big bug, they told me about the Xmas beetles, they fly endlessly blind around structures until they bump or sense a structure to land on. It left a few scratches on my cheek!

Dolly and I paid a visit to see Dr Bligh about 3 weeks after he saw her. He gave us the good news there and then, she was two weeks pregnant! We were surprised at getting such a quick result. No hospitals in maternity clinics, the Aussie was simple, your GP saw you for the whole 9 months start to finish, unless if you required hospitalisation or specialist treatment. We got another surprise, he would deliver the baby at hospital of our choice, either NHS or private. We chose private, it was not far from where we live.

On Fridays we all gathered at 3pm to collect our pay packets and the boss always organised a lecture for us on how the company was doing. He held us captured by dangling the promise of crates of beers. No drink driving problems then.

Now and then I was tempted and joined in. On one of these days I parked my van up after a few bottles and went with some of the lads to the pubs. I was in for a wee bit of a surprise when we piled into one of their cars, an old GM Holden (General Motors) American type thing, and what a bloody carry on!

When we took off it was dark, the car had a slide open sunroof, I was standing on the front seat with my head out of it, heading into the Harbour Bridge when all of a sudden, the buggers pushed me up and out. I ended up siting on the bonnet hanging onto the windscreen wipers as it raced over the bridge, only stopping to pay the guy at the tolls. Slowing down enough for me to dive headfirst back inside, on shit!

Another place we went to at the weekends or warm evenings was Lunna Park in an area below the North Shore of the Harbour Bridge, there is a tiny shark netted beach, also a fun park. The mothers and fathers who took their kids at night already had them dressed to go straight home to bed in their PJ's and gowns.

Having learned to snorkel it was a wee bit adventurous of me to climb over the shark nets surrounding the beach as the harbour itself was known to be a breeding area for sharks and in particular, the Grey Nurse (Port Jackson shark, so named after the Harbour Port Jackson). Well, I was in for a shock when I dived down the net, which was made up of large foot long interlocking rings, to find huge pieces missing, just rotted, away and all those innocents playing in the water didn't have a clue.

Later on, once I qualified as a diver, they employed me in repairing these shark nets. My uncle Doddie and Auntie Jessie, (my mum's brother, the Laidlaws) emigrated to Brisbane right after World War II, we promised that we would visit them at some stage. The day arrived just after Dolly found out she was expecting and of course, it was a long weekend break. That same week they gave me a wee minivan as my Morris was in for a service. This was, I thought much newer and more reliable. All the vans were sign written and for use within North Sydney. I did think about that and decided there was no risk, it was 600 miles each way.

We were all packed ready to go, the last thing on the Friday a couple of hours before we took off was the usual works meeting. I got my pay packet and managed to avoid having a beer, unfortunately I overheard my boss having a chat to one of the supervisors. The gist was, he too was driving up to Brisbane and was leaving right after the meeting. What a bummer! But I decided to leave an hour later and let him get ahead only with there being only one road and one lane each way, all the way.

The No 1 route Pacific Highway in such a wee van loaded with gas meters, stinking gas oil, but who cares? Strangely most of these meters were wet ones in real working order unlike the one I got the history lesson in the first months of my apprenticeship at the Training Centre in Edinburgh where they were considered extinct!

Ignorance was a bliss on this occasion. We left in daylight at about 5pm. The traffic was very light and this road a true adventure into the bush. As the evening wore on into darkness, we stopped for a quick bite to eat at a café in the only town between Sydney and Brisbane, that was Newcastle, just a hundred odd miles up the road. Topping up the tank our intention was to drive through the night, but by midnight we seemed to be the only car on the road with not a sod to see for the last 50 miles, not a house, café or garage. The sky was sparkling with stars, we could nearly touch them and the Southern Cross was brilliant. But we were getting worried. Not long after we passed a solitary petrol pump and wooden shack and shop sign, and the road was single both ways made up of tar with soft edges, our lights just shining into dense scrub and no indication except my speedo to say how far to go, enough! I pulled into the soft edge and we decided to sit it out till daylight. We both got out to have a pee, one of us mentioned snakes, shit! And we nearly did! With a delayed realisation, slammed the doors and snubbed them locked. With the lights out, Christ, it was dark black, couldn't see each other. Sitting there in the most uncomfortable seats ever, we slept oblivious to any noises, not aware of cars or whatever passing. Daylight came 6am. A quick decision, turn back.

Fortunately, we didn't have to go far until we found the petrol pump and great, queuing four or five cars and two young aborigine boys on bare back horses. We were last to get topped up. We joined the queue, at the front and to one side stood the two aborigine boys patiently waiting to one side to get served about 4 or 5 folk upfront of us. By the time we get to the front the two boys still stood waiting, then it was us. We told the boys to go first. The woman behind the counter told them to wait till she served us.

I looked behind me, there were a few folks waiting and all white. Dolly told her in no uncertain terms, serve those boys first or take the petrol back. There was a bit of a stalemate but the boys got served and the woman got her petrol money. Our first encounter with racist people and well-mannered blacks!

We went on a visit to Botany Bay, an aborigine settlement at La-Parouse south of Sydney, the native residents made spears and boomerangs, to my surprise even the smallest boomerang flew back. There was a live display of bush snakes where a brave guy demonstrated to us how they struck and how to identify them when in the bush. Poor guy died the following week in this pit, he stood on one!

Another of our experience with aborigines was at a place west of Sydney, Katoomba, part of the snowy mountains on the Great Dividing Range, this part known as the Blue Mountains, we were visiting a well-known spot high up in the Range with spectacular views out form the Three Sisters, a natural rock formation surrounded by thick scrubby bushlands. Only us two and our wee gas van when the silence was disturbed by familiar sounds of tribal music, aborigines and they were not far away, close enough for us to be concerned, being out there on our own but curiosity got the better of us. We decided to follow where it came from. The bush was that thick, only enough room to creep our way gingerly getting harder with each step. It began to sound like a whole tribe were dancing, singing and beating sticks together. When on every turn we made expecting to be confronted by war like figures, suddenly we broke through, there before us was a very low-lying stone building with this old guy sitting with his feet up smoking a pipe, just relaxing to the sounds of a record on a player beside him on a small table. Without his seeing us, we crept away. Bastard!

Dolly's boss' father was killed when a wave swept him off the rocks when he was fishing off the Entrance (as it is known) two high cliff faces the gateway into Sydney Harbour (Port Jackson) only weeks later, his mother passed away.

Out of the blue, Mr Kaluski offered us the let on their completely furnished bungalow at normally low rent, £10.00 a week, 5 Falls Street, Cremorne. A lovely red-brick detached bungalow, gardens (lawns abound) and garage. Well-kept inside and out, 2 bedrooms, living room, dining room, bathroom with shower, kitchen with full size upright fridge-freezer. We'd heard of them and seen them in the movies, great! Also a complete laundry with heated washing machine, no more boiling a copper. The house was fully furnished wanting for nothing, including a TV, our first one ever! There was a radiogram so now we had two.

Under these strange sad circumstances things were getting even better. We made very good friends with a couple of our age across the road, Andy and his wife Lynn. She was an Aussie, he was an immigrant from Liverpool, England. Another plus factor for her (Dolly) was that Dr Bligh covered this area, so we were on course. Cremorne, we were soon to find out, was a very posh area, the house was probably intact as it was before they both died, only their personal effects were removed from the house. We wanted for nothing! Even the gas company relocated my workload to this area.

We had already booked a cabin cruiser in the Hawksbury river up at Bararra, just north of Sydney. The last suburbs and dense bush with hills around Kuringgi Chase, prior to moving to our new home at Cremorne. We met up with a crowd of Irish folks, the Patersons from Belfast. I was one day called out to their house in the northern suburbs of Artarmon, it was an old wooden shamble of a house, they were the tenants, Mum and Dad (John and Nell), the salt of the earth. They had already emigrated before but had returned home. Not long ago they realised they had made a mistake and had come out again. They had a lot of bairns, ages from 11 years to 30 years old. The older ones stayed back in Ireland, some remained in Australia. Which was one of the reasons for coming back, the younger ones had to tag along with Mum and Dad. Old John and Nell invited us to join them as they were having a party and that was it. They smothered us with kindness, whether we liked it or not, we were part of the family. Old Nell had a bad heart, and was a bit overweight with a fag in hand, toothless smile. She was always to be found sitting in an upright armed solid dining chair, dressed in very fine underslip, in her words, "The heat buggers me." Always shouting to old John, "John, John, is that friggin' soup burn in?"

John was a wee skeletal figure of a man, scurrying around at her command. Answering her, "Cut out that bad language, for the Lord's sake, woman will ye now!"

They were a great double act. Always parties and broth soup. Old sing-song of home. Lovely! Everybody they seemed to be friendly with all us immigrants. One of them, wee Sammy, he appeared to be very much on his own, were it not been for the Pattersons, he had left Glasgow the year before. Old Nell told us that she thought he had Downs Syndrome, or as we knew it 'Mongol'. He certainly looked and acted the part, laughing then crying for what appeared to be no reason. He was of a fond nature; it was nice to have him around. He yearned to go home to Glasgow but could never afford to go home to his mum and dad, so we invited him to join us on the cabin cruiser.

With absolutely no knowledge of boats and very little instructions, other than stopping and starting the engine, the three of us set off in this 28-foot cabin cruiser, 2 berth, toilet and shower area and loads of living accommodation. Also, two under counter fridges. We were soon on our way with our weeks supplies and clothing. For the first couple of days on this nearly brown river, which got narrower by the mile we were soon to be on our own on the river. The mangroves that lined the muddy banks nearly arched over from each side, behind them we could view orchard of orange groves with rocky bush covered hills rising steeply on both shores.

Dolly had a craving since she was expecting and that was for my most hated fruit the orange! I detested the bloody things, the smell and spray on opening when squeezed, drew my cheeks and jaws together and the bloody stink of them was all around. But she wanted some, I dropped anchor midstream and with now only the sounds of the bush and our voices, Sammy and I rowed to the closest shore, clambering through the knee-deep mud and entanglement of the vine, trailing a wee wooden vegetable box with us, we could now see clouds of oranges hanging on their trees. Wary of snakes, we made quick work of filling the box and as fast as we got back to the boat, she didn't have to really devour them like they were going out of fashion. We were to repeat the gathering day in and out. Ignorance is truly bliss, with only a tourist map to go on, it was difficult to say where we were at any one point, only that we had a rough plan that was three days out and three back with the one to spare. We could never keep straight for more than 30–40 yards before we turned one way or another, and not knowing how deep it was, we had to keep up a good head of speed as we learned to negotiate the hidden sandbars that every now and then lifted the whole boat skywards as we blindly hit them, it didn't matter which part of the river we travelled, sides or centre, they managed to find us. One night we dropped anchor as usual mid river, got up next morning only to find the boat had swung round to point the other way, up until now we never knew the river was tidal, not that it would have meant much to me. we worked out that the anchor rope was completely wrapped around the propeller and had no idea what to do.

The night before we saw a shack high up the hillside above an orange grove. We left Dolly tidying up the boat. After about an hour or so we arrived at the cabin, it was like what you would expect in the movies, there was only an old guy with no phone. It was him that told us that it was tidal and said we'd best wait till high tide that night, beach the boat, then cut the rope away. This time we did ask if we could take some oranges. It took forever to row back upstream to the boat and pass on the news. He did give us a wee frightener in telling us that shark to be caught this far upstream. We all had at one point been swimming, it was only now we realised it was salty, so the plan was to wait until the boat was high and dry before we attempted to cut the rope from the propeller.

We spent the rest of the day rowing to and from a small beach, using all the brains we had between us in getting this boat ashore with only a rough idea about high tide and when it was. In the pitch black of night, things got scary. We only had one small torch, fortunately there was a spotlight on the top outside of the boat. After spending the daylight hours rigging up ropes to the shore, and with the tide incoming, we managed to cut away the rope linking us to the anchor, abandoning it to the deep. Sammy and I rowed to the beach where we pulled the boat, Dolly steering it as planned. By this time, we had to turn off all the electrics except the fridges to save the battery. Spending the next few hours inching the boat further up the steep beach, each time we thought we were beached, we would only find ourselves still afloat. My confidence was flagging and very worried. It was well after midnight before it started to lean over. Dolly having done a great job, was now bedded down in our cabin. So Sammy and I decided to take a watch up on the front deck for an hour at a time each. The back of the boat was still well under deep water, god knows when the tide would be fully out?

I went up first and by Christ, was it not spooky! I thought I'd do the right thing and turn all the lights off, shit no, although the stars blanketed the whole sky, it was the noise, the whole place seemed to come alive, I was being attacked by everything imaginable! Then it came to me, I had been given a loan of a .303 rifle in case I wanted to do some kangaroo shooting. So for my comfort's sake, I clambered down to where I had stashed it, and put the deck light back on. My nerves once again settled, I returned to my watch. Bloody difference!

We took turns about and by daylight we weren't sure if the tide had been in, and now going out. Decision time. Bugger the sharks! Sammy and I taking turns, well-fortified with Dolly's sugary tea and a rope tied to our waist, dipped underneath, knife in hand, bit by bit we cut away the rope from the propeller shaft until we could turn it by hand. With us all on board, the engine started, but the front had embedded itself deep in the sand. With Dolly and Sammy at the controls and the engine in reverse, the water churning up, smoke coming out of every window and exhaust outlets, I was on the beach my shoulder under one side pushing the bow over to one side and back again. I was bucketing with sweat, the whole boat shuddered when without warning, it shot away rapidly. I fell flat in the water, rising to see it circling backwards, fortunately in the middle of the river and at high speed. All I could do was watch as they struggled to understand what was happening, and how to gain control of the beast. The rowing boat was still attached to it, so I was stuck but they eventually got the hang of it. Fearing more problems, I got them to come as close to me, where it was easier for me to swim. My nerves were shattered. I'd lost a day. I headed straight back taking two uneventful days, but plenty of orange stops.

We had already agreed before coming to Australia that, not like many before us, did we think this was a one-way ticket, but only a trip of a lifetime needing to be done sooner rather than later. Although we lived in the northern suburbs and presented ourselves to the nicer side of Australia, our circle of friends operating within these boundaries which grew up all around our social and working environment. There were plenty of happenings going on and newsworthy events even though we didn't pay attention to papers or TV news, violence and drugs seemed worlds away in the unknown suburbs of Sydney where we only drove through them to get from A to B. There were huge communities of Greeks, Italians, Russians, Nicaraguans, Turks, so many (but not black), they never spoke a word of English, only their own mother tongue, except for the few who came north. But you could not avoid and hideaway from the murder, shootings, rapes and drugs.

On a Sunday morning, between midnight Saturday and 1am Sunday there was a TV programme on for 1 hour called Sydney Night Shift, which covered all of these crimes which took place, it was filmed as we slept 8 hours before. The TV crew and cameras were tuned into the emergency services and in most cases arrived at the scene before them. It seemed that nothing was edited. Bodies shot, knifed, whatever. People attempting suicides, rapes, nothing was left out! But all was accepted. Drive-by shootings seemed the favourite. Compelling viewing!

At this point in our life it had no real influence in our day-to-day living. By accident I started a small business venture. The fridge, freezer packed in so I bought a cheap second-hand one. We couldn't wait to get the parts. When we did get the parts I repaired it, so now we had one surplus. I advertised it in local shops and sold it for a wee profit. But an added bonus was I had the van so charged a delivery fee. Then the new owner asked if I could for a small fee, take her broken fridge to the tip. Instead I brought it home. I messed around with it and got it going again, so I sold it without any effort. This repeated itself over and over, never having more than on item at a time. I had plenty of time with this gas job. I done my work, now on average of eight a day, only going into the office on Friday for pay. Although there were supervisors, I never saw one in all the time only on the radio, I did feel a bit insecure at having all this unrestricted time. A typical day was at about 4pm at the official end of a day over the radio they issued us with our first two calls to go to at 7.30am the next day, and at 7.30am all they wanted us to do was call over the radio with our call number. My call number was 41 so I would say "41 clocking on", not even having to wait for a reply and that was the start of the day.

Then every two hours clear these jobs again over the radio, this was repeated till finish. But I had my own plans. As soon as I got the two morning calls at 4pm, I shot to them right away, and completed them that same night. Get out of my bed at 7.30am to radio '41 clocking on', then back to my bed and in case should some of my supervisors pass by my house I hid the van in the back garden.

I needn't have crept about during working hours, later I was found to be one of the only one's seriously working after 10am or 11am, and I found out they were (most of them) in the pub or club grogging including the supervisors and bosses, like true blue Aussie's they were guttered and standing, some even ventured to do a bit work then back to the grog. I felt a bit safer and at ease with my lot.

But I was getting bored. With Dolly at work all day, I started filling the gaps, window cleaning, this helped our bank account. I chose my houses carefully, staying away from bungalows and main doors, what with a sign written gas van, I'd be chancing my hand, so I stuck to multi-storied houses, mostly old gas customers who I thought were safe also the flats that hung out over the harbour, such as areas of Mosman, Manly and Kirribilli, hoping no one would spot me from the ground. I also enjoyed my snorkelling, I decided to take the next step, scuba diving.

So, the only people I knew of who gave instruction were a couple who were to become Australia's most famous deep-sea divers – Ron and Valerie Taylor.

They operated out of a shop in Manly and worked from a huge rubber dingy. The actual training was done over a reef a mile or so out to sea, where first we had to prove ourselves in snorkelling down to 30 feet, pick up a weighted belt which he flung overboard, putting it on then resurface. This was great! I had no problems. The water was very clear, the bottom was a carpet of seagrass which opened and closed with the motion of the currents revealing bleached-white sand and shoals of tropical fish, fantastic! Finding the belt was a wee bit of a task, we moved from one spot to another, the whole course was to take 3 weekends. In shallower parts of the submerged reef I was taught the basics on using the bottle, demand valve, pressure gauge, as that then was all the equipment used then, with a side sliding air reserve lever, which in emergencies gave you a couple of minutes of air. Once that was learnt, having got the hang of clearing your demand valve and face mask we'd go out to deep water again, I was sitting there watching as Ron tied up the loose harness and tied it around the bottle with my weight belt, he then dropped it overboard, it disappeared beneath the waves. I was pushed overboard and told to go after it and not to come up without it all on.

Down I went, after spotting it in the rocks and seagrass, I grabbed at the demand valve, blowing out what was bursting in my lungs, tried sucking new air, Christ, Mother! As I surfaced feeling ready to pass out, gasping air, the boat was quite away, once I reached it, Ron shouted he forgot to turn the air on, shit! He just laughed and gave me the thumbs-down, it seemed a hell of a lot deeper than 30 feet. This time first of all I turned on the air valve then pressed the demand valve, lovely, the blast off bubbles was reassuring. This time I breathed and was rewarded with plenty of air, great. I attached the harness and rose up to the surface. After a good few further successful dives, then practice the art of buddy diving, I got my certificate. I was a diver!

On one of my first dives myself, after hiring the diving equipment, I set off to an area north of Long Reef, my favourite snorkelling reef which was tidal. I had heard of another submerged reef which was accessible straight off the shore and not only safe but plenty of shelves for exploring. I recced the reef first using the snorkel, keeping my ¾ hour air tank for a good dive. Once I located a ledge with a huge surface area which steeply descended into the depths which was not for me! I changed to my diving bottle, moving along this white sanded corralled cleft, I saw a piece of tube steel sticking out of the surface. Some sand revealed more to an extended area of about 8 or 10 feet, coming around on itself to form a horseshoe shape. I was baffled to say the least. At one point I dug deeper onto the shifting sand to expose the tubing which was firmly bolted into a steel superstructure beneath, the shifting sands thwarted my efforts to get deeper. My air supply was now running low, I abandoned my efforts. Mentioning this to Ron, he just smiled and said, "Well done, you've found it."

It was a submarine coning tower. He told me it was at the end of the Second World War, one of the submarines they towed out of Sydney Harbour which was damaged in action and now surplus to requirement. It broke loose when it was being dumped far out of harm's way and was known to have drifted back towards the shore, but no one knew where it went to.

Ron and I, with others from the navy, returned to reveal the top of the coning tower. They discovered and removed an ID panel along with some cutlery strewn around, the sub was left to decay safely on the reef. What a find on my first dive!

My discipline in regards to 'customer relations' was to be tested on many occasions. Everything I was brought up to face, in terms of temptation which would come from the female customers, was more than abundant here in Australia. The bastards tested me at every move, it was a constant weekly dilemma for this poor Scot's lad.

On one call, first thing (which was when most incidents happen) up Mosman Way, I called at about 9am to a bungalow front door and knocked and waited standing there in my dustcoat with tool case in hand. Finally, the door opened, it's a wee lassie about 4 years old. "Go and fetch mummy."

She understood and took off down the long, dark hallway. In the gloom I could make out doorways on both sides. At the far end daylight lit up what seemed the main living quarters. The wee one shouting, "Mummy, mummy!" as she ran the whole length.

Without warning I hear a voice nearby, followed by this completely naked body stepping out of the doorway only 6 feet from me, her back was to me, shit! I had no place or time to respond to this, I froze, in an instance she spun around fully. I waited for her to yell or dive back into the room, no, not even putting a hand over her body to hide or cover any part (and by Christ, she was nice!). Instead she just said to me, "Are you married?" I nodded yes. "Well that's OK them." And told me just to go up to the kitchen at the far end.

I squeezed past her, leaving her to close the door, quickly finding her gas cooker and trying desperately to open my toolbox. Within a minute or so, I could feel her presence in the kitchen near me. Foolishly I turned trying to engage her in conversation now that she was clothed, only to find her walking about in the skimpiest set of see-through baby dolls. This was worse! Oh shit! I'm off and that was the quickest job yet.

Life was hard, trying to do a job and keep a marriage was proving very difficult. However, there was a release valve, Dolly and I had a good time relating these experiences repeatedly.

Stan the grog man called me to give him a hand in a wee flat with an under-sink gas water heater. This was located in what the Aussie's call a 'home unit', which is just a modern one roomed flat with a wall mounted double bed which hinges down to the floor. The room is open planned only separated by a breakfast bar counter, behind which the sink and cooker along with our heater, quite a cramped area to work even for one, but two, Jesus! The reason he wanted a hand was he'd discovered a stash of booze in the lower cupboards. The guy, a young man let us in, he only had a towel wrapped around his waist. There was a young female lying in the bed with a sheet covering her obviously naked body. OK, we could handle that, so we went about our business behind the counter out of sight below the worktop height.

Stan set about sneakily gulping out of the bottles in turn. I was fearful he would get caught in this cramped enough space. There were noises coming from the couples' side, whispers and giggles. I wasn't long fixing the unit when I decided to let the couple know, I peered up and over the edge of the top, oh shit! She was completely starkers, he was on his back with her bouncing up and down on his tackle which was obviously embedded within!

Stan opened another bottle whispering to me, "We're going to have to sit this one out!" and we did, at least ten minutes.

Stan was only concerned that the guy might notice the bottles have been nobbled.

Dolly, where are you? Not again!

As it's turning out, the average Aussie female doesn't expect to get married until over the age of 30 whereas in Great Britain, they were expected to be well married by 21! They were quite open about why, they thought if the men could sleep about then so could they without a wanting. Other than the obvious, in character they were a good match.

Grog was always on top. This was this way of life, so I had to respect it and accept it. No wonder we Europeans had no problems in getting work, you only had to turn up and if you did for sure you were earmarked for any promotions, no wonder I was told off for completing too many jobs a day.

We were well used as babysitters for the Aussie wives when in their droves went off on their own weekend binges.

Another myth, the Swagman was not an Aussie. I met quite a few bushmen (swaggers), again they were mainly Europeans, it was too much hard work walking the bush or working the mines, there was too much a career gap in Aussies. The ones working in jobs were normally to be in high management, big businessmen, who were more fond of the plonk (wine), and again their armed forces now in Vietnam and in the two world wars, was hugely made up of emigrants and 1st generations. Bull-shitters is as good a description of a true-blue Aussie as they call themselves, who wouldn't pee on you if you were on fire. Having said that, as a young man like most, I was very taken in by the movies and stories but was very disappointed in what I found, being invited to join them at weekends was for the most a male only BBQ with plenty of grog.

But on one big event, (for me anyway), at a pub on Anzac Day, they took to gambling on a game known an 'two-up', they locked everybody inside as the game was illegal. A bedsheet spread over the tiled floor, two pennies balanced on 2 fingers, quickly thrown up in the air and spinning; $50.00 on the cloth, $5 + $10 laid down by punters calling heads or tails, or one or the other, money turned hands at a good rate as did the grog and shouting, but they were worried that the police would do some arrests.

So I had my uses, I stood outside keeping watch, now and then a hand with a full schooner appeared. Just a typical male Aussie day out.

We had our own circle of friends so BBQ's were truly on the agenda and at one point every night of the week, it didn't take much to organise. Everybody brought their own drink (beer) wines and spirits were just not on at that period. The beer could differ as our English friends ventured to brew their own ales. Yuk! Can't stand the bloody stuff, it was alright if you were suffering from constipation, because that's all it did for me, shits!

The ladies were also beer hands, if anyone did fancy something different, well they brought it with them. The same was for the grub, BYO (bring your own) and cook it yourself. The host may only supply the sauces, so it was great. Again, like the rest, we all cooked on an open fire using a steel plate. Some folk brought extra booze, which was an excuse to shout another party if not BBQ.

Fridays and Saturdays once a month meant an even bigger full BBQ. Everybody was welcome, and the neighbours were always welcome, as if it got a bit noisy, there wasn't much room to complain. We never had any problems with this as my Scottish music seemed to go down well, kilts and all!

The only one from the gas company who came to our weekend do's was Olaf and his girlfriend Margaret. They only came to our BBQ as they had a 70 miles hike back to his place where he lived with his Mother Dolly and Father Lars. But after a short time, he and Margaret parted company, she was 18 years old and John 25. They'd been together for the past 6 years, I never saw anybody drunk at any of these do's, including us in particular me.

Dolly had stopped drinking since expecting. I was always the joker doing my Norman Wisdom or Jerry Lewis, great clowns of the day. Dolly at one point got fed up going to or getting invited to other parties of folk outside our circle. The reason she told me was that they always got a laugh at me, and that is why she didn't want to go. I put it down to side effects. But we kept our events. But thing seemed to change at our BBQs.

I was ending up at the very beginning of our night going to bed drunk, fast asleep, before even half the folk arrived. I could vaguely remember some of them trying to pull me out of my bed from under the sheets with their coats piled on the bed. I never ever felt drunk, just too tired and only wanting sleep. But on one of these nights and again only in my house I remember lying on the living room floor with my head resting on the skirting board trying to sleep and again hardly anyone had arrived.

On a couple of occasions during the night I was awoken by Dolly getting out of bed in her nightdress opening the bedroom door. I saw Olaf standing in the hallway light. I tried to get out of bed. Dolly called back to me to go back to sleep, the door closed, in my dark room I guessed the party was finished and he (Larson) may have decided to stay again as he never had to take Margaret home. But in the morning with absolutely no hangover and no Larson, I shrugged it off.

It was in a conversation with one of our friends who said it seemed I was being 'spiked'. At first, I couldn't accept this, I trusted everyone and if it happened it would have been for devilment and a laugh. But I had a thought on it and after going to other parties, folk were waiting on me going to their beds it never happened and there was only one person who I knew who said they spiked girls drinks, Larson! I never trusted him to any parties again and confided in Dolly as to why.

She says I was mad; the result was I never took to my bed again and lasted the pace. Once later at work, I said to him I thought my drink was spiked, he gave a wee snigger! Captured!

But previous to this I promised to be a navigator for him in a car rally. I hadn't a clue about rallies of any kind, my only link to navigation was map and compass reading from the military. However, the car rally was about the class of cars and consumption of petrol – well out of my depths! All the entrants met at the filling station in North Sydney, and it returned to this place as the finishing post in two days' time.

All the cars were topped up with as much fuel as possible into the tank, then it was sealed, a note of how much went it, then the speedo reading taken. All I knew was this point of leaving and our final destination out was Bathurst. Never heard of the place let alone where the hell it was.

Olaf told me it was way west over the Blue Mountains, a bush town. My navigation was very simple. I had a clipboard listing many 'way points' of reference and what they were. Leaving the garage we done a left-hand turn onto the road, travel 2/10 of a mile where we make a right-hand at a T-junction, then travel 1¼ miles where we go over a roundabout and straight on for ½ mile from that roundabout, I had to watch the speedo clock clicking over the 1/10 of a mile, calculating every digit and without looking telling how far ahead was the next point. The problem was there was sometimes two junctions only yards apart, getting it right meant everything. When we got into the bush the way point was a bush or boulder and at one stage fording a river. I told him any minute now we'd be crossing a river, he replied, "Look out window," oh shit! We were halfway across it.

His job was to keep a constant speed and a light foot on the pedal to use as little petrol as required. He had already spent days adjusting tyre pressure, carburettors, all the stuff I know nothing about. We arrived in Bathurst late in the evening and pitch dark, the final check-in point for the day was a petrol station where our tank was topped up giving us how much we used to cover the distance.

After a night in a local hotel with other entrants of the rally, we were off on the return leg. Finishing up at the starting point. It was a few weeks for the results. And what a surprise, we took first place in the economy and 2nd place in the class of vehicle. I was fair chuffed it was a shared trophy which he got.

Andy and Lynn Peel, our neighbours opposite, were also expecting their first born around the same time as us. He was a huge guy, 6 feet 2 inches, built like a brick shit house and you heard him before you saw him, also a Scouser (Liverpool, England) he made up for what I lacked, but Lynn, she was such a tiny wee lassie about 5 feet 6 inches. Although they had been given the same due date Lynn was huge in comparison to Dolly. They had lots to talk about.

Andy and I would go snorkelling while the ladies sat on the beach sunning themselves. On one Sunday, Andy came over to ask if we would like to join them for a wee run to Canberra, a 400-mile round trip. We were amazed, but agreed. We had never covered such a distance in one day by car.

The ladies sat in the back because of their condition. I was soon to find out why we never got even halfway to Brisbane. It was terrifying, he booted it all the way there, just a normal winding country road there and back, no wonder we done it in one day. We only stopped once for a pee stop and that was enough. In the area of bush where we stopped, I saw all these small holes about our feet as we were peeing, these small crabs began to come out of each hole, only their faces, arms with nippers, they were all around our feet. Being brave I picked up a stick to prod one of them which instantly grabbed it with both claws, it held on as I lifted it away out of the hole for a split second. I tried to focus on this thing, oh shit! I dropped it and jumped away. Andy was quick on my heels; it wasn't a crab but a scorpion! We couldn't believe it, and as quick as a flash we were on the tarmac, both near trembling. We had only seen these things in the movies. We plucked up the courage with a longer branch and from a safe distance managed to dig up a few more, just to satisfy our curiosity, there were hundreds! But we were all bored out of our skulls with Canberra!

I know it was a Sunday, it was full of modern buildings and empty of people, even the museum (war) although open but no one except us there. Not even a place for a cuppa! We were happy at any speed to get home. Andy provided that.

Just days before Dolly was due our next-door neighbour, an elderly couple, told us they were going away for a few days and their son who was just released from being in jail was going to look after the house! We were ready for an early bed, just putting the lights off when the house trembled, the noise was deafening which seemed to get louder, then lessen, then rise up even louder, we both thought at first it was a tornado as a couple of weeks before one had devastated a neighbouring suburb. Then it faded to a rumble.

Dressed only in underpants, I ventured out the front and on my right side came this bloody blustery roar and a small car appeared out of my neighbour's drive and thundered away up the road into the darkness. It didn't have any lights on. The noise never lessened at it disappeared into the night. It was then I saw Andy coming towards me shouting, but I couldn't make out what he was saying until he got closer. He was an angry man. We could follow the path of the car as it seemed to circle us at a distance round the immediate vicinity, heads and bodies came out of some of the houses. Suddenly the car swerved back into the street, still without lights, it just shot past us and quickly reversed up into his driveway just missing the two of us. With the engine still turned on. The guy well in his thirties jumped out ignoring us and everyone else, undid the bonnet hinging it up.

Andy shouted to the guy, "Shut the f*** engine off!"

The guy heard him. "No! I'm drying it off, it's racing tomorrow!" then disappeared into his garage. Even just ticking over, the noise without exhaust was deafening and the ground beneath my feet shook.

Suddenly without warning as the guy returned to the car and was bending down under the bonnet, a wave of water came from behind me and completely showered the entire front of the car, soaking him and the engine. A voice (Andy) shouted out, "Now it'll need drying!" Walking away with an empty bucket.

It worked; the engine cut out. Nobody hung around. I learnt later the car was a Ferrari!

Less than a week later at about 1am, Dolly got out of bed to go to the toilet. She came back and woke me to say she thought her waters had broken. I was out of that bed like a bullet. Running about like a headless chicken. Looking for the hospital's phone number. We chose the private one, the Caberoghsha, Edinburgh Road, Castlecraigs. We didn't like the NHS one, it was run mainly by some sort of nuns. But the private, it felt more like a hotel, palm trees outside, your own room and a bonus it was on Edinburgh Road, you beauty! Born at home.

She showed me the waters, I don't know why I expected a gallon, this was not much more than a couple of soup spoons of pinkie stuff. She wouldn't allow me to phone the doctor or hospital yet. She says she felt good, I had a bit of a panic, it was alright she could turn over and sleep. My nerves were all over the place, but I did have a wee plan! I lined up loads of towels, scissors, string for the cord. Disinfectants, kettles on standby! I was ready. It was 7am before she agreed to let me phone Dr Bligh. Oh shit, did he not give me what for, saying I should have phoned first thing! With that I piled her into the Morris 1000 pick-up truck (utility) and off to the hospital.

As the bairn popped its head out at 12.40pm, I held her hand and was wiping her brow when Dr Bligh declared 'it's a boy!' We all looked at each other, nurses and all, he wrongly assumed the cord was the willy, it wasn't a boy I was hoping for, Dr Bligh left. I left to let the nurses get on with things, high as a kite. But then deflated horribly so, there was no family to share this moment with!

I radioed the work and told them over the air. The radios listening-in were alive with congratulations! That made me feel better.

After going to see old John and Nell, then up to the hospital, made (or heated) mince pies and beans.

Andy came to the door, saying he had news to give us, he's a daddy! It's a girl, Caroline, 12 lbs 6 oz. Jesus, our lass was 6 lbs 8 ozs.

The next morning having decided not to stay off work, I went up to see her at about 8am, we were told being private meant this was one of the bonus's, getting a visit in before work. I got turfed out, and told to come back at 9am. I was obedient. When I did see her next, she told me she had had a visitor at 7am – Olaf – I was a wee bit put out. I hadn't seen him for ages before. Later that day after keeping on calling her (the bairn) Billy, I was told her name was Helen. I'd never heard this name used before, ah well!

After a two week stay in hospital, I was glad to have them home. No fancy cars, just the old gas van! She (Helen) was born 13th March 1968. Now it was definite, we were planning our return to Scotland.

Dolly worked right up until her waters broke, now we were living off my wages and our 2 years were up in October. To get the extra cash, I tried other jobs fitted around my gas job. Dead keen I pitched high thinking that another full-time night shift job would be good. I turned up at a Kellogg's cornflake plant 70 miles south of the house at Botany Bay. This was a huge industrial area right on the bay itself, I was one of a couple of hundred men gathered in some waste ground beside the railway marshalling yard. I was definitely a fish out of water, the crowd was made up of Greeks, Turks, Italians etc., the area stank of garlic and spices. Two white European guys holding clipboards emerged from a door onto a platform overlooking us, the place fell silent.

One spoke out into the crowd in a foreign language, some hands went up, this went on for an age, then one of these guys looked down at me and asked if I spoke English, "Scottish," I said.

"Right, start tonight 10pm."

And that was it. I'd got a job. Drove home all excited, tried sleeping after tea, no bloody good! The plan was straight forward at the end of my working day and having done my two first calls that night, I'd try and sleep from 5pm till I had to leave for my 10pm nightshift job, finish at 6am, motor back, radio on for 7am, that gave me at least 3 hours spare. It worked for a few weeks, but this was not for me.

No bugger to talk to, climbing all over railway container wagons all night in hurricane weather coming off Botany Bay and I missed my bed and family!

Then I tried my hand at cleaning. There was a vacancy for a cleaner, five nights in a bank up the road. Great! Having gone there to collect the key I was met by the cleaning supervisor, he showed me around, the place was busy. A huge long leather-topped wooden customer counter, 8 tellers desks behind. There were three of us cleaning this bank at night 6.30pm–8.30pm.

I had been doing this job for about 3 weeks when my boss in the gas job called me into his office. I was petrified, I couldn't think what I had done. However, this was to be the big turning point of my plans. He asked me if could take on some overtime, 5 nights a week which he called the back shift from 4pm to 5pm and emergency call outs all day Saturday. "Yes", I never even asked the hourly rate, the job meant I had to only do any emergency calls that came in, also working from the house over the radio (the bank job went instantly). I still had not asked how much I was getting, as it turned out, my wages more than doubled from $40.00 a week to $84.00. my dreams had come true. I even got to spend more time with my new family. We saved well, banking my overtime, completely saving this for our return home. We had decided on flying all the way, having flown in from the west, we chose to make a world trip and go to the east, Fiji, Hawaii, Canada, USA, Prestwick via Philadelphia and New York.

One of my Saturday call-outs took me down to the entrance area on the north-shore of the 'Harbour', where I saw the most impressive sights of my life to date; It was the American Fleet heading into Sydney, troops full on Rest and Recreation from fighting in Vietnam with many of their wounded one behind the other (line of stern), slowly cruising in between these massive cliffs on both shores. Sailor lined the Railing Deck. The gigantic aircraft carrier inched in through the 'GAP' with the help of Tinny tug boats; it took a good number of 3 point turns just to fit her within the cover of port Jackson; every available point on the shores, windows doorways and pleasure craft was crammed with applauding people to welcome the heroes ashore, returning to my duties of nappy's which were made of towelling bleached white 20 inches x 20 inches commonly known as "Terry-Toweling" we had prepared well, a huge stock of some 50 to 60, some stacked for use; others in the wash and outside drying whilst the remainder steeping ready for the wash like a little factory assembly-line the safety pins were huge and had to go through the multi folds where the corner met at the front of her wee-belly. On removing one of the pins I found it had accidently gone through her skin just missing her belly button. I had pulled it out before I had time to realise what had happened. Dolly was more than a wee bit upset, it shook her confidence; Helen however was not aware and didn't seem to feel anything. Thank Christ we were becoming aware of our own and her environment in particular, insects, they were a bloody nightmare from checking everything for flees, ants, cockroaches, spiders and snakes, we didn't realise just how adapted to them, we had become the fleas used to bite us on bed or on our under cloths leaving big blood spots on the bedding or underwear, snake and spider around but normally ran away but the spiders were in the grass and if you sat down on it checking shoes or whatever lay there was always a must red backs, trapdoor and black widow along with tarantula were very common spider some fatal to healthy humans and all fatal to bairns, checking and rechecking became instinctive and when the bairns cries for no good reason check them thoroughly no matter what… It proved effective, we found plenty of insects time and time again. We even made sure she was covered with a mosquito net when unattended, it could be a nightmare for some but when she had a nappy rash the sun done its job, leave her bum exposed for 30 seconds front and back and it was cured no problems… when she was only about 6 weeks old we went a car run with Andy and Lynn, with both babies on board what a huge difference in size they were, Wee Caroline was too big for any carry cot of that time so Lynn had to carry her everywhere but we headed north up by the HawksBury river; although it was a cool Sunday when we left things got really hot for this time of year. So much so that cars up front started to break down. With traffic on both directions now completely at a standstill and ours now overheating. We had ran out of water and juices supplies the only fluids the Bairns getting from the breasts of their mother with bush covered hills all around us, after a few minutes we could see coming over the hill tops what we thought was clouds against the pale blues sky's; folk were out of their car, just to get whatever air there was; then minutes later word spread that the clouds were in fact smoke bush fires we got out of the car and followed some folk who were heading down the slopes beside us and we all ended up sitting half submerged in a salt water creek of very wet and warm brownish water; (part of the water we had earlier been boating in the cruiser with Sammy). We were fortunate as what breeze there was kept the fire on the other side of the hill thank 'Christ' it wasn't long before the police came on the scene and told us that things were safe and the traffic was beginning to move. It was frightening just feeling so helpless with the infants being so exposed as there was no air-conditioning then!!! With time rapidly getting closer to heading home to Scotland, we successfully applied for the return of our passports, we packed up a few tea chests of our belongings and shipped them off, a couple of our Irish- friends welcomed us to stay with them for our last few days in there timber bungalow on the western suburb of the lane-cove, on the edge of Lane Cove National Park. the weather was hot and dry and a bush fire started up all over the park and had already burnt down a number of houses on the leading edges. Shit, we were worried, he had me help him hose the house down, during the night he and I watched along with very worried neighbours as the glow not that far off along with the sparks that covered the sky's and falling all around, some as big as our fist, I didn't know if we were going to get away the next-day when just as sudden the wind changed direction pushing the fire well and truly into the bush. I don't know how people can live so close to the bush that at least catches fire twice a year and property is always lost but to have the house made of timber 'NUTS'… We finally arrived at Sydney airport 8th Nov 1968, exactly two years after arriving. Now there were three of us, but we had 29 people who we made friends with in that period. Except Donny and Margaret, who had split-up and gone their own way, with 4 suitcases one contained some of the Bairns nappies and she had been weaned off Dolly and onto light solids for the sake of the whole journey to keep her on the same type of baby foods. The first leg was to fiji on a Boeing 707… it flew right over Sydney bridge and still not complete opera house… I suddenly wondered what the hell am I doing up here for some reason the first flash I got was of my mother-in law's screaming face; true; why? I don't know, then all those faces we'd just left behind, tears and all, our friends' people who wanted us for what we were? True friends had the pilot asked if we wanted to go back, without a doubt. OH yes! Soon the bridge and land disappeared only ocean, we just looked at each other, we were without a doubt thinking the same. but Helen took our attention and the folks on board, she was a 'novelty'; bald-head they never knew if she was a boy or girl, the hostess took her up on the flight deck whilst another took some of her baby food away to be heated to our surprise an old gentleman after talking to Helen and us about his children and grandchildren, thrust a $20.us note into her Wee jacket top. A fortune this was. This whole trip was costing us all our savings $1200 including our spending money which was only a small part we had saved this fortune mainly by my overtime in the last 6 months. After 3 hours we landed at Fiji's International airport in NANDI, just a handful of low lying single stoned white washed buildings without much fuss we got a taxi to our hotel which was only about ½ mile away; our plan was to stay here for one night and the second in SUVA; our hotel was colonial and cottage like, with lawns and an inviting swimming pool surrounded by tall trees and old freshly painted wooden deckchair , what was missing; people? Not a soul around. We spent the remainder of the day around the immediate area of the hotel feeling a bit exposed and isolated being the only white people. Thankfully we brought Helen's carry cot and netting, the place was alive with bugs, the inhouse entertainment for me was lying on my bed watching these see through tinny lizards running up and down the walls and across the ceilings. At first light we were outside waiting, on our hired-car a small air-cooled engine that didn't mean much to me. We headed straight out of town and what a shocker as soon as we left the last building behind we ran straight onto 'DIRT' 'Orangey-brown stuff' that was the last tarmac we were to see until we got to Suva some 200 miles away; this was adventure; I was slow driving on the Queens Highway one of the only 2 Highways on the island, the kings and queens as I drove on this narrow dirt road lined on both side with very tall fields of sugar cane with a huge trail of dust cloud of the stuff. Having to watch out for folk walking on the dusty ruts. The only vehicle I met on this track was an oncoming tractor. He was giving off massive clouds trailer behind him. I slowed down and pulled up as close to the 'Cane" as possible as he thundered past waving to me until a huge long 'Machete' in hand Christ before I knew it, we were blacked-out smothering all over with sugar cane. Dolly screaming her head-off the Bairn slept in her carry cot in the back seat. I looked in my rear-view mirror in time to see a massive load of sugar cane underneath which must have been and his trailer, disappear into the cane-field on it's side, he and his tractor shot to the other side. O' Shit, what have I done without another thought I was off before his 'Machete-waving' tribe got to me. moving up into the jungle-clad-hills I dared look back over the plains to see the dust settling 'Christ' I got Rat-shit from wife, it was my fault. Ok; Further on with jungle and tall grass on both sides, we came across an old-woman sitting under a frame work of bamboo covered on a roof of palm leaves, surrounding her with a load of 'wee naked black Bairns, We stopped to have a wee-look. Just to find it was a take away of the time. She was sitting on Woven matts, beside her sat lovely freshly cut pieces of juicy fresh pineapples. Helen was sitting up in her cot on the backseat and all the Bairns gathered around waving to her looks of wonder at the pure white Bairn such a lovely novelty for them all; this was one of the elders doing her baby sitting and earning at the same time; I was never fond of pineapple I found it stringy and cheesy, but not this; it was soft sweet and very juicy, after talking with this lovely lady she reassured me that all the men folks and some of the women carried there machetes as if it were part of there ever day dress and not to think otherwise, after that I spoke to some and yes they were pleasant and helpful people as they were the natural Fijians but they did not get on well with the Indians most of whom were born here but part of the old British colonies and were constantly warring certainly noticeable the Indians were the merchant traders, the natural Fijians laid-back always smiling and waving, even if it was with machete in hand! It was late in the afternoon when we arrived in 'SUVA', booked into a hotel, tried to get a shop open so we could buy Heinz or similar baby food. Finally we ended up in a small harbour front café, this was run by Fijians(native), they told us it was a holiday time at this end of the island, all the shops were shut for three or four days, we would get all we wanted from NANDI aaagh, we have only enough left for the night, they were very kind and made it what we had for Bairn, once she was fed and watered, the café owner called on one of her Fijian girls, took Helen from us and told the girl not to come back until mum and dad had finished the meal, and what a meal it was, they refused point blank to take anything for it. We returned to the hotel re-packed and off by this time it was dark, but I knew we'd have to return that night as our flight to Hawaii was evening the next day, after topping up with fuel we were off, the track took-on a different meaning as I sped through the bush and jungle, in some places the whole (road) dirt surface was covered in what appeared to the FIST sized stones, they weren't there when we came down, I ignored them driving at speed hearing this rapid Pop-Pop and felt a slight-rattle as I went over them.(only to find out there were (cane-toads); but we only encountered a handful of natives on the track itself, the rest were gathered around huge bonfires, thankfully we managed to get back into the same hotel, what a start to a trip of a life-time; after spending the day by the poolside we were off to "Hawaii", travelling across the international date-line the whole aircraft burst into applaud. Wakened the Bairn from here sky-cot, we arrived in OAHU next to Pearl Harbor, it was then a single storied terminal block, a taxi took us to our hotel/apartment on the ala-Moana boulevard around the corner from the famous Waikiki beach. We had self-catering and had decided not to hire a car as we only had 2 days here as well and we were tired out already, we went to the local-store; our priority was feeding the Bairn we grabbed eggs and tins of corned beef, bread, milk and margarine, I put some eggs on to boil, then took a spoon to get them out, shit, oh hell the cooker was live, I tried again, Zap! We decided to give up on cooking; I reported it twice, there were a couple of burger stalls at the beach (Waikiki), I think we were spoilt with the beaches in Sydney, here good 'Bit-surf' and lots of sand even the weather was pretty poor, warm, but lots of tropical-rain we just stuck to the pool side, even there we were the only ones at least the Bairn enjoyed it having to watch for the (UV) ultra violet rays' as she was so blonde mind no hair everyone thought, even at six months, she was actually a boy! 2 days was enough; I felt a bit Peed off leaving the hotel, the eggs so I put them on to boil, just switching the cooker on and off, then put them in the fridge. I'd like to have been a fly-on the wall when they took them home.; another Pan Am flight over night to Canada Vancouver to stay with her name sake aunt Dolly they had never met her cousins Marilyn and Wee Jack. It was day-light when the plane finally touched down and dreich (damp) this was more like it, lovely damp snow sleety snowy weather, it had been just over two years since getting a dose of real weather. We spent 2 weeks here at Burnaby a residential part of the city, going to bed was a bit of a novelty at first, the home, as was very normal then only had an open log fire in the living room and a cast-iron pot-belly stove in the kitchen, all to heat the whole house up and down so my long awaited dream came in the guise of loads of blankets and coats over the bed, co-oried-up just the weight of them was great not a thin sheet no wonder I never liked my bed in the hotter climate, but right up my street, Marilyn's husband wee Jack ran a small scrap-dealer business. He must have noticed I was getting bored babysitting whilst the ladies went out shopping, so I ended up out every day hunting for any metal he found. I was employed up in the gully's of the snow covered rocky mountains a massive quarry dug well into the surrounding mountain with the cliff top 200 foot high topped with tall spruce like trees he had a flatbed lorry with detachable back and side gates, every morning at first light we drove-deep into the snow covered Quarry to where piled high heaps of waste dumped the afternoon before, whilst he tore into them pulling out any metal articles throwing them to one-side anything from tin-cans bits of wood with nails stuck in them, any metals whilst his labourer and I started to build a bone fire as big as we liked great-stuff we no sooner had one going when he shouted for us to throw the scrap onto the flames to burn it all clean; removing any part, plastic or electrical wiring otherwise when selling it anything left on the metal was known as dirty and devalues the whole load, one morning when we arrived there was a large load of 45 gallon drums filled with unwanted gloss oil based paint pushing them on their sides he set about them with a spike, puncturing a hole top and bottom, the paint poured out and ran like a stream down-hill he took a flaming bit of wood from the fire placed it on the flow some 20 feet down from the drums; shouting "run"; we didn't need another telling 'swosh' one after another like the drums spat a flame thrower of roaring flame from the holes as the paint reduced in flow the drums took off like rockets, I kept running, then over the top of the tree-line appeared a police helicopter very low keeping clear of the thick black smoke shouting through a loud speaker to put out the flames I was told that everything was in order and that they worried to much about forest fires, But I didn't really think things were under anybody's control as darkness fell and more trucks full of waste rolled in to dump it all for us more money, we were off to get it all weighted in at the scrapyard my share $25-00 Canadian each day, great stuff, then off to the local for beer this money each day came in very handy to supplement our savings, I didn't know what we could have done without it, we set-off again via Seattle, Chicago and arrived in Detroit, It was a good flight, only a handful of us were civilians, the rest were USMC(united states marine corps) on leave from Vietnam most of them a lot younger than me 23 years old, Helen was spoilt rotten, rather they had her from the cockpit to the tail end. it was night when we arrived in Detroit, met-old mate Alan, Helen and there 2 year old Scott were there to meet us with their Car, we drove North over the Border-River right into Sarnia Ontario Canada to their Bungalow it was -20F. Alan worked in the nearby area known as Chemical Valley as an electrical engineer in one of the big oil plants; his brother, Jim, was a supervisor in the same company had been for some 10 years before. The place reminded me of botany-bay mile after mile of pipe-work and steam but yet nothing happening. At night it was very spooky, space-age all lit-up with the lights of port-Huron city showing on the fast flowing river, great flat bottom boats (known as Lakers) Ploughing against the floods of water pouring out if the great lakes I could have watched all day, I had packed into one suitcase my wet-suit and snorkel , the real reason being nobody in Scotland I knew owned such gear, let alone dived except those who were in the Navy, My qualification on diving was beginning to look useless So I couldn't take a chance on losing my suit etc., but I got all Kitted-up one night as Alan and a couple of his mates were going fishing on the lake where they kept an ice-hole open; they drove onto the 6 feet thick ice far from the shore, the hole was just big enough for me to get lowered into using a safety harness, a rope on me the other-end onto his car bumper, on the beam of their head-lamps, they lowered me Jesus not only was it freezing but what a strong current and up I came as quickly, We went to a couple of ice-hockey games, shopping seemed to be the main thing and as Alan was working 12 hour shift we decided as we were running out of cash to cut short our stay and bring forward our flight so we sent telegrams over the phone to our folks giving our new early arrival times, anyways we were getting more excited to show off our wee daughter. They drove us back to the airport in Detroit. There Bairn Scott was needing a Pee so Alan and I took him to the men's room in the airport loo's, I'm holding the door open the wee bugger running up and down the hallway, Alan says this will get him in (he likes Golly-woggs) So Alan walking backwards into the loo calling out loudly come-on Scott see the Golly in here, Scott shot past me and inside, Alan followed him and in a flash Alan was out again. In fits of laughter saying mike there's a real Bloody Golly in their shoe-shinning we just took the Bairn out the front. We had a fuel stop at Philadelphia as we descended towards it flying over a spectacular sight literally hundreds of American warships Broadside on to each other as far as I could see to the horizon, they were I was told moth-balled from the second war. Then onto New York. This was an all-day stop-over. So, we checked in all our luggage. We got a bus ride into east Manhattan $1-00 each, the weather was dull and damp; walking up all the avenues and streets we'd only saw in the movies we were surprised not to be able to see by just looking at the tallest building in the world and leave, the main reason for being here, the empire state building, the entrance was pointed out to us; we headed straight for the lifts; just as the door were closing the Bell-boy inside asked for $2-00 each shit! We were back in the hallway in a flash, instead we climbed the adjoining stair-case and up the first flight and down again; at least we could say we'd been up! We headed back to the airport after finding a couple of tins of food for the Bairn, this was truly right living; a separate room for changing and sleeping infants, 3 or 4 bassinettes on stands for the Bairns to sleep in we fed and changed her with no one else here, we put her down to sleep, turning the lamps off gently closing the door behind us; Click, we waited and listened with an ear to the door only to hear creaking and jolly 'goo's and googling' Christ! She was up. she'd found a new lease in life. I tried to turn the door-knob, it wouldn't budge, shit, one of us must have pushed the lock-button on the knob and Helen seemed to be having a good time, we could hear her rocking the Crib back and forth and it was a concrete tiled floor blind panic we ran off to the main counter, the women phoned the matron who was coming with the security key. (the matron was a tall black man in a boiler-suit) he had the door open in seconds, there standing bent over hanging onto the crib was madame, all grins, no danger of sleeping, Wee Bastard. She was awake until we were on our final flight, home, on a BOAC comet plane (British overseas airways corporation), we flew through darkness until arriving at Prestwick Ayrshire, daylight was just coming through. We were the only ones getting off here, the rest were going on to Manchester, so the pilot pulled up at the end of the main runaway, The ground staff came out to meet us with umbrellas it was peeing down after going through what was the customs on turning a corner hoping to find a big welcome committee, nothing, no one at all, not a bloody sole the whole building with lots of seats and balcony's only a handful of staff milling around. we had only a £ 5 note, half-crown (12 ½ P) and a three-penny bit (1 ¼ P) between the two of us, thinking they were late, I decided to phone, mother answered. She thought I was phoning from Canada, and just screamed dad, dad! Three-hours later, dad and Tommy turned up with the Humber car. They never got our telegrams after stopping for a quick pint at mid-Calder we were home at Stevenson drive, none of Dolly's family were there although someone went to fetch them, Helen took to mum and dad like a duck to water, but the whole thing was a bit of an anti-climax and damp-squib, but Helen, managed to stamp her mark within minutes of getting into her grannies (Mclenaghans) house. She was standing just keeping her balance holding my hands and just jumping on the spot, showing off, when suddenly a thumping noise came up from beneath her, granny was out of the front door like a shot. And down stairs all we heard was verbal rammy, she was giving downstairs Mrs. hunter hell for knocking up with a broom, It's a six-month old Bairn, only minutes of a plane from the other side of the world. Argh home sweet home, no change, but there were two other changes. It was now Ok to play football on a Sunday! The free church of Scotland gave the law permission and now we have a much more mobile police force fleets of Ford Anglia patrol cars. Two tone colour, light blue and white (commonly known as panda cars) with a single blue warning light on the roof, this doing away with the standard black jaguar car. we decided to stay at Dolly's mum in Granton, my mother thought she'd help by giving us a box of groceries to take down, oh shit her mother was not pleased, saying she could manage fine without the help of the Rich self-employed no change, with my tail between my legs I took them back to mum's! It didn't take many hours before we felt at home I was told or advised that I'd better sign on now I had a wee family, I didn't, so I got a job as a van driver with good-year tyre and rubber co, St Stephens St. Stockbridge delivering all sizes of tires, one of the Edinburgh's most famous dealers (1968) Sir Tom Farmer's Kwik -fit Corstorphine road. The realisation that my trade certification were useless outside Scottish gas, and they had a policy that they never re-employed old employees gave me no choices they had full control of installations and security of all the gas fields, I was offered to work with some plumber but as a second class plumber at most which was equivalent of a plumber labourer, On 24th Dec 68 we visited Jimmy's mum in hospital (Liberton Hosp) as we wanted to show Helen, Mrs. Cavanagh (54 years old) was 'Poorly' and in a side-room she seemed pleased to see us and the Bairn; Jimmy was excited as well, the four of us blethered ' a nurse came in and asked if we'd like to go home for an hour, Jimmy drove us to my mums only to hear his mum had just passed away! Dolly stayed with my mum, whilst we went back to see his mum in the mortuary wrapped in a sheet! Christmas eve! That was all his family gone, he was 23 only Dolly Jimmy and I attended his mum's funeral in mount Vernon Liberton! Jan 68, she was laid to rest alongside Margaret his Sister! So Sad, the next few months were very difficult for him, I managed to persuade him to go over to Australia for a couple of years and he did firstly to stay with the Irish family John and Nellie this got him off to a good start, he ended up staying in Sydney for 5 years! He had the Itchy foot like ourselves Dolly and I bought a couple of near derelict cottages for £ 800 to be paid-up at £ 5.00 each week in the west Lothian village of long ridge, they are situated near the church on the top of main street, one of them (semi derelict) was just a shell, the other was at least floored with a living room to the front, bedroom and kitchen at the back and about 15 foot into the back garden stood a single brick toilet and just enough room for your knee's This toilet was to cause a bit of a mystery never to be solved, we put a small candle lit in a jar at night in case of a freeze up, in the toilet bowl, so we placed it every night just under the outlet elbow, nearly every morning we'd get up to find the lot gone, not knowing why was it the value of the Glass-jar. surely I was not to do a night shift to find out who was taking them. But I never went out at night. It was too cold so I first peed out of the window the house had only one tap in the kitchen sink, and it was a mains cold water supply the cooking was on electric cooker no hot water system with two open coal fires one in the living room the other bedroom which was the smallest room and we could only manage a single bed. We needed both fires on in these cold days and nights were nearly cooked and couldn't sleep properly even with the fire dampened down if we let it go out the heat was soon lost and we froze all night we were lucky though! As this was a coal mining area; and our next-door neighbour old Bill Smith was a retired coal-miner and had a part of his retirement an agreed supply of coal weekly free, we got loads from him even at a cut price we managed to get plenty of kettles on the boil from both fires. Rather than sign-on I spotted a Job for a handy-man driver, the labour exchange (Job Centre) said I couldn't apply for the job as I was a Gas fitter tradesman, so they refused to get me an appointment, this I could not understand the reasoning! So, the next day I went in and the job was on the board, I took the application card up to the desk but I noticed it was someone else serving I played the daft laddie Bingo it worked I got the job with Rentokil the vermin extermination but my job was as a rising damp technician after a couple of weeks doubling up with another experienced guy I was issued with a long wheel based land rover complete with a second engine fitted in the back as large as the one under the bonnet , it drove my air compressor which in-turn operated my drilling tools, I covered the north of England and South of Scotland away from home too often living in Bed and breakfast my day was spent drilling holes in old stones dwellings suffering from rising-damp it was as dirty as a sweep job oily never getting to be completely clean, I missed the wife and Bairn too much we'd never separated, after a couple of months I got Dolly to put an advert in the West Lothian courier for chimney-sweeping at the week end, it worked I couldn't work as one in Edinburgh the city areas had their own sweeps, even father had his areas of the town and they had an agreement not to touch anyone else's patch, the town then was a closed-shop, dad at this time of the year had enough work for himself. But out here men work singularly not in teams no tenement's and most using the Rods (the English method) It was only weeks after advertising that I had enough sweeping coming in to enable me to pack-in the Rentokil job ; thank Christ, although the work was not very reliable and covering from shotts all the way into Kirkliston old Edinburgh airport. then I was offered a short-term plumbing contract job with William Brown down the road in Whitburn and the work was on new housing, in the new town of Livingston! Which at the time only covered Craig's hill and not much else with the promise of more housing being built on the surrounding country side this new housing was to be the overspill from the overcrowding in cities like Glasgow and such likes, with problems in me keeping clean every day sweeping some days earning £ 3.00 and a lot of travel and other on occasion moving above £ 5.00 which was great I had to stand in a wash hand basin Dolly pouring hot water over me and enjoying scrubbing parts I couldn't (no baths or showers) but with this plumbing I would be taken on as a first class plumber earning £ 15.00 for 40 hours and up to £ 5.00 bonus although his plumbers were not too keen to have a gas-fitter completely as they saw it with them, Mr. brown was quite happy as it was general pipe fitting and as he told me just go and look at an adjoining house that was already completed and copy it that worked. But there were completely new things on site that we all had to be together so the manufacturer could instruct us and one was plastic gutter with pre made joints I was used to lead and cast-Iron I like the others thought this stuff would not take on in particular the plastic piping for the waste pipes under sink. I was getting used to running in (Pouring) molten-lead into cast-iron piping this was becoming Redundant having said that it was embarrassing to come on site one morning to find my rainwater-gutter I fitted the day before sticking up in the air like fingers. I didn't know that plastic expanded and I should have left enough room on the joint for this, I'd never seen the likes of it before, I certainly learned fast and avoided a repeat! But the bonus system was fast and furious on site, everybody was on it, In one bathroom I put the taps and fittings onto a bath (cast Iron no plastic ones then) then, I pushed it into its space a success the right size for it the whistle went for lunch break when I came back a joiner had the bath completely framed and boxed in I had not piped it up. I had to get him to take it off (I wasn't allowed to touch it against the rules, time and motion) Once I plumbed it, he got paid bonus for putting it 'on' then 'off' and again on. What a bloody farce now we were a bit better off we could afford to rent our first TV 18 inch (corner to corner) screen there were now (1969) three channels BBC1, BBC2 and Scottish tv not long after I returned from Australia, I applied for an interview for a job, I was not sure if I qualified for I'd never heard of it before Gas-technician, I found it scary three members identified themselves as directors it was frighteningly impressive I was lost in questions natural gas my knowledge on electrics managing men and contracts. I didn't even get a sniff of a job even as a labourer but it left me thinking I could have done it, but it was overwhelming to say at least now months later just when I was getting established the bloody job came up again. I reapplied thinking they would recognise me but this time I couldn't care win or lose, I got it, I didn't know what but it was mine, wages based £120.00 a week. Plus, expenses and hotel or accommodation money supervising 50 plus personnel! Contracts base in Galashiels and covering the borders, working on pre-conversion (for natural gas) appliances changing them from towns-gas to natural gas once it was piped in from the North Sea (North Sea gas)! Some other great news Dolly was expecting (Billy a boy ???)! I took the job I didn't know anything about Gas conventions! What the hell it was about, I heard about this North-sea gas or natural gas and that combined with gas appliances kept my confidence up, not even thought about the unknown, Ignorance was such a bliss, truly I motored down to the headquarters which turned out to be half a dozen old wooden plywood cabins in my battered old Morris 1000 van(black) I'd never even bothered to clear out the soot and sweeping tools I was introduced to some of the men I was told I'd be supervising and assisting with my technical skills as I only had an interview asking about my job qualification and history I never got any detail as to my position other than supervisory, (which at this point I never had any) and my title natural gas technical conversion assistant and the money was out of this world. Once on site in Galashiels it became even less obvious what the hell was happening I felt very confident that whatever it was I could do it, I thankfully met up with a couple of guys also with the grand title all of us dressed in 3 piece suits no overalls in sight, one of them was also an old gasfitter and in his 40s so collectively we let him take the lead and be the boss thankfully I let the others ask the questions and by the end of the day and after drifting through what paper work that was available to us a picture conjured up in my mind what the hell my job was about it didn't not take long to access my position and the others. Regarding the gasfitters and converters (maintenance men as known in the gas industry the lowest skilled in the engineering and fitting side), both their jobs in pre conversion

Before pumping that natural gas into the pipeline we were to go from house to house on the domestic side, identify all the appliances and serial numbers of such! Cooker, water heater or central heating boiler and or any possibly old appliance which had no identity labels or number as these were the ones that could not be converted by a readymade kit, and would have to be 'ADHOCED'. Butchered to be able to burn safely the new gas the alternative was for a salesman (standing on the wings rubbing his hands in Glee, commission!) to call and gently persuade some old geezer to buy a new type appliance. It was the fitter or convertors job in the event of a no sale to strip the appliance down and list all the parts requiring altering injectors burner, governor, ventilation, whatever was required to get this thing to burn safely. This is where the lowest of the engineers shone through to be the most skilled and left the gas fitters standing, now I got a better picture as to why I was here, and qualified for the job at the age of 23, I was qualified gas fitter and my Australian 2 years as an appliance service engineer, put my working knowledge of pipework and installation now adding servicing and maintenance skills I was well and truly at the right place and time both of these areas overshadowed a lack of man management or admirative knowledge. My first test in man management soon came I was to take charge of 40 sparking new Wee Bedford Panel vans straight off the assembly lines all a two tone light and dark brown company colour Wm Press sign written, I stood in the newly fallen snow issued each man his keys with a word of warning, "your down the road if you even scratch it and off they went" I had the use of one till my own superior one came on site, once they were all gone I jumped into the spare one and up the snow covered road into town got my hot rolls then down the steep Brae towards the gas works at the bottom no one else in sight being as careful as possible, I touched the brakes to steady up 'nothing' it kept on going turning the steering left and right it stayed on a straight path downhill at about 20 mph. Oh shit, facing me looming up fast a T-junction with left or right turn and a steep snow covered embarkment Infront, I had no control fearing for another vehicle coming along in slow motion I was into and up the banking I somehow managed to reverse it out, looking around I was amazed that no one was around driving back into the depot no one in sight I planked the van dents and all shot into my own, Morris which was nearby and away, I came back later in the day to hear about this van which was damaged but no one knew who did it. Thank Christ, it was soon history. But the flat I was allocated at Bank street Galashiels at gala and used as a company flat in a small tenement 2-bedroom although it was the best I had and not good like 5 falls St Sydney all the furnishing were very old fashioned the bed was the old wooden slatted type with well stained hair mattress, and huge springs the only heating coal fire in the living room my one and only night was enough when I was awoke by banging on the door at 1am fumbling about draped in a blanket, I found myself staring into the beam of a torch behind a very loud voice of which turned out to be a policeman I noticed quickly that he was on duty by the sleeve (black and white striped band) on his wrist. "Is that your Morris Van down there," he sharply said taking me completely by surprise.

"Yes, yes, it is."

"Well you've got it parked on the wrong site of the road facing the wrong way and you have no parking lights on. Move it or I'll book you!" He turned and disappeared down stair I went down and moved it also putting my parking lights on (the first time in my life and never again) I did notice that what vehicles were in the street had their lights on. But I found out this was the territory of the borders police, not the Edinburgh city police. That was not to be done again after all my men returned back to the gas works normally at about 7pm I made my excuses to the office staff taking up the days reports saying I was going to do it homework style and I did; I motored all the way home to longridge to my wee family and own single shared bed and back again for a 7am start the trip would take a good 1 ½ hours each way even with having to stop and thaw out my frozen engine. But things were to change again, I was after about 6 weeks or so given promotion to a higher degree and of course extra money then the bomb shell, 'sugar' I was to help set up new contracts in England, Doncaster, Coventry, and Leamington spa not a bloody clue where these were and thank fully living in hotels although they were poor standard bed and breakfast B & B's might have been better in some of these areas, moreover I got to go home at weekends the only plus factor with my new position was getting to see the administrative part of the contracts although I was more than in tune with the practical side in the field side of this business. On one of my weekends homes I found a letter from another gas company inviting me to an interview for a position (which I couldn't remember and this letter did not say) I had applied for some months before as it happened, they wanted to interview me in two days' time. I phoned my office and made my excuse for a couple of days off. I went Glasgow the airport hotel I was met by an old man who was introduced as the personal office then after I finished a 10 minute on the stop watch questionnaire (I never asked or got a result) I asked him he could let me know what was the position I had initially applied for and he told me that is was for a converter on one of the natural gas contracts. I then told him of my present job without another word he picked up the test sheet ripped it up and put it in his waste bin he then apologised saying if he knew that in the first place he would never have done the test, he went onto tell me he had no such vacancies on his present contracts I got up we shook hands then in an afterthought told me of a new contract ready to go but it was in Sussex England and possibly if I was prepared to go South (moving) then he would find out more he produce a map of England because I had no idea where this was. Below London and down to the England Channel, without much more said he phoned the HQ there and then getting me an on-site appointment to meet up with the contract's manager. I was fly-down, my starting pay was to be £200 P week on top a house rental allowance of £ 12-10.00 per week, travel expenses also a return flight to Edinburgh for me and family once each month for the weekend (this was because my contract would be signed in Scotland) on top of this all moving expenses paid. I took the job (the average tradesman weekly pay was £ 20.00) This company known as HGS, Humphreys-Glasgow and Soufriere gas H and G an old British company, joined up with the French gas company based in Paris and now selling their skills to GB. Still only 23 years old flung out of school 9 years ago and now on my return home I gave notice to W press, and put the house in the hands of our agents, We agreed that I go ahead first to start the job and find a house I drove all the way down and spent my first night next to what was to be my first base a tiny hamlet in Sussex Broad Bridge Heath, in a Hotel of the same name I spent my first night before work having a meal and beer with 2 other older men and a good blether as it turned out they were my directors boss's Oh shit I must have had some sort of nightmare it was very embarrassing when I awoke to find out the bed sheet ripped, and in tatters around my neck and body, bloody thing must have been thread bare. my office was only some 100 yards from the hotel, as it turned out to be and old 2nd WW2 army holding camp purposely built to hold the troops before the D day landings, but now used for the fitters and converters accommodation blocks dining and kitchen areas within all the Nissen huts as bedding areas hundreds upon hundreds of men with parking for all our mobiles including workshop for adhocing appliances that had to be done offsite including 12 men mobile workshops each radio controlled with a clerk and leading hand toilets and cooking along with stores and mechanical workshops. Everything needed to complete any conversion kit showing to be a problem and each mobile shop allocated its own backup in the way of a technical assistant. After my first night at the hotel I daren't go back for two reason the sheet oh dear but the director I was told were booked in again I couldn't be arsed with more drinking with the old guys or drinking at all so I found emergency BnB in a suburb of Crawley called Ifield, East Sussex apparently my favourite singer took his stage name from this place Frank Ifield It was just a council type home run by mother and daughter Wynn and Ann a right double act but made a good stew I shared my room with another guy Tony he was a ticket collector for London underground Brainy too I was given transport allowance but I continued to use my own. Morris Van without the Soot in fact with the help of tony I went to the scrapyard and fitted 2 seats in the back great. As pre conversion had already been done in Sussex and all the underground piping was put under high pressure water testing previously which showed up any weaknesses now rectified it was all systems go for what was called C day which was to be the first Monday in every week of conversion and on that day the old town's gas was shut off area each week and the new natural gas flowed through; it would start at 6am Monday morning and in a chosen calculated estate suburb or whatever our men tapped on doors to get entry in order to turn off the meter supply if entry was refused or just could not get access to the property the road was dug up and pipe sealed. The people were warned weeks then days ahead of C day and date also the procedure as to their priority appliance. It was all done with military precision week in and week out until the whole of Sussex was converted this applied to the whole country over 8 years but we had our moments I found a nice wee rented gable-end semi-detached fully-furnished 2 bedroom front and back garden house on a residential estate Horsham Sussex. It was great and took up my whole £ 12 housing allowance (weekly) within days I had my wee family down beside me and running hot and cold water much more than I asked for! I hung onto my wee

Morris 1000 black van, my priorities were with my family and job which gave me such challenges Dolly's big complaint about me that I never carried or took any pocket money only nipping her lug for some out of her purse only when I was skint! From day one I never felt money was to be a priority for my gains but for a better for the house and it sticks or as it went in days gone by "the provider" at work my title was senior technical officer with a work force allocated to me 200 fitters and convertors with some 20 office and supervising workers and 1 radio operator, no computers at this time, sometimes getting what was known as a computer print-out these were large sheets of lined paper listing the names and details of customers and appliances at their addresses. Otherwise everything was manual and job cards, I was only one of 8 technical officer, we each were given our own office space on whatever area of land was vacant and could accommodate such a vast army of civil contractors and related equipment one thing was noted no women were ever employed during my time on any of the three contracts and it was never questioned what with thousands of men living away from home speaks volumes. My own office was one 30 foot long container on a trailer with on one side a full length desk top with 3 clerks all young hippy type long haired beatniks smoking there weed like fags, mine were regular one's tipped but these lads were good at their jobs at the far end sat the radio controller who had two way radio link to all vehicles in my group which probably at any one time was 20 linking our 200 men one wall facing us was sectioned into the crews names and duties on board my mobile workshops out there on area. Sites we held a duplicate print out of all their workloads with the use of our radio we had a complete update day by day I could check the process of the workloads as was the same of other officers, feeding it all back to HQ, our sector were down to purely population capacity one sector could be a very small village using up our manpower for one week or just a fraction of area in a small town and without question each and every Monday we had to be man and vehicle in a new sector for another week and if necessary our trailer offices would have to move to another location the largest move is when the men living in the old wartime camps had to move into other billets! The logistics were indeed fantastic in peace time my youth (23 years) did not ever give me any problems at any stage even though most of my men (a huge most) were older than myself and some were old soldiers a couple were former POWs of the Japanese. I think talking with respect! One other noticeable thing I began to find was that (only as a rule of thumb) time served and semi-skilled men were more reliable and trusting even producing a better standard of workmanship and attitude than papered tradesmen who seemed to take issue at having to work with the others and questioned when quality controls were put into practice. I had most trouble for some strange reason with light fingered Scotsmen I'm sad to say I was not the only technical officer with that view point but the one person overall disliked and seemed to thrive so on being were the Cockneys this was reflected in Australia. The average Aussie male could not stand them they were always there to be heard and no real structure to what they had to say but always trying to upset the work force there was many an incident where guys were caught in the actual act with the customers avoid the very thing I fought hard to get involved in.

And here it was like a Rash that had to be treated with dignity sending a guy home to his wife or family under this umbrella I didn't like to do it like others, so my way of dealing with this was to give the guy the chance to resign and it worked this was my way with most people including one of my guy's from Glasgow and aged 40, I was informed that he sold conversion kits to some customers when everyone was supplied kits free he was very grateful to have the option and went. Now with conversions well underway I felt more at ease with what was expected of me and work wise settled down very well I'd even got a new name 'MACK' well that was to my face. They got value for money not only did we have to stay on till the last man finished daily but until all the vehicles were back and locked up every leading hand checked in all the reports by this time on average 8pm, then the paper work had to be checked over as to what carries on to the next day and materials passed forward now 10 or 11pm off home depending on how far the sector was away. Back on for 6am the men had to be in there vehicles and on shift for 7am. This was based on a 5 day week and 8 hours day for them after which it was compulsory overtime time and a half Monday to Friday, double time for a Saturday and triple time for the Sunday, for which there were never shortage of volunteers. By the end of the week some were taking home more than me I spent many a night sleeping on the office floor and on some occasion doing 3 complete days on the Trott, the reason being I had to stay was the mechanics who were working on one of the workshop vehicles making sure everything was ready for the next shift I never found it difficult at work or coming and going and enjoyed the wakening time I got with my wee family. Catching up with all that was going on Helen was proving a bit too much for Dolly and corporal punishment was used by her on Helen , Dolly seemed to be doing ok with the pregnancy I wish I could spend a bit more time with them when I managed (a weekend off going to Horsham market place was top of our list, Helen had a habit of stripping off naked (1 year old) and trying on any clothing in the shop or the stalls, in one shop she and Helen had a set too, Dolly with a well skelpt backside, eventually put her clothes back on what a stooshie the women who challenged Dolly on child abuse nearly got her head in her hands and backed off. Back in the base outside working right on the shores of the English Chanel, I had my first ever encounter with trades union and politics two areas which by choice I was totally ignorant I had heard of conflict with the coal miners and the government of the day from Old Smith Back in Longridge. This went in one ear and out the other, I never at that point under stood the politics of either. I didn't even buy a newspaper (except the Sunday post for the Broons) or took interest in news events, having said that it's still the decade of us having out first ever TV. One morning arriving at this base in darkness along with senior staff told that we were going to have to drive our men out of the front gates the reason being, there was a flying picket gathering outside the gate by mine workers (this is 1969, ten years before Maggie thatcher's era). if I did have my view point in that area of time with jobs it was simple there is plenty jobs out there go and test the water but as it turned out our director did not want our men to drive through a union Picket line as the men's union asked them not to we weren't in any union after a couple of days in driving out the main gates taking all kinds of dogs abuse including rotten eggs covering the windscreen we began to notice a lack of miners with ingrained sooty back hands which was there calling cards, but Hired hands skin heads," Mods and Rockers" these guys were only thugs from Brighton and Hove, who were never happier than chasing each other on Scooters (MODS), and motorbike (ROCKERS) up and down the seaside towns causing havoc. Being an extension of the Rockers and Beatles era now jumping on the Bandwagon of the God fathers of the Union this Fly picketing was supposed to be illegal but when we approached the local police they turned a Blind-eye The news that did feed back to us was that this was happening all over conversion sites throughout the country Men were resigning in there droves just to return home and attend and support their families like millions of others I had to learn and adapt to the fall out because of the minor disruptions up and down the country we noticed a shortage of gas Mantles , lights, old and new gas cooker parts going missing in fairly large amounts, this was directly due to the lack of coal mainly for the power stations cutting supplies to homes, these guys making up gas (Butane and Propane) emergency appliances to take home we took their lead rigging ourselves out I did prefer when I'd have the opportunity to visit actual homes to lend my skills where the appliance of some strange origin gave us a headache in ad hocking a procedure if someone brought their appliance into the country where it burnt an unknown gas peculiar to that country. It was back to grass roots, I did not realise just how rich an area of Gb this was, my technical abilities were called on in the homes of some famous people such as comedian Frankie Howard from the 1950 onwards era, Cliff Richards, Pop star, a huge mansion house on areas of ground, but many more, Norman Wisdom, the world's top visual comedian (as far as I was concerned) the guy I spent most of my party times impersonating him, dressing up in similar cloths he lived in a detached modest bungalow on the lovely England picture village of West Chiltington with an outdoor swimming pool they all had the same thing in common which brought me to their houses, central heating system, I was tempted to tell Norman about how famous a person he had tending his boiler conversion. There was one thing I failed very badly at and that was cricket, whether I liked it or not I was roped in to play for the company's side after a couple of tries I made sure my name was top of the list to look after the base camp I was never interested in sports and as the cricket was on a Friday afternoon my trip home to Edinburgh my out excuse, we enjoyed the family get together and I am sure they got the benefits too as Dolly spent so well while I was at work on things for her family in particular this meant I'd have to use my van on some trips to carry the supplies which were too costly for carriage flying, I'd let her and the Bairn fly on their vacations, I must admit I enjoyed being on my own on their long trips. On one I left Brighton at tea time travelled up the A23 into London somehow managing to dodge the heavy traffic all the way I arrived in the outskirts of Edinburgh in just eight and a half hours later, no bugger to greet me. I had to bang them up they weren't happy, I never noticed my stress levels had been climbing up until Dolly said I was smoking a lot more and she was right where I used to buy up to 20 fags a day we worked out I was getting through 60 a day I was in denial but after keeping an eye on myself I was buying

3x 20 fags (60) but thought I was handing them around to others I was but I accepted as many back. I was still only , 9 stones in weight I just could not give them up. Dolly was due anytime now, The Sunday before she gave birth I lay in bed after she got up I shouted down to her to bring my fags up she never heard me so I thought the longer I lie there the longer it is before I take the first fag of the day, by 5pm and after many words of encouragement to get my arse downstairs I didn't let her know my plan, I gave in and went down, I only smoked 4 fags the rest of that night Jesus I could have stopped. I never ever felt like having the 4 fags, I went to work next morning still full of anger, with an open packet in my pocket, I never had another one , and at work I openly told them I'd stopped and I did never even had an urge but I did have a cream bun or whatever with my coffee still with six teaspoons of sugar, well I needed some comforter even after the stresses of child birth I was proud of not being a smoker my clothes were getting tighter then I checked my weight, 3 months later, Oh shit 12 ½ stones, three stones in as many months, I prided myself on my straight up and down look but when I had no choice because my gear never fitted me I went to the local tailor another bloody shock when he handed me baggy trousers, I thought they were for some old fat guy no me (Nov 1970) all of a sudden, I was awaken out of a sleep, Dolly shouting for me from the (LAVY) toilet area she thought her water was broken this was different from the last time but she collected the sample in a basin , two or three pints of blood, this was around midnight I phoned the doctor minutes later Dolly was on her way to hospital in an ambulance we had planned for a home birth and everything was going great, while she was under observation for the next 3 days and the first hospital in nearby Crawley a handful of miles away in East Sussex was full they had to take her into Dorking Cottage hospital over the border into Surrey as this happened on Saturday evening I managed to fly her mother down to look after Helen but I also decided to take a few weeks off the directors were not happy about taking all this time off Bugger them, I've worked more than a year with only days off and that was at weekends, family came first and that is where my loyalties lay. on the third day and at about 1am the house phone rang the hospital were taking her in for a caesarean section and Dolly wanted to see me before she went in but the nurse said I wouldn't make it Dolly told her I would 16 miles of twisting bendy roads tall hedge rows on both sides not a moment too soon they were loading her on a stretcher outside in the midnight air onto an old 3 wheeled Milk float being a cottage hospital the operating theatre was at the other end of the Parkland gave her a kiss and waved goodbye. I spent what seemed all night sitting by her empty bed side in a single room. After a long time and me nearly nodding off they all arrived back they put her to bed and not quite out of the anaesthetic a voice said don't you want to see your "Son", I had a mental blackout totally forgetting about a 'Bairn' They pushed this glass open top box towards me just a mass of wee covers a nurse pulled them back revealing a tiny crinkled face with a huge black eye I only gave him a glance and turned to his mum they took him away I sat for what seemed hours holding her hand she seemed in a lot of pain eventually I went home in the dark she was kept in for 2 weeks which was normal. I kept busy back and forth twice a day with her mum and Helen, being her only visitors, but I took her mum to see her favourite ever film star which was Norman Wisdom she knew all his films and songs in particular Don't laugh at me cause I'm a fool and she was in luck when we drove past his front gate he was just walking up to his front door, he turned and waved at her, and that was it, just a passing glance all those years and that wave to her was a real magic moment. I returned to work a non-smoker and larger than life. The most senior above my level were the directors who I got on with very well they were to my mind very elderly, gents, dressed in smart collar and ties, and how they managed to stand upright at any time of the day defied me they were for the better part just walking 'Gin and tonics' always slurring, one day, 'Pay day' for the men was a high security point they (the men) were paid on site outside their mobile workshop pay envelopes with cash delivered by Securicor armoured car, only us technicians knew what route they were to take and we were informed over the radio's using coded call signs. When it came to my call sign, I opened my envelope inside was a planned route I was to take with the security folk in tail behind me even they never knew where they were going however I noticed a white Mercedes car following us at a distance I told the guard about it with in a minute or two we were surrounded by Panda police car giving us a protective curtain after 20 mins we were allowed to continue once I was finished I returned to HQ for 'Cuppa' outside stood a number of police cars and a white Merc I went into my office low and behold there they were the directors and police standing around one of the directors came straight up to me and shook me by the hand after the police went, then I found out it was the directors that had been nabbed, they thought they would checkout their own security without telling anybody, the police were not happy. The Sussex contract was coming to a close, it was getting hard to keep the good men they were while there was still a calling, I myself, well, a bit cheesed off doing all these hours and with having a taste of family life when Billy was born, I really wanted a bit more home life, I was offered surprisingly a directorship with this company in Liverpool, I would have been more impressed if I'd never seen these directors in action. Drunk in the Boozers, divorced. Now, no thanks! Over this couple of years, we were still writing to my mate Alan Currie in Canada he mentioned that his gas company were looking for tradesmen. After writing to them I was offered a position in London Ontario, not far from Alans, they invited me for an interview, but first we had to get immigration, we took the opportunity and went to their consulate in London England only 1 hour from where we were, we were accepted, Dolly decided to stay with her mum, whilst I go ahead. After a couple of days with Alan and Helen I had a good interview with Ontario Union gas company, I got the position of senior gas engineer, working on mainly domestic appliances, then I asked the wrong question, when can I start, well were going through a bit of a recession here in Canada so it will be next year sometime hopefully (this was March 1971), OH Christ! I didn't even know what a recession was, I've learnt the hard way, and I didn't have a contingency plan I phoned Dolly to break the news, so we agreed that I stay a while to see if I could get alternative employment but after 3 weeks I tried the RCMP, 'Royal Canadian Mounted Police' I was an inch too short, then an ice making factory reluctantly and after missing my wee family, I returned to Edinburgh. But Dolly had not let the grass grow under her feet regarding a home for us, putting our name only under the housing in Edinburgh would have meant waiting a couple of years, so she applied to the new development in Livingston West Lothian and Bingo we were given a house within 10 days in an area Craig's hill East Just up the road from where I worked as a plumber 2 years before this was to be known as the concrete jungle a Maisonettes 3 bedroom and wee garden, we were grateful for any furniture we were given I think family were glad to keep us from the itchy-foot syndrome, But we did have enough in the kitty to buy a proper 4 door car, again a Morris 1000, but I couldn't find work. Dad was slack, I signed on very reluctantly which was paying me £ 13 per week, but I hated the thought of the fact being out of work, I saw a job advertised as a night shift baker at burtons the bakers at Sighthill Edinburgh. I got as far as the main gate to be told that I was not suitable as I was a tradesman, this being over qualified was not real jimmy once worked in here, earned good money, and everybody seemed to be entitled to cut price and sometimes free broken-biscuits. It actually sounded like more of a fun job, rather than stand in a job queue, I decided to go back the next day my luck was in, a different guy on the gate gave him a sob-story that I was a labourer down on my luck I got the job great £ 13/10/- per week. What a feeling back on track and out of the house. I had to start that very night, another baker in the family, other than the security guys, there were four of us, supplied with all the whites trousers T shirt and flat cap and up into an attic space doubling as a bake house well-lit loads of 200 gallon Buggy's on four wheels pipes and Ducts above my head I soon got the hang after establishing what we were making digestive biscuits with the most basic of instructions and with my ingredients menu! I set of with my Buggy, to each overhead hopper, punched in my requirements on the dash board alongside it, Whollup thump and in a cloud of flour stour (dust) I had my first load moved onto the remaining pieces of equipment on my list, finally after 2 gallons of milk, 1/2 lb of salt now the planetary heads mixer after 30 mins of this machine the mix was put to one side the floor by now was sticky with what missed the Buggy's I was now all white and a bit like soot, got into orifices; nose was totally blocked and crusted up! Now I was a baker onto another mix of whatever, I was feeling a bit lonely in the space, so I reached other areas to see where my buddies were, I found them after a while in the darkened Assembly line down below in a small room with an equally small table in the centre, they were hard at it, CRIBB 15 one, 15 two half bottle of whisky and a few cans, I did eventually found out that we all worked in the same small space but in shifts. One of them had been there for 17 years, and thought it was great, no wonder had I not gone in search for them I would have done the whole shift on my own, the one in the black hair turned out to the foreman, each night he came on duty as pissed as a fart, Tommy my big brother worked as a bus driver, down the road from here, he told me they were looking for bus conductors, not able to sleep through the day, I took the opportunity and went into his Depot, and put in an application, within two weeks I received a starting date at their training centre, Annandale street depot Leith, but firstly to get measured for a uniform, and apply for my conductors license which was no problem, I couldn't have resigned under better circumstances from the bakery, when I came on shift to find I was the only one along with the well sloshed Foreman he was nuggets (drunk) and depressed, effing and blinding to me to get a move on well just seeing someone coming into work in that state was enough for me I just took off my white hat put it in his pocket turned and walked out he was screaming and yelling dogs abuse I'd like to have been a fly on the wall in the morning, best sleep I had that night, after 3 weeks a baker I never got my free biscuits, now with my conductor uniform including my badge and number given by the council and police, firmly sown on my lapel of the long overcoat similar to the army great coats. Every piece of clothing was required in winter time standing exposed at the rear bus platform open footway at the foot of the spiral stairway most of the shift was spent in this position when I finished with the schooling and practice runs with an expert conductor on how to press the bell, clearly and properly our passengers were forbidden by law to press the bell press once for go twice to stop and three to keep going don't stop in others words we are full up, part of my fitments to go with of the uniform was the crossed shoulder straps on my hip the multi open leather coin bag and the other hip. The ticket machine with multi money setting dial, my base depot was the same as Tommy's, Longstone Sighthill being junior in ranking I had the split shifts to put up with taking out a bus at the start of the day 2am until 7am go home and back out at 8pm till midnight notwithstanding with freezing winter my car (no anti-freeze then) frozen solid also no heating systems wrapping a rug around my legs after scraping some ice from the screen in front of my face, enough to see a wee bit no other traffic on the road, getting (regularly) as far east Calder and forced to a stop as the steam from under the bonnet covered the windscreen blinding my view and the engine spluttering to a halt. I'd sit there till the heat from the engine defrosted the hose pipes sufficient for it to restart and with care make it to work the bus was not a great deal better at least for me upstairs and down was like a freezer, the ice was not only thick inside the windows but be careful on the stairs and back platform which only started to thaw out as the bus moved away, the driver was lucky his wee cab was separate and the engine had been running before we got to it to make sure it could go out at this time of the morning most of the passengers were men and nearly all smokers all having the first cough of the morning spluttering and spitting their lungs out (on their cough stick FAG) it didn't take long before a thick blue haze enveloped the whole of the bus and as it drove along the road a smoke trail was created behind it. You had your regular who squeezed a penny into the palm of your hand that was the signal that they didn't want a ticket so it went straight into my pocket you'd have to be careful not to get caught an inspector was seen at the next stop you made like a B-line for these passengers and issued them with a 1 penny ticket, they never issued me with gloves but mother was always one step ahead when she knew I was going for the job she knitted me up with a pair of finger less woollen ones, I never thought I'd see the day I'd appreciate something as useful as them since back at the Depot after my early part of the shift they had their own canteen hot meals fry-ups most of the men were on regular shift, others preferred the split shifts but nearly all of them lived in there uniform spending a hell of a time in here playing CRIBB but my first and only day shift came as an overtime spot no-one else wanted and that was new year's day I done a full 12 hour shift without breaks it was a snowy bloody cold day and a bus full of boozed-up folk drunks. Loads of broth sickness all over everything my feet splashed in it but everybody was great I was offered loads of nips of whiskey and beer it was hard work saying no without offending but the driver seemed well versed he had already given me an empty half bottle and a warning take all Drams, no matter the model, I could have filled twice that amount even given he had a few well measures sized gulps at break times I shudder at the thought of that stuff, bloody awful in my CUBBY hole (lock-up) under the spiral stairs there was at least 2 ½ dozen bottles of beer differing in sizes by the end of the day. The great thing was no inspector all day I was a bit red kipped (faced) when my final takings for the day were some 5/6 d (27p) officially that was but my hand was well pressed and red raw and pocket weight down with coppers (pennies) thankfully all that went well. Back at the depot they were 'eight sheets to the wind pissed and everybody's pal, and all drunk driving in safety and some using buses (driving buses) I was only in the job a couple of months when one day on the upper deck to see this guy sitting there drawing on a fag (smoking), and it was my old mate Ronnie Campbell in the uniform of a Scottish Prison Officer the last time I saw Ronnie was at Easter road barracks, 15th C company para, reg, he was the same guy the uniform was different what with my flat cap full peak hat and him in his but with Ronnie a new look slashed peak all the looks of a guards=man blonde hair and laughing fine sharp blue eyes a guy that was respected by many. Just before he got off the bus outside Saughton Prison he'd furnished me with the home offices phone number within six weeks I had a medical interview and assessment interviews with the governor himself of Saughton prison with only one question at the time left me a wee bit flummoxed, would I prefer to work with young people as I felt this interview was going my way and at this point go with the flow mike yes of course I didn't realise I had a choice. After another week of tooing and frooing to the storeroom being tailor measured for my uniform should say uniforms 2 great coats 2 trousers 2 Tunic's, Baton with leather strap brand spanking new bonnets (peaked caps)of 1x30 inch length of stainless steel key chains 2 black clip on ties (in the unlikely event a prisoner wants to take you for a walk) 1 police breast pocket whistle and chain for the top pocket 4 long sleeves blue (light) collar less shirts and a dozen stud fastening collars to be well starched on each wash the only thing that was different to the police was they had a chequered black and white hat band. Thankfully starch and collar studs were readily available at the Haberdashery's I received a letter with a date and place of start the Edinburgh young offenders institution her majesty's prisons known as the Yo's which had its own separate gate nearest the chesser corner of the jail. Well turned out in my uniform I was escorted down the corridor which was the administration unit leading off its doors all well marked to describe what was behind them including the governor chief officers the door opened sharply a short well dressed and groomed gent stepped out in front of us the officer escorting me snapped up a good snapper of a salute sir. I didn't need to be told I instantly followed suit. thank you, he replied looking the officer straight in the eye and nodded wandered off where we had just come from that's the boss Mr Berty Nobles also well known as Square Go 'Nobles' my governor who rose through the ranks from Barlinnie Prison Glasgow. We continued down the corridor for some way then arrived of at a wooden double door which for all looked like warehouse doors except a normal height the officer pulled out a key linked to his chain opened one side of the door he was blocking my view but it was very noisy on the other side he took a very short step and opened another Iron Barred door clearly I could see what everybody thought a cell block or prison hall really looked like this was my entrance to Saughton Hotel as it was known in the local pub song this was Forth hall there was a second hall Pentland and closed in and more modern both held the 16 years to 21 year olds whereas the jail housed the over 21s adults. I felt as though I was on a film set although the place was noisy it was well organised the slightest foot step echoed shit even the lad with a mop and bucket had a ringing of its own and even officers speaking from the top flat to us below spoke loudly and clearly in order to give clear instructions. No one seemed to be hanging around all very busy doing their tasks over and above that the opening and closing the heavy steel cell doors with the coming and goings of a few prisoners some of them carrying out tasks like cleaning the hall floor industrious and silent I was to act as spare officer for the next weeks trying not to get in the road whilst I awaited a date to the prison officers school although the environment was very strange to begin with I found it easy to work with being very military. Yes sir, no sir.

Prisoner's Song (Saughton Song Night)

I was picked up in the high
street one Saturday night

I woke in the morning,
with a hell of a fright
the judge said to me
you can go for a spell
six months hard labour
in Saughton hotel (prison)

Versus:
too—raa—loo-
to—raa—leigh
Oh, how would you
-how would you-
like to be me.

They drove me in carriage
They drove me in state
And never stopped once
till they reached the big gate

when I got there
I rang the big bell
That was my entrance to
Saughton hotel

Too raa loo
Too raa leigh
Oh how would you
how would you
Like to be me

With bars on the windows
And bars on the doors
And lovely red carpets
All over the floors

So now I've been there
now I can tell,
there is nae place in Scotland
like Saughton hotel

1971 saw me at the Scottish prison service training centre Polmont near Falkirk which was more like a hotel which was to be home for the next 8 weeks Monday to Friday 40 of us trainees from all our Scotland even the ones who were working at Polmont Institute and lived half a mile from here had to stay over during the working week. We all had a room to ourselves, which was inspected each day we were monitored all the time discipline was of the highest order haircuts a must you had no warning the results were kept until the last minutes of the last day this was right up my street marching and inspections of turn out all male they did have or we heard women's courses like being back at school in the class rooms working out a prison sentence into the last day of sentence watching for leap years adjusting for remissions all seemed garbage but was well used in practice lecturers from psychiatrists doctors police chief and social workers and very useful instructions and certification for first aid. The centres only night time recreation was a full size snooker table and only one payphone which had a timer on it as there was always a queue we were allowed out at night but not to the local pub but local established officers who used it were well warned that the centre took a dim view on anyone using it this suited me and some others on a couple of evenings I sneaked off home for a few hours after tea only managing half an hour as the centre was locked up with us inside on curfew that was doggy. However after 8 weeks and many exams we gathered at the main notice board to read the results it was impossible to read them from behind the throng of bodies some at the front shouting our places as listed I heard my name being called a number of times along with others but I thought I am hearing things, it can't be right but not paying much attention to all the ranting I finely saw it for myself I was 2nd and not from the bottom but 2nd place at the top I don't know how that happened lots of well-dones from all the guys and staff I felt very strange!! Some of our calculations in dealing with prisoners cash unpaid fines etc. we had to re school ourselves due to the new money decimalisation 240 pennies to our old pound now 100 pence although it first appeared simple it gave some of us a wee-bit problem especially when it came to their wages and spending power in the prison canteen it upset staff and prisoners who did think a miscalculation (fraud) was happening I returned to do my 2 years as a discipline officer (the qualifying period of any officer) after which or during this period you could be dismissed or promoted until this point you were only a junior officer senior only to those whose starting date was behind yours, Now on 2nd division and just by chance this was Ronnie Campbell's great as far as prisoners were concerned we were called sir or mr and them by name or number and no swearing by either of us, no matter what these rules they were simple and very effective, easy to apply on an early shift starting on the gallery (junior officers like myself began their career on the top flat) 3rd floor in the forth-hall at 6am sharp on the gable-end cathedral like windows extending all the way from the ground floor and high vaulted roof space all windows securely open to get rid of the stench of urine and sweating bodies and other stinks, my eyes watered at all this in the dark and coldness of the morning any heat in the hall was lost great coat collar turned up some officers had scarves and gloves on it was so cold we went door by door to each cell a small coloured card attached to the outside (colour donates religion) one card one body inside the maximum prisoners to a cell were 3 even at this early stage after returning from training school I had to shadow a more senior officer during this part of the shift and it wasn't long before I got to why we had to call live bodies at this time in the morning down to the control desk below. I opened the door at the same time flicking the outside light switch on I was close behind him as he stepped just inside the cell calling to the 3 prisoners lying asleep , to stir them into movement to prove them alive. This was my first sight of things to come he near jumped back and over the hand railing his feet left marks of fresh blood shouting down to the desk for the M.O (medical officer) in a panicky loud voice he regained his footing another senior officer pushed past me to join him in the door way I couldn't work out in that instance what the hell was going on but the sight of blood at any time was one of the most feared sights. I moved away and back to the central bridge desk and stairhead down below all the doors were slammed shut officers on each landing gathered around there desks some glancing up looking for an answer as to what's happening the two officers at our cell door stepped to one side letting two blood soaked covered figures exit wrapped in blankets with blood covered bare feet the medical officer came up the stairs two at a time on seeing the two boys he hesitated ready to question them but the officers at the door called to him shouting into the still open door what came of this was the third boy still in the cell on the top bunk had at some time through the night slashed his wrists and bled to death the blood drained down onto the bed below both these boys were treated for shock, I really wanted to run, the cell was sealed up until the police checked out that they were happy. It was a suicide outside the cell all the blood was cleaned up very quickly by pass men (trustees) and when this was done everything went back to normal, but even the prisoners who saw nothing acted even more meekish than ever later in the morning they were all locked up until the body was removed the cell cleaned up and that was my very first taste of what was to come, but my next one was a stabbing which happened in the same forth hall ground floor. As I was just entering through the barred gate into the cell block a skirmish of officers and a couple of boys was taking place at the far end other officers entered a cell one came out with a boy held in an arm-lock the boy had some clearly visible blood on him he was frog marched past me, I could hear the principle officer in charge calling out for him to be put in the strong cells they disappeared towards them, In silence as I stood by the main desk awaiting instructions as we were trained to be in these circumstances and not run around getting in the way, observe as they say assess what happened one boy was sitting in his single cell (all the cells on the ground were single some for observation or other reasons) another boy who had a dispute with him stabbed him in the chest with a homemade knife the mo.(medical officer) who examined his lifeless body reported he couldn't find the knife the police said they couldn't find knife. it was found at the post-mortem inside his chest. The first boy stabbed him and left immediately followed in by a second who saw the knife sticking in his chest so he just stood on it that was the boy I saw being taken to the strong cells. The coal miners were still disrupting the whole country the home front was still affected the government began to ration electrical supplies as the miners picketed all coal supply depots and power stations so the power was cut to named areas each week by as much as 3 to 4 days depending on the amount the population was using, we had gas controlled heaters but as the controls were electric we lost everything, heating and cooking lighting torch's and batteries were in very short supply and the cost went through the roof, the poor old candles ran out of supplies much earlier in this period but Dolly began to use other methods one was a Jam-Jar with a small amount of water cooking oil and a couple of short pieces of string which was dipped in this fluid and when the power was off we had light we had a number of large flasks filled with boiling water to heat baby food as much as could be done with the power on washing ironing bathing or find a friend whose supply was on and likewise for them. Going home after a back shift was a completely weird experience. The prison was not spared during this period even getting to and from work could be a problem petrol pumps were electrically operated so keeping a fuel tank full and a couple of gallons in the boot was a must as even the petrol depots were picketed and supplies limited the heating in the cells was by a 9 inch diameter pipe carrying stream which ran through the whole blocks from cells to cell, the boiler house somehow with the help of a generator kept this going, and when the power was on they could get out to the workshops to work, but on the days the power was off they spent 23 hours behind the locked doors except for slop out (emptying chamber pots etc) and exercise once the power was off they had no lighting in or out of the cells or halls, we had to use old fashioned hurricane lamps they had long lonely hours even the kitchens at the time could only turn put white bread sandwich's and no hot meals for days but the kitchens somehow manages to keep drums of hot surgery tea to wash them down, no bad behaviour was tolerated by the governor and only a few skirmishes behind the cell door took place but he was even harder with punishments that anyone, one of my jobs as the junior officer which I did not relish was the shit bomb patrol, which was normally done at about 7am where I would escort a passman (trustee) who would be armed with a tin bucket and small shovel, collect up all the droppings that were deposited out of the cell windows through the night as there were only 'Po's (chamber pots) to have a Bowel movement during light out, nobody wanted to sleep with such a thing whether it was theirs or not it didn't matter what the containers were anything from a sock tobacco tin or rolled up in a sheet of paper if nothing was at hand, then it got the 'heave ho' out of the window, but with a lock up for 23 hours during the duration of the miner-strike I'd repeat this task up to 3 times a day.

It wasn't only convicted or united prisoners that we locked up but at the start of a shift one of our ,most senior officer who has been out all night at the masonic lodge meeting arrived on duty as full as a boot (drunk), he came staggering up the stairs bouncing off the rails, he just bumped his way past me as I stood on the bridge next to the desk oblivious to anybody pulling the chain and door keys from his pocket, fumbled at the lock of an empty cell, crashed down on a bed his hat lay on the floor he was out for the count a quick acting officer grabbed the door handle slamming it shut before the prisoners wandering about Shopping out were aware of what was happening, I was totally taken back by this on peeping through the spy hole it was very obvious he was in a drunken comma, we went about our duties for the next couple of hours, when without warning a call came from the main desk, below, the governor sometimes he did put in a surprise appearance it was bad enough getting spare prisoners bodies who were not already at work back behind their cell doors to smarten them up. But shit, he was still fast asleep the governor if it suited him would sometimes inspect empty cells worst still he always nearly started with the top flat, and took as much time as he liked, up he came I was positioned right next to the empty cell(closed door) the senior officer advised him that 28 cells for inspection sir also as normal told him 2 were empty when he said that I nearly shit myself I was more terrified that this bugger would be disturbed and bang on the door to get out. The tension continued right up until the governor left the gallery it was near the end of our complete shift 1pm before this sorry for himself officer eventually came out and what a bloody state. Another of our junior officers tasks called upon to do was because of the troubles in Ireland there was a war going on because some political ongoing issue people were being blown up and shot at on a very regular basis, many on both sides were held in jails throughout mainland GB prison officers clambered to serve in the Northern Ireland island jails, where Irish officers refused to serve where political prisoners where involved for fear of their lives our officers were on fantastic double wages and expenses, but many were under threats, some seriously assaulted but when the overspill of prisoners came across to mainland Britain we had officers working both sides of the water some became marked men by the IRA at the time of all threats made against them were taken seriously wherever a phone call of a bomb threat in the prison officers' car park just outside the gates using a mirror tied onto a golf club I had to check car to car, once a senior officer who had just returned from Northern Ireland was a bit loud in speaking out on how he handled political prisoners in their own land returned home one might to his married quarters house and family to find his cat nailed to the garden gate by the tail dead its throat cut and the letter 'Provo' painted beside it. They didn't always get it all there way another well liked young officer happened to cross swords with one of the political higher ranker whilst on the exercise yard in Saughton, and was quietly threatened also his family, the officer could and probably should have reported it to the governor but instead when we were going on duty one morning at 6am we let this officer go down to the gallery's ahead he had a cell key and gently in the darkness opened the single cell where this guy was sleeping, took out his baton, and taped him gently on the head, see I can get to you too any 'fucking time'. And that was the end of the matter, the day I lost 22 prisoners, not long in the jail I was handed a set of perimeter door keys, as I was the only spare officer and still very green, I was told to take these prisoners out to the Football Pitches I hadn't a clue where the pitches were and said so the reply was just follow them they all gathered around in the boots, shorts and a jumble of football shirts, and not a sign of good order the door was opened into the yard they all took off right beside the 15 foot perimeter fence, gathering around a small locked gate, only 10 or so feet beyond was a 20ft high concrete wall caped with German razor wire, panicking was in the word, I opened the gate and managed to count them through into this gap 'yes, all 22' as I locked the gate behind me I was taken by surprise that I was mobbed as they were jumping and running on the spot calling come on sir, my mind was expecting them to be off running round between the fence and wall in one direction or another, but they bloody well hung around I struggled to get the key out of the lock without shaking as I turned to face them I noticed a cluster of them pointing to a very small doorway in the wall, I could hear the voices of my fellow officers talking to each other over the radio I had attached to my breast pocket. OH shit, I was sorely tempted to call for help, but with the instruction, just follow the prisoners, ringing in my ears I pushed my way through them into the 4 foot narrow gate key in lock it was opened towards me eager hands helping it open and without warning they one by one dived out through this opening, I was struggling with my priorities, keeping hold of the keys still in the lock and me attached by my chain I couldn't even see at this point what the hell was beyond this door I had not a clue finally I got the keys out and by this time most had jumped out between them I saw a figure of a woman with a pram walk by only a few feet away oh shit, they've escaped my whole mind froze! the headlines of the newspapers 22 prisoner escape as the last one disappeared out through the doorway, the women pushing the pram, with another Bairn walking beside, strangely waved to me, knowingly I gingerly peered out to see the prisoners running away and fanning out in the distance the women had stopped and I heard a voice calling daddy, daddy then in one frame shot of my eye I saw between me and the woman the fine wire meshed fence looking up high I saw it was topped with German razor wire, and the woman was my wife Dolly with Billy in the Pram and Helen shouting to me by this time I focused on the huge dirt area surrounded by fencing, the football area was indeed outside the perimeter wall but surrounded by a high medium security fence, also we had just moved house from Livingston to Kings Knowe in Edinburgh which was set behind the prison, my mother lived near the front of the prison and a much favoured short cut by the way of a foot path between the prison and water of Leith just by a coincidence Dolly was there, my anxieties of an escape with the embarrassment of Helen calling to me, the prisoners reacting by whistles and jeer! I had a right (Beemer) red face! But 22 prisoners all correct and Ok! Panic over! I was the only one panicking! You had to have eyes in the back of your head, a fight could break out in front of you the natural basic instinct was to get involved and break it up. My policy was based on other older officers stay back keep an open eye on what is happening around them, I was, I saw, I did, Unfortunately officers blindly go into the mallee of fighting prisoners, the prisoners on the edge of such fights take advantage of the uncovered backs of the officers and throw anything at hand into the scrum. The place that gets the biggest response was the dining hall many an officer covered in custard and soup! Talking about soup it's not the first I've seen an old MOP being used to stir the soup, I did like the break from the routine of the prison, where I had to go on escort duties like the old Royal Infirmary at Lauriston using the old heavy Iron D handcuffs with a screwed bolt type key I was sitting in the back of the van with a young lad going to the hospital along with others (4) I stepped down leading the way with him attached to my right wrist wrong. I was on my own, he just sat there laughing, he had slipped his hand out of the cuffs, did I not feel a twit, normally he would be put on governor's report and lost a couple of days remission, but I saw the funny side of it, but what a red kip me putting him on report. explain that to the GOV, I learned my lesson, on another visit I had a strict escape on the Cuffs upto the hospital VD clinic and I was under instructions to stay with him. Normally I had the final word on whether I let them off the cuffs, but with those ones strictly escapees even the medical staff had to take me where ever he went, we were called into a fair-sized room in the centre stood an examination couch with me still attached he dropped his pants and lay down a nurse and a doctor working away at his penis, eventually she took a large sheet of tissue paper made a hole in it and pushed his penis through it, I was beginning to feel in the way, and I could give some privacy to them(talk about being a spare prick) he (the prisoner) was doing what I wanted to do, shut my eyes without much warning the nurse put some liquid on a cloth and holding his penis firmly dabbed the end of the fore skin the guy and I near leapt with the aggression she put on it. After a few seconds the doctor turned to him grabbed hold and with a gun (like welding iron) touched the end his penis, I was horrified to see what looked like a skin wart on the end of the foreskin burn away in blue smoke, Oh Jesus Christ, I thought that was bad till one afternoon two young guys had a stand up 'square-go' fight in their place of work, the metal salvage yard one had used a hatchet and made a right mess of the others head by the time I got to him in the prison surgery his whole head was swathed in blood stained bandage again I had the strict instructions to stay cuffed at all the times no matter; he lay on the operation table only given local anaesthesia I tried my damnedest to look away as the bandage came off as the doctor and nurses moved around I was more than in the way and I felt like dropping every time I looked down at the huge gashes right down to the bone as the doctor pulled all the flesh together bit-by-bit all the time they all had surgical clothing and masks I only had my complete uncovered uniform worst still this guy never expressed any pain or discomfort I was with him handcuffed until we returned to the jail. Although I started as a discipline officer his whole working life revolved around good order and discipline in the daily running of a prison, I had set my sights on becoming a plumbing instructor who's duties lay with in the industrial and fabric of a prison everyday installation and maintenance practices using prisoners skilled or otherwise but firstly I had to complete my probationary duties on the galleries, then complete a trade test for 4 weeks in the area of my choice, plumbing, after putting in my application Mr Berty Nobles (my governor) called me into his office and gave me a stern warning that no officer of his was even applying for or going over to the industrial side of the service and that was final, Jesus. And he was not a man to argue with. Strangely just a few weeks later I received a letter at home from the home office telling me to attend the clerk of worker's office, and under there instructions to follow and complete a four week ability test on instructing plumbing the chief engineer a wee man white hair showing from under his peaked cap the peak itself covered in white silk like ribbon (snow as we knew or called it) and resplendent with a ribbon of war medal awards chief Stewart introduced me to Bob jones and Bob Mcintosh, Both middle aged plumbing instructors to whom I was attached to during my stay here in the jail itself (Saughton Prison Engineer Department) I was issued with a sandy brown Bib and brace dungarees also jacket worn out over my uniform which was always worn by the works dept. Also a handful of tools (all hand-tools—hammers, saws, files etc.) with the added rider, all tools counted at the start of the day, and at the end. Any broken saw blades or tools were replaced by the stores one for one. I was taken up to C hall 21 years and over male hall all lifers (capital criminals). At the top floor I was shown into the archway (ablutions area) which had been completely stripped out of all its old plumbing and fabric, only the top of waste pipes just sticking out of the floor along with the hot and cold valves attached, I was told I had 4 weeks in which to fit it all on my own, no labourers all toiles and cubicles (8) wash basins hot and cold (10) slop-out bays and (10) urinals and all had overhead cisterns! This was my test piece! During the whole week (1st week) I only had one small incident one morning while working away in the arches the prisoners were wandering about unsupervised as was the way of lifers, they operated on trust and good behaviour with only one discipline officer in attendance at any time this young prisoner beckoned me to his cell door then inside when you went away last night sir, I saw you had left these behind, so I hid them in my cell so that others wouldn't take them, he pulled back the blanket on the bed exposing a clean white bed sheet on it lay a small file and 12 inch hacksaw blade. I have got to admit that I never checked my tools before or after instinct kicked in I knew he had me dead in the water quick thinking I nodded at him but not giving much away I took the tools thanked him, and walked away the next morning I went to his empty cell and placed a Mars bar under his pillow, when I passed him later, he looked at me and I gave a wee-nod. then again I passed him later he looked at me and gave another wee-mod that was the end, I learned to count my tools, I realised that he could have made big problems, honesty and discipline work both ways and are to be seen. At the end of the first week everything was assembled ready for testing, even the cubicle partitions were in place, but when I went to get the keys for the lockup where the water values were located on the ground floor level. No keys both the plumbers who had them were, one on leave, the other helping out in another prison I couldn't test my work no water. chief told me I'd have to cover all the maintenance on my own but using the two squads of the prisoners who work with the plumbers the six of them were all plumbers when on the outside I was given a tip by one of the engineers mind and bring in a pot of jam to go with their toast on morning and afternoon breaks, one of their previous instructors refused to give them their wee-treat when they laid some drainage, on back filling the trench, and bringing the drain into use, the whole place flooded after digging it all up he found a bag of cement stuffed in it they got there Jam from me, I never had problems with them although on one day I got an old lag (old school prisoner) of a plumber not a lifer, just to keep him happy and out of the way, he requested of me to put him on Governor report why I asked him. I'm going out in 2 days and I've just had a visit from my wife she's in the middle of decorating and wants me to help, he told her to bugger off. Now he wants to lose a few days remission so that it's all done by the time he gets out; his request was denied, but I came in the next day and there he was all smiles, he only went and thrown a plate on the floor in the gallery's, and was awarded 4 days loss of remission. At the end of this 4 week spell, the last 3, maintaining all the plumbing, water leaks washers blockages and renewals and keeping a 'hour-by-hour' log book and time table, also report on each prisoner abilities during my time with them, I returned to next door to await my results, (back to the Yo's) after about 3 or 4 weeks I was called to the chiefs office in the prison where I was met and interviewed about my results by some head guy from the home office, I was taken aback by his news and comments that normally they expect the job, (test piece) completed within 4 weeks, and to be fair to me would I be willing to come back and given another 2 weeks to complete it, I couldn't believe what I was hearing, it was my turn to explain that it was completed but untested and that I had been looking after his jail with 2 squads of prisoners. Fortunately for me I showed him the works records, poor guy he was not told this, he was full of apologies, and asked me to forget all what he said, but asked me to help him by doing the two planned weeks, just because the head office sanctioned it but ignore it as a test, and that I has passed! This done, as with any new position, is also meant a move to another prison and married quarters, within weeks, I was given a posting as plumbing instructor in Barlinnie (Glasgow) had a look at married quarters that went with it but I found I was on a hiding to nothing. we had our bags packed carpets up all the systems ready to go. then told that a guy senior to me in service has taken the quarter only for the reason he had more time-in over the next couple of months I was offered Polmont then Peterhead. Finally, the nail was in the coffin Perth prison. The top security jail in Scotland this was a good family posting so the four of us went up on one of my day off to see the jail and hopefully the quarter. my wee Morris 1000 drove me right up to the Big wooden gates. Dolly and the Bairns just waited in the car while I joined some of the resident officers (all in uniform) waiting to be let in at the picket gate, I had a wee blether whilst waiting, I introduced myself to some of them, the door opened and we filtered inside and gathered at the larger iron gates for the same officer to open them, I just mentioned to him why I was there, at that he opened the gate, letting us all into the inner courtyard closing the gate behind us, after wandering around from closed doorways looking for the works office, I found an officer who was very helpful and pointed the way, I eventually entered into the building to meet up with the chief work officer, he never questioned for I.D or anything and seemed to take this man in civvies as he was, he even gave me the address of the house I was to be allocated, one of the men took me for a tour of the jail layout when done I returned to Dolly and the Bairns, before coming home we had a look at the house from the outside it looked great, I turned down the advice from the fellow officers on my return to Edinburgh telling some of the failings of security in Perth, but I regretted in not taking it and reporting this to the home office, what a story, the story came filtering through that Perth quarters was being disputed by senior officers stationed in Perth prison itself and I would be fifth or sixth down the list and not even at that would not know what house we would get. As it stood a member of the family spotted an advert in the evening news for a job as gas technician that was it. I applied for it and was offered the position, what with me successfully completing my probation, and my pay packet advancing to £28 per week!! And the offer of an exchange to a main door house, front, back, and side garden also keeping her indoors, happy was too much to ignore, I resigned after moving into 41 Oxgangs Farm Avenue. I took up my new job as gas technician with Scobie Mcintosh catering engineers at fountain bridge work shop. I was one of three engineers, the others were electrical and mechanical we covered the whole of Scotland and supplied with a van each, I was to be flung in a the deep end and well tested on my lack of electrical skills but I wasn't the only one requiring introduction as there were only the three of us, we were on many occasions at different parts of the country on the same day, at first I was horrified to find myself in a highland hotel, working on gas appliances then the manager would complain that an industrial food mixer had broken down, I was soon to find that if it were not for a skills sharing agreement between the three of us engineers the company could not function effectively or financially, but I like them gained valuable skills when confronted with uncharted appliances electrical mechanical or steam, it was a case of picking up the phone speaking to the appropriate engineer, don't panic and stay with the job till the problem was solved, I was hungry to learn, too bloody hungry I was in the kitchen of the world famous golf hotel North of Edinburgh working on a faulty gas cooker when the kitchen was near to closing, and only stayed open to serve the legendary film and comedian star Bob Hope, he had just been served and the waiters were bringing back some of the serving equipment, my eye caught sight of a four wheeled heating plater with a silver dome top the waiter had just removed the remains of the roast putting it in a fridge nearby, I was always interested in what heated those things and we were advised by our boss to have a look at equipment when in kitchens to build up a working knowledge, so here was an opportunity the whole body was of hard wood well-polished I hinged back the huge silver dome lid, revealing the spiked silver platter, with bits of cooked meat remaining I struggled to lift the plater off its framed base it was very warm to touch so I made sure there were no trailing electrical wires, there were none after prizing it up with a screw driver slowly it gave way, I peered in to see a naked flame from a candle, slowly revealing more, too my horror, the candle sat in the bottom of the 'shallow well' completely caked in burnt fat and grease, 'Yuk' I shut it quickly went over to the restaurant door and peeped out to see Bob hope and company finish their main course, I was learning well. not long after I was awaken one night with murderous pain in my lower back and ended up in hospital after 3 days on painkillers I passed what I was told a kidney stone, so small it was only a tiny black dot on tissue paper(white) I got home only to be followed close behind by a professor from the hospital asking if I would return right away to take part in some study tests which would take upto 8 days with my firms knowledge and agreement for them to allow me to take the time off they gratefully agreed to paying me in full pay and a taxi service for Dolly to visit me when ever, I was to spend 8 weeks in hospital it was a nightmare all there tests went completely wrong, on the end they were going to operate on my bowel, thankfully I refused, I had no problems until this period with my health, the end result was they never knew what caused the stone in the kidney as he promised. When I got back to work the miners' strike was crippling the whole country to the point every part of Britain was under a three day working days, whole areas were allocated power supplies for up to four days a week, It meant always having a full tank of petrol all over the place pumps not working tankers stuck in refining, I never knew when I was called to a premise on site, that it may have been a genuine fault of a piece of machinery or power cut, having to stay days with it until the power was put back on just to test it, our office staff and workshop machinists only turned up to for work on the days when the power was on, but us three engineer worked the full week as we were mobile but Scobie Mcintosh were great to their staff and paid them there wages in full, on one of my trips over to Fife to a wee family bakery in Kinghorn I always liked to visit the local boat yards dreaming about having my own boat someday well I was at the right place at the right time a wee wooden cabin cruiser was high and dry on the beach, and well with in my budget, it never had an engine but I was promised the loan of wee out board it was an open boat with a small cuddy cabin, I arranged for Tommy and my dad to come with me, and sail it across the four miles to Granton Harbours Corinthian Yachting Club, a friend drove us over on Xmas Eve just after mid-day although the sun was shining in FIFE a sea harr (fog) blotted out the whole of the Edinburgh coast line but we could see Inchkeith an island half way and hoped to see Edinburgh once we got to that point other than my experience of the cruiser in Sydney, I had the most knowledge even Tommy couldn't swim so was busy baling out the rain water so we could drag the boat into the water the two of them decided to watch me from the comfort of the boating club bar, after more than halfway across to the island we had to keep bailing out and it wasn't raining but we could just make out the dock yard cranes of Granton on the Edinburgh side, with no lifesaving equipment or fuel, we limped into Granton Harbour only to be met by the man himself, Harbour Master, standing high above us as we sailed in through the twin entrance walls where have you come from, he shouted with a wee bit of more that annoyance in his voice when I shouted back kinghorn, what, your bloody kidding there's bugger all else out there but you, now that he mentioned it, I never saw another craft I called up to him that I thought we had a wee leak, he just pointed to a slipway farther into the harbour lucky for us the tide was not fully out so we tied up in a instance along came two guys from our sailing club, the master had phoned them telling them to get us out of the water, they were well versed and had brought a tractor pulling a trailer and wooden frame we stood back and let the experts do the necessary, what a start to Xmas 1972 I spent quite a lot of spare time at the weekends lying under the boat out in the freezing cold trying to repair all the wee holes, in the Hull, but every time I filled the thing using a hose pipe, water just dripped out, but one old boy who seemed a wee bit of an expert told me to get a bucket of runny pure cement, pour it inside the hull and it will find and deal any wee-holes shit it worked I was well pleased, but I was in for a nasty surprise, the IRA were busy smuggling stuff from mainland Britain to Ireland using small boats one day before my wee boat now names the Wee JEAN was ready to go into the water I was working in a café up in Hanover street Edinburgh I was just wrapping up my tools out on to the pavement to put them into the van, when I was aware of the young women in the company of a middle aged man followed me out of the café and as I was opening the back door of the van stepped upto me. Hi Michael and in a quiet strong Northern Irish accent continued to ask, when you put the Wee Jean in the water, he'd like to hire your services are you game, I stuttered and stammered in complete horror at what was being said, I must have even looked the part, as he never waited for a full answer, the pair of them just took off and disappeared into the crowd, leaving my mind in a very shocked and confused state, so much as that I went straight up the High street, where the police city HQ formally was, I was soon interviewed by special branch who told me that this was happening up and down the country, where they were ferrying everything they could, from one part to another right around G.B reassuring me that they helped to get me to act out sympathy in the hope of employing me rather than violence or force, what bothered me, how they know my name and how come they met at work, they must have followed me, shit! After that and with some doubt in my mind that with my involvement in the prison and my old parachute regiments bad press against the Irish folk my enthusiasm for boating had really taken a bad blow, I sold it for a small profit, Dad he was getting work in from all directions on top of this army sweeping contracts he won the national health boiler cleaning contracts for the Lothian and border hospitals, but getting the men was difficult so I volunteered to help at the weekends along with Tommy in between his shifts on the buses. It was animalistic work most of the Huge Lancashire boilers were solid fuel hand stoked boilers, as they could not shut them down completely and 3 or 4 boilers in each hospital sitting side by side we only cleaned one at a time and had only 8 hours in which to do the job the amount of soot removed was so much that more than one large skip was used to remove it all from site, as there were at least six of us employed for this and part of the agreement was that the boiler being cleaned was drained and flushed out using cold water too cool it before we climbed inside the chimney, Health and safety were not known by any of us at this time, but it was well accepted by all that the boiler men were not about to cool the boiler down for in their reason was it would take days to get them back up to temperature which was very true. No more said, once the flame bed was out and empty of cynders we'd strip down to our underpants open the flue door entering head first the heat was of such a blast like when you open your oven door to check a casserole, try climbing in, the first reaction was to with draw catch your breath then slowly re-enter into the dark oven leading with your right hand with torch, arm extended forward left one trailing by your side lying completely horizontal on top of the burning soot your head touching the roof the sides only some twenty inches apart, steel soot encrusted plates, quarter inch thick with boiling water on the other sides all around you, by the time you had dug out all the soot, passing it out through your entrance way bit by bit you would be able stand upright and walk along this back to front some twenty five feet by 20 inch by 6 ft. there were at least four or five areas in each boiler, using your hands and feet only no room for tools passing it man to man as space was cleared another man entered, you never even sweated as the heat evaporated it on your skin, blisters appeared after touching the hot plates, now and again the encouragement by dad(who never ever went in) with a good supply of beer at hand and words of encouragement when it was getting time for the pub going for a shower was a waste of time we scrubbed each other only to find the soot turned to gel for a week after we still had mascara eyes and engrained hands with lots of cream on our slow healing burns, although it was hard work I liked working with dad and his men a great bunch of characters and loads of story lines in the Pub later but dad had a queer way of paying me most of the time he'd stop at a butcher or bakers and come out loaded with carriers bags of goodies, he'd pay off his men in hard cash but as usual I was last to be dropped off its mince stew or rolls, pies I enjoyed It and Dolly was happy enough this was always a stickler for him food if there was enough on the table he was happy a throwback to the days of destitution but mother made up for him as she was in charge of the cash bag so without dads knowledge she would give Dolly or I a £5 note quietly pushing it into our pocket mind she done this to all of us whether we worked or not both were great providers, dads firm Lums-dun shifted from Haymarket to 22 Ardmillan terrace Gorgie (1969), giving dad a handout with all kinds of work including general building and roofing slating and flat roofing, in particular when his men failed to turn out I even had to take days of work or even cancel my workloads replanning much of my own work I couldn't let him down, the country was in a heck of a state, the strike seriously effecting most walks on life, flying pickets running up and down the country Scobie Mcintosh was being effected badly what with the three day working week planning work was a logistical nightmare the guys in the work shop although paid a full working week somehow saw us three engineers were black legging and should be working 3 days somehow the boss saw fit to ask us to take two off which meant if only Edinburgh and our area were on a 3 day that week, inverness or where ever we are working the full week and one of our customers had a breakdown we couldn't attend that's how much control the miners had on the country. But I couldn't just sit so I decided if I can't still do sweeping then I will try window cleaning and never having washed any in my life. (other than in Sydney 60s) I asked a friend how do I do it, he told me to boil the cloths first, and get the starch out first polish finish with shammy cloth, so I set about knocking a door in Colintonmains four in a block, doing each house once a month at 50p once I got one or two in a street then others followed as long as I was regular between this and Scobie Mcintosh things were busy, but word came through from a couple of prison officers I saw from time to time that things were changing in the jail transfers were no longer mandatory for officers everything was for the better, chimney sweeps in particular were dying breed, even the new customers in the window cleaning couldn't afford once a month and were dodging being in when it came to wash day asking if I could come back Friday nights after tea time to pay so I had to call to most on a Friday to collect, some bastards sat with the lights out pretending they were out, on top of all this the country was well entrenched in the cold war with the eastern bloc continued threats of nuclear missiles being aimed at Edinburgh and Fife to repeated warnings of a 4 minute warning four minute for the missile to reach us people were digging in lead lined nuclear shelters, plans on how to get from work school where ever in time to get under cover I had enough work from window cleaning to safely resign from Scobie

Mcintosh adding to the fact I was getting some roofing and slating work, 1973/74 the unions were playing havoc with everybody's life style a great firm like Scobie Mcintosh was being damaged and with no end in sight having to stay away in hotels first to be in areas where people had a clear working week, my home life was suffering also peace of mind that I was around in the event of a Bomb strike, with my weekends I was now out window cleaning something had to change so it was back to the prison as a discipline officer and this time working in Saughton prison 21 years and over this was meant to be easier not all those young nutters trying to get the better of any situation what with my new fresh uniform hat chain shining bright and the leather hand loop dangling down from my hidden baton I wondered what kind of comments I'd get from the con's I was soon to find out when on the landing at locking up time on my very first day a couple of Cons were having a wee chat when I told them to move into their cells they just gave me a sideways glance and totally ignored my 2nd request so I called on another officer nearby and without any fuss I told him to put them on governors report why he was taken aback. The two cons, looked on in total amazement; I just stared at the officer in complete silence he blinked wondering what to do calmly I just said both of them thankyou now sir and he did slamming the door behind the cons, I think I even took the officers by surprise, it was not even the case that I was senior, as I still had over 2 years up my sleeve, which was awarded in the line of seniority but that was the way it was always done, you never booked a prisoner yourself when on gallery. It was not the right way to do it get a fellow officer to do it and it worked next day the governor gave them 2 days loss of remission and I got all round respect and they got my respect it just makes life easier but only a few days after this news filtered through from the Yo's next door that an old friend Bruce a much liked officer had been found dead in the river side at Musselburgh, he was fully dressed in the uniform such was the way the Job is as for some in the next couple of years 4 officers from Saughton, committed suicide in there married quarters just up the road, there was without doubt a huge shift in discipline and poor support for the officers my wee incident seemed to be one off officers were now openly swearing at prisoners and each other there was little self-respect even with the most senior officer the whole thing seemed to be from the home office prior to my time in Yo's. There was unwanted shift of attitude away from the USA structures and onto the Northern Europe Scandinavian soft laid-back touch on how to disciplining of prisoners and sentencing, and in my short period of time away seems to have some effect. One morning I was told to go down to the strong cells where there were 2 prisoners banged-up I entered the 8 cell in the block locking the entrance door behind me, directly above my head I could hear the shuffling of chairs and human feet as my mates were in the muster room enjoying their breakfast break. I opened up and slopped out, the first guy giving him his open razor blade to shave which he returned to me after completing his wash the guy was quiet and only took a few minutes before he went back to his cell I closed the door behind him as normal only one at a time were allowed out in the digger (nick name for cell block), after letting the second one out, he slopped-out I just stood by the cell door watching him finish washing and shaving he was about 24 years old bigger built than me quite big stripped to the waste towel slung over one shoulder he walking past me Turing right at the door I had my hand out in order to take the razor, when suddenly he spun around with the razor in his hand at my cheek sneering into my face come on fucking take it I froze to the spot, thinking my end had come, on my own locked in the cell block, still the only noise, the foot taping only inches away above our head, completely unaware of what was going on down here now with this guy gritting his teeth, I couldn't see the blade his hand was near to my left cheek the open cell floor way inches from his back, I summoned all my strength hoping not to show it my left hand thrust forward and with as much force that I could muster, thrust him backwards successfully getting him off balance he staggered back into the middle of his cell, I reached forward grabbing the door brass handle snatching it shut with a very loud bang he was quick of the mark kicking and banging the door so loudly before I could regain my senses a very senior officer was at my side, I explained what had happened and exactly the action I took that same morning I was told that I was to put on Governor report for assaulting a prisoner, it was not what or the content of the charge but the way the principle officer told me I was not even allowed to question the charge, however in the said manner when I was lined up outside the Governor office alongside and in line with Prisoners standing to attention waiting their turn to go in for their punishment, the door to his office opened the same P.O. just walking up to me and told me to return to my duties as the prisoner had withdrawn the charges, what bothered me about this seemingly most turn around was the prisoner was nowhere in sight, if as he would have been lined up escorted by two officers, the truth came out in the next few days that the P'O would have to answer why was that officer on his own in the digger and I was not giver the prior update on both prisoners, the afternoon before they were given 28 days solitary confinement by the Governor which then automatically means they are covered by two officers at all times whether in or out of their cells I'd like to have been a fly on the wall, when the Governor brought this to the P.O's attention! There only seemed to be a small number of officers working within common sense rules, and they were the basic officers where the senior officer appeared to be relaxed and on first names with prisoners but applying discipline to us, it was a very strange atmosphere and openly talked about amongst ourselves. In very quick succession events were very alarming one morning I opened a cell door to find a prisoner lying on his bunker bed on top of the bedding from the waist down he was naked and covered on blood another was sitting on the edge of his bed and in the Gloom of the lighting I saw him trying to hide his blooded hands I shouted for assistance I at least remembered not to go into these situations within seconds the one siting was quickly pulled out, then the full horror could be seen through the blood he lay there with pins and sewing needles pushed through his penis, the other guy James Ward, threatened him so frighteningly so with other torture and death if he uttered a word, finding guys who hang themselves during the night, I walked in on 2 such events, each one had another sleeping cell mate oblivious to what happened as they slept, I had to suppress my feelings and act it all out as a matter of fact my insides were turning in knots, it was a case of contain the situation priority to the whole situation to the point I didn't get a chance to assess myself officers didn't break down (only hung themselves). It didn't matter what the situation be professional, it didn't matter what it was I walked into my mask was the same, blank matter of fact complete control how brave, I began to think it was only happening in the jail. But the grape vine from the Yo's was saying it was all happening also the discipline was not happening, when on one day coming to the end of my shift, the prisoners were all locked up behind the doors after their dinner waiting to go out to the exercise yard when I was slowly pacing up and down the empty walk way on my gallery other officers gathered around the desk chatting away, suddenly a door I had just passed exploded into loud metallic banging the buzzer and door light flashed on without any thought knowing this was an emergency, I quickly got back to the door, which by this time vibrated with the blows it was receiving from within and the screaming voice calling for help I tried to peer through the peep hole but all I saw was an eye staring back at me, my yell's to him to move out of the way went unheeded, once I got my key to turn I had to shoulder the door to get this guy out of the way, just in order to get it open enough when a hand from the inside grabbed it, before I knew it he was out and past me, being held by other officers who by now came to my assistance I was left staring straight ahead at a silhouette of the other guy, hanging by the neck from the window frame I instinctively rushed at his legs and shoulder lifted his waist to take his weight off his neck, a couple of other officers struggled to untie whatever was choking him a leather belt after placing him down on the bed, freeing up the buckle which was well hidden in the flesh of his neck, he looked like at rest peace full there was no pulse or other sign of life as I was the last one going out of the cell leaving him lying there I don't know why I hesitated and glared back at his body lying there but I remembered what an old doctor who was instructing on first aid during our training said you can't kill or damage them anymore if they are already dead go for it don't worry if you break the ribs or damage the heart I turned unfolded his arms and with as much force as I could muster punched his heart a couple of blows I grabbed his wrist feeling for a pulse or at least where it should be I gave a further blow still holding his wrist like an electric shock going up my finger, a pulse just one or was it? I was about to let go when my fingers vibrated to rapid pulse beats his whole body began to move and his face turned many colours of purple, like a monster it was bloody horrible at that very moment it or he frightened the shit out of me, that I wished I had left him dead, I cried my eyes out driving on the way home bought my first packet of 20 fags in years, chain smoked five before I got home and finished the rest that same day. But there was a prisoner who was in the Yo's and now in the jail having become of age 21, Mick McLeod when he was only 16 he dug a grave west of Edinburgh out Lanark Road brought his young pregnant girl out to the country side for a picnic hit her with the spade and buried her alive, he got HMP being under 18 (her majestic pleasure) he was a troublesome lad to begin with settled down learning the trade of hair dresser at which he got his London city a guilds whilst at the Yo's the governor took interest in him as he did others but Mick took an interest in Budgies and in the grounds he established an aviary, breeding and using his growing knowledge with them, more scientifically and became known as the bird man of Saughton but our paths were to cross in the mid 90's when he became resident hairdresser only a couple of streets from my house and also socialising in the pubs in the same area although he was larger in body frame, a huge head of hair and full beard his eyes pierced into mine, whilst he was at the other end of the bar from me otherwise I would as I possibly had already walked by him. One day walking down the street he came towards me giving me big glares this happened a couple of times till I cornered him, sliding up to him in the noisy bar I quietly warned him that if he continued his behaviour I'd have to report his breach of release license adding its better we live for the future, and try leaving the past, it must have had an effect as after that he actually struck up a conversation of sorts, from time to time when one night I was at the bar completely on my own the bar man was down in the cellar, when Mick walked in, he came and sat on a stool beside me I couldn't make out what he was saying didn't seem to be drunk just very low, depressed we had another pint and I left him with the barman, but all I could hear or make out of what he was mumbling was something to do with his kids, the next day I learnt that his body was found in the river, apparently he was successful this time as he had attempted it before, such is life, the vast majority of the officers were in the job for all reasons the main one being early retirement at the age of 55, instead of the normal 65 years it was very apparent that in the short number years that I have put in there were only a handful who actually made it to 55, but a great deal disappeared well before there time with ill health. I'd had enough again especially for £33 per week, I had seen and heard too much. I gave the Governor his hat back, Fortunately I still had most of my window cleaning still up and running, Jimmy had come back from Australia after nearly 5 years, he came back with a wee fortune £1300 he stayed with us at the farm avenue. until he bought my brother(Hamish) flat at 41 Caledonian Cross for £650, which at the time was (1973) twice what they were going for, things on the Chimney, side of life were getting, worse for the older sweeps, many just closed down, dad somehow due to his extension into contracts never had to rely on the private sector as much, as the others closed shop he crossed into other areas Vacated all the way from Morningside down to Barnton, I was still helping him from time to time also window cleaning mother spent most of the day sitting in the shop taking the orders by the phone but she told me of sweeps who had gone out of business in other areas of the town that dad didn't want to touch and would I like to take any calls that came into her for those areas yes and that was the start for me, dad was not happy he never said so, but slowly stopped getting me out to help he turned to use Jimmy which suited me, I was window cleaning in morning and sweeping afternoons, I started to put cards in shop windows as dad had done before advertising my home phone number trying to find out just where dad began and ended was difficult, but it wasn't long before I asked mum not to give or take any work in for me, and not to tell dad so it worked, slowly he began to socialise and open up when he realised I was not touching or a threat to his well-earned workloads only one thing was left, Jimmy came to work for me, I obviously learnt much about Chimney's and chimney parts, but not only did sweeps work on the Flues and lums, but were well learnt Roof slating and I did know a fair bit of repairing and slating them, but I never felt confident enough to talk the langue of the qualifies roofers, and how to calculate the removal of a slated or tiled roof, so I booked myself into doing a 3 year part time day release at Telford collage on the slating and trowel trades London city and guild course, one day a week I was well encouraged by the fact that the instructor an old slater by the name Jimmy Fivvie a grand old man hands on, he told me after only completing about 2 months that he was putting my name forward for the next up and coming city and guilds exam, I was well amazed at how much I'd learnt from dad and his men over these years and as it turned out I passed with credits it boosted my confidence no end, not the fact of having the certificate but in doing a job properly, sizing estimating and employing a slater at a later date, to support my income as with the miners still causing disruptions all over the country the smokeless fuel zones, spreading wider all over Edinburgh, as a result of natural gas conversion still going throughout the country Scottish Gas man power was stretched very far and wide their own men could not keep up with all the private and local authority servicing contracts as a result sub-contracting these workloads sprung-up this suited me fine on this basis I hired out my labour at a good hourly rate and flexible hours so I could fit in window cleaning sweeping and any roofing the only thing working for Scottish gas that was in my favour was that all of the four(4) sectors in Edinburgh were managed by the men who by luck were apprentices in the same year as me and the overall senior manager was a trainee manager at the same time but they all had one thing in common they hated contractors and spent most of the time trying to fault there work and time keeping I had a battle on my hands from the start I needed the money, and most of all I had my good name, you had to have your wits about you, there men were just fitters, we were all qualified fitters and technicians any of their quality controlling was done by their own fitters as it turned out a wee bit of a nightmare as us contractors workloads was attending and fault finding work left behind by their own fitters at a time us guys were walking on thin-ice we couldn't report there shoddy and sometimes dangerous work standards just had to bite our tongue and hope for the best as their knowledge of the technical side was not too good they targeted times on job. That was my biggest problem doing my work in there time, however I by luck found a major fault in there standards and I drove a hole through it by a stroke of good luck I detected a faulty flue liner whilst carrying out routine serving on gas fire and back boiler central heating units when I smoked tested it the smoke went up both the inside and outside of the flue liner on closer inspection at Roof level I found the liner had been fitted (10ft) ten foot short of the top. This was a three chimney stack, all three, I could look down them and see the other two were also short by the same amount, the gas board(Scottish Gas) had been servicing all of these boilers and initially inspected them passing them as all safe to use five(5) years before and all aspects of repairs. This covered all the council housing sectors my business boomed without much of a say, and very quietly the service manager instructed all his men, in particular supervision to direct all suspect flues directly to me, I had to pack-in my other jobs and focus all my time to my growing sweeping business I had to try and bring all this work into some kind of control as the gas board were never off the phone a situation that I had only dreamed off all this work thousands of pounds a week never mind a year, I was in danger of being swamped and just not prepared for all this it was as if my wee house and life became an extension of theirs, they were quite rightly ditching there headache on me, knowing my technical gas background but also my whole knowledge of Chimney's I had only me and Jimmy so I struck a working partnership with them, that they at their cost, give me two or more gasfitters to remove the gas fires and back boilers ahead of me, then follow up behind me after I removed and dropped the liners, and the other main factor was they had a delay of 3 months in paying each job. But it was guaranteed money. Things were taking off prior to getting this work I had placed adverts in the yellow pages under chimney sweeping and now this was steadily producing much wanted private work, something had to go so I gave the window cleaning to Jimmy when I say gave him the run well it was a bit of a nightmare he decided he couldn't climb ladders and after what seemed months I had to double up on the run, repeatedly showing him to boost his confidence on how to carry and setup the ladders safely and without breaking windows at one house he was bringing the extension ladders down he got both his thumbs stuck between the rungs, with a heavy handed pulling force ripped them free and the skin down to the bone, he came back to the house with two well bloody red white bandaged thumbs the customer kindly done the first aid and gave him a cup of hot sugary tea to calm his nerves what a bloody shame Jimmy, but Dolly was the main other part of our team, with her clerical side back ground when she worked as a typist when I first met her then again in Australia running an office, she's only worked part time as a home help, in the evenings my mother taught her all she knew about book keeping as mum did most of her other Daughter in laws who helped out with Lums-Dun when they were on holidays so now all her hidden talents I needed to support us with our own business, now called Scots sweep and Scots services she was never too keen on taking on a full time job, and much preferred being a house wife and mother she did a great job, even controlling Helen who was as head strong as her mother, Billy on the other hand is pretty much like me, happy to keep the peace at all costs I wasn't one for having pocket money all my earning's always, from the early days of the Milk-run till now and onwards went straight to the house, Dolly always got annoyed at me not having money in my pocket but unless I had a good reason too, I never felt comfortable with it, but on special occasions started when on holiday I always turned to her for spending money, also I was not a sports fanatic other than diving which I kept up close to home, diving on the union canal at Slate ford 3ft of water on top of 6ft of Silt and a bloody stink but great fun diving into the mud blindly feeling for old bottles, tea-pots and unfortunately and old skeleton, boots leg bones and after pulling up a pair I bravely got out of the water on doing my duty reported it to the police who came up with the theory it was an old tramp who fell in but I never told them about the pistol found within inches of the bones the locals called these areas in the canals a Victorian Tips , I decided to take up a proper sport where the Bairns could join in, it was a good move at the old age of 32 years karate with an old instructor Kenny Black aged 60 within months Kenny progressed me through the belts up to green, I became the proverbial punch bag for all the younger ones including one in particular Kelvin Greenside (or something like that) Kelvin was in his early twenties and now a brown belt. He was a tough nut to crack and on one occasion he sent me off to hospital with a bruised kidney it took weeks to recover, he never knew when to draw his blows, he went on to run his own club as a 2nd Dan Black belt and seemed to being doing well, till I read in the paper he received 20 years for throwing acid into a woman face he was apparently hired by her husband to do it recently was released after serving 10 years on parole! I myself went on to win my first ever sports medal, the runner up on the South East Scotland championship even beating black belts which was my reason for packing it in, I gave up to much of my real blood that day, the business was doing really well and so much so faster than we could think phone systems then were poor you couldn't even switch it off the cable came right in without a disconnecting point like mum and dad we decided to try and take the business out of the house so we bought a shop at 15 fowler terrace Dundee St Foundation Bridge but it never worked the telephones would not divert from one area to another in those days but again we had a good idea and bought all the left over clothing from jumble sales and advertised used clothing wanted I got a broker's license and went into the rag and bone trade we made a few bob from that then decided there was more than enough sweeping so we sold the shop 6 months later for a reasonable profit the shop was converted into a main door flat but at a later date when the sweeping got very quiet, I did the same thing in 5 Wardlaw places, Gorgie, It done the trick and kept us in work during a quite spell, there were no real things as charity shops at this time so little competition. Tommy (1975) decided to pack up and try New Zealand. He got offered a job as a baker in Auckland, and thought it the best thing as he was fed up with the buses driving. Dad became the most sociable I've known him, also Dolly and I on a Friday late teatime were regular at the poshest restaurant in Edinburgh at the time, the Caledonian hotel west end. It was a great way of unwinding, a couple of pints, followed by a huge steak on some of these days I never even had a wash completely black with Soot , now becoming a regular sight they never once asked me to leave even when the place was full to the Gunnels, and sitting beside us was the famous pop group at the time Hot chocolate Helen and Billy were with us on that momentous occasion, Helen nearly flipped with embarrassment(she was only about 9 years old) when I stared to talk to them over the table. I was very self-conscious when all black, when I washed at any time then, my hands were always engrained with soot, and showed up more so when I was dressed and showered, mum and dad planned and paid for a trip to New Zealand also whilst there they planned a couple of weeks over to Brisbane Australia to see here brother Jimmy who emigrated to there just after the second world war but at the last minute she took panic attacks and the holiday was put on hold and didn't look like it was going to happen, dad was not a happy chappy he was going to lose all his and mums flight money already paid for after a couple of weeks listening to them and Xmas 1977 had just gone by the final day of reckoning was coming up Dolly told me often enough to take mums place and keep him happy also shut his moaning up. I wasn't happy to being away from her and the Bairns for 5 weeks, the only thing that added up was it was just after new year, 78 and there would be no work coming in, so no financial aspect to prevent me from going but in one of our Saturday night music drink sessions in our house it was agreed that I would accompany him. He had arranged with a friendly shopkeeper that when in Singapore for 2 days he'd look up his long last brother a MR. Lal Singh. The only other time that dad spent out of the country other than a week Spain, was 6 years with the Argyll Sutherland Highlander's Regiment 1933-39 fighting in Palestine, on this 2 night and 2 days stopover in Singapore we were well occupied, Dad found out his suspicions about what happened to his mates in the argylls, after the outbreak of WW2, when they got back to the base after 6 years in Palestine he failed another medical for another tour of overseas where his regiment went to where he never knew rumours went about they ended up in the tropics whilst he spent most of the war driving all kinds of army vehicles up and down UK, but here in Malaya, we visited a war graves cemetery at Karangi by the straits of Johore, where we wandered about the neatly kept head stones totally surrounded in tall jungle and stinking humidity, we discovered many a Scottish soldiers last resting place here, how on earth they must have suffered just living from day to day in this part of the world, let alone fight and so far from home poor souls, in the forty eight hour we spent there we were never away from the toilet we visited changi, prison where the Japanese held captive most of us British Australian and other troops from the Island, also had a beer in the famous Raffles hotel, passing on our way through the jungle Kampongs native villages the whole place was still as it was after seeing it in war films but on every opportunity dad stopped and spoke to the Rickshaw drivers asking about MR Singh Christ dad, the bloody place is full of Sikhs, but he continued on this bloody mission, on the last day he said he'd follow some leads he was given, and after an age, we ended up on the dock side alongside some huge ware houses the Rickshaw driver buggered off, MR. Singh you will find him in there, so we did by Christ within minutes we were introduce to this huge turban topped Sikh and to my amazement it was him a huge guy massive black well-groomed beard and he took us into his office Plush affair leather chair glass topped desk, he sat down, picked up the phone beside him and ordered refreshment for us all exactly what we could do with in this stifling hot day sweat constantly dripping off my face dad looked a state knackered but and Ice cold beer our staple diet not even trusting bottled water at least we knew the Tiger beer was universally OK, the door opened in the came another Sikh and younger carrying a tray with opened bottles of Coke! I looked over my shoulder at the open door to see if anyone else followed with the real thing. I've never heard dad keep so quiet; I took my Que from him, he rushed through the exchange of pleasantries, and we were out the door, the coke was working on our tired bowels, never so glad to find a bush and the flight out to Auckland, NZ, we had a lovely warm welcome from the family Tommy, Chrissie, Anne and Susan and the Bairn's Mark (7years old), straight into an early morning BBQ but my priority was the Doctor, and I was surprised being seen only hours after landing, Dad refused to go telling me to get double dose, and I did. It took us a couple of days to get reasonable control of our Bowels the family were please as well they could approach us as normal and not with caution. Whilst Tommy was at work, he gave us the use of his, what we thought an old 4 door Banger. But standards were backwards even by our standards and a way behind time. The reason we were seeing so many old model cars and in really good condition was nobody but the extremely rick folk brought in newer cars it was because of import taxes so nobody really could afford them, there wasn't a trade as such in buying and selling which even limited spare parts this applied to most, even domestic appliances, so dad and I set of with Chrissie and Bairns out into the Country side and onto the Metal roads in hilly country, bloody hot weather, not after long dad pulled over as he found the steering hard, no wonder we had a flat tyre, that's when we found all his tyre's had absolutely no tread. Chrissie reassured us this was also common practice used tyres, but we were used to remould or tyre with tread by law this was NZ rules once changed with a completely Bauld one, we were off again not for long another flat but now we had no spare and in the middle of the bush fortunately there was a house at the top of a long track perched on a hill and we could see life so we all tramped up and introduced ourselves only a lady at home, dad and I trying to hide our embarrassment explained our predicament no problem there we were all sitting around her swimming pool and a generous supply of beer and fruit juice for them she phoned the AA breakdown who in turn phoned some local garage who put in an appearance some two hours later the lady refused our offer of reward for her kindness we would have been overcome by the heat without her hospitality, when he did arrive with a car towing a huge trailer the reason being he never had our size of tyre, but hopefully he could repair ours, back at his garage not only that his car doubled as a van, where the back seats were lay piles of tool box's, we had to get in our car once it was winched on to the trailer, a trip on a life time, for the next hour we all sat with the windows wide open just to get a wee breeze in our car high up on his trailer the kids thought it great fun, Dad and I slightly fortified which covered any embarrassment but the mechanic true to his word and courtesy of the AA repaired both tyres, Tommy now a true Kiwi thought them in good nick for a good few miles Dad was suffering a good bit of depression that I'd never seen him with, he was not handling being away from mum, all of us were beer drinkers and it was flowing constantly during wakening hours, we shared a bedroom and a couple of mornings 1 or 2am I'd awake to find him sitting on the edge of his bed sighing and muttering. I planned with Tommy and his pal to go away for a few days as it was already getting near the time to visit Australia, and we'd better try cheer him up beforehand. Great there was bugger all for us in Auckland. So we headed for Rotarua Maori territory with a couple of tents for our accommodation this change was needed for dad but his home sickness and depression came over him time and time again he hid it well from everybody but lent on me to excuse him from doing some things but true to form he was a great comic, and had us in stiches, when we visited a bird sanctuary near the hot springs, chickens and lots of ground dwelling birds ran around our feet for a few cents we bought at the entrance a wee poke of seeds we scattered about the place feeding them when suddenly there was this squawking and screeching there was dad he had a chickens head in his hand the rest was flapping about, he's going see lads that's how we used to catch them when we were boys(now aged 62), Christ with loads of folk and Bairns around we all at once rushed him out through the gates we'd just come through what a man. If that wasn't enough we ended up in towns hot-springs boiling water gushing out everywhere bubbling mud pools at the road side spewing steam out of every hole in the ground but worst of all the stench of rotting eggs you could taste the dammed stuff. As we walked up the hill side trying to follow the mud paths that were most solid feeling underfoot dad somehow lost his flip flop and his bare feet were proving to sore and burning he was leaping about all over the place, out over a crust of mud, shouting that he's stuck and feet are burning, I shot over to him and gave him a collie Buckie, piggy back a few yards ahead there was a post and blackboard I headed for it just skirting around boiling mud, went around the sign-post to read what it said under no circumstances go past this point danger collapsing surfaces shit 'faither Tommy who saw us delighted in telling us of people just disappearing when walking over these soft crustations of lava. that done it Pub, then it was off to visit uncle Dode and auntie Jessie, who he had never seen since they emigrated to Australia after WW2, the same folks Dolly and I failed to see in 1967. Now I was taking mums place to see her big brother. It was only a 3 ½ hour flight, a good greeting from them in Brisbane, arriving at their timber bungalow, we sat on their veranda beer in hand going over the good old days and some stories with Dode at Anzio, and dad in Palestine there were plenty of stories, he was a bit of a Bushman they never had any children's. He spent most of his time wandering in and out of the major bush mining camps working at any labouring job he could find although he was a well-qualified storeman even venturing up to Port Morsbay in New Guinea , Jessie learnt just to wait on him coming through the door after months of not even hearing from him, she did have some of her family who came out from Niddrie and Craigmiller in Edinburgh, on one of his visits home and just before he left for a mining camp at mount Isa, In the bush he bought a lottery ticket and left it with her, and he didn't know till 6 months later on his return, she had bought a bungalow, his ticket won $33,000 the top prize. She said he was unhappy, he was happy with renting houses, she had a hard time convincing him he was better off. Now 3o years later he's still fighting his corner, but they were a happy understanding couple, after a few days, dad decided it was time to look up, Uncle Jimmy Flockhart, an old mate from the days of the concert parties, he and his wife emigrate to Brisbane in 1951. Dad warned me that Dode and Jimmy hated each other so I'd to keep things quiet my turn to get depressed dad as quietly as possible told Dode of his plans to see Jimmy, I was surprised that they wanted reassurance that he wouldn't bring him to their house. I never did find out the reason why, such feelings. The next morning having tea and toast with Dode and Jessie, before they went off to their part time jobs which supplemented their pensions as they left turning on the radio just in time to catch a bag pipe tune it was Rabbie Burns day they left for work leaving us with the heat and humidity was almost unbearable even at this early hour and no relief came from the overhead fan, Dad like me dressed only in short the sweat running down our wee bodies he opened the freezer door and backed into it as much of himself he could get into it. Dad had a wee problem, he never knew where Jimmy lived but the Last news he was the manager of the unemployment in the city of Brisbane armed with their address we took the Rickety old commuter train in, dressed just shorts and white vests the train was jammed full of well-dressed office workers as the train schoogled and groaned into the city, dad loudly remarked he'd given away a better train set, some did find the funny side and sniggered, finally we found ourselves inside this entrance to the labour exchange we walked up to a long front reception counter dad asked the young Girl if a Mr. Flockhart worked here, she disappeared into an office doorway behind her reappearing with this gent in a 3-piece suit bauld-headed looking at us two half naked twits we heard her quietly say there's two Scotsmen are asking for you, he hesitated then his expression changed and at the top of his voice, showing no control, bastards Willie Mclenaghan he shouted in one move he birrled around to his Desk, picked up the phone briefly slammed it down, coming towards us dragging his legs he said to the girl. I'm off sick for the rest of the day. Before we knew it, we were in the PUB. The remainder of the day on one big Pub crawl, he had already phoned his wife with the news we spent the rest of the evening at his place. A couple of days later days as planned Jimmy picked us two up from outside Dodd's place and didn't come out of the car. Jimmy had the vocal cords of his mother loud. He drove us up into the great dividing range a jungle hill top Pub in the area known as Tam Borine Mountain wonderful opening times out there 24-hour license after a good few beers there, we were on our way to another of his watering holes bloody miles away. Surfers paradise on the gold coast his favourite bowling club, and true to Aussie style not a bugger on the bowling greens. But queuing up for the Pokies the most boring past time I've seen bloody fist fights over who's next and Jimmy seemed in his element. Dad and I managed to fall asleep with all the excitement then we were off again and this time it was Dark finally after a good steak and chips in a small café Christ, somewhere in Queensland the owner, closed the place up and invited us to join him in a beer on the Veranda, out the back Jimmy, asked me to help him get something out of the boot of the car, Guitars, he had two that was it , we were in our elements, I only play 3 chords, but Jimmy was a belter not surprisingly we found out he had his own country and western show on the radio at the weekends what away to finish a meeting Christ knows what time we left but dad and I had booked a hire car to be delivered the next morning sharp 9am we lined up a week away to Sydney but the last we saw of Jimmy was when he drove off leaving the pair of us lying on the grass verge, outside Dode's it was only a handful of years later we got the news that Jimmies wife Kathleen had died very suddenly somehow Jimmy lost his house and job and took to busking at a flea market with his guitar and cowboy songs. He was found dead alone in a room of a local motel, how sad! That night I slept on a Veranda just to get some fresh air or movement as I was getting bitten to death with the mosquitos at some point I was awaken with dad beside me ragging his single mattress behind him he too was looking for air we were soon on our way to south towards the Gold coast again and the border of NSW (new south wales). Both of us were ill, shit not just a hangover we made each other a promise NO more booze we're both not worth Rat shit.

I previously told him to find a good café for a full Aussie, breakfast but as we drove further south and into the bush civilisation rapidly evaporated bringing back memories on this road 10 years before and within minutes the road disappeared under dark sky's soon to be followed by wave upon wave of tropical rains which bounced back of the road well above the height of the car slowing us down to a crawl. Just tall scrub on both sides suddenly a boarding come flashing by us, I had just managed to read something about food at the next stop great, that lifted our spirits no end. With the rain thundering down, spotted a huge shadow of a building just set a few feet of the road excitedly I pulled up beside what appeared to be the entrance wooden steps leading up to a Veranda, and awning overhead on both sides wooden posts and rails where you'd tie up the horse, stacked along the Veranda, I could see some open sacks of grain, peas, implements for farming and gardening in the middle two half swinging door I could just make out that the lights were on through the edges! Right, dad out you go and I'll have the same as you, I'll park round the side, Ok so he slammed the Door behind legged it up the stairs, I shot round through the puddles and mud, I was soaked through by the time I got under the awning, in through the doors the place was empty no dad no bugger this was a typical country supply store everything you need to live in the Bush, I could hear dad gingerly I edged over to a curtained off door way at the far end I pulled it to one side revealing a woman standing at the sink opposite washing dishes and to my right sitting round a kitchen table a couple of kids an old man and dad shit, I forcefully called him out we were out of there like a blow shit fly as if a crime had been committed he was trying to explain that he's put in an order for us, I had a job explaining that he was in someone's home. On the way down to Sydney, dad has a rush to the toilet the nearest part to stop was alongside very tall and dense sugar cane plantation as he was scurrying around in his wee shorts bare top and sandals desperately trying to find a way into the maze of sharp leafy sugar stocks I was just about to tell him about snakes in these places when he shot out with his drawers at his ankles what a mess fortunately there was a trough of water nearby he said he saw a snake, I think he did poor thing (snake)! after an overnight stop, I was moving into familiar territory driving down through the Northern suburbs of Sydney pointing out as we went where we lived and Helen's birth place I was about to make a life changing visit and that was drive into the car park of my old employer the North shore gas company, and immediately ran into two old work-mates everybody seemed to be in a supervisory positions, after exchanging pleasantries and contact address some others came out to see and including Olaf who was a superintendent we left after about 10 minutes! We headed South over the harbour bridge, our destination was to visit Leslie and Elsie his wife, two daughters and Granny Stevenson, who emigrated from the next stair to Dads in 1964, Dolly and I visited them a couple of times at their home in the Southern outer Suburb of Liverpool West Sydney in a high density Low Budgeted housing area most if not all the houses even now had no sanitary drainage chemical Loo's they were known as the weather board sheds or Dunny's, but anything compared to the emigrant camps was heaven! Granny Stevenson came out sometime after we left 1968 Dad and I arrived on a very hot and dry day only the main roads were tarred all the side ones including these were still dirt tracks, dad told me we were staying with them but we found they were not prepared for visitors, we managed to get a nearby motel we got a very warm welcome Granny Stevenson in particular standing there in a silky full length slip showing all the signs of heat exhaustion clammy and sticky. She captured dad trying to get the messages from home has someone got her house it was like walking a land mines trying gently not to get her any more home sick I was out the back being shown around, they had an above ground swimming pool looking all the part a plastic tub of green pea soup! Stagnant never seen the likes of this sitting in a sandy soil of scrubby bush, but after a home cooked meal and a good few beers we all took to the pool what a great night it was well after midnight when dad I headed up the road where we decided to grab a bit super at a road side burger stall our eyes were bigger than our bellies we chose steaks on a roll sounded nice but dad only had his false teeth no match for their buggers we tried everything to help tenderise them, finally smacking them of the bonnet of the car no good we ate the rolls and returned to our beds at the motel for the night when we got up for an early take off back off to Brisbane, well hung over again I went out to put the baggage in the car, ah shit our nice lemon green bonnet was tomato red with onions and the rest we must not have been able to a park outside our door but a few away I've never loaded up so quickly leaving the washing up till we found a garage! We took a couple of days to getting back up to Brisbane said our farewells and flew back to Auckland, it wasn't long before we picked up the pace of life in NZ, again when Tommy and his pal took us on another Pub crawl in Auckland to an area known as Papatoetoe Jesus we were the only white men the place was heaving with Maoris. Bloody black and huge but being ignorant Scotsmen we pushed our way to the jam packed bar and ordered a round the next thing a portable radio was placed on the bar right Infront of us by the big Maori barman familiar sounds blasted from it, bag pipes Paul McCartney, Mull of Kintyre his new tune before we knew it we had a gathering around us what a brilliant time we had it was like being found by long lost brothers. It was sad leaving them all behind but it was good to be home and back into a routine but dad kept on instigating me to write a book on chimney sweeping eventually I popped into libraries to see what was written on sweeping I'd never really used the services before so I was finding things very hard to follow every one of the librarians I spoke too just looked blank when I mentioned chimney sweeping but time and again I drew a blank no such thing as computers then, No written work on the subject not even a reference, what the hell was dad going on about he is a great reader and of history then he told me that he hasn't seen anything. It all added up to the fact that there was nothing under the heading Chimney sweeps sweeping or otherwise. Little did he know the seed was planted and it was to take a good bit of my time in the next 10 years to get one published and on the shelves every move I made to research this subject was new territory, I even wrote to the press with what stories I had uncovered to date these were with the help of complete strangers telling me they had read a book or an article many years before suggesting where I might look for it and that is where and how I got dates of happenings in particular the criminal records child slavery burial records hangings and transportation of sweeps trades or callings it was a huge task I only had one objection directed to me after one of my articles in the Sunday post. It was from an old rival of dad's, John Swan, who dad chased around the HIBS ground at Easter road with a shovel, swanny apparently called dad a bastard his complaint to the paper was that he was a master sweep and for years was going to write a book on the history of chimney sweeping it was his story the thing was he himself has never swept a chimney, it was his family who were sweeps but nothing more was heard of him, but I was given a word of warning from true chimney sweeps even the ones who I grew up with not to giveaway any of their trade secrets. This even reduced my material further eventually I had a manuscript then published on to 3 editions of a history of chimney sweeping, by Michael McLenaghan, I never made any money directly from it but my businesses got plenty of revenues and advertising many tv spots newspaper write ups and talks lectures with many calls to weddings as the lucky sweep but I spotted an advert in the newspaper, wanted trainee actors I always had a hankering for the stage not as an actor but comedian so I joined a theatrical group I didn't disclose my true interest in comedy I was given a screen test as they called it to read a page from a book I must have failed but given the part of stage manager how the hell they worked that out? I was to find out that they were preforming at the Edinburgh Fringe festival a play called wait until Dark! The play ran for three weeks in the halls at Chester street, I ended up organising the stage scenes props and in the case of myself the part of a policeman using real uniforms supplied by the city police walking into the pubs during shows dressed in full uniform I enjoyed not having a larger part in the acting most of them were young keen budding actors a bit too serious for me at the end of it they had another venue at the Church hill theatre and I was ask to be the director, things were getting too serious I just wanted a fun part I backed out! When it came to my 33rd birthday I decided to treat myself to a parachute jump I always held a yearning to return to this subject, Strathalan was the nearest parachuting centre complete with my borrowed boiler suit scooter crash helmet and ankle supporting roofing boots I was ready I'd have to go through most of the ground work learning to fall and roll feet together not in military style there were three of us training Dolly and the Bairns buggered off to shops coming back after lunch when after only some 3 hours we were ready to fly in a Cessna 702 light plane minus its door I was in my element no pressures from RSMs corporals nothing all pretty laid back then we boarded the light aircraft just the pilot has a seat I was first in sat in the space up front where he co-pilots seat would be the next man had his back to me on the floor and between my legs and the third he sat on the floor with his back to the pilots seat lastly the guy squatted down on his knees facing us he was doubling up as our dispatcher the plane circled the aerodrome in wide circles until the dispatcher who was by now looking out of the door opening hanging on with one hand the other waving to the pilot directions to the left the right the pilot responding with jerking movements of the plane as it fine-tuned to line up with the DZ-below I was to be last out ready to exit the plane you could tell when this happened or was about to happen the pilot cut the engine to slow speed, so slow that the ear piercing high pitch of the stall warning sounded then the dispatcher grabbed the first one who slid the couple of feet to the door way hardly a pause and he was out as quickly the pilot gave the engine more thrust turning it steeply to one side and came around repeating this manoeuvre till it was my turn as I slid on my arse and my legs dangling out in fresh air. This was fantastic what a view 2500 feet below it never felt a height but a distance everything looked soft I could feel the plane jockey for position then the engine cut my feet felt for a ledge or step in which I could launch myself clear but shit nothing, not even the side of the fuselage, by now I was hanging on by my tail bone. Totally unnatural, as instructed on how to exit I looked back at the pilots head then I was out into the free fall arched back. I could feel the snatch of my static line this was great, on my way the plane banked away and disappeared out of sight. The chute opened I soon found the DZ on the grassy air strip below it seemed I had all the time on the world, not another chute around me. The other two had landed, the surrounding country was vast and horizon far off. I tried to assess my directional drift, the runaway was a dot in the vastness of green. These chutes had as little steerage as the military ones, after what seemed an age I made a perfect landing just short of the woods but quite near the small hanger. I hoped the Bairns were impressed, I'd waited all these years to do just this, I was back the next day for a second jump. This time no waiting about for the family, kitted up it was only me and dispatcher out. I went magic, the only difference this time my approach due to wind factor was across the aerodrome which was very narrow and lined with huge trees probably 60 feet high. Giving myself bags of room I slowly turned into the wind skirting the trees with plenty of height to cross over the runway and land before the trees on the other side. Suddenly out of the corner of my eye the aircraft I had just jumped from appeared from my left and in an instance shot past me after he had just landed, fortunately he was passed and travelling at speed. I held my approach, still with height I pulled my left lift web to help descent a bit quicker. To avoid the trees now Infront in a flash I caught sight of a wire or cable just below my feet, it ran parallel to the runaway on this flight path. It would catch me at about the waist, quickly I released my left pull and grabbed the right one. My feet clipped the wire as I bent my legs upwards, the ground was rushing up fast OH shit Christ another fence, a field sheep fence 3 or 4 feet high and I was coming right down on top of it straddling it cutting me up between the legs. I could visually see the pain coming up with a horrible crunch and what sounded like my legs snapping at the knees, I lay there folded up in agony and as quickly, I was surrounded by others (a normal landing using this type of chute would be around 22MPH this on must have been nearer 40 MPH). Before I knew it a crowd from the hanger gathered round me a couple of the guys checked me over, I heard them whisper there're broken. As I lay there in agony, they splinted both my legs together, Dolly had by this time brought my A3 car over close they all seemed to have a hand on me putting me on to the back bench seat giving her directions to the local hospital. I told her to get me back to the Edinburgh Royal Infirmary where they diagnosed that my knees had a nasty collision I must have landed with my legs slightly apart, the impact brought them together at the knee joints smacking them with such force they now looked like huge black and blue balloons, fortunately not broken with both of them well bandaged and aided by two under armpit wooden crutches. I was happy to agree no more parachuting, now I had to deal with this injury and my workloads staring me in the face. After a few days of trying to get my legs to work going painfully up step by step in my own house stairs using the hand banasters for support and releasing the tension of the bandages I decided to tackle the increasing work load on the roof by selecting one that I thought I could get access to within my limits. Also the pain aspect of this, I managed to bring under control simply by ignoring it as I had to do when being ill on the milk rounds with a good dose of the flue and mothers helping driving force and echoing words Michael get up awe ma, but for me it worked Tommy and my three wee brothers always got to stay in bed when they complained of being not well all they seemed to do was moan a little and that was it another day off school or whatever. It just seemed easier and more peace full going to work we were doing so well with business that we splashed put on a holiday to see Alan and Helen Currie in Canada with an extended trip down into America via Detroit Kentucky then Tennessee. After driving through Detroit on a lovely day Ronald Reagan was somewhere in the area campaigning for the presidency, but before we left Scotland the whole country seemed to be on a state of red alert. The cold war was at boiling point, the news was full of endless threats of nuclear bombing from the eastern bloc mainly Russia. Nuclear shelters were going up all over the place, endless instructions on how to deal with a 4 minute warning as a bomb approached. In our case they told us Rosyth in-fife was the likely first target, this was truly a nightmare subject. The news on tv was full of the US president and our pm slagging the east, we were being well warned by all our family not to travel to the USA as they would be first to be bombed or we could be shot down on the way there or back. It was a serious thought and on the facts at hand could prove true, we went all gee'd up and feared for our Bairns and a lead lined bomb shelter planned on or return. To our shock, horror on landing at Toronto with the first leg of our nightmare journey successfully behind us and the news from the eastern block just a few hours past and very alarmingly but fresh in our ear, we were prepared for horrific news about Scotland being smashed. We were Gob smacked, Alan and Hellen met us with cheesy faces and a warm welcome we looked at each other and gingerly asked what seemed the obvious, we drew blank questioning looks what the hell are you talking about. I had to tell him to put the TV news on. Christ not a bloody word, nothing about the nuclear or eastern block, it was a hard job explaining about the state of the UK just only hours ago and the HIPE, No they knew nothing, not a Dicky bird. And yes the whole of our stay was void of such news sadly on our return. Christ it was still happening and as strong as ever, a bloody eye opener as to how America and Canada were truly worlds apart. Or was it just Europe, the result was we cancelled our nuclear shelter. We had a bit of a problem trying to tell our friends and folks our country never had a problem and it was all stage managed (tongue in cheek style). On the drive south nearing Cincinnati on a motor way the sun was shining brightly, we were all feeling the heat so I had the air conditioning on full blast, we noticed a long black line of clouds coming up from the horizon in front, within minutes they nearly blacked us out the car began to shake as rain and wind whipped all around before I knew it we were the only car left on the road. I put my head lights on as we were now driving in the pitch dark, the rain drove hard against the screen, the wipers could not cope all I could see what was the edge of the road on the right hand side only a few feet away the whole family were screaming frantically my speed was near standstill. Then again on my right an orange like glow appeared out of the storm followed by a complete calm and clear blue skies, no wind or rain but yet blackness all around only this beam of sun light pointing down on us as quickly it came it went shit it all began I was so taken by this change and the only car on this road this orange glow appeared again as suddenly the screaming started up again I turned the car straight off the road and right up to the light source, luckily I was creeping up on it. As my front banged up against it a wall crunch looking up to a couple of faces staring down at me. It was a McDonald's Diner only a few feet separated us from these folk having a burger inside, again within a couple of minutes it was calm and bright. The black clouds had moved well away from us revealing a trailing spiral tail, I'd only seen in the movies a Tornado before. It moved off and I found the plastic front fender cracked slightly. The folk on the other side of the window gave me a wave, our one and only tornado and we had been through the eye. Later according to our car radio a number of people had been killed, also whole houses lifted from their foundations. The rest of our trip was much more enjoyable, Elvis Presley died last year but we managed a trip to his birth place tupelo and his burial plot in Graceland's. Sad but a trip to the country hall of fame which housed a huge theme park the people were welcoming and warm. It was very different to try and gauge what the atmosphere was at home regarding the cold war and not a twitter, nothing but true to reality 'bang', it was all systems go when we stepped off the plane at Prestwick, the war was still on and from that day onwards I refused to engage in this propaganda and it never happened. Nothing, not even a burst balloon along with a few eastern-bloc leaders lying on it. Not long after our return we got a surprise letter from Australia Olaf and a friend Alan Walker were on a European tour and would like to pop-in, they had booked into the Braid hills hotel not far from us and were in the Edinburgh area for a couple of days. We invited them to join us and Jimmy Cavanagh, to the house for a drink also to meet the Bairns, not having met Alan before he came over as the perfect gent although we only had 2 bedrooms upstairs ours and the Bairns's we invited all three of them to stay sleeping on the floor and Settee, no problem. In the morning we stood looking out of the front living room window as one of our young female neighbours walked by, Katrina. She was well known as a bit of a girl with the boys, Dolly said something to Olaf that she was a bit of a whore, Instantly Alan replied those who live in glass houses should not throw stones. We all sort of looked at each other I thought what a strange remark. Nothing more was said (it was Jimmy who at the time remained silent and for the next 20 years when he told me what was meant). The two of them left that day, on their return home we received a thank you letter from Alan on his return that was the last we heard from him. Not long after a neighbour Mrs. Cochrane from across the road at no 34 Oxgangs Farm Avenue. came over and bluntly said would we like to exchange houses with her as hers was too big, 4 bedrooms ours being 2. No sooner after seeking permission (and getting it) from the council we moved, not only 2 more rooms but a huge garden but I had to ask permission and submit plans to erect a small Greenhouse also install Central-heating bullshit. Maggie Thatcher conservative was in power, she instructed councils all over UK to allow tenants to buy the houses at a huge discount, not that I voted for her but with the red tape flying all over this place Dolly my driving force decided that we will buy the house that scared me shitless. What a commitment how the hell could I afford to have a mortgage, however the cost to buy was £27,000 but we had a discount bringing it down to £9000, shit, we had a good bank manager who gave me a short term loan over five years even that was too much for me. Panic attacks galore I put my head down arse up and had it paid off in 8 months, for some reason I thought we'd have a celebration party, the green for Go kept shining. The whole thing was an anti-climax and at no time did I feel I had achieved anything. There was one thing that I had to agree to and that her mum and dad were no longer welcome at Xmas, I found that a cruel decision to have to come to having gone through the past 4 years of ruined Xmas days just because of her mother's drunken aggressive behaviour, old Boris was as usual great fun he was just another Bairn at heart, Helen and Billy thoroughly enjoyed his lovely childlike involvement when he opened his presents and a couple of cans of lager just kept him going, Wilma she started off as enjoying herself keeping up with everyone else. The fatal turn came when Dolly opened a bottle of whisky for herself reluctantly giving her mother a glass, which at first seemed ok, followed by second, all seemed great and what the hell it was Xmas day. Everyone was happy, soon to change after the third one. Her mood changed, slurring and then getting a wee bit verbal with old Boris. He'd go quiet then her mood changed to anger and an attempt at violence on him. All this Infront of the Bairns, as normal Dolly got involved in a good old slanging match with her. A taxi called and out they would go, what a nightmare. I'd get well and truly told not to invite them ever again. Shit, it's her parents, next year no one wanted to know them and on xmas eve we'd go out and collect the Bairns' presents from them and fall into the old trap. What are you going to do tomorrow, old Boris was fine, she would be sheepish, hooked again but know more said as it was her mother died(aged 60). As it turned out there were two good reasons why she always got violent with old Boris when the whisky was flowing, she had four Bairns whilst he was a prisoner of the Nazis in Poland. Dolly's brother young Boris and a sister Liz who by a coincidence turned up a year later in Sheffield although this gave account for her mother's behaviour towards her father but was for me, he had a hellish life and dad (old Boris) died some 20 years later alone on a Psychiatric ward, a completely down trodden broken man. We weren't long in at 34 Ox Farm Avenue when we were invited by the whole Olaf family to spend a Xmas in Sydney with them. We arrived at his mother and fathers house where he lived with them on Xmas morning leaving Edinburgh in the depth of a big freeze up --21°F. Fortunately for us we had just put in gas central heating, one of the first such system in the whole area leaving it on 24 hours constantly at a low setting because of the freeze up. It was hot in punchbowl Sydney NSW, Olaf had installed an above ground swimming pool and converted their excess space in the garage to a spare bedroom for visitors we were the first to use it. Helen and Billy slept in the bungalow. This was quite a novel holiday for our Bairns there first visit to down under. Billy was a bit more than terrified to get in the water at the beach, he was totally convinced the sharks were going to have him, not surprising as he'd just watched the horror movie JAWS. Mind you, on our first outing we visited laparouse cliff tops looking down on a crowded beach near Botany bay. The reality was there for Billy to see JAWS come true, a shark moving about beneath the surface only a few hundred yards from swimmers and nobody bothered. After what seemed only days into the holiday and possibly a week I became unwell with flu like symptoms and also a whole body rash which Helen took such an interest in it to photograph it all over my back. After a couple of days Lars, Olafs dad, suggested I see his GP about it. I was reluctant at first but agreed, the GP seemed concerned that I should be hospitalised immediately. No way, as we were going home later the next week he told me to come back and see him if my joints got sore or swollen. That evening Dolly decided for her own reasons to sleep in the house I was running a high temperature so sought the coolness of the swimming pool. I awoke in the early hours of the morning alone in bed to my horror on trying to make a turn I couldn't seem to move without extreme pain in all my leg and arm joints. I thought I was having a nightmare realising what the Dr said panic set in but I was on my own, not knowing what time it was and unable to get help, I just lay there trying to understand what and why was this happening all I could do was try not to move. Daylight was a long time. Then the whole household woke up, my joints were all swollen and bruised even my fingers and toes began to take on an agonising look and shape. The fingers were actually beginning to twist in to different shapes with knuckles swollen and very red and hot, just 2 weeks before I was weight lifting training for the Edinburgh marathon and karate. Why was this happening, I was not just frightened but bloody terrified. Yes I struggled to get to the GPs in the morning I refused his offer to have me hospitalised immediately, his diagnoses was acute arthritis, and he was surprised to hear me say I did not take drugs. He could only offer me painkillers till I returned to Edinburgh which I prayed would happen but I struggled until the day of my flight, I slept alone for the remainder staying mostly in and out of the pool and eventually I got the use of the wheel chair to board the plane home. My GP diagnosed Rheumatoid arthritis, my world collapsed. I was given an appointment at the Northern General Hospital with a waiting time of 3 months, by this time my hands were twice the size with fingers twisting and swollen red joints every move painful. But at last after a couple of weeks I began to recover, by the time of my appointment I was fully back on the roofs. I was given the all clear, again I was asked as to what drugs I'd been taking now! I packed in the karate and stopped running since the first GP consultation just so frightened to push any barriers. This whole thing at the time was a mystery the doctors would only say that it was in there opinion chemistry or drugs related which I never took as far as alcohol, well I had a sociable few beers as it was the kids holiday I could not afford to be hung over. But being home certainly made to a speedy recovery. I had never thought about free masonry only like most who ever mentioned it was a club for jobs, and I never was a clubby person, but a supervisor from the gas board openly declared himself a mason we knew his wife and Bairns the big question came up! After some doubts tooing and froing mentally I decided to apply and was accepted after my degree as a mark master mason taking upto 7 or 8 months of meetings and degrees which I found both interesting and very tiring. Mentally loaded down with signs, handshakes and passwords, yes I met many pleasant guys and the myth was broken. I found only a hand full kept the lodges up and running which was as good for them as was the sanctity of the wife and daughters. Olaf and his family were regulars on the phone getting all the news on one of his calls, I told him about me becoming a free mason only to be told that he too in very recent years had become one too. Within a couple of months he was back over here apron and all, and stayed with us at 34. His father was meant to come with him took unwell and remained in Sydney, this was a better visit as I took him to a few lodge meetings. I was surprised to find that he was a past master of his lodge this gave him a senior seat in the lodges we visited, I had organised a BBQ in our back garden which was becoming a regular thing, but, I did became aware of one thing. When he was visiting and staying for his usual couple of weeks having a drink or just socialising was ok, I'd lost the whole night and get up for work without a problem. On the BBQ nights with neighbours and such like visitors invited, I never got around to see them all arrive let alone light the BBQ and it was morning, I was being called a party pooper, again! By him and Dolly, this smarted of old tricks I challenged the bastard about spiking my drinks, his reply, it's only a joke. Some joke, of course, Dolly just laughed. It was a bit of a relief when he went, he was getting old and lazy complaining that his work was boring and looking forward to retiring. Helen was doing great at school and passing all her exams, when she was asked by the school what she wanted to be, an RAF, fighter pilot. But there were two problems, the first being her teachers had talked her into doing her 8 o levels in all the wrong subjects and none of which helped get on to the starting block for the RAF, never mind fighter pilot, secondly on their advice if she got a private pilot's license, this would help. And she nearly did bankrupt me in the process at the age of 14, she was landing a light plane all under her own control but with an instructor present, not bad at all. After all of that sleepless nights she was told by the RAF at her interview, there were no women fighter pilots, it shattered us all poor wee bugger her whole life just fell apart, and mine! Billy however, took a fancy to motor bikes, where he got this idea from Christ knows. An old customer Ernie Page dealer in motor bikes in yeaman place helped him a lot, pointing Billy in the direction of motor cross biking. His young son David was probably 4 years younger than (Billy, aged 11 or 12) was well Intune with moto cross and actually brought Billy on a great deal (unfortunately his son died only a few years later of some illness) Billy went into trials then road racing then it all thankfully became a good pastime married life brought it to a halt, although they both had expensive ambition and Past-times for their age. I found it an equally exciting time, being able to afford financially helping them succeed in whatever venture they liked to try they were good Bairns. the business was going from strength to strength employing 2 slaters and labourers and moving into a large redundant warehouse at the former Kinleith paper mills in Currie, even our social holiday style moved into an area which was well out of my wildest dreams I now drove my own long wheel based land rover a huge status statement in those days fitting in a couple of highland shooting holidays in mid-winter and our own deer stalker, me armed with my own 243 rifle at Glen Cannick next door to Glen Affric, Billy and I spent a few good days up in the heavy snow covered mountains with Donald, the Glen stalker who taught us toonies the way of the hills and Glen, and not just the art of shooting at random anything on four legs, but keeping the Herd healthy the hills clean what the shooting was all about, and it was a way of business Meat culling the injured and weak removing any carcass from the hill, to keep the place clean! The whole point was echoed and seen to be true when for a change of scenery I hired the whole estate and house plus stalker at Glen glass, near inverness on the east side of the highlands, Duncan was a young huge figure of a man taught his skills by his father in Glen Affrie where he was born and bred, this wee man in Glen glass was tiny all the tweeds and shite catchers with hill boots and shepherds crook. Two very usually different characters I should say Duncan's foot apparel was size 12 wellie boots and a bunnet. (shite catcher are, trouser which fit to below the knee's with long socks up to them) so if you have a number 2 it will collect at the knee's this wee man stalked from down in Glen looking up the mountain, oh yes there's two up there in the corrie, Christ I had binocular I couldn't see a thing then we'd set off in another direction I was fit but by christ the wee man had an endless supply of energy, after what seemed hours he caught up with his selected beast! I was well out of puff even up close to my target with a fixed bayoneted, I couldn't keep the gun steady enough no bloody energy left, Bang missed it (I was well pleased, I wasn't equipped to drag it off the hill) oh shit missed it as it bounded over the hills out of sight, he remarked the bullet just went over its shoulders his sight was that keen even without tracers I wouldn't have noticed (where's my bren gun!) before I knew it we were off and after it shit! My thoughts were in a 'can of beer'. I seemed to be out on the hills with this keeper most of the extremely snowy weeks. 'However, he supplied Billy and Richie (his wee school pal who joined us) both were only about 13 years old, with a shot-gun and permission to shoot anything that 'flies', they didn't need to be told twice… He told them to 'walk-down' the river with one of them beating the shrub 60 feet ahead of the man with the gun, 'we followed Billy who had the Gun, Richard was way ahead, tramping through the snow covered boundary with the river glass, on our left, dad, mom, Dolly and I blethering away not a care in the world. Next thing, this bloody big bang followed by a shadowy flash and thump at our feet lay the lifeless body of a 'Duck'…the boys were all excited until they took it back to our "lodge" where they ID it as one of the country's rarest species, a golden eye duck… It wasn't long till they plucked it clean of all ID. Then in the oven, no one ate a bit of it. what remained was secretly given to the keeper's dogs. at least this was value for money spent I never shot a thing (thankfully). What it did for me, was to trade my rifle for a camera which was much more enjoyable, but these keepers, they do a really good job, and take pride on the service and set a high standard… still seeking more adventure, Boats were part and parcel with me, I had a few, Plastic and Rubber dinghy's for fishing and diving, but was well governed by the weather when getting caught-out as a storm came by seeing sail boats continue on their way, I got a bit mystified with them, so I decided to take night-classes at the Marina in Port Edgar south Queensferry, learning the art of sail. After a couple of months out in the small-way fairers (Dingy sail boats), I was smitten, I found a 30 feet Bermudian -sloop. Long-keel… a way, above myself after some 4 months of work with the advice of local yachties, I had it launched and stepping the mast "all bull and no shit'… with no help from the family, except dad, who managed single-handedly, put it on the rocks, fortunately without damage, and still within the harbour. Poor old Bugger forgot to tie off the rope, secure it to the jetty when he was alone on board, the wind helped it drift away, the one-ton lead 'Keel" prevented the wooden hull from damage as it bounced off the rocks, My sailing days didn't last more than one season. Business and family life took priority, now that the smokeless age was well and truly taking hold of the whole country (UK wise), but in particular Edinburgh, Chimney-sweeps were going out of business, leaving there family areas vacant; smokeless fuels were the rage, gas-fires and central-heating were now the main focal point in heating, but new ruling made by the governing safety body's ruled that only, Gas related Chimney-sweeps, were to attend to the mandatory servicing (cleaning) of all chimney's. it seemed that I was the only Gas engineer with Chimney knowledge in Edinburgh and wider afield. The work started to come-in from all areas of the city and surroundings, within months, I was employing, slaters and roofers to keep up with that side of work-load, as I tried to keep up to the fast changing face of Gas and Fuelling. the gas industry and national coal board were at logger-heads, could not agree what was to be expected of a chimney, heating and ventilation, even dad struggled, as he, with all his experience in the lums failed to come up to what they said, was the standard now laid down by themselves, qualifying working as a modern chimney-sweep. I was getting the blame from him (me being a gas-man). However, somehow, he struggled through helped by his army and National Health, boiler cleaning, … I even managed to capitalise, when the city crematorium's went on strike, they refused to do the cleaning of the ovens-flues; (direct result of the main flying picket strikers) climbing in and out of ovens where the skeletal ash remains still took the full form of the person just cremated. very spooky… but treated with respect after working hard to pay-off our house-loan (mortgage), Dolly decided that she would like to move away from the council-house scheme and into the private sector but we were not sure if anyone really wanted to buy a council house and what was its true value, I wasn't really too keen on getting into more debt just yet but the money was coming at us thickly; her niece Netty and husband Brian, were looking for a bigger-house and we agreed on a swap. so, into the private sector at Sighthill with a value of £27000, a spring board onto another house, hopefully given in a step in the right direction. I never took to living upstairs in a block, a long walk to back garden, but it wasn't for long… I was getting even more publicity in my research and writing for my book only what seemed weeks away after moving into Sighthill, and our accountant was asking us to spend our ever growing capital on property or other investment when an old customer of mine and Dads passed away, Miss

Wren of Thorburn road Colinton village, one of the most up market parts of town, her 5 bedroom house was on the market large garden, tongue in cheek Dolly and I turned up at viewing strangely, another lady present at the viewing was one of my old window cleaning customers just a couple of years past, she actually though I was here to do repairs, and was a bit put out when she realised I was looking to buy it. The whole house needed re-wiring/plumbing and brought into the 20th century, seeing the look on her face, I think it made me a wee-bit more determined to go for it, offers over £36000 and I got it for £50000 and without having to take out a mortgage.

This was the turning point in our lives; Highs, lows, and unseen hells.

Now at the grand old age of 39/40, my life was entering into an area that put me onto a level of life I never even dreamed of, going along with the 'flow'… Sighthill we rented out, putting into the hands of an agent for a couple of years, it all just seemed to happen too bloody fast, we had enough capital to buy Thornburn road outright, so I had now built up running parallel to this, a contacts electricians, plumbers, all traders and at very affordable cash rates, for a month we sat it out at Sighthill, until the house of Thornburn road was up and running down to the décor carpets and new furnishing, a room laid aside for Billy and a full size pool table, Helen had a furnished room to herself with walk-in wardrobe. Dolly had her very own house-keeper (old Margarette), the cost of the upgrading £4000 all we had to do was supervise such a luxury, this at the time was the poshest street in Colinton village much sought after but it felt right… On the work and business side with only about five or six tradesmen, I was operating under a number of titles which worked well over the past handful of years, scot services – scot sweep – all areas and lately Blackadder-Bell all in the area of chimney and roofing and each one had its own telephone number advertised and above board with all the phone-lines, coming into one phone-base, such as the technology then, no computers or mobile phones, all done by phone (land-lines). we had our best Christmas that year and a huge Christmas tree. But no family were invited on Christmas day. Enough drunken squabbles caused by her mother at our previous, but we did have a trip up to 'fort William' area for a week in a log cabin… after this the accountants called us in to point out to us that we were facing a massive tax-bill of some £20-30000, this wasn't a problem for us as it was already in the bank, he suggested that we would have to consider expanding further, the over-riding factor was we earned most of our income over the winter months, the remainder of the year, we lived of the fat and with little turnover of work meant we had to lay off our work force then until the winter came around again, re-employ and train up new staff, we were also told that we would be leading into a higher-rate of income-tax… the answer was to only work no more than 5-6 months leave the country, and then we were not liable for any income tax, I thought this was only for millionaires to be told yes we were soon to be taxed similarly but with our income really only happening in winter then again we were told or advised that why not work here for 5 months, then 5 months in Australia where the same sort of tax rules apply, but not as stringent, the other two months spent in another part of the world. on holiday, after all, we could work two winter seasons in the same year and pay no tax at all. Then we were introduced to an Edinburgh couple who had lived this method for years and were very successful, we took the bait. our first move in this Direction was an application to Australia house for immigration, laying out a business plan, then it was submitted. In the meantime, we got to know our next door neighbours, one of whom was the director of the national-coal board for Scotland, any elderly couple who we had a few drinks with at the week-ends, I was a fish out of water when it came to talk about business our other neighbour on the other side as Charlie Whitker in his early 60's, Charlie was a loner, again he was an old customer of ours. He was living on his own , his mother died and he was never married, being a bit of a hoarder, the house and front entry porch full of empty cardboard boxes, being larger than an average garden green – house and I full it was impossible to get in the front door, his other project was his well-kept rear-lawn nearly a full ¼ acres in the spring time on a fine sunny day. Charlie was on his hand and knees with an eye dropper and wee bottle full of chemical (brownish stuff), squirting wee-drops onto the up and coming daisy's, the whole lawn when done, looked like a green leopard. a job that took him days on his hands and knees, but the poor man frail and always unshaven and unkempt took fright one night, when we had a bit of a storm, the electric power was cut to the village and our lights were out to make it worse 'thunder and lightning' as we settled down to candle light, the front door, knocker rattled in alarm, it was Charlie panic stricken, we sat him down, he said, he was always terrified of the lightening, however, he settled down at the fire and joined me with a beer, this was the first time we had a good blether and to our astonishment it turned out Charlie is a retired professor of psychiatry but still does lectures where he worked at Bangour hospital (village hospital). It was nice to have such well-established people for neighbours here we were treated as equals.

During this short time I had taken on the lease of our office and storage building at the old Kinleith paper mills now redundant and mostly derelict by now, without any warning, a letter from the Australian emigration arrived. 'oh boy'… they weren't messing about; all our planning was now fast tracked. They gave us all six weeks in which to arrive on Australia. This seemed to bi-pass all these expected procedures, interviews of all applicants, medical of same, then social assessment, criminal records and much more. Even the accountant and our lawyer were wrong footed the timing was perfect, our workloads were going down as winter changed to spring, and a new autumn and winter was now looming, most of all in as many weeks we were due to be subjected to a £27000 tax billing, but not so if we showed our intentions using our lawyer and we did, now we decided to have a trip out and have all our passports legally stamped and have a general look around. and take things as they came, our work force was now reduced already to myself, Dolly, her secretary, 1 slater and Billy our apprentice; leaving the slater and secretary to pick away at the last few calls and Helen to look after the house, she already had her Aussie passport, leaving only the three of us to head off for a planned 5 week return trip. then decide which area in Aussie to take up residency. Keeping in mind, we were advised to even keep all our receipts for whole of this trip as it was classified as expenses against tax, however this was not our aim or priority. We headed for our first stop as is normal on the way to Aussie 2 nights in Singapore mind full of the deli belly but on every trip in the region, it had developed so much away from the small towns surrounded by jungle and kampongs (villages) to the mass of sky-scrapers which grew out of every corner on the wee-island, taking expected food standards up with it. we arrived at Perth western Australia. On arriving had our immigration papers rubber stamped officially now residents of jointly Australian and New Zealand. We were intending to visit Perth, Sydney then Brisbane to access the opportunities in work, jobs firstly and social life, along with self-employed aspect. . Sydney was proving to be the most likely area which could provide us with what was needed, it covered all aspects, even Billy's obsession in dirt-biking; I even re-introduced myself to the (North shore Gas co) now the Australian Gas light company. I was offered a job, should I return, being in Sydney we stayed a few days with the Olaf Family, Olaf was now a superintendent with Gas Co but in his own area in Liverpool (Punchbowl) some two miles, south west of where I was offered a position on the north shores... things were now beginning to visually fall into place. the offer of a job on the north-shore, very highly populated white European decent and English speaking people, as many areas, in Sydney, south and west, were of swaths, of Greeks, Italians, Turks, and others, whole areas where English was not spoken inside them... keeping the kids in the north shore was very helpful... an old saying of these times was, SPOT THE AUSSIE. very true, scots, Irish, English and Welsh, made up a great deal of the residents in the north shore keeping, an open mind on the fact we were only going to be staying for 5 months of the year, after 4 weeks of looking around, the agreement was for Sydney, we headed out to NZ, Auckland, to stay with Tommy and his new wife Peggy, for a remaining last week holiday. New Zealand, turned-up with a few surprises, Billy disappeared for most of the week with his cousin's mark and Anne. we stayed with Tommy in Pakuranga, a suburb of Auckland, I took the opportunity of sussing out the Gas Industry, to find yet again, Scots and English well employed in that field and that I was more than qualified, to the point of being over qualified for positions open, and have been vacant for some time, the money was way above the average. In the event, some thought I may return, made huge monetary offers, also employing Billy as an apprentice, I declined all comers, I've never known the likes. And, hours before our departure I received a phone-call from one company offering me the sum off $1000 for a week should I return... again, I was grateful, but meekly declined... Sydney, Australia was our choice! Once returning to the Edinburgh collectively, Helen and Billy along with our business advisors. The final package was put together, keep the house at Sighthill let out, sell Thornburn road, using whatever that brought (£75000) to buy another in Sydney, close the business, final accounts, submit, the 4 phone lines (I each on all areas Scot Sweep, Scot Services and Blackadder bell) retain them with the phone company (using Sighthill address) as our return base, come winter time, after taking the house back! all this had to take effect with-in the next couple of months, again we agreed that I should go out ahead and taking up Olaf's family The offer for me to stay with them, in the meantime taking-up a position with the Australian Gas light co, in the north shore, which meant a 70 mile return (each way) train journey every morning at 5am over the harbour bridge and back again, that was very acceptable to me. after a number of weeks down-grading the Edinburgh side and getting the Thornburn road house on the market… whilst the house was going through the due process, I flew out via the two day stay at 1987 Singapore, although I was feeling very positive, but after a few days staying with at Olaf's house, I started work at the Gas Company. I was feeling more at home in the north shore, the train journey at 5am each morning, was not too bad, but my fellow passengers could have done with a Tub (bath), the coaches stank of Garlic and stale-sweat, it was like being in a foreign country, I was the only pale-face on board, all the way into the city Sydney where it emptied out, being replaced with my look alike thank god. in all my years of travel, this was the worst regular journey I had ever done. It's not that I don't like spices and garlic, but second hand yuk. After picking up my van and workloads which like old-times were completed in an hour or two. this gave me plenty of time to look around at the available houses to buy or lease in the north shore area but unfortunately, how they were bought, which was very different from Scotland where it was offers over, not here… they always tried to at least double the asking price of any property… if I had $50000 to spend, and saw a house at this price. they tried to sell you a pressure guaranteed mortgage of the same on top (total $100,000) and they would not budge once they knew what money I had, with some advice from my (Scots and English) customers who lived in the area I wanted to live in, I now came to grips in how to get around these agents and I was beginning to enjoy haggling retreating my plan B, to rent which was very affordable, and make a buying, move once the family and resources were at hand here. Every day, I phone Dolly, sometimes twice, Thornburn road, sold very quickly, within the first week she had accepted an offer of £75000, bloody good stuff, over £10000 more than we bargained for, days after it was signed-up, she had a container completely loaded with all our furniture and goods! Everything! I decided to put plan B into action, and took on a short termed lease on a Colonial Bungalow in the Lane-Cove area of north-Sydney when I returned to Punchbowl, and told Olaf that I'd done this., I was taken aback at his sudden unexpected out-burst, for some reason he was not at all happy that I should have decided to take up residency in the north shore, somehow he had it in his brain that I was staying in the punch bowl area, we settled down as usual that night to a few glasses of wine. To begin with, after his mum and dad retired to bed, we stay around the pool-side with the outside lights on and good old country music, blaring away after downing at least a couple of cartons of wine, we were both getting well pissed. As the time moved past midnight, I said I was going to my bed to try and get a couple of hours before an early rise, but the subject turned back to us staying in the north shore, his mood was getting deeply black, then his whole dialog changed to Dolly and his previous contact with her was easier for him to get to Edinburgh than the north shore, he was getting totally unamused in his uncoherent mumbling drunken state, what began to come over to me was the clarity of what he meant, he then moved onto the physical side of how that only I and a doctor would or should only know, I don't know why, but I joked about spiking my drinks to get his evil way he just nodded and laughed telling me I was easy meat. I went to my bed sober, my head was swimming. I just did not know what to make of the whole picture. My first reaction was trying not to take any of that on board, but shit, my thoughts were going in every direction. all I wanted now was to see her and the Bairn's. as much as I tried not to think about what he said about Dolly, shut it all out and facing him again was more than difficult, I never considered this at all! I quickly moved out and into the rental house in Lane cove. the next week waiting on their arrival was terrible, I never made contact with the Olaf or his family, my heart went out to his parents who never were aware of what was going on, he was usually knowing just what I was doing; I made my excuses to his folks turning down the offer of a lift with my cases in favour of a taxi, all the way… in no time, did I think badly of Dolly, this bastard deliberately spilled the beans on the past, I was preventing him from lining his nest by putting her on his door-step, not long after I was re-united with my family at the airport… as the Olaf's family knew of their time of arrival they were at the airport. He was very quiet, but things went alright, finally we were alone at our new home, within the first week, I got Billy a start with a local roofer, Helen was out and about testing the job market in banking which was her chosen area of work and enjoyed. They seemed to settle as best they could into routine around our immediate environment… There was no mention of Olaf, but to move on, I felt I had to ask her a question… one night I approached the subject I felt hellish, Helen and Billy were bedded down. I asked her first what did she think of living in this area and not down south in the Liverpool region. she just shrugged her shoulders seeming by not to fussed where we set up home, when I came to telling her what he said, I actually told her firstly that if she said no, then subject was closed. She never showed any emotions, other than a slight smile of what seemed relief, and a firm yes and that was that, she again was happy to confirm some of the past, including spiking my drinks but she could not tell me if it was all over… I too even at that point felt a sense of relief.

Why, I don't know, we had a good drink, and let the subject slip-by… next morning Billy and I were up first, I dropped him off at 7am, near his job, then as usual drove on to my job, picked up my paper work, visited the Gas sites, then headed back home about 8:30am for breakfast, the relief was still with me, I drove up to the back-door, into the house by way of the Kitchen and into the living room, shit, there was Dolly and him sitting on the settee, both just looked up at me, they didn't look surprised, I was totally taken aback, I could only look at her and blurted out "Get him out of here", I turned and went back into the kitchen, I heard a door close, she came into the kitchen, I could not find it in me to utter a word, other than continue on from there as if nothing had been said or happened, she too, never showed any anger or emotions acting as if all was okay… but that was always her way, Helen was still bedded down. now the air was much clearer, a decision had to be made what happens next!

Up to this point, mentally, I was hoping and prepared for her to have given me a no, denying everything putting up a bit of a fight, but this through my whole plans and objectives in searching them a life style here in Australia. I couldn't ever contemplate a return to Scotland at this point. our container was on the high-seas, bound for Sydney, I had to secure my kids and wife but no longer here. we talked openly to Helen and Billy that maybe our best plan was actually New Zealand, they seemed well at ease with this, talking about staying and socializing with their cousins. and that was that. within a couple of weeks, I had gone to the shipping agent, and redirected our container to Auckland. To try and keep things neat and tidy, for the sake of the Bairn's, a last visit to the Olaf's folks to bid our goodbyes to his mother and father and his sister, I corrected the reason for NZ was simple, I was offered a good deal. try as we must it was a sad occasion, thankfully I managed even to make eye contact with them… even trying not to leave forwarding details was bloody difficult as they did ask, Dolly appeared to be her natural bubbly-self plenty of chat to all, but again that was her,, I didn't know if I admired her strength or what, a few days later and we were at the airport, shit and they were all there, all the Olaf's family, how did they fuckin' know our arrangements. This was murder even to the death… but at the check-in desk, the woman doing the weighing-in, asked us to put cases on the scales one at a time. so I did, blindly she stretched down and tied on the labels one at a time, when it got to the six or seventh case or hold-all, she sat-up straight and said how many do you have, I pointed behind me to where many more were beside Helen's feet. 21 in total, she looked a bit dumfounded.

But your only allowed I bag each, four. then she demanded that we have to pay for the remainder, I said fine $500 NZ, she just stared at me then said are you from Scotland? Yes. Oh well, my daughter was over there and had a problem, I was sick with worry but the kind folks in Scotland looked after her very kindly. so, this was a gift to Scotland, and tore-up the billing there and then, and wished us well. such kindness. my lasting memory on Australia's Shores. Such a relief on getting on board that aircraft, having gone through the ordeal of sitting in the departure lounge, with Olaf fully recovering his composure, the life and soul swilling back the shorts. I never at any stage acknowledged his presence in fear that I might let known all, do something or saw something and Dolly carrying on as ever, both of them happily to chat away loudly. How any of the two of them could keep a front going like this, the bastards have practiced this well. after a 3 ½ hour flight, Tommy, with his son Mark and daughter Ann, met us at Auckland airport, fortunately he brought an open flatbed truck which just managed to hold all our luggage. His kids were of the same age as our two, they were dropped off at their Mums house 'Chrissie, whom he was divorced from, Billy and Helen stayed with them and I with Tommy. They only had one spare room which we used before, within days I had bought a 12 seater mini bus to convert into a van, but firstly we decided to remove some of the seats to make-way for a double-mattress, taking a few days to go up and around to Top half of the North-Island Auckland to Capé Rangie (something like that) where the pacific and Tasman sea collide, Tommy and Peggy came with us. I was not keeping very well, (mentally) and on a short fuse, unfortunately Peggy was in a talking mood, mostly about her ex-husband Alan, a womaniser, the pair of them were not aware of the true reason why we were in NZ, but what she was rabbiting on about was so near the bone, I snapped at her "Alan done himself a favour when he got rid of you'. Dolly turned to me "Michael" just as Peggy shot out of the café we were in Tommy just happened to be away for a pee when it happened.

we all went out into the dark to find her, shit it was pitch black, above the sound of crashing waves, we followed the sound of her snivels, we still never let on what we were on about, touchy bitch. But Helen was quick of the mark, she was working as a teller for the bank of NZ, in the village up the road in Howick, I decided to contract my Gas labour to two Kiwi plumbing brothers who had a long-standing family business on the go. Part of my deal was that they took on Billy as an apprentice plumber which worked out great as a I got to use him as my assistant, they paid his wages. My job was very boring remedial gas-appliance trouble-shooting mostly on the domestic side, with some Chinese kitchens flung in. I was working with 3 gasses, old towns gas (coal gas), natural gas, the new discovered fields were coming into use, and LPG, Butane and propane. My big brother Tommy was getting a wee-bit upset as he was earning as a double-glazing fitter foreman $250-$300 a week, and I was getting $1000 for 10 or 12 hours a week but at no time was earning or finding work a problem to me, but my direction, ambitions general bearing were completely lost, just narrowed down to the very basics, stability on working was the number one particularly for the Bairns it was working they were well focused, and appeared to be enjoying things. It was only a couple of weeks till we got lucky with a house and our container had arrived on the docks. it was a 5 bedroom Two tier bungalow with double garage, laundry and ¼ acre orchard, with lime and oranges and a couple of banana trees, trust me to be burdened with God awful, fruits ever grown, oranges and limes, when Dolly peels one, which is quite often, I have to vacate the bloody area, the smell from them draws my 'Jaws, yuck. so cutting the grass was left to others, unloading the container was fun for all, in particular Billy and his cousin Mark, me not being there when it was packed, I wasn't surprised to see his moto-cross bike sitting there first to come off, that was our two helping hands down as they spent the rest of the time trying to start the damned thing, by the end of the day, everything was in its place, even Billy's Pool-table, stood in place at the side of the bar downstairs, one thing we practiced 'well' when moving house. The drawer, everybody has all the bits and bobs normally found are in the kitchen, we tipped the whole contents out into the bag and I just like now, its emptied into another drawer, feels like home within minutes, within 3 or 4 hours, all our helpers were gone, with all the familiar furnishings, clothing, and even the bedding it was almost like home, but I left all my collectables, (stuff that I had found in attic spaces over the years, not quite antiques in Scotland, but over here in Aussie and NZ they certainly were, I had no intentions of selling them), they felt more homely and now a room (bar-pool) to display them yes a dream come true. Billy, the wee B , went to work as usual on his moto-cross bike, and still only 15, that was the starting age for driving, he came home with a bloody road, bike, shit, as usual everybody including his mum knew about it, but after the going through all of this, I granted and guaranteed it, after living this lie to everyone who were great, putting up with my mood swings, I'd never ever lived such a false-hood, but it was nice to have the Bairns back into the fold… Christ, It didn't last-long with our new phone line put on hopefully to start advertising for my own work, Tommy phoned, he sounded excited, "hi mike, I've just had Olaf on the phone. My whole head and being froze, amazingly I found myself sliding back into the gear. But being unable to get excited as Tommy sounded, was near impossible, I let him finish his spiel, Olaf he says was wishing us well in our new home and wanted our phone number and address, Tommy obliged, before we left Sydney she (Dolly), showed me a note she was presenting to Olaf (to put my mind at ease) saying mike, knows about us, it's finished, yet he turned up at the airport and now the bastards still on the go… did you post that letter to him. yes. (that seemed like a no), showing no signs of remorse, I haven't a clue what her intentions were or even are, not even a word of annoyance at him causing us this endless grief! Not only was it mental torture, and my joints began to feel pain, I was becoming crippled again, I didn't hang around and saw my GP stripping down to my underpants she checked-out all the joints and came up in diagnoses of Arthralgia (painful joints), but before she let me up, she asked if she could have a look at my crutch, telling me my wife had been in as she had contracted thrush, I got the all clear… but Dolly never said and I didn't ask. until now we shared our Paranoia and Anxieties although there was some structure in which to address them and rectify, we could basically read each other's minds and somehow arrive at a reasonable answer, then move on. But on this I felt alone and inept our relationship was purely mechanical, she never seemed to share this with me, I seriously did not want to push her, or dig-deeper, not wanting to uncover my worst nightmare, and on other issues she was always very vocal, where at least she gave responses. Finally, I came to a conclusion all on my own, I told her to phone the travel agents and book us a couple of weeks holiday just for the two of us on Fiji (just up the road). I opened a beer and went down-stairs to the pool-room, leaving her on the phone in the kitchen, as I sat there, supping on a bottle of beer, she shouted down the stair-well, "mike pick up the phone there, someone wanting to speak to you" the phone base at my elbow, I picked it up! Hello? I asked 'yes is this Michael' a young ladies voice sounded my ear, yes, your wife has just told me you need a break, I couldn't understand how this woman suggesting I need to be treated, she doesn't understand the complexity of this situation, what the hell does she knows, I listened and agreed I needed a break, but I could not even understand that anyone could help us both, she had the answers, bloody find them, she left me agreeing to speak to a friend of hers who could help, Dr Culpan an, consultant psychiatrist. my first thought was 'who for'. as she promised he'd phone in a few minutes… and again in nearly as many minutes, I was sitting in the passenger's seat with a wee overnight bag of stuff. after about 20 minutes Dolly pulled up outside the brick built bungalow, it was illuminated by a single overhead lamp, being now dark, I was taken into the office just outside the office door, this young nurse (cherry) dressed in full white uniform asked me to follow her into a small, well-furnished single bed-room, cherry handed me pajamas and asked me to put them on and into bed, asking me what I took in my coffee, she left, this was not real, what the hell am I doing here, Dolly comes in, saying goodnight that she'd see me in the morning. sitting up in bed after cherry gave me a tray with coffee and biscuits, I had a great feeling of well-being and what seemed to be a clearer picture of how to go about this, cherry came in again and asked how I was, I told her how much better I felt and it might be better if I went home, now. she quietly said Dr culpan was on his way over, and rest till I see him... that spooked me, other than my neighbour Charlie Whitiker in Edinburgh, I'd never seen to my knowledge a psychiatrist, and for me... shit... he came into the room...Christ, What the hell has the cat dragged-in, the bauld-headed, tall and skinny old bugger, dressed in jungle green shooting jacket and wide shorts. fortunately he introduce himself, thank Christ, as I was beginning to regret being here, he sat down in the armchair next to the bed, lounging back, cross legged, white nobble knees (surely this wasn't right, I should be sitting there and he up here). Then what seemed a very short period of questions and answers, ending abruptly when he asked dates of birth and death of my brothers and sisters. when I suddenly got to jeans (my sisters) details, I got very chocked up at that, crying as he left he'd get cherry to give me some sleeping pills or such like... again I was left alone, sobbing uncontrollably and for the first time in my life, it felt great almost enjoyable, nobody telling me to stop crying the last time I now remember was dad with a finger on my face, not long after Jean died, 'stop it' ' stop it'... that's what I remembered, that's all. At least for the first week, I spent in the darkened room, only aware of someone coming in, walking quietly round the bed, and the door gently clicking closed, the curtain was kept closed. Even in the morning, somehow 2 nurses, with Scottish accents, somehow managed to change the bed with me still in it, I don't remember them even acknowledging me in any way, but in soft tones kept-up their own conversation while keeping busy. One of them came back with some sort of breakfast on a bed-tray, when they came to collect it, and if I never touched it, not a word was said. but there was one persistently noisy bugger, she stormed in, clanging and banging, horribly cheerie old Maori woman did her hoovering... she always seemed to pick the right moment, when I was in the depths of warm self-pity a good-old greet, by the time she was finished, I'd forgotten what I was greeting for, painstakingly, trying to get back into it, it never was the same, actually the old-sow, turned out to be a Gem, well into my second week, no visitors, except messages via the nurse's ... but bit by bit by bit the old Maori woman managed to get my permission for her to open the curtains and windows, which to me was that bloody air spray that she was always blasting in my directed; up until then the only time I got out of bed, was for the toilet or wash-basin in the corner of the room. when all was quiet, my nose got the better of me, sneakily opening the door, trying to get any bearing on what surrounded me, but I could only see vegetation, and hear running water, later I found this convalescence home was made up with four bungalows set in a square all inter-connected by corridors, the central inner square was all of a tropical garden setting, there were trees and bushes, also water features with seating and footpaths where patients could sit, I was located in the restful area, others being for people recovery from operations, dementia, a good mix of patients, slowly but surely the nurses pulled me away from my sanctuary, my pit, then without much ado, I found myself being ushered into the shower cubicle now my whole body shook with tremors, the amount of energy that this simple action took was exhausting, mentally and physically, I had to have help in finishing the remaining soap from my hair, there was no way I could hold the razor to shave, it took two of them to do this task and a good job they did. It was a couple of days before I risked going through that again. The tremors and the leg wobbles increased the more I moved around. What the hell was going on, I walked in here, I'll never walk properly again. They were trying to convince me things would come right, I was told Dolly did come a couple of times but I was sleeping, into the third week, Dolly arrived with a picnic hamper and took me out for a drive. Jesus, what a life, which turned into a night roller-coaster, the destination was an old Maori fortress, one tree hill, aptly named one conical tree in shape, grass covered and a couple of hundred feet high, with its famous pinically shaped 'one, lonely tree' this place being a well-known land mark which I'd seen on a daily basis, from a safe distance, simple as it seemed a winding road led to a tiny car-park on the summit, true to form, she legged all the way, or that's what it appeared to me, everything, was well out of focus, just a blur by the time we got to the base of the hill which was only probably 1 mile away, my head was shot, spinning even at the sight of other traffic moving, she took off like a bat out of hell (well it bloody was to me), screaming and yelling at her, had only increased her speed accelerated all the way up., howls of laughter from her. closing my eyes seemed to make it worse, it seemed endless, the whole phenomenon was a blur, once at the top facing this lonely pine-tree, we pulled up to a halt, but my head just could not stop spinning, realising that she couldn't part my hands from the overhead-handles, she made the right decision, I was back in my room, my sanctuary, by the end of week four, I was ready for discharge, once home, it wasn't long before I got bored out my skull, although I still shook my mobility over all was far from good, no matter how I tried cutting the grass or washing the van was both physically and mentally, draining but I hankered for real work, driving was all down to Dolly, I was more than concerned about meeting people. I knew, in particular, those who I contracted myself to what the hell would they do or say about this, sweaty, shivering wreck, I noticed by the phone in the kitchen, the writing pad notes on calls of recent, a few were for, repairs needing done and mainly for gas-heaters and pump filters for swimming pools and good money waiting to be earned, I had a talk with Dolly and we reached an agreement, I would use my brains she would give it a shot using my tools under my supervision. She was great, as I sat in a deck chair by the pool side, pointing to this and that gas, electric, pumps, plumbing and how to hold and use the correct tools placing the importance on let the tools do the work. she too was impressed with her abilities and success rate even to the point, on how to gain the customers confidence, we agreed after a few weeks, that we were successful working like this, but in all honesty, we could do with a complete break!

    With Edinburgh the only place in mind, even the thought of it in particular the flight I was having panic attacks galore, at the thought of it. Helen and Billy were quite happy to stay by themselves. Tommy's, daughter Susan who stayed in Gorgie Edinburgh area, had a small flat furnished, vacant. so, we had a base all to ourselves, no work distractions, come and go as we pleased, visit who ever as we pleased. the flight turned out perfect. The travel agent was advised of my health, they passed his information to air NZ, we only booked and paid for the basic passenger class for some strange reason to both of us, we were told to take a seat in the lounge, we could see the guests slowly disappear into the boarding tunnel, we were approached by a stewardess and told to follow her, now I was panicking shitless as one does, we followed her right into the passage heaving with bodies, she stopped at the foot of what appeared to be a spiral-stair case, she pointed for us to go-up. I was by now wanting my bed-space, bugger Edinburgh. don't panic. Up top, we were shown to two black leather arm chairs, just Infront I was amazed and yet confused anxieties whatever, sat the pilots, this was our first ever flight on a jumbo jet and how we got into first class (another first) kept me guessing the whole flight, and bugger it, this increased my anxieties greatly, waiting on some, bugger noticing, we might be in the wrong seats, another first, we never had a drink of spirit, under normal circumstances I'd have been reasonably oiled by now. otherwise, a good trip we had an uneventful four weeks in Edinburgh, lots of walking sleeping and visiting (family) at least we agreed to one thing, that as a return back home to Edinburgh was the best way forward… but I decided that I would try for a full time job when we got back to Auckland, the reason was I was feeling, stronger and felt I should get the best out of a regular commitment, 5 day week, more as a treat, let someone else take the reins we had established money was not really a problem or at least earning it. When we got back and had a talk about returning to Scotland, the Bairns seemed very happy to do so… the first thing we did was to put the house on the market, then I got started with an Auckland plumbing and gas engineering, company cooks, they seemed to be well established outfit. the only thing that they gave me a problem was Gas-welding, I had never done it before, it was the welding of black iron gas pipes, which had died out in the UK even before my time, I had all the skills in, brazing, soft solder, and lead work, but not this, so I decided to go back to college (night classes), to get some good experience, and it worked… adding this to my jointing knowledge, I enjoyed something at last, I was nervous of my tremors the older instructor did notice this and soon put me at my ease. he told me that the tremor was an advantage in gas-welding, if used properly, keeping the heat on the move, was important, the tremor certainly done this, it actually became a bit of a novelty for me at work, using it to my benefit, I sought-out as much black iron work I could get my hands on. I was enjoying my work, communicating even putting in a full day's work. the work force of about eight was a nice mixture, Kiwi's (white), pacific islanders, and one eskimo, I was working on a building-site inside the huge 'warehouse' type area, loads of workmen, in particular I noticed next to me, two young pacific islanders, electricians, working away on their own, they walked by me I done the natural thing, and stopped and talked to them. They give me a disgusting look and body swerved past me keeping on going, I had never encountered that in all my travels. come break, I made my way down to a particular tearoom with my flask and pieces (sandwiches), the place was empty, I sat on the bench next to the only window and my back to the door, poured my tea, spread out my newspaper and got stuck into my pieces, I was so aware of guys coming in around me but never looked up even some sat at my table, I was so engrossed in my paper that I was suddenly alerted to the silence… on lifting my gaze upwards, shit there was this sea of different shades of black faces, and they were all looking at me. and not a smile amongst them, one of them pointed towards the window beside me, shit, outside and only a couple of feet away was another window into an adjoining cabin, through which sat all the white guys, I deliberately slowly turned to all the black-faces and asked the obvious question, do you want me to go in there, only the one who pointed nodded, so I got up gathering my gear together, I just said… well, I don't have a problem sitting here with you guys, where I came from we all get on together. nothing was said, I joined forces with the white mob, who didn't even notice what happened, later back at work, the two young islander lads approached me, shook my hand and we had a good old blether, the white guys did not know how to handle it. 'Quite amazing getting drunk. it took a wee bit practice but I found the bottom of a carton of plonk wine, very rewarding but a wee bit too regular. this I found the best therapy for a good greet sitting there down in the bar and pool room, with great music, which thankfully drove them all out, Andy Stewart, pipe bands, galore, blaring our over the room, tears of joy streaming down my cheeks, and off my chin dropping into my glass. oh, depression is great… the hills of home. shit. squeezing the carton to get the last drop. good lass, I've found another one behind the bar, I awoke to find my head glued to arm of the chair (again) bastards are in the beds left me in the dark. time for a wee greet, like everything, we decided on a wee changed. since we had no real intentions of plans to return here, NZ. A holiday around the south island seemed a good choice, and now since we are working to a bit of a budget, back-packing seemed a better way than any. but we received a phone call from my mum and dad in Edinburgh. they were bored in their retirement and asked if it as ok to come out to NZ, for a few weeks, so we agreed to put our trip south off in the meantime, mum and dad were keeping this a surprise, only Dolly and I were in on it not even our Bairns but someone else did know, we received a brief note from that bastard, Olaf, saying he had a few days holiday and was coming over to see bill and jean (mum and dad). My head was in a spin, I thought I'd shaken this 'get-off' my state of mind could or would only harbour the thought he knew of their visit by that my mother and his mother spoke on the phone from time to time, all of them as far as I was aware, knew nothing about their affair. Here he was sneaking about under the raider, bastard. One thing was for sure, I was on his case for the three-days, he was here much to Dolly's disgust (tough!) I made sure he was in my sight all the time and refused him the spare bedroom, which was unoccupied all the time, making him sleep in the open on the floor by the pool-table with only a sleeping bag… for some strange reason the bedroom door was locked and the key missing (planked by me). I was alcohol dry for the whole of his stay. I have never seen him again even to this day The day mum and dad arrived at Auckland International Airport, Jesus, it was bloody heaving don't know how many flights arrived at the same time, but hell we could hardly get into the arrival-hall, hundreds, shoulder to shoulder, more than 20 deep. both of us trapped at the back with me jumping, up and down, only a trickle of bodies coming into this area right at the front, then I saw the wee-man, he was just standing there looking out into the crowd, then I hit on it, I gave him the Chimney-sweeps, distress call, cupping, both hands to my mouth, 'Ah he hee he' three time loud, lots in the crowd turned looking at me. what the hell. I only had to-do these 2 or 3 times, then I heard his reply 'Heeeee!' After strange looks at me, he kept shouting till Dad's wee face appeared with a wide grin. we used the sweeps call, distress signals, where one is on the roof in a sea of chimney-pots, his mate in the house gives the call up inside the fireplace which is only a muffled noise at the top, this shouting kept up until the correct chimney-pot is located, and it's working. (Read my chimney-sweeping history book)! We kept their arrival from everybody except Helen and Billy, as a surprise. as it was still mid-morning and once they got their cases in the house, I took dad on his own to meet Tommy (unannounced) at his work-place, a huge work-shed, 10 mins from our house, dad hid behind a landfill-skip, I asked Tommy out into the yard, placing him with his back to the skip about 10 feet away, he was looking a wee-bit anxious as to why I was there, just telling him I was just passing, then I started a shorter and much quieter 'Hee, hee...' Christ, he looked at me strangely, what's wrong with mike... then dad copied with a very quiet reply Tommy face was a picture, he recognised all this, his brain was working overtime, looking around!! Then back at me, that's when I changed it to, hee-up!!! which meant show yourself dad, appears. Tommy was truly in shock, we all hugged and laugh uncontrollably, then Tommy asked the obvious, where's mum. oh, she couldn't fly, son. Having gone through this before Tommy understood. This was the next surprise, Tommy phoned Peggy at her, work asking for us all to meet in my house, for a wee-drink (I had already arranged with Dolly to hide Mum down the stairs from the upper lounge. we all met back at the house even as Tommy's kids were there, they were all in on the surprise install for him, I sat him at the top of the open stairs head, gave him a beer, he sat there chatting away, everyone acted as naturally as mum's head appeared behind him, and she held that spot for what seemed an age. slowly Tommy sensed there was something behind him... it was pure magic. tears all round, what a day. 'mum and dad on the trip here booked up a visit to see uncle Doddie in Brisbane for a week, making up for when she took panic attacks back in the 1970s, when I went with dad in her place... unfortunately even this trip was not to happen, just days before they were to fly-out, dad took unwell, some sort of heart problem, he went to see our doctors, who told him that flying now could cause a big problem, now he had a bit of an unrealistic decision to make, he was fearing dying out of Scotland, in his opinion he wanted home whether it killed him or not, so after a few weeks out in NZ he took the gamble, and completed the return safely home, where he made a good recovery, poor uncle Doddie, it was another 10years when Doddie and Jessie made their own way to Scotland for a reunion.

After Mum and Dad left, we decided to do the trip to the south half of the north island, and the whole of the south island, our first overnight stop by bus was wellington the windy city, the weather kept up to its name, arriving just before dark, arriving at the local youth hostel with our huge rucksacks and all the dress gear to go with it, prepared for a cross country event, which by the way, was our intended and preferred choice, much to our disappointment, we found that there was a law which made it as difficult as possible, to halt anybody who had such ambitions, Christ more bloody, do-gooders...we had mapped ourselves a route on the south island up the hills and down the glens, which we done (mostly in Scotland), camping by the river-sides, but no, unfortunately just before we set off with our tents. I happened to mention our intentions to our travel agent, it was the look of horror on her face which struck us like an alarm-call, she gingerly asked, have we booked our overnight stays and spaces in the Huts. then she told us it was against the law to stray off the foot-paths, particularly in the south island, and the huts slept 8 or 10 people which meant only that amount of people were tramping between huts at a time. also, you had to book-up well in advance. and no straying of these paths or camping. we had given ourselves no alternate but to coast-it… the land of the free our first hostel here in the windy city Wellington, I yearned for my tent, our beds stank of sweat from the bodies before, the place was just a shock, thread-bare 'curtains and carpets", I also found we could not be seen to leave in the morning unless we had completed a chore, I chose hoovering shit a mistake, I had a stressful fight with the carpets holes and tugging up the shreds of pattern, it was the enthusiasm of the young ones using the place, or it was back-home…. We were the grandparents amongst this lot, fortunately we shared their sense of humour.

Our best source of information as to bus and ferry-time, came from these kids our fellow backpackers, they also warned us as to where not to stay on our trip-ahead, and also told us about some, who like us, planned a cross country only to find themselves in the police cells and courts, for the troubles… but we caught the morning ferry-boat all the way across the choppy water, the cook straits… we had a good crossing down onto the south island it steered between these massive beautiful mountains which just rose out of the seas around us, then the breath-taking sight of Picton township our first step off-point, then a bus trip of a good few hours into Christchurch a low lying township with all its colonial structures, every bit English. Now we popped into the local grocers to stock up on some eggs and beans to have for our breakfast the next morning. Before the next leg to Dunedin, also bought a sealed pack of cheese and small loaf of bread, being husband and wife, we were given a double bedroom in the Victorian type youth hostel, timber-built, a wee-but tidier than wellington, and we had a double-bed. next morning was Sunday, we were either the only ones in this place or just up early what-ever. we had this multi-table come, kitchen all to ourselves which was great, only a small-electric ring for all, we put our bacon-on, both of us bursting to the toilet. what seemed only a few seconds away on re-entering the kitchen, we were met by a cloud of smoke making its way out of the room, shit, the frying pan… agh. the whole room was choking with smoke, not wanting to get caught, I shouted to Dolly to close the door, I grabbed the handle of the pan, Christ it wouldn't budge, with both hands, it came away with the burning ring attached, as the pan had melted onto it. quick a flash! I reached over to the old wooden framed – window, turned the handle. help ma-bob, the whole window frame fell-out, I just managed to keep a grip of it before it disappeared outside, in one move the pan disappeared into the backyard, I pulled the frame-work inside, we were amazed not to hear or see anyone, what with all the smoke and noise, without a word, action, like sneak-thieves, we were down the road and out of Christchurch. and onto the only part of the journey done by train. I think the country had a surplus of sheep, all the seats were bedecked with the stuff… they could have washed them from time to time, but not one for complaining, we got tea from the buffet bar, opened up my rucksack to make our sandwich cheesy. shit, in a flash a mouse jumped out and scurried over our table, we didn't get time to scream. But the wee-bugger had a belly full of cheese, at least it was on its way to another town. I think it was at this point of our whole trip to NZ, I was to see something from this trip that shocked me and surprized me about how uncaring they possibly were… looking out of the window going down the coast, looking landwards to the distant-mountains, I saw ever increasing numbers of sheep, many thousands in each area, and flocks everywhere, we were at the right time of year, as lambs were dropping-out of the mothers in large numbers, but to our horror, as many dead and dying ones including their mothers with dead lambs hanging out, blood all over the place looking in horror because of this 'sea of red' against the white wool, , we were aware of the silences in our carriage at this site, which seemed to go on and on, mile after mile, but stranger still, not a shepherd or human insight to help these poor bastards, amazingly, sheep were part of the tourist attraction!! Dunedin, I was a wee-bit disappointed, I didn't know what I was expecting to find, it didn't resemble Edinburgh in any way at all, other than similar street names, it was late in day, so we left it to a taxi-driver to take us to what we thought was local YH, once there (in the dark), we were taken up the side of the building and shown our sleeping quarter. bloody hell. an old standard 6x8 feet garden-shed or batch as they were known in NZ, batch holiday home/huts, and a second which doubled as a kitchen come toilet. we never got to ask how many shared. I found an old-bucket. Thankfully our batch had only 2-fold-down camp beds, we took turnabout standing out in the cold, so we could sort out our gear for the night and prepare ahead for the morning. night! Fortunately we had our own torches, we didn't hang around! The next day we were up and away on the bus to the very south Invercargill again, we arrived as darkness fell, there was nobody in the town, the bus dropped us of in a dimly lit street, empty except some shops frontages closed but lights from their windows helping to cast an eerie shadow, at least the directions were right following a foot-path between shops, it led us down to an even spooky dark area littered with an assortment of caravans, this area seemed lit-up by the high lamps, we followed curve of a very high wall on our right to the only small caravan sited beneath this wall, which had light coming from its window, this was the office of the site manager. In the gloom he handed me a key pointing over to a long static caravan in the distance. after trying the key in its door, a good few times, we returned to tell him, it wasn't working. after a few grunts and groans from him, we got the message, not that one, there's one behind it. found it! and the key opened the door to the smallest caravan we'd seen, the light switch was where he said it was, we shouldn't have put it on, and in the name of the wee-man, Christ, straw everywhere, kind of piled up to one end, with just enough space for us to lay-out on what cushions were around, we laid out our sleeping-bags, strung up our rucksacks from the central ceiling light, in the event of small visitors or even there big brothers Rats during the night, keeping fully clothed we snugged up in our own bags, pulling the cords tightly around our necks, making sure we were the only ones inside them. lights out. having hardly closed our eyes and ears all night, the calls of the wild were all happening inside this wee-van, we dragged ourselves and got outside, rainy and misty, what an amazing sight, we were on the edge of the southernmost agricultural showground (out of season) beyond which lay the main runway for the airport and a scattered batch of old-battered odd sized and shaped caravans I'd ever seen, but the alleyway we entered by way of with the high-wall, was the Invercargill prison, with row after row of cell-windows looking down upon us, they were better off in there, we returned a friendly wave to them who seemed to notice our plight. they probably had a good breakfast; we chose to forgo ours all the way down to this southernmost town in the whole of NZ. South-island, there was we noted a distinct lack of coloured or black faces, all we could see was white Europeans although we were told that there were many old-tribal areas, there may be, but where are they hiding. a completely different picture in the north-island. and the country side on this side of the island was picture post-card, flat-lands with the pacific on one side open plains spreading out to the distant-mountains, but at no time other than snippets of the imagination, did I see a resemblance to my highland home, which to me had more character, but it was more acceptable than the north island, sub-tropical, monsoon weather, humid damp and bloody-cold, the south to the white European must have seemed hugely better and struck your mind, without a doubt the better choice, to be like home, I must have been brain-washed at geography in school into believing this was Scotland on a grand-scale. shit, again, being evicted from our highland-homes (clearance) the south of the south islands, which weather alone does remind me of home, throw-in some familiar street names 'Magic'. ship up the black tribes to the north island and tropical jungles, move in some sheep. sounds really familiar, I've got an imagination, but it doesn't stretch this far…

We caught the bus on our next leg, to Queenstown, getting a wee-bit more desperate for a sleep. driving by bus from the south up through the high mountains was spectacular to say the least, as the road wound its way in and out of the passes, opening up into inland waterways, 'Fjords' alpine looking. Arriving at the town late afternoon, the place was jam-packed with most of NZ tourists, unfortunately, mount-cook was shrouded in mist, so we abandoned the ski-chair up to get closer to it, although on the way up here it came into view from time to time, at last the YH turned out to be very good, and sleep at last, next day we headed north of the west coast to grey mouth, a small town on the coast, we gave ourselves a treat and booked into a motel-room with our own TV, shower-room, fridge, and double bed with clean sheets (white), Jesus, I never enjoyed a hot-shower as much a treat, I sought-out a licensed liquor store, 6 pack for me, ½ bottle grouse for the boss, sleep came easily or a coma more like it. the next day, bus again, heading up into the canyons of the Buller-gorge, north to Nelson, where we spoiled ourselves again, and booked into another motel. fast getting back into the good-life that night we went to our first movie for years 'crocodile Dundee 2'. crap. we must be bloody desperate to go and see this stuff. the next day it was back to Picton and the ferry-boat back to the north island and our final night in wellington, when we phoned home and got the good news, the house is sold, $190000, nearly $40000 in over one year gained. The main point being it sold at all, as we were well informed there was slump in the market. there wasn't much to pack-away, Aug 1988, we arrived back in Edinburgh. to find our flat in Sighthill, reasonably in tacked… really only the bath-room flooring needed some attention, whoever our tenants were, we are told they spent most of the time in the bathroom, apparently they belonged to a religious sect, and were carrying-out some sort of baptism on a regular basis, the neighbours down-stairs were not happy at getting flooded-out. then there was a disagreement, when Dolly took the washing down to the back-green at the rear, she had to run the gauntlet of their abuse downstair neighbours, but she gave us much as she got, she attacked there wee-dog, the guy chased her round the garden and thumped her. it was left for me to deal with him, fortunately for both him and I, he retreated to his house, and refused to come-out, Helen and Dolly were back into their normal fighting mood, never happy unless they were pulling-out each other's hair and generally ripping their faces to bleeding shreds, Billy and I gave them a wide-berth peace came about when Helen, went round the corner to Dolly's sister Senga's house to stay, but this was an on-going period, where Dolly, Billy and I made great progress with our new business, Scots-Sweep/ Auld-Reekie chimney sweeps, the very day the phones were put on the yellow pages arrived on our doorsteps with our advert looking great and as a planned we were top of the column, that very afternoon as I was giving the skirting board a new coat of paint, the phone burst into life, hello. I asked. is this scots-sweep, Auld-Reekie chimney sweep. Jesus, I felt great, the effect on my being was fantastic, the first injection of adrenaline 'oh boy'. I'd never had such a feeling for the past couple of years. Helen was also working with the banking. she also had met her love of her life, Joe, RAF great coat and all, coupled with a full head of long-black wavy hair. but I was now to make a fatal move at this period. we all signed on with the local GP practice of Colinton, health centre, my young GP innocently suggested, that because I had, had a successfully treated depression episode, that I see their resident psychiatrist (consultant) Dr Ian Putin. so, I did. he asked me to take part in an exercise, the reason being, he said was we had never met before therefore, doing this may prevent a reoccurrence, simple, okay I agreed, using a graph type chart , I was to keep on hour by hour mood swing gauge on myself and he would see me monthly, we would spread the page-out over the floor and see what pattern if any was developing, in mood changes, I should have kept one eye on this bugger. later he was found to be, (by the media) the drugs spokesman, for drug company 'Prozac'. the nightmare anti-depressant, which was accused of causing a huge amount of deaths world-wide, and I was one of his guinea-pigs. he was caught out with his hand in the till and disappeared from Edinburgh, later I found him in Melrose Borders, in early retirement, bastard. still at Sighthill I had bought a small red (cherry-red) van, just to get us going. on our very first call, Billy and I pulled-up outside the house in Craigleith, mounted the pavement reversed with two wheels on the Kerb up to the gateway behind us, "bang". the whole van shuddered to a halt snapping our heads backwards, a shower of glass covered both of us. then motionless and silent, we looked at each other, what the buggery was that. I got out to find a lamppost wedged imbedded in back doors, in the now dented rear doors, 'Oh dear' no wonder I hadn't seen it in my rear-view mirror, not being put off we recovered our composure, as by now the customer was standing in the door-way, alarmed at the noise, we completed the very first job, got back home, phoned the council to advise them of our wee-accident, with the lamp-post which fared better than the van, to be told our honest customer had got to them first. smart bastard. but the guy thanked us for our honesty and told us to forget it, our monies from NZ came through ok. and the business was already within weeks, filling our expectations 'great'. we already had our sights on getting back on the housing market in Colinton. We offered Helen and Joe the chance to get on the housing market to take out a small mortgage, about £10,000 and we would give them the keys to Sighthill, buying it from us £10,000 (the house was valued at £36,000). but thankfully for me they turned it down, Joe a nice young lad decided that working was not worthwhile, Helen a true believer followed this, and chucked in her job, then she found out she was expecting (John)… however, between them they got a council house on the multi-storied flats 9th floor in oxgangs and seemed to settle down for that meantime. just weeks before Xmas 1988 a bungalow in Colinton came up for sale, Bingo. And we moved in ahead of Santa, just a small 2 bedroom and box room, in need of upgrading, wiring, plumbing and no central-heating only gas-fires. a nice wee project. with a well-established back garden all around, great. plenty of work coming in, a tiny wee self-built staircase up to a well floored combed ceiling attic, Billy, grabbed this area as his hideout and room. painting it gold with the letters of his pop-group. AC-DC. (who the hell are they?) Dad now aged 76 years, was always nipping my legs, about coming out to work with Billy and I, so one Saturday morning, we relented, he turned-up in his best Bib and brace, dungarees, we only had to go up the road to a lovely large posh house, Billy and I walked up the long-driveway and knocked on the side-door tradesmen's entrance, dad followed a wee-bit behind, the lady of the house answered. We hardly introduced ourselves, when this raging guy in his dressing gown came from behind the ;lady who seemed prepared to feebly stop her ranting husband, blinding waving his fists at Billy and I, both of us in a wee-bit a shock, dad suddenly guessed what was going on and from a few yards tried to encourage us, not to take any lip from this customers, and deck him (punch) we backed off grabbing dad who was by this time rarring to have a go. With dad still shouting up the driveway we forced him back up into the van. as this was our only job for the day, it was back to the house, that was the last time that dad put on his dungarees, to our surprise, we were called back to do the job, some weeks later, the lady apologized for her husband's behaviour, he was a lawyer and didn't like tradesmen, in particular on a Saturday morning, we weren't bothered, we just doubled the bill, magic. Billy was now attending day release for roofing and slating at Telford College, and doing well at work, I decided to share the business with him and Dolly, as an incentive to the three of us, so I put in £12000 each (£34,000), making us equal partners! And as he was into road-bikes again I bought him a cherry red Volvo estate car. trying to keep him on 4 wheels with safety in mind. Helen had our first grandson 'John' Michael McLenaghan DOB 09-11-89', and what a pleasure, my enjoyment was the times with him, pushing him in his Pram all the way to and from Whitson to visit my mum and dad, change his nappy and off again. I fully understand where the old-ones said that they enjoyed pushing a pram for miles, even to the wash-house, steamies even in the first couple of months Helen found it hard to cope, with everything life through at her, as a result she and Joe were falling out a great-deal of the time and by the end of the day, she had no energies left again she couldn't cope, John stayed most of the time with us, we were all suffering as a result, John became my priority. things with her got even worse when she found she was expecting she had our second grandson Peter and both the boys were great characters and were fun to have around, Dolly established her own space in the small spare room as her office, I made one big mistake at this point, I let one of my customers talk me into re-slating part of his huge mansion house-roof, as this was an old Victorian Villa, set in what seemed a cliff edge down near the water of Leith beside the Dean-Village, it had many roof sections at first he only wanted one done as it was well weathered, I decided to let Billy work away at the sweeping and jobbing, which kept the cash-flow going. this part of the roof took me two solid weeks to complete. he paid up with no problem £6000, but he hit me with a bomb-shell. And that was he wanted the remainder done, oh shit. the better part of me didn't want it, I would never have touched it if I knew, I much preferred smaller jobs, however I felt tied down. Dolly wasn't happy. But I done it. weeks later I had it completed, too late I was done in I didn't really understand how bad I was until GP suggested that I take a rest and book into the Andrew Duncan Clinic! Or better known as the royal Edinburgh psychiatric hospital in Morningside! I had heard a wee bit about this place, and was seriously worried that I was this low. the GP and Dolly came with me up to the top flat and ward 5, it was dark outside, we entered along long dimly lit narrow dirty flag stone paving, passage oh god! I was overcome with panic, horror, only passing another person from time to time, climbing endless, cold stairwells, coming to a single solid door, it opened up into a warmer atmosphere but again dim-lit, even narrower corridor… a young girl clutching a clip-board and pen, sitting just inside the door, stood up and challenged the GP. they spoke quietly then she pointed to the distant end of the passage. We followed the GP down past curtained doorways and onto the end, where bodies lying on the floor, having to step over and between them, young folk, totally ignoring us, smoking and talking away, at the time I never realised. I was walking in amongst staff and patients socializing, I took a seat in a large darkened room, scattered about were other arm chairs under which lay a thread bare carpet on the chairs they were sitting and slouching what I took to be patients, some appeared to be sleeping, none of them even gave us the slightest glance, the GP called on me to follow him. We arrived at one of the curtained doors, which the person pulled to one side, to reveal what was to be my bed-space, 'ah, Christ. staring at us was a wooden ply' rectangular box sunk into it a battered old mattress, all stained, beside this stood a smaller one acting as a side-table, that was enough, I was out that door, like a bat out of hell'… with Dolly and the GP, calling and trailing close on my heels. not a word had to be said all the way home, and into my own bed! But the GP never gave up (this was very like NZ repeating) he called into see me the next day 'Lorimer House', in Merchitson, Brunstfield, a massive stone, three storied detached townhouse run by a wife and husband team, specializing in psychiatric care, and only hundreds of yards from the royal Edinburgh hospital, I arrived there shattered, a single room to myself, I couldn't understand why I was back in this situation, but different in many ways to NZ. Yes I felt it a sanctuary, but from what? There was no drama or real conflict with myself only a feeling of regret that I was here, coupled with that I could not see where else. meals in my room, and a shower with toilet, no nurses just civilian staff coming and going, issuing pills, changing beds, cleaners, very much that of a classical hotel, after days, or a week, I ventured out into the carpeted corridors, but not really aware of the places locality until after the first week, I ventured out into the huge back-garden enclosed by a 8 foot high stone wall. many a time during the day I'd sit with a coffee and sketch book pencilling out my surroundings, my mind still well focused on the grand chimneys of this and surrounding houses, in my third week I'd only came across two other residents, both male. one a tall well-spoken middle-aged gent. who was the son of an estate owner out by Stirling... Blair Drummond safari park, his problem was that he drank all their profits, he had a slight liking for Gin, so he was having to dry-out? this was his in umpteenth visit and already thought he had established a nice life-style which was worthy of keeping up. The other guy. he had similar problems. he worked out on the north sea oil – rigs, 2 weeks on and 2 weeks off, although, when out on the rig he was dry with no urges, but he got slaughtered stupid during his stay on land for the next two weeks, he was here courtesy of his firm BP (Britain Petroleum) who thought he was such a good investment, and pay for his dry-out period. he then produced a letter from his company, in it was also a costing of what they were paying for his 6 weeks stay £6000. 00. my brain and heart took a turn. I was on the blower (phone) to Dolly who confirmed by saying she had just sent off a cheque for the first week, £1000, what a recovery, shit, I wasn't that sick, and to qualify this, I never saw a doctor of any kind after the first-night. I was packed and home in hours, with a total bill of £3000. Billy and his cousin got a flat, Like Helen's multi-storied flat at Sighthill then had a white-wedding in Corstorphine, she was expecting soon, and it was a wee-girl, Sally so I volunteered my expertise, after getting Peter and John to nursery at view forth. Billy was concerned about leaving her alone whilst he was working, I would go up to see her after getting the boys to nursery, get Sally ready then bring both of them up to our house, leaving her there in great hands take a few jobs for myself then take them home and pick up the boys from the nursery. October 1993, dad died, as the result of an operation which was meant to give him an added 5 years to his 76. It came so suddenly only days before John, Peter, Mum, Dolly and I were fishing at a trout-farm in fife. we were having a great-time after he finally caught a big-trout, he took a plastic machine gun (toy) and clubbed it senseless much to the alarm of John and Peter. Grandad's deeded it 'stop it granddad, when he took it to the owner of the fish-farm who on weighing it to charge him. she shouted bloody things, still alive. dad grabbed it, and thumped into head on the counter. I think it's dead and now. dad was buried beside his wee Lassie Jean at mount vernon round about this period in time, things were not going ahead as far as I was concerned. Although I was doing my job and lots more. I found things at home being more frustrated getting difficult, Dolly was not coping with the boys down to the fact that she locked herself away for hours at a time in her wee-office. The boys were completely banned from going inside and to oversee this and keep her anger in check, I was allotted the task of keeping them busy and away from her feet when they were at nursery later Bonaly School to the point, I was put in the same exclusion zone. The office as it were out of bounds, only Billy and ones chosen by her allowed entry. even my workloads were issued to me in my living room. This was not a problem for me. book keeping was not my choice of earning a living doing the work on site brought the money's in and that was where I was at my best and happiest, she was at her best at a type-writer and on the phone. Billy, he was happy and at his best doing his own workloads with his mum… during this time we took John and Peter on holidays, to what was to be our favourite haunt Dalbeg bay on the extreme west coast of Lewis in the outer Hebrides, it didn't matter the weather, they spent hours on the beach, rock climbing (infants that they were) rabbit shooting, then trout fishing. I got peace in the out-doors with them and she had the caravan to herself. venturing out when the sun shone. then we would always gather up drift wood for the night time, (having said that, it was nearly always twilight at this time of year), the fun part of the day really began, 'boys will be boys', a big bon-fire even if it did not stop the attack of highland midges. both of them pitching their wits against each other, Peter straight in there, John the thinker, a great balance of minds… for a wee change, we would go to Butlins Holiday Camp at Ayr. but there wee minds were not harnessed there following the pack, being exposed to the highlands, they were well struck on the out-door life. and still are. when they returned to their nursey after two weeks in the outer Hebrides, we were called into see the nurse, why was John acting depressed as he was alright before he went in holiday? we were being challenged. I had to ask them the obvious. how did they feel like when they returned to work after having a great holiday… say no more? end of meeting, and in a couple of days, John was back to himself… back at Red Ford and on their mornings off from nursery, one of their favourite haunts as down to the Blackford ponds, which occupied a good 2 to 3 hours if no-one had been there feeding the ducks before us, and there bellies were not already full of bread, Peter was always the one leading the way down through the muddy pathways, splashing through the puddles on the way, keeping them dry at this point was a must in that they didn't get too cold, moaning to get home quickly and I was under instruction to keep them away as long as possible. with a ton of stale bread, down the duck's throats, they (the boys) could get as wet as they wanted. Many a time they nearly went head over heels in beside the ducks, great fun was had all the way back home, soaked…

    Mother was a book keeper by profession. so applied all her skills in running Dad's business… all the books, estimating, daily records, right through to the final accounting balance books and banking records, placing them before the tax-man for his examination and assessment. Her accountant's comments were that they never really had much work to do, as she was well knowledge. These skills mum passed onto Dolly who in her own right had her own clerical skills, typing, phone answering attitudes, and communication in general, required to run a family business. and Dolly's foresight even took her into the land of investments insurance and bonds, where the hell was I?

My knowledge of reading and writing has always had given me a problem, that is more so when figures or calculations were involved. My practical skills even on mental arithmetic are well noted, and excelled well above those of the theorists. bastards (couldn't hang a nail) I could and still even, look at a roof, visually work out the size of nails, slates and quantity, also the amount of under felt required then visually assess the whole site for access, loading, unloading, everything, all without pencil or paper. unfortunately, the reality was I had to put it all on writing so create it in a way I understood it, also so Dolly can understand it... estimates prepared easy. the same as with plumbing or gas fitting, I had a mental plan which I worked too. when it came to earning, I could work out mentally day by day earnings and spending, to a rule of thumb, which was very accurate, and not far off mark. couldn't read balance sheet.

Wedding – Lucky sweeps
'Self' kneeling (Roper)
James Cavanagh (Bottomer)

Later that year came the nursery, I was to fulfil a lifetime ambition when I was asked to be their Santa, they sat me up in the large open corridor just inside the front-door, to welcome the kids as they come in, sitting there on an old upright chair next to the Xmas-tree, one of the nurses, played my helper handing me the already marked, name tagged gift so I would be able to call these names as if by magic, Santa knows their names. all went well, each and every one of them sat on my knee and mums taking their photo, enter John and Peter, I put on a hopefully unrecognisable voice, 'hello John and Peter'. shit. they were the only ones to refuse to come forward, they never even twigged an attempt to drag them, shove them, all foiled, then eventually I had to own up, down with the beard! And they shot off 'right into the hall, amazing'…

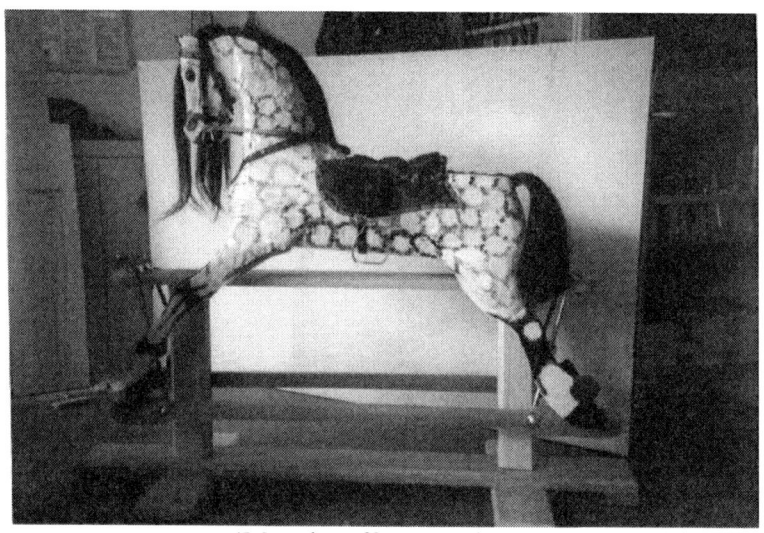

'Must be off my Rocker!'
'Asylum at work, more of the same please'
O,T's really work

Returning from a job in March Mount, I spotted a wee Grey van A35 (Austin), sitting at the side of the road, with a sticker, for sale and a landline phone number, (No mobile phones at this time) (1993)! And I bought it £400. what a smile. it gave me a buzz. I could see it in all its glory. within a month and another £400 spent on it, sign written and a coat of black paint. it transferred things instantly, it was getting well, and truly noticed all around the town, and as we were to find out photographed. and not by just tourists. I was soon to become a member of the A35-A30 automobile association club. something I never was really into clubby… but these people were very nice and plied in with as many spare parts, we virtually had all the bits to make another van, as it stood this one was always in demand for even tv programmes that I bought a second as back-up. which in reality spent as much time out and about as other but at least we had one in service at all times, Billy was not keen at all driving any of them, no heaters and rattled over every bump! My GP noticed I was having problems after a meeting with Dr Williams (psychiatrist) at the surgery, he asked me to come into his ward 2 at the Royal Edinburgh, but not the sector words like 5, I was invited to have a viewing first, this ward was different in as much that it was attached and serviced by the university of Edinburgh! The professorial unit as it was known so I did. It seemed very relaxed. I had two stays in a number of weeks, as a voluntary patient! Given so much medication along with antidepressant was all foreign to me, the shock came at the end of my second stay. Manic Depression. I had heard of this, but was a wee bit more than shocked, and prescribed Lithium, by the time I got back-home, I was more than a bit drowsy with all the medication, a different planet, altogether.

It was at this stage, Dolly was becoming distinctly aggressive with not only me and John in particular, making strange statements on the passing, your worth more to me dead and disappearing into her office, leaving me sitting wondering what the hell is this all about. I was just getting in the way, I did mention this to the doctors, who suggested I go to their day unit for occupational therapy. again, another turning point. even at this point Dolly got Helen involved by putting the boys to her. this put us well and truly back in the past. instead of me going for a few days each week at OT, I did one a fortnight so that I could be available to work with the boys and stop the nonsense of Dolly and Helen fighting again. Oh hell! By luck at the OT. I got in tow with their Joiner Norrie my well hankered for childhood trade joinery I set about it with a vengeance and headlong into making a full-size rocking horse! Another good point was the boys thought it great-fun running around in the wee A35 van, taking it ill out having to get into the car with their mum or granny, as long as I kept the boys occupied she was in a more manageable mood, also if and when I took a handful of work, she was off again. there was a danger I wouldn't get home in time to get them from school or wherever and entertain them till bed-time. things may have been getting difficult for her, but it was bloody impossible for us even Helen. but, sitting around the house was not my idea of living. now with the joinery aspect and a double garage up the back-garden, I set myself up in my own workshop, making all sorts coffee tables bird boxes and some small ply-wood rocking horses. coupled with the large one nearing completion in the OT; s joinery, I was making a second in my own workshop. great above that a handful of jobs, running around in my wee vans. and now doing talks on the radio, BBC – radio Scotland, radio forth, 10 mins to spots and building up a circuit of talks around halls, retirement homes, schools, even followed by Scottish TV, news. managing to get back in time for the boys. The business was getting good money for all of these outlets, the ones I had to manage tighter were the weddings, the lucky chimney sweep again it paid well, and all the great publicity for Scots-Sweep, they were mainly at the weeks end… somehow we managed to get her maneuvered into the right frame of mind, but for Christ's sake, don't push to it Mike, don't push the boat out. having my workshop was a double whammy, no matter the weather, the boys joined me at the work bench, it's amazing how occupied they were with a hammer piece of wood, and a load of flat headed slate-nails, they spent hour after hour belting the hell out of them. and if one only came into the workshop, a piece of wood, quick wee demonstration with a wood saw, again they'd be well occupied and no worries. peace and quiet. one ritual I kept the boys too, that was when they were 4 years old as like the rest of us, a trip up a tenement roof as a wee-bit of an initiation ritual happened at this stage, I took them to a safe tenement roof top in Leith, roped them up and let them wander, in safety. 90 feet up. I like them was 4 years old, they enjoyed it, I'm sure if they weren't it wouldn't have mattered. more and more, I began to notice as did others, I was developing tremors, in the hands and legs were more noticeable, the speech was not right, I was getting more concerned this as effecting my talk in the halls to, I was asked to return to the ward 2 for a couple of weeks, which I did, to be given a written diagnosis of Parkinson's disease (1994) Aged 47, I was devastated, discharged with a 'bank of painkillers'… I continued to do my chores as best I could, strangely my mind and thoughts about ambitions, still functioned, it was the tremors and general grim mobility that seemed to come and go. to make things worse, various people from time to time, asked me and told me he met him, and his dad Olaf, they said that they were on a stop-over on their way to see Lar's family in Norway. Dolly did have on many occasions stayed out late from time to time. but never mentioned Olaf, it didn't take much for me to work it out. I could only let it go by. as far as I was concerned nobody knew of our troubled-times, we did have a regular visitor, Danny Thomson, an insurance agent, Danny was a good friend of Helen's and Billy's when they all went to school together, but on these weekly visits it was purely business as he and Dolly took up meetings in the office-room, sometimes a couple of times a week. insurance investment was always a favourite of Dolly's, I was never invited to the meetings or discuss the contents, but from time to time she'd declare an investment had matured again nobody saw the colour of it. one afternoon, Dolly awoke me whilst I was having a lie-down on the bed to tell me it was ok, the ambulance was on its way. What for! Before I knew it, I was being led out down the driveway to an ambulance. this was hard to take in that this was really happening, I had just, what seemed not long after enjoying managing my workshop then having my usual couple of cans of beer, then gone for a sleep, and now this… I over heard her say she would follow behind in her car, then the door closed, the last I remember was lying down on the stretcher bed, and it slowly took-off down the road with no excitement. then I had this magical dream. I was sitting cross-legged up on the roof of an ambulance, beside a largeish flashing-blue light, as it sped along through Lauriston, weaving in and out the road-traffic, this dream finally stopped as we entered the hospital and under the overhead canopy at A and E the old royal infirmary. I awoke lying, covered by a white-sheet in what I later learnt was high dependency ward. with a few tubes stuck into me, so I glanced down at my chest, it was easy to see, two round like red ring mark on the surface of my skin, looking with an arched head and neck. there hanging ID card, which showed him in large letters DOA. but my attention was suddenly taken by a female voice, hello. You awake. a nurse sat at a small desk with night light. Dolly was standing by the bedside. I relayed to her my strange dream. She then told me that when following of the ambulance for the first mile and normal speed, it without any warning pulled into the side of the road at Locharton, she thought it unusual but decided to pass it and go ahead, by the time she got to Gilmour place, she could hear its siren blast, weaving in and out of traffic and disappeared when she arrived at A-E, a young nurse escorted her into a side-room, which she thought was well-furnished and boxes of tissues – littered the coffee tables, she was asked a few questions about next of kin, she might want to be with her, at that the nurse told her she'd be back in a few minutes… and left her, on her own.

and now we met up. I never waited around, not long after being moved up to a general ward and without ever getting a reason for being here from anybody, I signed myself out. a nurse arrived at my bedside with my belongings in clear plastic bag, to which was attached a label with my name and details, again in bold-writing. D.O.A. I was anxious when I got home by taxi, to Dolly surprise… I had to ask her straight-out, have you spiked my beer again, all I got was a sideways knowing Grim. bitch. The Parkinson disease, grew rapidly, it was getting more impossible to function on all areas, when our biggest TV spot came along. The name of the show (Ken-Fyne… 'Scots' for you know well), documentary series apparently the A35 van was photographed on the passing by an agent. in my ignorance everybody spotted the title Ken-Fyne from a mile-off, it took a while for me to connect it was speaking Scots, mentally I felt up to doing this programmed, filmed at different locations, grass market, Tollcross. The filming was done both to capture the chimney sweeps language, and the chimney roof-tops, where all the film-crew were roped up together with a professional mountain climber on site all the time. Billy and I devoid of all harness', walked and crawled along chimneys and roof ridged top, I couldn't hide my tremor, I tried fighting them but they won through, the worst part was when all got stuck inside the cramped roof-space (attic), the camera shots were unfortunately for me close-ups, my hands-shook uncontrollably, so I picked up a small empty ¼ gill, whiskey bottle for my hands to focus on. not having Parkinson before or even knowing anyone with it, that was the hard-part. but the whole thing was uneventful and came out on TV, great. adding to my involvement with the chimneys, along with my increasing workloads on sites, and the joinery, built a lean-to, storage and workshop area hidden from prying next door neighbours views (being residential snobs) for fixing up all chimney accessories, cowls, pots, liners, for Billy and his growing team, spraying recycled metal cowlings. My concern was that my joinery workshop was now being taken over by increasing storage and howf for sweeps, but it was really great, it kept me out of the house and her feet, a bonus was John and Peter were getting more pocket-money helping me in this increasing new workshop and they were picking up a lot of information on sweeping, that was the best way to learn any trade… unfortunately, Billy was adopting an aggressive manner, in not only looking at me directly but tapping my ankle the toe with his boot when he passed me by, also some marked comment, I tried to make light of this, although I felt very hurt. on a couple of occasions when out and about when I met him and his men on a job, it was more noticeable, as I spoke and laughed with them, he would not say a thing, but he just shrugged his shoulders and walk on by, I never received any direction or reason for this at the time or indeed ever again, I had a change of direction, I was asked by a new group to chair the first meeting of the Manic Depression Fellowship, for the south east of Scotland, meeting at a church hall in the west end, it was for carers and sufferers, we invited a couple of psychiatric nurses along the congregation of maniacs came from all walks of life, GPS, managers, plumbers and their carers. right from the start I felt a wee bit awkward, why. I never felt connected. I thought these meetings would be very tearful and oppressive, no very much the opposite laughter all the way. With their real-life stories, I just could not connect with even the depressions seemed out of my area. but I noticed too, that for both many of the sufferers and carers. it appeared as if this was the highlight point of their life. and it was great to see how much of a relief value this was for them and not just relying on pills or hospitalization, I never connected with these poor bastards, it was more than depressing, I re organised and concentrated on my unmapped future. although I felt that most if not all my attempts to understand just what was on Billy's mind he would only hang around the wee office room and leave giving one a parting kick or indirect undistinguishable comment, all one move, we bought them a bungalow in Lanark road west, even my time completing all the new installation of a central heating and completing a new designer kitchen which a friend of theirs started, and all because they exchanged words, he walked out on them. all the work was making me ill. Unfortunately I was never offered a helping hand, quite the opposite, I noticed Maggie his wife has more plans than Rommel. and normally kicked up a tantrum till she gets her way. but only they for sure, his customers were of high esteem for him. which was the only ray of good light, I noticed, but dare not question 'why everyday he brought a change of clothes, and had a shower in our house, later it became clear he was under pressure at home, not to bring back dirt into her house. another reason for me not to interfere and understand he was working under these pressures. there was a whole parcel of problems for him. so, I began to get more affected by the disease, physically. My mental state seemed my biggest enemy, why. because it didn't relax its grip on reality, I was fully aware of everything. but the pain, and movements were unbearable, I could barely do my duties, getting up at 1am, doing the kitchen duties (whilst they all slept, the Bairns and Dolly) preparing the main meals for the next day, ironing and washing. trying not to disturb them… I even, under hellish protest completed an extension to the kitchen, this housed the washing machine, dryer, fridge, freezer, space we really needed along with a huge garden decking and 6-foot gas, BBQ. (Manic, who knows, but I could do it for others, so why not for us). it was good fun for the boys as at 6am, the Teletubbies (Kids programmed) come on TV with a soft catchy tune, I turned it on. opened the doors and let the sound waken them up. I'd take up my place in the armchair, one by one, dragging their dressing gowns behind them, they climbed up beside me, snuggled in, not a word spoken the three of us wakened up nice-fashion, great, what a way to start the day! Bairns's are great. it seemed that all the medical profession could do was supply me endless amounts of pills, and another to overcome the side effects of that one, more effects, more bloody pills. Cocodamol 500mg, painkillers were awash. I had bottles of hundreds if not thousands stashed away, on a high-shelf in the garage, I was paranoid as to what the hell to do with them, I even feared I'd contaminate the bloody sewers, I was worried shitless. on a really good day, as the Bairns's school holidays. came up, I pulled myself together in order to convince everyone (it didn't take much) that Dolly needed a rest from the boys. a friend had at one time offered me to use a wee flat he had in southern Spain. so, the boys and me, flew off for 3 weeks free of bitching. but I had a worse time with the medics (GP). Who were concerned about the hot-climate and inter reaction with the Lithium, what a bloody nightmare, not about the debilitating

Parkinson, oh shit no, but like a bat out of hell, no one would stop me, it worked with the threat of going without the lithium, was too much for them to imagine. Dolly was near shitting herself, endless, we had three weeks in heaven. my biggest worry was feeding them. soon over come when we found a McDonalds, and Kentucky Fry chicken outlet. the flat was on a private complex with swimming pool, what a great three weeks, not one problem with the boys, we slept in 12 hours shifts. with a hired car we even stretched onto the rock of Gibraltar. up the chair lift, only to be attacked by the barbary-apes frightening the shit out of them when they stole there crisps and holiday past-cards, their football skills were well tested, when by the enclosed poolside a gathering of other owners and tenants from what seemed the whole of the African continent, were amongst us, proving that we had no race-problems, all the boys herds of them with John and Peter the only whites present. it was pure magic. the two of them were spectacular wizards. goal after goal, they were cheered on by their opponents. I never had a need for a beer the whole three weeks. with good snorkelling on the rock pools, up in the hills where the people lived, I had warned both of them not to go near cats or dogs, the reason, rabies. deadly don't bloody touch. we were sitting on high-stools in an open-air café, jam packed by the local Spaniards. we were minding our own business when my boys let out a yell. and as quick mounted the seats on these high-stools, both them clutching each other! Shit, they had taken me at my word. Literally trying to climb the wooden-leg of the stool, a hair-less skinny kitten. they screamed and yelled. nobody needed an interpreter to work out what the chaos these two scary anglaises were going on about. I was not going to touch it, I never had a jab, bugger that for a long laugh, fortunately, an old gent stepped forward to rescue the situation. and picked up the playful Kitty. I recovered my composure. Gracious! I had my handfuls explaining to them all was well. at night bedding down was no problem, we were knackered. sleep was like a welcomed comma, for the three of us, one morning we got up, tidied up, as the morning progressed, we realised some of our belongings were missing, including our camera. but it was all our stuff at the balcony side of the room, the other side of where our beds at the opposite end, we'd been burgled during the night. this was confirmed at the front reception that over a period of time someone had been entering the balconies. my answer, I slept by the door. They went from international footballers, potential large cat trainers to granddad carers, but we managed, like all the good things come to an end we had to return! I wasn't long back from Spain with the boys, when Dolly asked me to take a cut in the wages, down from £60 per week to £50 this was because she wanted me to take full wage to myself. which I didn't agree to, a wee bit pocket money yes. I wanted her to take my pay as she was running the house, and therefore gave her more scope, or leave it in the business as working capital. but why a reduction. she was at it again. I was told I was wasting my money on the boys, buying clothes, 'what a bloody freak', I pointed out without return comments nobody else buys them clothes. Tens of thousands going through the books weekly and what the hell was I to spend a full wage-on, never mind £50.00 but the Parkinson disease, came back with a vengeance for some strange reason.

John O'Groats Start

I was becoming crippled with my feet swelling and my arches had collapsed, I couldn't get into regular shoes. I had to get Velcro fastening ones made to measure, but a relief, only to be confronted with all other problems, getting in and out of my arm-chair it was too low, my shoulders and arms folded every time trying to get up from it, a framework was fitted beneath and with the help of someone standing on my feet (toes) and pulling me up I would be stuck.

Land's End Finish

The toilet seat for me had a high-insert, the shower had rails on the wall, my side of the bed had a metal frame around it, the tremors and swelling of the hands made feeding time very much impossible, with special trays for my plates, spoons with exaggerated handles for grips and a plastic BIB, with a catchment tray for spilled food, which there was plenty of. spilled! My weight shot-up from around 13-14 stones to a hellish 18-20 stones in just few months, with the aid of a Zimmer I managed to walk outside the house only about 30 feet when I had to stop, I never noticed that I was walking up hill, till I tried to turn my feet to come-down!. oh hell, pain, tremor, sweat dripping all out, stuck until some-one noticed and helped me. oh god… what next, my mind was still active. it was trapped. I looked forward to the Bairns coming home from school, my little helpers. Then one day on TV, I saw something about these new mobility – scooters. that was it. I ordered one… and it was delivered. These four wheeled red plastics mobile, after a very brief instruction and test drive. the guy buggered off, my greatest immediate problem which loomed insurmountable was the accelerator was a push-button operated by holding it in for forward using the thumb. oh shit. problem, my thumb was taking, a fit with the tremors, with practice I tied it (my thumb on with an elastic band)! It took some practise in the privacy of my back-garden, crashing out of control, trying to release my thumb in order to stop the bloody thing but I soon mastered it, by reducing my speed-control, which gave my brain the time to assess when to stop. I had already purchased a proper, zip-up warm all in one tank-suit… so I was off on my very first adventure… such freedom. out into the big world that I had actually given up seeing again, I opened up, down this pavement at 6mph, going flat-out. when it suddenly narrowed down. silly me, I kept going as the cars on my right sped past me getting closer and closer. shit without warning my world turned over. I don't know if I screamed or yelled, but I lay still locked in the seat which along with me and the scooter lay stationary on our sides, in the middle of the road, then I was aware of me and the scooter being bodily lifted back onto the pavement.

By people, who somehow managed to stop their cars just in time, then rescue me, no fuss, no bother, just plank me back on board, and buggered-off. this was great, all the way to my folks and back with a good bit of learning done. with now getting out and about, taking the boys to Bonaly School, no longer tied to the house, this is extended to getting space from Dolly. and keeping her face straight, I had her make me up shopping-lists, then I'd sub-divide them into small purposeful journeys. stopping outside shop-doors and wait till someone took the list, bringing the goods to the door then collecting the money, I was getting a dab-hand and well known, people proved themselves to be kind, what happened next took me by surprise. I had a final ambition and that was to sit at the bar of the Colinton Inn with a beer in hand, and a blether. I took up the challenge when I passed one-day and a familiar face at the doorway of the pub, just as I was passing. without a-do. more came out, and helped me up the short steps leading up and inside, 'oh boy, they even lifted my shaking carcass into an upright tall-stool, Gordon Hendry, the bar owner, (snooker world champs father – Stephen Hendry), was pulling the pint-glass with a straw, somehow with shaking the beer nearly from of the glass. it was the best I ever had. Just the atmosphere alone, the laughs and the banter. Jesus, I thought that this day was never going to happen again. within a couple of weeks and on another re-visit. sitting there at the bar, I announced that I was going to go from John-o-Groats to Lands' End, in this scooter. But this was impulsive. without thinking, a voice in the corner chipped-in. and I'll be your driver. it was Sandy an old retired Royal Scot soldier. and it was all well-done and cemented, right there and then, when I reported this back to Dolly, she just gave a dry laugh. I don't think I really knew what I was saying… but she just through down the gauntlet. say no more, the very next day I attended my spot at the bar seeking-out Sandy. who remembered hesitantly his offer to drive (he never got a chance to think about it).? anyway, I had him hooked. and the others reminded him. you- promised 'Sandy'. true to his word, he was in. great. it only took a few weeks in planning and proposing. Vauxhall gave us the unlimited use of a long wheel-based, high roofed brand-new van… my old catering, engineering firm Scobie McIntosh, covered my scooter with sheets of stainless-steel, I bought a load of plastic collecting cans. I never wanted any negatives. I think she thought this was a none-starter. but went in the Huff, when she realised it was on. how long are you going to be away? probably three week or maybe four. Depends. it took 2 weeks to get all this together, including kiting out the van with beds, cooking, lamps all the kindness of Vauxhall and Scobie McIntosh.. In Edinburgh a signs company supplied me with magnetic signs for both the van and stainless steel on my scooter after speaking to Sir Tim Farmer of kwik-fit car parts, with outlets in cities and towns in every corner of the UK, he supplied me with 20 spare batteries, and chargers for the scooter, also the use of any equipment in any of his departments, adding to the fact, they would cover the cost of any vehicle breakdown, and overnight charging facilities. with all that assistance, I had the easy job. hold the button. great! I told Stephen

Hendry's, dad (Gordon) after he invited us to leave from his Pub the Colinton Inn on the Saturday that I would try and get the local-press to see us off. oh no! leave that to me, Mike said Gordon, we have all the contacts, TV, nation-wide press, they'll all be there, Fantastic, what a relief.

    Days before, my aunt Jessie and uncle Dode, came over from Australia, they said that they wanted to see me off, 'Magic'. Saturday morning, Gordon Hendry was busy setting all his tables with white-clothes, cups and saucers etc, Dolly and John with Peter along with Dode and Jessie were all there along with Sandy's wife. Time to take off in order to get up to John O'Groats for night fall. We were just happy to get away from Dolly and her constant negative vibes. I was close to calling it all off during the week. we arrived at John O' Groat's late at night in the car park next to our starting point. got everything ready for our photo official take off one, which, when at the other end 'lands' end' another will be taken as part of the evidence to say dates to and from completed and the route we were taking was only down to inverness, so far planned, we would wait until we got to underway to find exactly how things preceded. but we both had very positive vibes to accept what lay ahead. We left John o Groats on 8th July 1997 (aged 51 years. Me. don't know how old Sandy is, about the same age. I never asked) and after completing 874 miles, we successfully arrived to have our official photos taken at land ends. not a bugger there to meet us. other than the photographer up at the north-end, we were the only ones up there with the seagulls. down here 'thousands, the place was like a bustling holiday camp. I had no time to really reflect on any part of this trip from start to finish. day in and day out. I was totally focused on the next couple of yards, continuously by looking for glass, stones large and small, holes on the surface, and in particular the very edge of the hard-shoulder, as most of all I spent only a few inches with hard edge with this on my left, and if on the main highways, such as the killer A9, and many like it. my space was only the width of my scooter, a continuous white line on my immediate right, huge multi-wheeler juggernauts, nearly brushing my right-elbow (how mad I was!) my wheels clipping the grass on the left. across the Forth Road Bridge south, only a small part of the way, Sandy shadow behind me. how I concentrated, I haven't a clue. ignorance was truly a bliss. on approaching Newcastle, I sent Sandy ahead to find the Kwik Fit depot before it closed for the night. there were no mobile phones in any great use, so communications were as normal and basic, however we had our own standards? I could see by our maps that we should take on the 3rd slip way the left, from this roadway, and we'd link up at that point, but some bugger had changed this road into the motorway shit! I was committed, keeping well close to the left barrier, lorries thundering past, I spotted ahead a low flying helicopter oncoming traffic on the far right heading towards me disappeared behind out of view, seconds later behind me on my left I could hear one hell of a racket, and could feel a blast of wind, the long grass moved about. out of the corner on the left this helicopter slowly drew level both in height and parallel. continuously I looked at it as it hovered only a couple of feet from the ground. I made out the word police. the pilot was pointing to me, directing me to follow him. I did. to the exit ahead and down the slip way, bastard. I was lost for 3 hours! It was dark before I finally found sandy sitting at the 3rd slip road, patiently waiting on me.

we then continued south to North Allerton, crossing over to Shrewsbury, south again over the Bristol-channel via the Severn Bridge, onto lands' end, the weather all the way, was great. Sandy done fantastic, he done all the groundwork like a true soldier no problem, not a crossword between us. It wasn't until after a few days home and comments from some folks, did I have time to realise the full extent of a recovery. my mobility had all but returned to normal, except for some slight-tremor. all the fitments in the house, I through-out the back-door, John and Peter! Played up and down the garden in the scooter. I never used it again. I had a phone call from Sandy, he was clearing out the van before returning it, he asked about a pile of medication, I'd forgotten to take it, he binned it all. progressively, I felt better. when I saw my GP, she was taken aback. But could only say, like some after her, that it was in remission it would all return. and times it did, but I had a quick-fix continue to issue. I re-stopped the pills which the GPs issued automatically, this was the key, bloody medication, I instructed Dolly to stop fart-arseing around with spiking. when I came home, bit by bit. it leaked out! My team had bought a shop Ardmillan Terr, right next door to my old dad's empty shop. I don't know what their secrecy's all about! one thing, that didn't take long to re-establish itself. my duties with boys was quickly re-establish great. now she gave herself a reason to disappear down to the new office, all day. no computers at this time strictly our land-line phones. I was kept at bay also, my workloads were all issued from the house, Billy was also pressed to shower at his home, so I never saw much of him at all, only when she decided for whatever reason to operate that day from the house, which was rarely, contact with the business finances non-existed as far as I was concerned, Billy, as far as I was aware at this stage was taking on huge jobs, roof-tiling, demolishing and re-building complete stone gables! With only a labourer! He was making a great-job on them, financially it was crippling him, fortunately he returned to the bread and butter more profitable work. strongly, Dolly asked me not to go to his jobs, when he was on them. no real reason was given, she said you know how Huffy he gets. yes, he does get his knickers twisted easily. now I felt the tail was wagging the dog. the road to recovery was not a happy-one, the business has nearly physically moved out, but the problem deepens. I wish they would clear the decks, we're in different worlds, if she's not fighting her way or shouting her way. what does she want, I had enough I can't get out? only one thing for its John, Peter and I another three-week holiday to Tencrife, more quality time with the boys. they were easy to please and were old hands, I hired a car. fishing and snorkelling, once back. we were invited to the A35 European championship held at scone palace, Perth. The club really wanted the two-vans (now called sooty and sweep), just to represent the Scottish club, I couldn't let them down, what with all their support. But I was the only one willing to go, as it stood, it was obvious that only one van was going, I was not into this car Rally stuff and on my own for 2 long days. there were a few acres of field hidden under the wheels of A35 and A30 cars and vans, of all colours, immaculately turned out, highly polished under the bonnet, inside sparkling dashboards, mine was a cracker, outside, under the bonnet, my rubber hoses wrapped in sealing-tape to stop the drips, oils leaking and lumps of rust, the inside all sooty full of chimney pots and cowls, and my custom made front to rear roof rack, weighed down by a multitude of ladders.

A35 Sweeping the Trophies

What a bloody sight. I sat in the driving seat in my bib and brace overalls, and flat-cap, sipping on my cup of tea, when I caught sight of 2 judges coming my way with pens and clip-boards, moving from motor to motor, Jesus, I started to panic and was planning my get away, but they were on me. I threw my hands in the air when they ask if they asked if they could look under the bonnet. and they did what a waste of time, I didn't know I had brass and copper pipes under there, till I looked at others. again, on the second and final day, I was on my own. quite pissed off and looking forward to getting it over and done with. with only an hour to go, I was drinking my last cup from my flask, sitting there up the hill looking down on Row after Row of these wee vans and cars, some travelled under their own steam (as this was part of the rules), from Germany and Switzerland! Ian the club chairman came up to me, 'Mike, I hear your leaving soon, but were having a meeting after the prizes have been handed out at the entrance to the big-tent and we'd like you to be present there was a huge crowd of many hundred folks, all clapping and cheering as one by one the winners of their classes picked up the trophies and awards, his lordship and lady of Scone palace, were handing over the huge silver cups. and giving short replies over the intercom. I stood near the long table which was now bare, except one very large shield. my attention and gaze were all over the place. when, someone patted me on the shoulder, I was aware of the words coming over the microphone "Auld Reekie"!! and applauding again, I glanced over my shoulder, it was Ian, pointing for me to go up and get the shield, I moved mechanically, my mind a total-blank.

so, I took the shield from the lord, he asked 'where have you come from' this stunned me, even blank again. Auld Reekie I replied, he had the microphone at my lips, he looked even more blank, asking where's that. down the road Edinburgh I replied "unfortunately I had my back to the crowd, still applauding and clapping, my eye caught Ian, jumping up and down! I was totally gob smacked. all the way home I couldn't believe it even, glancing at the huge wooden shield with lots of heart-shaped. lesser shields attached to it with the names of the other winners, previously on it. just trying to even understand, why have we won it, what was it for. It was explained, the overall winner, chosen by all the clubs, the main reason, because it was genuinely on the road every-day. True. and there was two… all the way home, which took a couple of hours. with no such thing as mobile phone' fearing the van would over-heat and have a complete break-down, I reluctantly kept on stopping to top-it up with water. To steady my nerves, I pulled into the Colinton Inn to share my excitement with whoever was there, had a pint and a carry-out. it was an anti-climax. John and Peter were there to show and share the thrill. Dolly did not even respond when Billy arrived next morning to see what it was all about, and poo-hood it as junk. then she started to agree with him. This just seemed like a defence attitude with them, but a couple of weeks later, a reporter and photographer from a major classic car paper called in and interviewed all of us, and photographed Billy and I alongside the vans, we got front and both centre pages for that month, and as a result, radio spots and another 10 mins Tv Interviewer, the work-loads bounced back-up. next year we or I, as part of the trophy arrangement, had to represent, it to the next meeting, in person and drive the van direct to the show. again, I was on my own, there and back to Cardiff in Wales. but on my return, I was soon invited down to my shop. The toilet wasn't working and they needed shelving put-up in the basement, as the men were leaving all the tools and equipment lying around and whilst I was about it, could I alter the staircase! It was all pals, but once it was all done, it was business as usual which by now suited me best, at least I know where I stood and found out whilst there, Billy wife was working there too, how come Dolly was there, first thing and sometimes not getting home till 8 or 9pm, a busy day she always told me, I was daft but not that much,. I had or seemed to have one major theory in my life that up until this point carried me through. and that was work was my key, to happiness, and satisfaction, also it was the easiest route to solving most problems, paying bills, fuel motor tax etc. I avoided all the writing on electric, gas, balance sheets Tax-Bills, and seemed to work very well. She done a good, safe job, that was not only that, but kept the customer well informed. that way everybody had a good idea what was happening and what they were paying for, there seemed no secret to this. I was taught my trade by craftsmen, who would never have their work questioned like my dad used to say he liked to put his head on the pillow, and sleep at night. following their rules, seemed the best logic. I know, and watched Billy employ these methods, and on that account, I could not judge him! Billy had a good-recognisable attitude and application to be 'proud off' that was all that could be asked of him in reality. his attitude towards me hurt, but was not accountable, although dementia (senile and lewy body) were diagnosed, over the years up until now from doctors who diagnose but it was never explained and I didn't ask and why should I, they're wrong with everything else. If things are worth doing, then do it right. what was becoming more noticeable was hearing her complain that she could not reach her work force, when emergencies of any kind came along. and losing out on viable, good paying emergency calls come in, who was where, on an hour by hour or who was closest. now that there were now anything up to 4 or 5 vehicles on the road at one time, even in 1998 mobile phones were not in any recognised use. Out of my own pocket (the solution was always there, tried and tested for past decades. radio link!) I sought-out all the equipment required to install a base-unit in the shop, also a receiver for each Van and car and one for the house, this gave the office (being the shop and or houses, whatever day, which was used) complete contact minute by minute with all her operatives no matter where they were and when. this I had used all over the world! Standard and good practice. it cost £1100-00 for all the bits and pieces! And the radio license £21. I had installed the base-unit in the shop and house, when Dolly and Billy decided for whatever reason they didn't want it. I just put it down to operational ignorance on their behalf. I backed off the equipment lay in the shop gathering dust. with everybody doing their own thing. Dolly whatever comes up her back regardless or whatever. Billy has his bikes and the boys their pals and football. it came one day when I happened to be working in Grove Street around the corner where I was brought up in upper Grove place, I was taken aback, when I noticed the St. Cuthberts dairy stables, were gone. I got more concerned that the best part of my child-hood has gone, I made enquiries to find indeed they had reduced to just a handful of horses and were now operating from a yard just south of Penicuik just outside of the town. as it turns out the guy that now runs them 'Bill Simpson' ages 28 years had just bought the whole lot from the St. Cuthberts, dairy. Only months before, only 13 horses out of the last year remained, but he bought all the remaining horses that was left also half-dozen of their coach's and one flat-back, milk float. Bill was their head coachman the last of them and made redundant with his pay off money he bought the lot. now he was starting a horse driving school, I was his first pupil. This was his first business venture, he was previously a jockey, then the head coachman with St. Cuthberts at 92 fountains bridge their depot, where he drove all kinds of horse-drawn carriages from up to 6 horses in hand, weddings, trips, films, and the lowly-milk carts. after getting back and forth by mobility scooter (License revoked) to his stables and fielding, way out in the moors south of penieuik. he put me through my paces in everything from picking out hoofs. stabling grooming and harnessing up, then driving on my own out into the moors, losing my way in hazardous snow blizzards. but I was smitten, this only took a few hours each week, before long I was out on the main road. learning good reign handling, and voice command, great. he was easy to follow and his horses well-schooled. As I still had tremors in walking and hands? what a great relaxing way to proceed through life as it now was. one day out at the stables, a huge horse transporter lorry turned up, I'd never seen the likes of it, the guy had to unload about 8 horses down the ramp just to get to the horse Bill had ordered. The guy had just arrived off the boat from Ireland, this was his first drop-off. They were all heavy type horses. Bill finally got his one off a Gelding, dark brown, white hairy legs, took my eye, muscular quiet as the herd shuffled around waiting along with him to be reloaded, I asked the driver if he was for sale, yes. he was mine £600. Bill was in shock, the lorry-left and I was the proud owner of a horse, that was, we were told a ¾ Clydesdale, ¼ Connemara. what that meant I hadn't a clue. he was mine. it was a bit of an anti-climax when I broke the news to the family, just another day. I kept it at Bill's stables and found stabling down in Colinton dell, only hundreds of yards from the house. but the horse was only complete when I purchased van harness from Bill and nothing but the best, 80 year old St Cuthberts and still in working order to complete the set. I bought the old flat back milk lorry. only weeks after, I secured field grazing up the road on the edge of the Pentlands near Bonaly scout camp, adding to the fact I had finished my second full-size rocking horse for my 2 granddaughters, Sally and Lizzy, by Billy and Maggie. this seemed to complete the circle for me at that time, I was getting literally back on my feet. this was also a double-whammy, for John and Peter, a great diversion, John as usual a wee bit wary and laid back at first whereas Peter was right in amongst the action, like a duck to water, full of confidence, he would climb up this huge Clydesdale like horse, never had any previous contact in this area he was a natural. John thought things through first, a wee-bit more cautious, which I think in line with a calculators mind, it wasn't long before I equalled the books-up a wee-bit again with the help of Bill, we found an old highland pony, (yellow-dun) who went by the name (Boo-eh!) or such like a spelling old scots for yellow dun and a mare. and a lovely nature, she took to the harness fantastic, so exercising them was very easy for me on my own, out in the silky cart, in and out of the backroads and tracks. Peter took to riding her out without any problems, Peter as usual, couldn't resist a gallop with John cautiously trailing behind keeping a tight reign. On one such occasion. Then Peter and I were riding out over the playfields. he suddenly took off at speed, I was on Smokey, and not quite sure in the saddle, ended up hanging on for dear-life as Smokey kept up at a good pace behind Peter. the wee-bugger grinning ear to ear, shouting his charger onwards totally ignoring my screaming please to stop, my crown jewels were being crushed. The most unexpected interest for the attention of my horses, came from others. People around the neighbourhood. it got to such a point; I was in danger of losing ownership. which was great to a point. getting someone to keep an eye on them was never a problem. as I still had my normal work and school runs. even without any help, they took no time each day to hard-feed and exercise, nearly every day, harnessing up, and out on the road for1 hour, even feeding in freezing weather when no grass was available costing no more than a dog or cat. especially with high protein feed, but I met, when out in Colinton village one day, the pony major with his regimental mascot Shetland (black) Pony Cruachan in hand walking it down the road, he took an instant liking to Smokey, and as a result, I was in invited to use the paddocks and regimental stables inside Redford barracks. in return, let the colonel and his wife use my horses at their leisure. Brilliant. I'd landed on my feet, and for sure lost my horses, but John and Peter were over the moon, in amongst the soldiers as there were built as Redford Calvary barracks (only designed for India) they were fully equipped for horses but until Smokey arrived only had the Shetland pony mascots and his pie balled companion pony in residence. only when they were visiting tattoo horse performers, they stood empty. we had the officer's stables. John and Peter helped me carry out my duties at Christmas playing Santa to the troops kids, the pony major Colin, drove Smokey. up to the functions because we had created a wee-bit competition with the Royal Scots regiment around the corner in Dreghorn Barracks. my exchange rate for these grand jobs were for John and Peter to be given 'Glen-Garry's, with the appropriate regimental cap-badges. and the boys were over the moon, one other gain for me was that the horses were always in Seeing and hearing, the constant bustle in the Barrack, Pipe bands right through to helicopters landing very near the stable blocks. alongside all of this going-on, I was helping Bill with some of his growing work-loads, on quite a few occasions using Smokey, some of his jobs, which included me driving coaches, were spending a few hour at a time up the lawn-market, taking tourists down the high-street, along princess street. dressing up for the part of coal-lorry horse driving on the set (film) 'great expectations', advertising campaigners and at the worlds championship pipe-bands, at Glasgow Green, adding weddings and funerals, he was well sought after for his expertise and hiring of equipment and horses, but like me he had all the practical skills, but toiled in keeping an eye out on the business side. He openly stated this to Dolly and I, offering her a half-share in his enterprise. a meeting was set up, with him and his chartered accountant. a figure of £20-000 for 51% share was his asking price, and Dolly keeping an eye on the figures through a joint accountant. On the bases of £20,000 this was a good deal and on this guaranteed workload at hand, even without, just more than the small-advert in the recognised method of advertising at this date, Yellow-pages, also with mobile phones being used more, but the preferred land-line still many firms' main communications! £20000 investment should be well and truly regained in the first 12 months. included in this way, all the horses (8 or 9), harnesses, saddlery, stabling and 4 various dress wedding coaches, horse lorries, land rover and horse-boxes and me hands on, on the ground, with my 2 horses. (one wedding coach alone was valued at £19000). independently! Valued! but to everyone's annoyance Dolly, sat on the fence only wanting the whole lot for £12000. This was monkey-feed for us, I didn't understand it, even trying to get an answer myself from her was nigh on impossible… as things were, I continued on with all my chores, along with the boys and with my hobby, the horses. Bill had moved lock-stock and barrel, to a stable block and yard with 85 acres just outside town a coach house with 2 bedrooms over the coach house and large stables complete with tack-room, and hay loft. He was more than over the moon, both my horses spent weeks on end on loan to him, he had a squad of keen helpers for most duties, but over the winter of 1999/2000 which was very cold and Icey. every time I visited him, he appeared to be operating under much stress, although the work scemed to be flowing-in, this weather seemed to give-way to a lack of support, he was becoming more isolated and appearing lonely. one morning in Feb 2000, it was a total white-out and severely-hard January morning, after dropping the boys off at school, I decided to drive out to see him as he stables. after driving down to the stables through the hard-packed snow and ice, looking at the outside stairs to the house door I could see through the gloom that the front door was slightly open. but no sign of human life anywhere. the only movement being the two grey horses leaning against the field fence on my left. I entered the flat knocking loudly on the open-door, no reply then I went from room to room, again gingerly taping on all the doors before very cautiously looking in the place appeared nice and tidy. lastly, I came to the living room / kitchenette, no one, my eye caught sight of a small piece of writing paper on the empty dining table, a blue pen beside it and scribbled on it, "sorry, I can't take anymore, Bill". I shuddered! I edged my way to look out of the window and down onto the driveway track, I could see clearly that other than my tracks, marking my entry down here, no other signs of coming or going were evident and all the vehicles still had a blanket of undisturbed snow. and me being the only live person in the whole area. my true senses told me that the worst was happening. it took me some 10 to 15 mins to systematically search cautiously each area, hay-loft, stables, tack room and garage, expecting at each corner I turned to find his body in whatever state it may be, I deliberately left the coach room directly beneath the flat till last with the two corrugated iron doors when open never really illuminated any daylight other than these doors, the point of foot access lay at the extreme-rear by way of a single doorway. Finally arriving at these doors, and the last place to check. I noticed that the snow had not been disturbed and drifted inches at its base… and no foot-prints. with a great deal of tension building up in me, I gave the left-hand side of the door a sharp-tug knowing that it took this effort normally to move forward and gently it scraped the icy-snow surface outward, only about a foot and jammed but it was enough for me to get my head through the gap into the darkness, without me moving an inch further forward… I drew back sharply as a white-hand only a foot and a half from my face, suddenly came into view. and gradually as I plucked up the courage to look at him from the feet up his toes pointing downwards only a couple of inches off the floor and very close to a chair. he had on his full-livery suit, black riding boots, jodhpurs, bright red jacket and white shirt, my eyes focused on the lead-rope which had bitten almost completely imbedded no sign of stress in death, not like some poor souls in the jail… but I never expected ever to see this again. my nerves just gave way, alone in the middle of nowhere, without touching Bill, I could see he was well and truly gone… fortunately, I came back to my senses and realised I had in my pocket one of these new mobile phones and only knew one phone number, 'Dolly'. So, I phoned her, I told her where I was and the situation asked her to phone the police. she said here's Billy. he just said phone them yourself and hung up. I never realised that I could do this on these phones. then to my amazement after dialling 999, it answered to the voice of a female police controller, I then explained the situation. to my horror, she told me to stay with the body… and let no one touch it! I was stunned, this was the last place I wanted to be, only 15 feet away I suddenly noticed Bill's two white horses standing at the fence. They knew, all the time I searched for him, they had stood there. knowingly. my mind froze as I obeyed their instruction. it took a full 20 mins for the first uniform police arrived. quickly followed by 15 more and lots of plain clothes people who seemed to be well organised and in control, I was taken up to the house, and very quietly interviewed also showed them the wee-note. then I watched them as I looked out of the window, putting him into a plain-white panel van, then we all dispersed! 4 days later, I helped lower him into his grave in a village cemetery in Lasswade. Poor lad, 150-200 turned out to see him off. sadly, no reason other than just suicide was given. but why. two days after he was buried, I took a drive out to the stables. my god, the place was alive with odds and sods, where they came from, I never knew, every item, horses and carriages were sold cash, it was disgusting. I left as quickly. I never saw or heard of any of them again, not even Dolly put in an appearance, prior to all of this, life was at home becoming a wee-bit erratic to say the least, Dolly came home one day and announced that she had come into a wind-fall, one of her hidden insurance policies had matured and a handsome pay out was due. But she never said when or how much, all seemed to be forgotten, when a few weeks later, she again came home and strongly suggested out of the blue that I should take John and Peter on a holiday to Queensland, Australia for some 3 weeks. what the buggery hell is going on with this woman!! And I asked her if she was mad. what the hell do I want to go to Australia for, even if she really was paying, no danger. she didn't like it.

I found myself making up a reason for not going there because it was bloody winter at this time of year June. but she planted a seed in my brain and that was, what a grand idea, to get away for a while and with the boys, so a few days later, I sort of cap-in-hand suggested I take them to the US of A, instead. bingo. we were off, John 9 years old and Peter 8. taking America by storm, after a nine-hour flight to Memphis Tennessee, arriving late at night, I managed to get us bedded down in a motel near the airport, with a hire-car already waiting for us in the morning, lucky for us, the motel was right next door to a 'diner breakfast' joint. 'waffles' by name, I'd never ever heard of them, fortunately the boys had, and settled down on the tall-stools at the breakfast bar alongside all these huge, Truckers with equally big fry-up breakfast, I hadn't a clue what the hell a waffle was, but with the help of the boys, and a nice motherly lady assistant, all was to be revealed and I was truly relieved the boys enjoyed the mess, sticky-syrups and cream yuk, I stuck to doughnuts and coffee, it was a wee-bit of a relief from the night-before, when after the plane landed and it opened its doors, the whole interior was suddenly engulfed with that outside air, and as I knew it, the smells and aromas that come with a new country, but not for John. he hit the panic button, 'oh, oh granddad' he shouted out loud. He couldn't understand the foreign odours, combined with the heat. oh shit. he froze to the seat. refusing to move. I couldn't understand it, I'd never seen him react in this was. Peter and I just looked at each other wondering what the hell's wrong. he just wanted to go home… a quiet word from an air-hostess coxed him out and into the main terminal, bit by bit with promises of getting home on the next flight, we arrived at our motel, and now breakfast. thank Christ he forgot about going home just now. That was my first experience with John and panic attacks even in his early years. poor lad, poor us. we spent each other night in a different motel, everyone with a swimming pool attached, very necessary, we were at the height of summers, the air-conditioning, both in the car and room was on all the time, I even managed to trail them around the home and burial site of Elvis Presley. and the 'grand old oprey' the home of country and western. the treat being a slap-up meal at the nearest McDonalds or Kentucky fried chicken easy to please, followed by hours in the swimming pools, but they weren't daft, on a trip-past Dallas, they spotted an open-air theme park, six flags of Texas. huge roller-coasters seen from miles around except me. I hadn't a clue. but we found a motel next-door to the park. so, I promised to take them the next day. fool. they were up and out the door at the back of 8am. only hundreds of yard to the main entrance and boy it was real-hot the doors weren't even open, but we found a small-que which had gathered, maybe as well we were early, within minutes, the que stretched-back and out of sight. after paying $85.00 for the three of us, I was trying to get in tune to having a very long hot day. we followed the wee-crowd in through a ranch style doorway and into a very small area which seemed to represent on old 'cow-boy' town. very narrow with fronts of buildings, like the saloon on the left and bank on the right, only some 15 feet apart then this street jinxed to a bend, being boxed in the sky directly above the sun beating down on every body, boy it was hot and the organisers were prepared for it. sprinklers high above, showered us with a constant fine-spray, we weren't prepared… suddenly a wooden door opened up to our right, we followed the heaving body of folk through and took-up a seat on a make-shift rail road train. the boys were looking how I was feeling buggered. this was not fun, in this make-shift enclosed desert mountain terrain fun-like western rail track, it was all lit up with artificial lighting, once all the carriages were loaded we were off, round and round, in and out of canyons, then out through a short blacked out tunnel to arrive at a platform, back into the toy-town street, now with loads more bodies shuffling in one direction, I heard both the boys say 'granddad', yep. can we go back to the motel, we've had enough. I've never found an exit so quickly. within ½ an hour I'd found another motel, and the boys settled into the pool, great! And they were well happy. at one of the pool-sides, they were to get there first racist encounter, when one morning they got straight into the pool as I sat inside keeping the air conditioning good company but being able to have full sight of them with a view through our patio double doors only feet from the pools-edge, they were on their own, throwing a ball back and forward, when two kids African American, looking all the more black against these white boys, the other common factor being they were about the same ages. 9 or 10 years old, one of the new boys was very big in stature, they were very quiet and entered the water at the opposite end, and just viewed John and Peter suddenly the ball slashed them, so the bigger boy took hold of it and kept it, John swam over to him, and put his hand out to receive the ball, the small boy seemed not wanting to take any part, clung to the pool-edge, the big boy pushed John away and under I got out of my chair in a flash but Peter was quick of the mark, and fronted the big boy face to face, oh shit! Peter, no. a square go was in the air. Boys, I jumped in between them, by this time John and the other one were standing side by side, quite calmly watching the proceedings, I tried my best to explain that John and Peter were only being friendly, and we should all shake-hands John and the smaller had instantly shook-hands, Peter and the other one were a wee bit more cautious, but took up the challenge. they played happily for the rest of the day. I managed to relax with another beer. race relations now satisfied. all along, I hankered to find some real cowboys for the boys to see. But all my enquiries as to where I might find them, led to the same answers, not in summer time. How strange. eventually we arrived in an area I had heard of Fort Worth. Just the name was enough to conjure up the imagination. the cattle crossroads of the wild-west, and yes. our luck was in, they had a complete indoors rodeo, apparently the only one on in the summer-time in the whole of the USA. Thank Christ. the pressure was off. I'd done my duty. we booked a ringside, box for that very evening! Again, we were first in the que, and dressed for the weather, shorts and tee-shirts. it wasn't long before the show started, real cowboy style. Lasso's, guns! Horses and riders galloping only inches from the boys, truly an amazing site all enclosed in this massive stadium, the boys were fully taken-up with the whole atmosphere and the cheering of the crowds sitting in the raised platform seats up to near the roof, behind us, they too were as entertaining as the show. But after only 30 mins into this show, we began to get cold, even with all this excitement, it took a wee while for it to register with me. air-conditioning, glancing around I noticed we were the only ones in shorts. awe Christ. trust the yanks to even condition such a huge-area, now the boys were getting restless and moaning, its freezing granddad. then in dawned on me, I had all our clothing based in the boot of the car outside in the car-park, stay here boys, I'll be back in a minute. And I was back, laden down with claddings. sitting there for all to see these three mad Scotsmen. dressing for the occasion! Great. what a difference and truly enjoyable night to remember. The coolness must have gotten to John's ears. The very next day as we motored through the town-ship of Texarkana heading into Arkansas. after spending the night in the township of Hope. where the boys spent most of the time in the swimming pool cooling off. John was in agony with his ear, now far from home, a kindly woman directed us to a nearby private clinic. the doctor attended to him immediately. Peter and I stood near his side as he lay on a leather couch, the Dr spent more time telling him how privileged he was sitting in the same place as Mr Clinton, president of the USA. or soon to be. big deal. sort his lug. and he did. our 3 weeks stay was soon bye… I couldn't have asked for better company, relaxed and refreshed, I soon got back into my routine, giving talks to more schools, clubs and the newspapers looking for 'sweeping news'. I was offered two orphaned welsh Ponies, ideal for my granddaughters 'Sally and Lizzy'. which was not a problem for me as I had taken on a field for my two horses and another two would keep the grazing down and better managed not only that the field was at Blinkbonny Currie only a few hundred yards from their home, they'd be able to access them whenever they wanted to. however this was not to be, for whatever reason to my knowledge they never saw them at all.in the short couple of months since we were back, things seemed to have grown wide apart, paths never crossed, but I was seen to meet what has been waiting for decades. there was mention in the air of an old-acquaintance of hers Margaret Scott, who a few years ago was caught out by her husband Harry Scott in the arms of his pal, he flung her out. But now I was hearing whispers that my Dolly was seeing him in the old pub, the good companions at oxgangs. after her work, which would account for her lateness and our wet-sheets. she screamed abuse one night when I confronted her, telling her to get out of bed and clean herself, she went ballistic and disappeared for the night, she showed no other emotions or feelings, not even in denial. my mind was in a turmoil as to what to do, thankfully the boys slept through this. I had no plans, nothing just bouncing along the bottom. but things were soon to change, when a few days later I found I had to call reluctantly into the shop (office) to check on some paperwork, as I was approaching the front doorway I heard a very familiar voice a bit loud to say the least, and my name being blasted out of the slightly open doorway, it was Maggie in full flow. Mike, Mike, Mike. just as I turned and stepped into the door. there was Dolly facing me as she sat at her deck. she was looking up at Maggie, who stood with her back to me, still with raised voice only using my name, the subject matter was beyond me. Dolly's glance turned to me completely vacant of expression, Maggie must have noticed her change of focus. and turned to look at me letting out a yell, on suddenly seeing me, my reaction was spontaneous, I swung open the door, and turned my whole attention on Dolly. This is what you get up to in here, well get your gear out of the house and over to Harry. now. I never even acknowledged Maggie, I spun around and straight home, such was the relief. at last. she wasn't long in following me, with not a word said, she packed up some bags, then quietly left. Not a word said, I acted that quickly. it wasn't till later that day when I went up to the school to get the boys, did I find that she had taken them. the bitch. my worst fears are happening, I never wanted them to be used as footballs, thankfully, over the next few days, I found that she was meant to be using Helen's flat in oxgangs, while she was in hospital, so I chose not to follow them at least they were on familiar territory! I just had to accept the boys were ok. after a few days, Dolly put in an appearance, when she used her key, whilst I was in the kitchen, picking up some stuff for the boys. and then into her office. our sparse conversation was uneasily relaxed, as if nothing had happened, this encounter happened a good few mornings, nothing was mentioned, the boys behaving. yes, fine! And that was that. she was too happy, and so was I, the thought of them being ok. was not what I expected. then I received a letter from her lawyer, she wanted a divorce. although we never even entered into any talk of such, but strangely I had an order put on me to stay clear of her. I still never challenged her comings and goings. I never even speaking a word about business or doing any work, I ignored the fact that the office room in the house was still locked and that she had the key. but I decided to go down to the shop one day to speak to Billy and he was at the van outside the shop, when I went up to say something. he saw me and instantly spun around to walk away shouting. I don't want your business just fucking keep it! I never expected this behaviour or statement, he disappeared into the shop, leaving me stunned, I just left the scene. Gobsmacked. what the hell was that all about! I plucked-up the courage whilst in the area of Gorgie and Dalry to go up and see Jimmy Cavanagh, who lived in Caledonian Cresent Dalry. he was in. I tried to break the news as softly as possible to him, as he was more like family, than family. I was embarrassed to tell him that we were getting divorced and that the problem all started years ago with Olaf. Ah, told you so. well I tried to. He spluttered out; his face was full of recognised anger. I let him continue, he was in full-flow, he continued of. That night in your house in 1979 when Olaf spiked your drink. you went to bed upstairs early, Dolly joined you much later, then the three of us, bedded down on the living room floor, Dolly had given us pillows and blankets. I was wakened in the darkened room, when Dolly came in, she was naked and headed straight for him (Olaf) Both of their noise kept Alan and me awake. next morning that's when she was slagging a female neighbour going past the window that 'Alan Walker', commented to her 'those who live in glass-houses , should not throw-stones!. (this was all true) and fills in the whole period of time. Jimmy continued, I didn't want to tell you, in case it split you and the Bairns up, but I went straight to my Lawyers and had her removed from my will. after that talk with Jimmy, I never saw him again, only because of circumstances, but for next-meeting was when I, John and Peter lowered him in beside his mother and sister Margaret! How I miss him! I felt proud of the boys! And so, would Jimmy. (that was 2009 Mount Vernon Cemetery). Filling my time was no problem, I had all the horses between the Barracks, and the field at Bonally, with a good number of talks at shows and old folks' homes, where I used smokie and the flat bed Lorry, where possible and my A35 van. mainly to carry my sweeping tools and equipment, Helen contacted me, she was out of hospital and sharing the duties of looking after the boys. with her mother, and she said she bad-news for me. her mother was seeing Harry Scott. but I reassured her this was very old news, but gave her no details! She seemed taken-aback at my lack of response. Helen and her mother appeared to manage the boys or so I thought, then I was to learn that at some stage Dolly changed the schooling from Bonally to hunters tryst another school and that they were very troubled with bullies and were not coping, even Helen was getting concerned but was now dumped with the boys as Dolly had settled into a house of her own. sharing it with Harry Scott. although Helen could drive, she had no transport. I contacted the headmaster at Bonally Primary School. he told me that the boys places had been kept open, and they were welcomed back, Helen said she wanted to try having the boys back again, so I decided to use my wee-van, as down payment for a car so that she had transport to get back and forth Bonally. I've never seen the boys so happy. to get to school. at this point, the Garage phoned me to say they wanted the car back as they had a complaint that the van was possibly stolen. Dolly had claimed ownership… we could have done without this. fortunately at the last minute I was able to have the documents were in my name, as it turns out, the garage I was dealing in Lanark Road on the route Maggie took into the office-shop from her house and she noticed the van parked there not finished at that, Dolly came by the house that morning, claiming, she was broke and needed £4000, so straight-away, to help pay for the flat she had just bought. as it so happens, that was the same amount that we had in a joint account, which I held in my name only for the past few years, as she was not asking for it, but demanding It, it was a pleasure to go there and then and give it to her. (I shouldn't be near her, what's this all about). there was a couple of weeks school holidays coming up. so, before they got all worked up about the boys hanging around, I decided to take them up to the outer hebrides for peace and quiet. it was great, I had some girls up on the field who looked after the horses while the boys were sheep shearing, fishing, and rabbit-shooting. the three of us were on very familiar territory, camp-fires and midges. on returning to Edinburgh, I suddenly found my house keys were missing, oh shit, it was getting, late on at night, I had to get the boys bedded down for the night. luck was in. as I drove into the oxgangs, I spotted Dolly, coming away from the chip-shop. I quickly explained my predicament, after a bit of huffing and puffing, she agreed to put them up for the night as long as I was there for 8am sharp. she had work to go to (Big bloody deal) so I followed her with Harrys supper, down to her flat. he wasn't too pleased to see us, though. after putting a change of clothes in their room, I said my goodnight to them and left. I had just pulled away for the kerb-side when a police-car suddenly appeared, and cut Infront of me to a stop. what the F.! all In one move two of them were out and without a word being said (that I remember) escorted me back into her flat, and her bedroom! I was in shock, when they stated quite clearly the problem, they were responding to a call that I had kidnapped the boys. Dolly Harry and the boys just stood there watching. I was totally silenced as quickly as this happened and without a-do. I got myself a 6 pack of beer! And headed up to the field by the horses. I spent the night sleeping in the car, in the morning I searched the car and my rucksack of clothing eventually I found the keys to the house. and at 8am got the boys. still not a word of what happened. some bugger was at it. Bill had not long been buried, now with all my horses just up the road by Bonaly, easy at hand, I finally decided one day to alter a Clydesdale-size horse driving Collar, I got for smokie, but it was just a wee-bit tight getting it over his head. Opening up the cloth material pulling out some of the old-straw, new packing was in order. A good job to be done in the comfort of my home and no nagging. Peace I covered up with sheets, after fetching, some fresh straw from the horse's field to re-stuff the collar, it was a lovely sunny day, cold and fresh, but warmer still indoors. Very pleasant, a job well-done, only 2:30pm, tidied up good job with my stitching. I settled down to 3 beers watching TV… next thing, I knew… I came around, awoke, the TV was the only thing that lit the room, darkness around about 8pm. I got up and walked into the kitchen, which was only some six or seven feet away. once inside I switched on the light picked up the kettle to fill it. then as suddenly the light went out… instantly. flames appeared coming into the kitchen from the living room, creeping high up at ceiling-level, and illuminating all around rolling soft transparent flame. as quickly I reached out, and tried to open the back-door which was only three or four feet away…It was locked! I turned to face the flames which were all around, and I was inside them. I don't think I panicked, this was not happening, thinking don't inhale, I put my hands up to my face and walked deliberately holding my breath, no heat did I feel, this was a dream. just walk… and I did, through rolling sea of flames, all around the living room, the door of which was open and into the hallway, I could see right into the bathroom, and bedrooms, the boy's beds were made-up, thankfully, not occupied. the front door was just ahead I grabbed the Yale lock and felt-pain as I yanked it open, I stepped clearly out into the front garden, the street seemed usually quiet. and like the bungalows opposite well lit-up, I took a few paces out into the garden before I turned to see the flames following, but shit. I stared in disbelief back into the open-door and down the short-hallway! Mother, no flames, smoke, bloody nothing. I felt no heat or pain. nothing. this was just madness. I stood there wondering as to what had happened, I glanced around me, no traffic. nobody. everything was peaceful. quiet. normal. not sure what to do, I made my way out into the middle of the road to get a bigger picture. The hallway and windows were clearly visible and no signs as to any fire, flames, or whatever nothing, I looked up at the roof-line for signs of smoke, the sky was brilliantly clear not a cloud, lovely stars sparkled. I was beginning to feel stupid. what the hell has happened. but one thing for sure, I wasn't going back in… and I wasn't going to a neighbour to explain nothing, but I needed a qualified opinion and suddenly remembered a phone-box a couple of streets away and that was that. My mind was now clear, 999. so, I walked down the road, turned left and in the distance, some 300-400 yards away, the phone box. I was not in panic, I was feeling a bit stupid, halfway down the road, walking and not a soul, or vehicle in sight. my sight was drawn to a huge puddle of water that nearly covered half the roadway. it was at this point I realised it must have been raining, the moon glistened its reflection, suddenly and without warning my hands, stung in sharp-pain. I was now realising that something had happened. I made a dash for the puddle and submerged both hands into the muddy-water within an instance the cold water reduced the pain almost instantly then my face started to sting again I washed the water over it, I looked down the road towards the phone-box, glancing around to see if anybody could help me. nothing. I made a faster walking pace. into the box, my hands hurt as I struggled with the door even pressing the 999 buttons stung my fingers, a voice ask what service. I manage to try and stay in control; I think there's been a fire in my house. within seconds, she was saying they were on their way. Jing's I instantly panicked. 'no, it's not that urgent' I'm at a phone box there's no one in the house, I replied with urgency. by the time I got that out, I became aware of the sounds of distant sirens… I hung the phone-up… the sharp pain returned, nearby I spotted another smaller-puddle, crouched-down splashing water on my stinging face, suddenly, shit, what seem a large fleet of fire engines, ambulances, and police cars sped past me and up the road, only feet from me, I made an effort to try and wave to draw their gaze onto me, but they just disappeared in a huge convoy flashing lights and hell of a racket. I watched as they, turned into my street and disappearing. out of sight, a police car drew up beside me, two officers got out, one opened the rear side door as the other grabbed me by the lapels pushing me backwards onto the seat with my feet staying on the kerb-side, quietly he told me just to stay-calm, an ambulance was coming. within seconds one appeared alongside, this was all a bit of a blur. one of the crew who wore a badge 'doctor' took full control. I was laid out on a stretcher like trolley at the road side, then lifted by a good few bodies up and into the ambulance, it was at that point I first notice my trousers had ended up looking like fish-nets, netted fortunately onto my long-johns, which had saved me more damage plastic bags were placed over my hands that was the last I remembered. until I awoke in an intensive care bed. at Edinburgh Royal Infirmary. again, things were hazy to say the least, but I was aware that the doctors around my bed were agreeing to transfer me Livingstone hospital, the burns unit. I spent all of three-weeks there in a single Isolation room. my only two visitors that I recall were Helen and Tommy. the at least Tommy told me the house down-stairs was not at all damage, only the attic and a small part of the roof. even during this period in the hospital, my concerns were regarding my immediate well-being most of the time there, my hands were kept in plastic-bags only cut away a number of times daily to release the build-up of fluid from the blisters during this operation, my exposed damaged-hands were submerged into a basin of soapy water solution. the blistered dead-skin as cut away, then new bags applied, sealing at the wrists with bandages. initially my eye-lids gave a problem, in that they would fuse together, and have to be snipt free a couple of time a day. but my attention was taken-up in a finger exercises God. that was the dreaded, part of the day. I never realised just how easily we took advantage of the simple mechanism on how our fingers and hand operate and just how difficult could it be to touch your pinkie and thumb tips on one hand, unbelievable. even though I couldn't stand the sight of this, psychotherapist bi-daily visits. come on, you're not trying hard-enough, assisting me by taking hold of my wee pinky and crushing them in her vices. Fuck but she was right that bit of encouragement helped, bastard sadistic. all of this took my mind off the fire itself. I could only guess at what possibly happened adding what Tommy said, and what I remember, and later saw myself. everything downstairs was intact, only some edges of the upper wall-paper where water from the Fireman or just exposure to the weather from part of rear-roof was exposed. and with no real indication by the Fireman report as to the cause. I could only put the central-heating boiler which is located in a tight corner of the actual roof space and directly above only inches away from the main electric fuse-box and immediately behind the boiler, and two or three inches, piled up against a false ply-wood wall lay a multiple assortment of emulsion and gloss paints used for decorating, being stored here from recent painting by our painter. the boiler was a conventional fired appliance, which purposely has a draught diverter fitted to its back which means in poor draughting weather, such as the rain that I was unaware of, can halt up draught, so allowing the flames to seek oxygen to burn... the flames, will (invert) turn upside down and out in order to continue burning then burn through the main-wiring, beneath the paint tins already being warm, the gloss in particular evaporate and become gaseous (causing a flash type gas flame). if this was the reason, then I was at fault because I had noticed the boiler was lacking a asbestos fire wall which I was always intending to put up halfway through my stay in hospital, a divorce lawyer came to see me, some member of the family thought it better I have one. I think it was Tommy. not sure. however, all I had to do was sign some paper work to let her (the lawyer) act on my behalf. once I was discharged I stayed with mum at Whitson and after a few days I took my first look at the house, it was quite remarkably intact, all the windows still curtained looking all the part lived in, even on entering it everything, was in its place, the beds even looked freshly made-up, I opened the wardrobe doors the clothing was well-hung and OK, other than the top edges of the wallpaper in the living room showing a wee bit water damage the only place with obvious well, and truly burnt debris was the short stairway up to the attic, it had been well and truly demolished, lying in a heap inside the cupboard which housed it, which thankfully halted me viewing the scene upstairs, but again once viewing he roof at the rear from the back-garden, there was a large hole where the sky-light had been, on the decking and immediately beneath another heap of burnt-out wreckage obviously thrown down from the hole above. It gave me an idea of what it was like up there. I had to enter and leave the house through the front door; the back was still locked and no key ever was found. I did notice that 3 empty cans of beer still stood upright by my chair, I noticed too that the wee room door was open (office). I went in and it looked very bare as I could have expected it to be as all the shelving contents were now down at the shop. But I couldn't resist a peek into the 4-drawer filing cabinet. like a sneaky wee-school boy. The first three were completely empty, not a scrap was left, but when I opened the bottom, it was jam-packed, full. I took out hands full of what appeared to be old cheque stubs and such like rubbish. No, looking closer at well wrapped up receipts literally a bin liner bag full, they were from TSB (trustees saving bank receipt and statement) just figures. I laid them to one side and pulled out a familiar brown envelope type package which contained our partnership paper from 1989 me, Dolly and Billy. beside it a fresher white large envelope. once I pulled out its contents official papering. My Brain I just could not properly focus or take in its heading. 1993 partnership agreement, Auld Reekie, Chimney sweeps, Dolly and Billy's new joint partnership agreement. I bagged the whole contents and departed leaving 4 totally empty drawers… after getting back to my wee-room at mums. I spent hours going over all the paper work. I was in total disbelief at this new partnership deal, but it was there to see, trying to think back over these years as to why. Parkinson's, that's what kept leaping out on me a terminal illness, I was beginning to give them the benefit of the doubt. but when I studied her TSB statements, Christ. this was her personal account, cash payments to the CIS insurance company, one alone for £50 cash each month starting from her 50th Birthday, and for 10 years till her retirement, all the policies endowment. I went over and over the paper work, no bloody wonder I was banned from her office space, she'd been dipping into the cash-bag, I handed this all over to my lawyer. Then only days after finding this, Mum came into the room, Michael, the police have been on the phone. Vandals have wrecked the house. They want you up there now. Once at the house. I noticed all the front windows, were smashed outwards, the front door was wide-open. There was no one around, not even the police. They made a good-job in smashing every pane of glass, I gingerly walked into the two bedrooms at the front, Christ, the beds had been ripped up all the clothes from the wardrobe strewn about the rooms themselves face down on the littered beds. There back walls, smashed-in. curtains from the windows including the poles pulled-down, what a mess. the bowl in the bathroom smashed curtains pulled down and windows again smashed out. It was like a war zone, the office rooms. Windows were also smashed out, furnishings and filing cabinet tipped over, the living room, suffered most, the leather suite and chairs were slashed, patio doors destroyed, the antique side board on its face and smacked into splinters, but the whole marble fire place and gas-fire were ripped away from there wall mounting… it was utter shambles, even the kitchen suffered, wall units and contents scattered about the floor and worktops and cooker face down, fortunately the gas-meter was already turned off... as I made my way to the front door. The policemen were coming in, when I was about to ask them if they got the buggers, they stopped me mid-sentence and told me it was my wife, and it was a neighbour who phoned them, they let her go without charge as it was her house. when I saw my lawyer a few days later, the police had already advised her as to what happened, and she had more information for me. The lawyer had discovered that an insurance pays out of £20,000 had been paid to Dolly for the fire damage, and the policy house, and business were in her name. Dolly told the lawyers that she had already spent half of the £20,000... no answers as to why she had done all of this. The lawyers husband, who was a criminal lawyer put in an appearance, saying he has looked at some of the events in our marriage and recent event, listing some of these, her past statements. I as worth more dead, spiking drinks, dead on arrival which was never given clear airing, to cause, the fears for the safety, enough to put on order on me to stay well clear of her. But she was coming and going from the house knowing I was in all the time, then the business in her and Billy's name, the shop in her name, insurances in her name, including the house. He (the lawyer) made it clear to me that this warranted closer investigation, initially I agreed but I was then told my divorce would have to wait possibly anything up to 5 years. Shit. No way. I've come through all of this, I want an end to it, got to get clear of her. I gave them permission to, not involve Billy. Knowing her, she would manipulate him... this has been going on for too long, and knowing Billy his attitude appears to be from his lack of how to handle the fact that he knew the firm was out of my hands, and he has been sworn to keep it secret. That is what I think, and what I now know, and the guilt has grown on him to be unreasonable. Hellish. I told my lawyer if Dolly gave up her share then so would I, effectively giving it all to Billy, and no other deal... the lawyer told me Dolly agreed, but would have to stay on for some 3 months to help him take-over. I agreed. I never saw or spoke to Billy in all this time, to me, for what reason his mother gave him. Signed up a new partnership for the right reasons. But in the following 7 or more years the truth of it all crept up on him and he entrenched himself in guilt. He is too honest and kind to be a crook... the divorce went through under these conditions. without any consultation with Billy.

After the divorces went through, I was happy with the boys, during the next couple of years, Dolly tried to make her presence-felt, once whilst I was shopping in Wester Hailes shopping centre, she and Ashly (her grandniece) followed me from a café and into a shop calling abuse. The manager evicted her on the spot, again, but this time with Harry they both came into the pub at my local. Again, they were both ejected and a ban put in place... as late as 2013, she entered my house in Fernieside when I was out and removed an envelope containing my will, how did she get in. Under the umbrella of giving John a lift in her car to my house, where John was staying with me, she followed him in. Finally, I'd had enough so I done what I should have done years before, reported her to the police. and since, I have not heard of her, it's been great. Dolly, contrary to what the divorce said continued on with Billy in Auld Reekie for the next 10 years. As partners.

Long may year Lum 'Reek'.
Aye
Using someone else's coal and cash…

All through my writing-up of my life thus far, I have probably not included all diagnosis of dementia.

In 1996 I was given my first diagnosis of Senile Dementia. Then in 1999, another of Lewy Body Dementia. Followed in 2009 confirmation of vascular and Alzheimer's.

I found no reason or purpose in including them in my story thus far…as living alone, like others given these diagnoses, I do not reflect or feel at all as different, or indeed act like being so different, as those without…getting on with life is still my goal. Forgetting is a normal practise as with others…there is no one to tell me different.

Only Time Will Tell

You will have to be my judges…the early years are easy to remember…but at what stage do we decline.
Or just chose to forget!